*Theological and Aesthetic Roots
in the Stone-Campbell Movement*

THEOLOGICAL AND AESTHETIC ROOTS

IN THE STONE–CAMPBELL MOVEMENT

Dale A. Jorgenson

The Thomas Jefferson University Press
Kirksville, Missouri

The Thomas Jefferson University Press

1989
NMSU LB 115   Kirksville, Missouri 63501 USA

British Cataloging in Publication Information Available.

Distributed by arrangement with
University Publishing Associates, Inc.
4720 Boston Way
Lanham, MD 20706

3 Henrietta Street
London WC2E 8LU England

Library of Congress Cataloging-in-Publication Data

Jorgenson, Dale A.
    Theological and aesthetic roots in the Stone-Campbell
Movement.

        Bibliography; p.
        Includes index.
        1. Restoration movement (Christianity)--History.
    2. Christianity and the arts--United States--History.
    3. United States--Church history--19th century.
    4. United States--Church history--20th century.
    I. Title.
    BX7316.J67   1989   286.673   89-4486
    ISBN 0-943549-04-3 (alk. paper)

    The following publishers have granted permission to use quotations from copyrighted works: College Press, Joplin, Mo.; Earl West Religious Book Service, Germantown, Tenn. For permission to reprint poems and portions of poems from the *Collected Poems* of Vachel Lindsay (1925), the author is indebted to Macmillan Publishing Co., New York, N.Y. The Museum and Library of Maryland History has granted permission to reproduce *View on the New Turnpike Road from Chambersburg to Bedford* and *View Eastward from the Gap of the Allegheny on the Sommerset Road,* both by Benjamin Henry Latrobe. The prints by Barbara Joyce Fiers were provided by the Bethany College Heritage Resource Center, and *Inscape II* was provided by Trudy Jones McRae. The Vachel Lindsay Association, Inc. of Springfield, Il. has provided the photograph of Vachel Lindsay, Troubadour.

    Composed and typeset by The Thomas Jefferson University Press at Northeast Missouri State University. Text is set in Garamond, 10 on 12. Printed by Edwards Bros., Inc., Ann Arbor, Michigan

To Dale, Becky, Mark, Janet, Eric,
whose songs and whose lives have been directly
influenced by Christianity within the
Stone-Campbell Movement, and who have
indirectly influenced the shape of this book.

Table of Contents

List of Plates and Illustrations   8

Foreword   9

Preface and Acknowledgments   11

CHAPTER 1   Hope of An American Millenium   15

CHAPTER 2   Old World Context: The Reformation   29

CHAPTER 3   Old World Roots: The British Isles   49

CHAPTER 4   Parable of the Sower: American Soil   69

CHAPTER 5   Sin and Redemption: Reformation Theology, American Understandings, and Restoration Ethos   97

CHAPTER 6   Toward Restoration: A Movement Emerges   127

CHAPTER 7   Education, Culture, and Restoration   149

CHAPTER 8   Aesthetics and the Reformers: Public Worship   177

CHAPTER 9   Aesthetics and the Reformers: Art and Life   211

CHAPTER 10   Reaction and Conflict: The Peripatetic Generation   246

CHAPTER 11   A Case Study: The Troubadour from Springfield   279

CHAPTER 12   Art and Christian Commitment in the Twentieth-Century Stone-Campbell Tradition   304

CHAPTER 13   The Heart and Brain of Restoration   324

Selected Bibliography   341

Index   347

List of Prints and Illustrations

Pl. 1 Barton W. Stone   27

Pl. 2 Thomas Campbell   28

Pl. 3 Alexander and Selina Campbell   68

Pl. 4 *View on the New Turnpike Road from Chambersburg
       to Bedford,* by Benjamin Henry Latrobe   74

Pl. 5 *View Eastward from the Gap of the Allegheny on the
       Somerset Road,* by Benjamin Henry Latrobe   76

Pl. 6 Walter Scott   96

Pl. 7 Thomas Campbell   126

Pl. 8 Dr. Robert Richardson   148

Pl. 9 *The Tower of Old Main,* by Barbara Fiers Joyce   192

Pl. 10 *The Old Bethany Church,* by Barbara Fiers Joyce   197

Pl. 11 *The Campbell Mansion,* by Barbara Fiers Joyce   240

Pl. 12 Moses E. Lard   254

Pl. 13 Vachel Lindsay   278

Pl. 14 *Inscape I,* by Clarice True (Trudy) Jones McRae   314

Foreword

It was a midweek broadcast of the most popular radio talk show in our city. The context eludes me yet, but I still recall my wonderment as the host—a remarkable woman with encyclopedic knowledge and a Renaissance breadth of interest—responded to her caller by reciting line after line of Vachel Lindsay's epic poem, *Congo*.

It was obvious that the radio personality was fond of Lindsay and knew a great deal about his distinctive work and his tragic life. A miscue came when she said that she saw a "great deal of religious content in his poetry" even though she did not really know much about his particular beliefs or affiliation. How I wished she could have mentioned Vachel Lindsay's close ties with the Stone-Campbell Movement!

One wants to "claim" a noted artist for one's particular religious community not just for the prestige and public relations value of such attachment, but also as a way of gaining some self-awareness, some deeper insight into who we are and what motivates us. But as a life-long "Campbellite" minister and professional communicator, I must admit to a craving for that *former* reward that remains unsatisfied because so few artists of Vachel Lindsay's stature have emerged from our movement! There have been but a handful of famous poets, painters, writers, designers, or craftspersons to whom I could point and say with pride, "That person is one of us. That talented individual has been inspired by the same understanding of God's purpose that I have found to be life-changing."

We can talk about the fine colleges we have started, the well-regarded publications we have founded, and some prominent civic, scientific, and cultural leaders who have been "products" of our Sunday schools but we have had few great artists within the Christian Church-Disciples of Christ-Churches of Christ communities across the years. Is the reason only that we have been a largely "working class," rural, and midwestern movement where aesthetics have had to give way to more practical, earthy, immediate realities? Is it because our young people have had little contact with those great cities and campuses where creativity is fostered?

I was delighted when Dale A. Jorgenson announced that he was planning a book on this very issue. No one is better equipped to write such a work, for he combines scholarly diligence with deep Christian commitment in a quest for answers to the vexing question: "Is there a theological reason that the Stone-Campbell Movement has inspired a few recognized, celebrated artists but has also failed to contribute its fair, proportionate share to the North American scene?"

9

To get an answer, one must dig deeply into the historical roots of the Stone-Campbell Movement. One cannot start with case studies or "success stories," but must look first at what our people have believed over the years about truth and beauty, mind and heart, practicality and idealism. Dale Jorgenson has given us a book that will enrich our understanding of American religious life and particularly the way in which faith was shaped by, and also *shaped*, the frontier.

After reading his solid, perceptive study, I have some hope that there will be budding artists, innovators, and dreamers among us who will find encouragement in knowing that our sometimes somber, straitlaced movement is not by doctrine opposed to joyous creativity and artistic innovation. Perhaps the followers of Barton W. Stone and Alexander Campbell have just been too busy in trying to construct the Kingdom while paying little attention to how we will brighten the city of God with song and celebration and all the bright colors of heaven that will make it habitable.

And let us raise up more Vachel Lindsays to praise God and to strike a blow for the "ancient order" with their magnificent but enigmatic poetic images!

James L. Merrell

Saint Louis, Missouri

Preface and Acknowledgments

The Stone-Campbell Movement was a major effort by a group of early nineteenth-century religious leaders to further the cause of Christian unity. Ultimately, the movement's leaders attempted to achieve such unity through "restoration of the ancient order." This was to be achieved by using the New Testament to discover Spirit-given principles and patterns in the first-century Church, and then applying them to the contemporary Church. Thus, both a zeal for Christian unity and a desire for an authentic restoration of the New Testament order were viewed by these reformers as being symbiotic. Many felt that unity could largely be achieved by mutual discovery and practice of the the "ancient order." Some recent scholars, however, have perceived the two purposes, unity and restoration, as being more opposed than harmonious. This has been especially true when parochial views of restoration exclude Christians whose understandings are at variance with the prevailing view of what the New Testament really is.

This work is concerned with the implicit and explicit significance of the arts and aesthetics to the ideas of the key leaders of the Stone-Campell Movement and the second-generation leaders of that movement. A cursory examination of the works of the movement's key leaders does not reveal drastic differences between their attitudes and those of other American frontier Protestants. A more careful study, however, does reveal the influence of the ideas of John Locke, the recognition of empiricism as a key epistemological tool, and yet a concern for the spirit of the Christian faith. These three components were used by the second- and third-generation followers of Stone and Campbell to bring about rigidifying tendencies in the aesthetic development within the movement.

Many excellent histories have been written about the Stone-Campbell Movement. As a mainstream American religious entity, the Restoration Movement, as it became known in the late nineteenth century, merits the close analyses of those histories. Barton W. Stone was a leading participant in the revivals of the Second Great Awakening in Kentucky in the early nineteenth century. He exerted a witness for fraternal acceptance of and a human tenderness toward those beyond his own circle of "Christians." Alexander Campbell was a primary moving spirit of the "religious reformation" which took shape on the American frontier. He was recognized in his lifetime as one of the country's outstanding religious, intellectual, and academic leaders. Both Stone and Campbell have faded from general recognition outside of the three religious fellowships

11

which take their points of departure from the Stone-Campbell Movement. Few works of American history, or even American religious history, give more than a passing nod to these men.

The Movement was originally a bold attempt to unify Christians into a true fraternal relationship, but it has suffered deep fragmentation. Generally, three church organizations are recognized as descendants of the Movement. Yet, within those organizations are numerous sub-groups which seem to have lost the original desire for unity. Some of these groups emphasize "restoration" in a continually diminishing pattern of doctrine which, for them, constitutes acceptable parameters for the New Testament Church. These groups find no religious organizations (except their own limited fellowship) which will fit the parameters. In this spirit, many have abandoned the leaders' desires for unity. They seek unity only in the unlikely prospect of getting all other followers of Christ to come to their point of view.

On the other hand, the most liberal and inclusive heirs of the Stone-Campbell Movement have abandoned any attempt to "restore" the "ancient order." The "rage for unity" has often become a "rage for union," a goal currently pursued by active involvement in larger ecumenical movements. Their view of Scripture has been amended from belief in the Bible as the center of church polity and personal faith to a much-diminished view that Scripture is an important collection of humanly produced literature. The use of Scripture as a divine norm for a central unifying faith has also been greatly diminished. Consequently, many leaders of the Christian Church (Disciples of Christ) have lost interest in reunification with their conservative brothers and sisters of the Christian Churches-Churches of Christ and the non-instrumental Churches of Christ. Recent regional forums and pulpit exchanges between the latter two groups offer a modest hope for a desire to return to the first-generation emphasis on unity.

Several agencies continue to offer opportunities for sharing ideas and hopes. Among them are the Disciples of Christ Historical Society which serves all three groups through its excellent library; the European Evangelistic Society for the Study of Christian Origins, and its associated international church congregation, at Tübingen, West Germany; and the World Convention of Churches of Christ, where the Christian Churches (Disciples of Christ) and Christian Churches-Churches of Christ continue to share dialogue.

Disciples of Christ, like all people, are part of their own times. Alexander Campbell often acknowledged his debt to the Protestant Reformers. Later restorationists, however, posited a virtual hiatus in the history of the church between the Apostles and the Stone-Campbell Movement. This book explores the European, British, and early American antecedents of early Disciples views in order to obtain a historical basis for Disciples approaches to theology, the arts, culture and the relationship between aesthetics and religion. Chapter 5, Sin and Redemption, is an effort to identify elements in both theology and art which make possible a Christian aesthetic.

Vachel Lindsay (1879-1931), a powerful Midwestern poet, is chosen as a case study, not only because he may have been the best-known Disciples artist of any generation, but also because his tragic struggle characterizes several of the experiences of other artists of Restoration heritage. The fact that he sometimes sought spiritual refreshment outside of his own fiercely-maintained Disciples frame of thought reveals something of both the man and the inadequacies he perceived in his own religious tradition.

The artists whose statements comprise the bulk of chapter 12 are living evidence that the Stone-Campbell influence, interpreted in contemporary churches which endeavor to continue this influence, still has the power to provide creative people with a Christian frame of reference for artistic expression. I am deeply grateful for their participation. Their personal achievements and the variety of their media of expression provide, in the spirit of Alexander Campbell, empirical evidence of the need for contemporary Christians to create and perform.

The librarians at Bethany College, West Virginia; Northeast Missouri State University; and the Disciples of Christ Historical Society Library in Nashville, Tennessee, have been most supportive in sharing the sources each had available for the pursuit of this study. The photographs are acknowledged individually where they appear.

Others who deserve recognition for the completion of this project include Perry E. Gresham, whose lectures on Vachel Lindsay and encouragement for the project have been vital; James L. Merrell whose Foreword provides tangible evidence of his support; President Charles J. McClain and Dean Darrell W. Krueger of Northeast Missouri State University who have provided encouraging words and some short term assistance in administrative duties in the University's Division of Fine Arts.

Other colleagues and scholars have been gracious in giving some sharp dialogue over ideas related to the effort. Joyce Brown has read many pages of impossibly mangled manuscript to get the text into trusty word processor form and polished draft. Bob Schnucker, director, and Paula Presley, assistant editor, of the Thomas Jefferson University Press have given both encouragement and needed technical criticism for the finished text and notes. Londia Darden Granger has contributed a professional note to the book through her sensitive work as copy editor. Mary Lee, my wife and best friend, has characteristically offered help at convenient times and importune hours as well.

Alexander Campbell, who impacted the author's life through churches and educational institutions representing all three principal branches of the Stone-Campbell Movement, has always been an exciting stimulus to both my spirituality and my intellect. Doctor Robert Richardson, clearly the most winsome blend of Christ and the arts offered by the Restoration fathers, has powerfully influenced both the Movement and this book in healthy ways. Since Campbell and Richardson have both entered into the next phase of the Christian life cycle, it is impossible to thank them personally. Gratitude, therefore, is expressed here to both their God and mine, in the hope that this book might provoke some fresh insights into the relationship between Christian unity and the "new song" which represents Christian redemption. I hope, and believe, that Barton W. Stone, Thomas and Alexander Campbell, Walter Scott, and especially Robert Richardson would have approved.

Finally, I must express thanksgiving for those Robert Richardson kind of people who touched my life at crucial moments: Leonard Kirk, Andy T. Ritchie, and my late uncle, E. L. Jorgenson, whose journey from a Nebraska farm to the preparation of a major hymnal for the Churches of Christ led through biblical and musical studies, and a life of the heart. His *Great Songs of the Church* delineates, with other worship and hymnal treasures of Stone-Campbell fellowships, the distance traversed since the Disciples' *Christian Hymn Book* first made its appearance.

Most of all, my parents who, under the shadow of dust bowl, depression, and illness, encouraged their children by precept and example both to trust God and make music, taught me that man cannot live fully by bread alone.

Dale A. Jorgenson

Kirksville, Missouri
January 1989

1

Hope of an American Millennium

On April 8, 1807, the sailing ship *Brutus*, commanded by one Captain Craig, rounded the northerly tip of the Emerald Isle on the first leg of her long voyage to Philadelphia. She carried passengers who formed a small contingent of that nineteenth-century flood of Irish emigrants bound for America. Included on the passenger list was a forty-five-year-old Seceder Presbyterian minister named Thomas Campbell. Captain Craig had little reason to suspect that this passenger—together with a gifted son who would follow him to the New World some two and a half years later—would ultimately represent the genesis of a movement which continues to impact the lives of millions of Americans and thousands of other people throughout the world.[1]

Thomas Campbell had embarked at the Irish port of Londonderry, from which he wrote a last-minute letter to his family exhorting them to "come out from the wicked of the world and be separate. . . . take Christ for your Master, his Word for your instructor, his Spirit for your assistant, interpreter and guide."[2] His next message to his family was written from Philadelphia May 27, 1807, after a "speedy trip" of thirty-five days.

Campbell's ancestors were Scotsmen, but his family had lived in Ireland for several generations before his birth. Although his parents were poor, he received both a formal university education at the University of Glasgow in Scotland, and theological training at a school maintained by the Anti-Burgher Seceder Presbyterians in that city.

The Anti-Burgher Seceders resulted from two divisions among Scottish Presbyterians, neither of which related directly to matters in Ireland, but which were carried over from the Scottish Synod to the Irish Presbyterian churches. The *Seceder* separation from the national *Kirk* resulted from a controversy over the patronage system for choosing pastors. In 1733, several ministers formally seceded from the national party to form a new Associate Presbytery, ultimately called the *Seceders,* which affirmed the right of each congregation to choose its own minis-

---

[1]Robert Richardson (1806-1876) *Memoirs of Alexander Campbell,* 2 vols. (Cincinnati: Standard Publishing Co., n.d.), 1:81. Richardson has written the definitive biography of Alexander Campbell, based on his personal association with Campbell, especially in journal editing and on the faculty of Bethany College. I have relied heavily on Richardson throughout this book.

[2]Ibid., 80.

ter. A second schism developed when the town burgesses in Scotland demanded that citizens support the religious party professed within the realm. Those who considered such an oath unlawful and unduly repressive came to be known as *Anti*-Burghers; those Seceders who supported the oath were *Burghers*. It is ironic that these divisions, which related only to Scottish polity and had no direct relevance to Irish or American Seceders, ultimately resulted in a movement to restore Christian unity. Thomas Campbell had begun his ministry as a Seceder minister in Ireland; in America he continued, but the divisive controversy in Scotland resulted in his dismissal from the Seceder clergy and, ultimately, in the Stone-Campbell Movement.

During his ministry in Ireland, Campbell did not serve any large church which would have provided a comfortable income. Rather, he served several small Seceder congregations where, to keep his family financially solvent, he also conducted either private school classes or an academy while fulfilling his ministerial responsibilities. In 1787 he married Jane Corneigle, who was a dedicated Presbyterian and a descendent of French Huguenots. In 1788, Alexander, the oldest of their seven children, was born. In 1801, Thomas moved his growing family to the town of Rich Hill in northern Ireland. There he planned to operate an academy in his home, in addition to conducting his pastoral responsibilities, to provide for his ever-increasing financial burden. It was part of his plan for thirteen-year-old Alexander, who was rapidly mastering the fundamental subjects, to assist him in the operation of the school.

However, numerous pressures over the next six years led Thomas to try his fortunes in the United States. The religious division in Ireland, not only between Catholics and Protestants but between the various groups within his own Presbyterian fellowship, was clearly a heavy, heartfelt burden. His concern about Christian division, based upon his experience as a pastor and a churchman in Ireland, was a driving force in his thought and actions throughout his life. Besides the weight of his religious burden, Thomas's physical health was undermined by the sheer energy required to maintain his schedule of teaching, ministry, and family responsibilities. Finally, his physician recommended drastic changes in his life and perhaps a sea voyage.

Campbell's family and friends convinced him to follow his physician's advice. Although the elder Campbell was naturally reluctant to leave his family, work, and country he decided to investigate the possibilities of America as a future home. The fact that several of his neighbors and acquaintances had already preceded him to the New World encouraged him to follow. Leaving Alexander at home to maintain the academy and assume temporary responsibility for his family's welfare, Thomas arrived at Philadelphia after his quick voyage on the *Brutus*. Fortunately (providentially, as he regarded the situation), the North American Anti-

Burgher Synod of Presbyterians was in session in the city. He presented his credentials from Ireland and was immediately received kindly by his American brethren.

The synod assigned him to the Chartiers Presbytery in Washington County, Pennsylvania, near the western edge of the Commonwealth. Several of his former neighbors from Ireland had already settled in the area, and more were on the way. Campbell's ability, education, and generous spirit caused him to be considered by Seceder congregations as "the most learned and talented preacher in their ranks."[3] His fraternal actions toward Presbyterians who were *not* Seceders, however, caused him to be regarded with a degree of suspicion by some of his denominational brothers.

The inevitable break came early during his ministry in his new country. It was precipitated by a visit Campbell made to a rather isolated church north of Pittsburgh. Alexander Campbell's biographer relates the story with sympathy for Thomas:

> It happened that, on this occasion, Mr. Campbell's sympathies were strongly aroused in regard to the destitute condition of some in the vicinity who belonged to other branches of the Presbyterian family, and who had not, for a long time, had an opportunity of partaking of the Lord's Supper, and he felt it his duty, in the preparation sermon, to lament the existing divisions, and to suggest that all his pious hearers, who felt so disposed and duly prepared, should, without respect to party differences, enjoy the benefits of the communion season then providentially afforded them.[4]

A young minister who accompanied Thomas felt it his duty to charge Campbell at the next meeting of the presbytery. The principal charge was that "Mr. Campbell had failed to inculcate strict adherence to the Church standard and usages, and had even expressed his disapproval of some things in said standard and of the uses made of them." Already in a frame of mind to receive such charges, that body censured Thomas for not adhering to church polity.

Campbell appealed his case to the Associate Synod of North America, basing his defense upon the biblical plea for Christian liberty and fraternity. The synod's response was somewhat ambiguous. It removed the censure, but refused to censure the presbytery because it was felt that there had been sufficient ground upon which the presbytery could base a censure of Campbell.[5]

---

[3] Ibid., 78

[4] Ibid., 224.

[5] See Charles Alexander Young, "Historical Introductions" in *Historical Documents Advocating Christian Union* (Joplin, Mo.: College Press Publishing Co., 1985), 31-32.

Based on a Calvinist heritage, the outcome almost seems, in retrospect, to have been predestined. Although the synod sent Thomas Campbell back to the Chartiers Presbytery for reassignment to ministerial service, the latter body ignored him and repeatedly evaded or delayed in providing preaching assignments for him. Consequently, Thomas withdrew from the presbytery and from the Seceder denomination. As a vindictive but meaningless gesture, the presbytery suspended him from ministerial office.[6]

This dispute resulted in a program that provided a basic foundation for future Disciples thought. The suspension of Thomas Campbell as a Presbyterian minister made it essential that a new forum be established for his stance concerning unity, freedom, and the proclamation of Christian witness. For Thomas Campbell, his neighbors, and his supporters who shared a commitment for providing such a forum, the choice was an ecumenical *association* rather than a new church or denomination. After preaching for a time in the homes or under the trees of some of his Irish neighbors, Campbell proposed that a special meeting be convened to define the direction of the effort.

The intent of Campbell and his friends was to see all the Christian denominations united, using the Bible as their only rule of faith and practice, and to avoid controversies which involved only personal opinions. Neither Campbell nor the others voiced any objections at this time to any Christian confessions of faith or formularies of doctrine.[7]

The planning meeting resulted in the erection of a log meeting house at Mount Pleasant, not far from Washington, Pennsylvania, and the resolve of Thomas Campbell to write the *Declaration and Address* which would provide both a rationale for the group's position and the identity of the organization as The Washington Christian Association. The creative and destructive tensions which have characterized the movement from that time first surfaced at the opening meeting. Campbell made a strong dialectical affirmation of two concepts, intending to place them in alignment; instead, a juxtaposition occurred which has affected unity, theology, fellowship, and aesthetic attitudes throughout the history of the groups tracing their lineage from the Washington Christian Association. Those concepts are (1) the unity of all Christians and (2) the restoration of the "ancient order" of the church based upon the New Testament.

The theme of the Association's opening meeting was the centrality of scripture over creeds, church polity, or any other man-made conditions of fellowship. That rule was to be that "where the scriptures speak, we speak; and where the scriptures are silent, we are silent."

---

[6]See Leroy Garrett, *The Stone-Campbell Movement,* 2d ed. (Joplin, Mo.: College Press Publishing Co., 1983), 139-40.

[7]Richardson, *Memoirs,* 1:232.

The first problem of practical theology which surfaced in the group related to the matter of infant baptism. One Andrew Munro, postmaster at nearby Canonsburg, Pennsylvania, and a Scotch Seceder Presbyterian, observed, "Mr. Campbell, if we adopt *that* as a basis, then there is an end to infant baptism."[8] The answer of Thomas Campbell suggests that he had not completely internalized the problem at the time. The matter was eventually settled some three years later, with the immersion of Thomas and Alexander Campbell and members of their families, the adoption and preaching of believer's immersion as one of the basic ordinances of all Disciples traditions, and the uncertainty about whether to extend fellowship to those who had been members of churches that practiced infant baptism or adult sprinkling.

The second problem, basic to this study and perhaps even more fundamental than the baptism question, related to the statement on the silence of scripture. Much of what Christians practice in the way of the arts and aesthetic concerns—both in the church and in other areas of life—occurs in the large domain of scriptural silence. The *Declaration and Address* which Thomas Campbell wrote as *apologia* for the Washington Christian Association outlines more fully the principles of Christian union which the Association proposed to espouse. The *Declaration and Address* is regarded as the cornerstone upon which stands all the literature that defines this movement which evolved into the Disciples of Christ, the Christian Churches, and the Churches of Christ in America. It states the theme of unity, which is central to that movement's purpose:

> That the Church of Christ upon earth is essentially, intentionally, and constitutionally one; consisting of all those in every place that profess their faith in Christ and obedience to him in all things according to the scriptures, and that manifest the same by their tempers and conduct, and of none else; as none else can be truly and properly called Christians.[9]

In separating the explicit and overt requirements of the New Testament from the areas of silence, Campbell called upon unity in matters of faith, and liberty in matters of opinion. Charles Young points out that while the traditional terminology of the distinction between "essentials" and "nonessentials" was studiously avoided, the actual difference in meaning is retained. Various definitions of "faith" and "opinion" by those who endeavored to speak for the church immediately became a problem which dogged the Washington Association reformers throughout their

---

[8]Ibid., 238.

[9]Thomas Campbell, "Declaration and Address" in *Historical Documents Advocating Christian Union,* ed. Charles Alexander Young (Joplin, Mo.: College Press Publishing Co., 1985), 107-8.

lives, and continues to hound the various branches of the Movement until the present. Numerous articles in Alexander Campbell's journal, The *Millennial Harbinger,* are indexed between 1838 and 1869 under the heading "Bible Interpretation." The reformers clearly believed that if the Bible were only read with faith in its divine message and an expectation of its intelligibility, divisions in the Church of Christ could be eliminated.

Robert Richardson, a close friend and the biographer of Alexander Campbell, also stood squarely on this ground in his advocacy of Christian unity through his writings in the *Millennial Harbinger;* however, he exhibited in his *Memoirs* a recognition that Thomas Campbell's distinction—made so confidently and with such expectation of positive acceptance by the larger Christian community—might be difficult to implement:

> The distinction between *faith* and *opinion* was here clearly indicated, nothing more being purposed in order to communion and unity than to believe "the scriptures only," and to endeavor "to believe it in the *true sense.*" In laying down this principle, the intelligibility of scriptures was necessarily implied, and it was not for a moment doubted that its true sense could be gathered from its words taken according to their established use and in their just connection; since to have thought otherwise would have been to regard the Bible as having no determinate meaning at all.[10]

This principle, which was the heartbeat of the Washington Christian Association, embodied at once the freedom and the great power of the appeal made by the new American reformers; but it also embodied divisive tentacles, which would tear at the unity of the movement long before the death of its first generation.

Thomas Campbell's distinction between *faith* and *opinion* is made explicit early in the *Declaration and Address:*

> Our desire, therefore, for ourselves and our brethren would be, that, rejecting human opinions and the inventions of men as of any authority, or as having any place in the Church of God, we might forever cease from further contentions about such things; returning to and holding fast by the original standard; taking the Divine word alone for our rule; the Holy Spirit for our teacher and guide, to lead us into all truth; and Christ alone, as exhibited in the word, for our salvation; that, by so doing, we may be at

---

[10]Ibid., 12.

peace among ourselves, follow peace with all men, and holiness without which no man shall see the Lord.[11]

Alexander Campbell's underlying distinction between faith, based on a clear biblical proposition, and human opinion, resting on undocumented personal beliefs about Christian principles, was based upon his understanding of John Locke's *Essay Concerning Human Understanding.* Richardson described the course of study outlined by Thomas Campbell for his son, Alexander, and mentions Alexander's admiration for the work of the seventeenth-century British philosopher.[12] As the works of Locke became a strong generative force in the evolution of American government, they were also basic in the development of polity within the Washington Christian Association, and later for the entire Disciples of Christ movement.[13]

In his 1690 *Essay Concerning Human Understanding,* Locke divided opinions and knowledge by separate definitions:

> *First,* I shall inquire into the *original* of those ideas, notions, or whatever else you please to call them, which a man observes and is conscious to himself he has in his mind; . . .

> *Secondly,* I shall endeavor to show what knowledge the understanding hath by those *ideas,* and the certainty, evidence, and extent of it.

> *Thirdly,* I shall make some inquiry into the nature and grounds of *faith* or *opinion:* whereby I mean that assent which we give to any proposition as true, of whose truth yet we have no certain knowledge.[14]

Thomas Campbell, if he was indeed a thorough student of John Locke, underestimated the force of human opinions in his naive belief that sincere Protestants would happily relinquish the baggage of non-biblical doctrines which they cherished as part of their denominational beliefs to join a fledgling movement centered in Washington, Pennsylvania, which sought Christian unity. "Who, then," Campbell asked rhetorically, "would not be the first among us to give up human inventions in the worship of God, and to cease from imposing his private opinions

---

[11]Thomas Campbell, *Declaration and Address,* 73-74.

[12]Richardson, *Memoirs,* 1:33.

[13]Lester G. McAllister and William E. Tucker, *Journey in Faith* (St. Louis: Bethany Press, 1975), 44-45.

[14]John Locke, *An Essay Concerning Human Understanding,* ed. John W. Yolton (New York: Dutton, 1978), 1:6.

upon his brethren, that our breaches might be *thus* healed?"[15] Locke's
answer, if weaker in faith, is a lesson in realism which the idealistic
American reformers were slow to learn:

> I easily grant that there are great numbers of *opinions* which, by
> men of different countries, educations, and tempers are received
> and *embraced as first and unquestionable principles;* many
> whereof, both for their absurdity as well as oppositions one to
> another, *it is impossible should be true.* But yet all those prop-
> ositions, how remote soever from reason, are so sacred some-
> where or other, that men even of good understanding in other
> matters will sooner part with their lives, and whatever is dearest
> to them, than suffer themselves to doubt, or others to question,
> the truth of them.[16]

Questions relating to the arts, either in worship or in the personal
values held by individual Christians, generally tend to be in the category
Campbell considered "opinion," or where scripture is silent, rather than
speaking. Thus, when one considers the history of this movement, it can
hardly be surprising that questions relating to music, liturgy and poetry,
church architecture, painting, and the environmental setting for
worship were among matters which later contributed to divisions from
within the movement—a movement founded in hopeful anticipation of
Christian unity.

The Washington Christian Association was formed by an eclectic
group of Christians with a variety of religious backgrounds. Although a
log building was erected for the Association's meetings, the emphasis
was upon principles developed in Thomas Campbell's *Declaration and
Address* and the consequent witness that the Church of Christ upon
earth is essentially, intentionally, and constitutionally one. This coura-
geous stand, which provided a forum for Christians of various denominational backgrounds to worship, study, and grow together, represents
the first emphasis of the emerging American religious movement. Bound
together simply by belief in Jesus Christ and a common core of "faith,"
while subordinating their sectarian "opinions," its members worked
together for nearly two years in this loosely bound covenant. It was
during this period, however, that Thomas Campbell's separation from
the Presbyterian Seceder Church became final.

In 1809, Alexander Campbell, after a year's study at the University
of Glasgow, arrived in America with his mother and Thomas's other children. Alexander was married on March 12, 1811 to Margaret Brown, and
he was urged by his friends to be ordained as a minister. The lack of any

---

[15]Thomas Campbell, "Declaration and Address," 93.
[16]*Human Understanding*, 1:40.

Protestant fellowship for the newly organized congregation was of increasing concern to the Christian Association's leaders. Thomas recognized that in order to enjoy the privileges and perform the duties of a local church, the congregation should be organized into an independent church.

It was precisely the shift from a Christian *association,* encompassing a variety of denominational commitments, to a church, with the attendant necessities of doctrinal definition, development of polity and theological position, that created the change of focus for the young movement.

The *Declaration and Address* is filled with references to Christian love, exhortations to "receive ye one another," and other inclusivist statements of fraternal care for Christians of all groups. Thomas Campbell believed that a mutual move toward acceptance of a New Testament pattern of doctrine and life in the church was the *means* to unity among Christians. In the *Declaration and Address,* he wrote, ". . . the New Testament contains a perfect and complete model of the Christian institution, as to faith, life, worship, ordinances, and government." By this he seems to have understood that Christ and the apostles had anticipated every exigency in the career of the church and had made provision for them. Therefore, there was nothing left for the church to devise or develop in terms of church polity.[17]

Thomas Campbell perceived the process which became known as "Restoration to the New Testament pattern," as the means of achieving unity among Christians. People committed to "opinions" or denominational doctrines which were not clearly based upon New Testament example or teaching—were expected to forego those opinions. They were to then rally around the standard of the "pattern" of the new reformation, and, by so doing, to find that precious unity—the ideal which motivated the original search. The decision of the Washington Christian Association leaders to leave the eclectic fellowship of that rather informal group and to organize a church congregation implicitly dictated a shift in the bottom on which the ship sailed. The emphasis became centered on "restoration" and conformity to what was perceived as the New Testament pattern, and less on the basic thrust for unity among Christians who held to sharply differing doctrinal positions.

Thomas Campbell perceived the two poles of this dichotomy to be a type of dialectical balance. The tension between unity and restoration has affected almost every facet of the Campbellian Movement. Conservative constituents—the "scholastics," as McAllister and Tucker call this group—have opted primarily for the "primitive pattern," sometimes at the expense of fellowship and the great thrust for Christian unity which

[17]See Young, *Historical Introductions,* 61-62.

generated the original movement.[18] The liberal branches of Disciples
have emphasized the conciliatory aspects of the *Declaration*, together
with the ecumenical spirit of the other primary leader of the movement,
Barton W. Stone.[19] Sometimes, one-sided enthusiasm for liberal ecumen-
ism suggests a lack of appreciation for dependence upon the New Testament as expressed in the *Declaration and Address*—or religious unity
with no theological guts, as it has been called by some critics.

The process of arriving at a conclusion about the meaning of scripture was, for both Thomas and Alexander Campbell, one pursued by
human reason. The age of rationalism strongly influenced their approach
to epistemology. The use of deductive logic later dominated the debates
Alexander had with opponents on various religious issues. Robert Richardson, along with the Campbells, was clearly influenced by both John
Locke and Scottish "Common-Sense" philosophy. He acknowledged the
use of human reason in the attempt to separate faith and opinion:

> Not controverting at all the fact that human reason must be exer-
> cised in comprehending the scriptures, the effort is made to
> draw a distinction between faith and opinion, between an
> express scriptural declaration and inferences drawn from it.[20]

"Full freedom of opinion" characterized the development of the new
church that succeeded the Washington Christian Association. The
church was founded at Brush Run in Washington County, Pennsylvania,
in 1811. Thomas Campbell proposed a test question for charter membership: what is the meritorious cause of a sinner's acceptance with
God? In actual practice, however, this question was dropped. In the
months that followed, the congregation's polity evolved concerning the
ordinances of the Lord's Supper, which came to be observed weekly, and
believer's baptism by immersion. Questions about the second ordinance
became especially cogent for Alexander Campbell upon the birth of his
first child. After struggling with the question for some time, Alexander
and Thomas, with other members of the family, were immersed by a
neighboring Baptist minister.

The tensions inherent in the cornerstone principles of the movement
were, perhaps, creative tensions. Nevertheless, residual possibilities for
serious and often bitter disagreement, abundant in questions relating to

---

[18]Lester McAllister and William E. Tucker, *Journey in Faith* (St. Louis: Bethany Press, 1975).

[19]Bill J. Humble has summarized the contrasting mature viewpoints of Alexander Campbell and Barton W. Stone in this way: "Whereas Barton Stone emphasized the unity of the believers in Christ, Alexander Campbell's stress was upon the other aspect of the Restoration pleas, the reestablishment of first-century Christianity." (*Campbell and Controversy* [Joplin, Mo.: College Press, 1985], 274).

[20]Richardson, *Memoirs*, 1:265.

"silence of scripture" and an attempt to demarcate the line between faith and opinion, grew swiftly during the lifetimes of Thomas and Alexander and with an accelerating pace after their respective deaths. The separate census reports first offered in 1906 by the Churches of Christ and the Christian Churches, and the restructure of the Christian Churches (Disciples of Christ) in 1968 which sharply separated them from the Independent Christian Churches represent only the tip of the iceberg in comparison with the cultural, theological, and aesthetic barriers which stand between members of the movement that began with such confident faith in the possibility of Christian unity.

The dialogue between culture and theological moral commitments has been present in both the Classical and Judeo-Christian worlds throughout Western history. The philosopher Plato experienced a strong, doubtless creative, tension in his own attitude toward artists, poets, and their work. On the one hand, he loved the aesthetic impact of poetry; on the other hand, ethical commitments led him to suggest the exile of poets from his ideal Republic because of the power of their often false messages.

Saint Augustine reflected this tension in a Christian context:

> . . . when I recall the tears which I shed over the hymns in Thy church at the early period of the recovery of my faith, and now today when I am affected not by the singing, but by the words which are sung, provided they are sung in a clear voice and with the most appropriate modulation, I again recognize the great usefulness of this practice.

> So, I waver between the danger of sensual enjoyment and the experience of healthful employment, and, though not, indeed, to offer an irrevocable decision, I am more inclined to approve the custom of singing in church, in order that the weaker mind may rise to a disposition of piety through these delights of hearing. Nevertheless, when it happens that I am more moved by the song than the thing which is sung, I confess that I sin in a manner deserving of punishment, and then, I should rather not hear the singing.[21]

The tensions inherent in the roots of the Disciples Movement have been both creative and destructive. Future chapters will explore specific ways in which attitudes toward the arts and aesthetic values—both in public worship and in private artistic practice—have related to the

---

[21]Augustine, *Confessions,* tr. Vernon J. Bourke (Washington, D.C.: Catholic University of America Press, 1953), 307-8.

values of the reforms advocated by Barton W. Stone and Thomas Campbell.

Plate 1
BARTON W. STONE
Courtesy Disciples of Christ Historical Society

Plate 2
THOMAS CAMPBELL
Courtesy Disciples of Christ Historical Society

2

Old World Context: The Reformation

The concept of Restoration as it applies to the Church, especially by the most literal advocates of the idea, approaches an existential ideal. The most extreme among the "scholastic" followers of the Campbellian tradition held little regard for the church history from the age of the apostles to the early nineteenth century. This attitude is chiseled in the cornerstones of many a twentieth-century Restoration Movement church building: "The Church of Christ: Founded in Jerusalem c. A.D. 33. This building: 19--."

William Blakemore observes that:

> the earliest leaders of the movement were, like all reformers, . . . more conscious of the points of their discontinuity with the past than of the continuities. It was never necessary to defend what they had retained of their former beliefs and practice, it was necessary to defend their abandonment of previous beliefs and practice, and to defend whatever was novel. The result was that the early generations of Disciples, like all new groups, emphasized their distinctiveness, and almost lost sight of their continuing similarities to the reformed traditions of Calvin and Knox and to Protestantism in general.[1]

Ralph G. Wilburn considered the question from a liberal stance and suggested that this approach to history is not characteristic of the Christian religion:

> . . . this unrealistic attempt to put on a pair of seven-league boots and leap back to Jerusalem, to use another metaphor, letting the intervening centuries drop into oblivion, was doomed to failure. For Christianity is a historic continuum; it

---

[1]William Barnett Blakemore, "Worship among Disciples," *Christian Church (Disciples of Christ): An Interpretive Examination in the Cultural Context,* ed. George Beazley, Jr. (St. Louis: Bethany Press, 1973), 116. The Catholic-Anglican doctrine of the continuity of the church through apostolic succession was the second proposition denied by Alexander Campbell in his 1837 debate with Catholic Bishop Purcell in Cincinnati. In this belief, both Martin Luther and John Calvin would have taken the position occupied by Campbell. See Alexander Campbell and The Right Reverend John A. Purcell, *A Debate on the Catholic Religion* (Nashville: McQuiddy Printing Company, 1914), 11.

persists in continuity in history, by the presence in power of the Holy Spirit. And historic time is irreversible.[2]

Walter Scott, one of the four principal leaders of the Restoration Movement, is credited with having developed the most effective organization of gospel facts for converting people on the Western Reserve to Christ, and to the "new reformation." In his major book, *The Gospel Restored,* Scott unabashedly claims a "restoration" by the Movement on three fronts:

First the Bible was adopted as sole authority in our assemblies, to the exclusion of other books. Next the Apostolic order was proposed. Finally the True Gospel was restored.[3]

Alexander Campbell's views about church history, like other characteristics of the Movement, seem to have been contradictory or in tension. Between 1823 and 1830 he pressed his novel claims for a restoration movement in the first religious journal he edited, *The Christian Baptist.* Reflecting his energy and candor, the editorial volumes of this journal are much more feisty and extreme than later pronouncements which he wrote between 1830 and his death in 1866 in *The Millennial Harbinger.* In the second volume of *The Christian Baptist* he began an extended series of articles entitled "A Restoration of the Ancient Order of Things." Critical of evolutionary religious reformation, he wrote:

Human creeds may be reformed and re-reformed, and be erroneous still, like their authors; but the inspired creed needs no reformation, being, like its author, infallible. . . . Human systems, whether of philosophy or of religion, are proper subjects of reformation; but christianity [sic] cannot be reformed. . . . In a word, we have had reformation enough! The very name has become as offensive, as the term "Revolution" in France.[4]

Even though he often used the modest term, "present reformation," in reference to the religious movement he helped bring into existence, Alexander could still naively write in 1835:

. . . not until the present generation did any sect or party in Christendom unite and build upon the Bible alone.

[2]Ralph G. Wilburn, "The Role of Tradition in the Church's Experience of Jesus as Christ," in *The Reconstruction of Theology,* ed. Ralph G. Wilburn (St. Louis: Bethany Press, 1963), 117.

[3]Walter Scott, *The Gospel Restored* (Cincinnati: printed by O. H. Donogh, 1836; reprinted Joplin, Mo.: College Press, 1986), v.

[4]Alexander Campbell, *Christian Baptist* 2 (1825): 128.

Since that time, the first effort known to us to abandon the whole controversy about creeds and reformations, and to *restore* primitive Christianity, or to build alone upon the Apostles and Prophets, Jesus Christ himself the chief corner-stone, has been made.[5]

"Ancient Gospel" and "Ancient Order" are terms used frequently by Campbell in *The Millennial Harbinger* for concepts which identify the restoration ideal but also denote a more respectful treatment toward church history than strict restorationists will allow. "The present reformation," is another term which concedes that there is at least some common ground with church reformers who preceded the Washington Christian Association.

In 1831 the Disciples—people associated with the Campbells, Walter Scott, and others in the Pennsylvania-Virginia-Ohio churches—effected a union with churches centered in Kentucky under the leadership of Barton W. Stone.

Stone, who was one of the four principal leaders of the movement, had left his Presbyterian roots to advocate the cause of "simple Christianity." The Kentucky group used simply the name, "Christian," and was energetically involved in the quest for unity along lines similar to those of Thomas Campbell's plea in the *Declaration and Address*. Whereas Christian unity was Campbell's primary plea, Stone emphasized exact conformity to the primitive faith and practice.[6]

Recently, members of the more liberal branch of the Disciples, with their zeal for unity, spiritual freedom, and ecumenicity, have focused new interest in Stone's pioneering work within the Restoration Movement.[7] Conservatives, who favor restoration over ecumenicity, tend to consider Stone's leadership in a less important light.[8]

Alexander Campbell was critical of all previous reformation efforts in church history, because, in his view, they all proceeded on the mistaken assumption that existing structures could be reformed and purified.[9] Nevertheless, he gladly gave credit to the sixteenth-century reformers, and acknowledged that the Church of Christ was not the

---

[5]Alexander Campbell, *The Christian System,* 121.

[6]See Richardson, *Memoirs,* 2:199.

[7]Leroy Garrett's excellent history of the movement sets a precedent in being entitled *The Stone-Campbell Movement* (Joplin, Mo.: College Press, 1982).

[8]M. M. Davis, *How the Disciples Began and Grew* (Cincinnati: Standard Press Publishing Co., 1915), 122, recognized that Stone's movement was older than that of the Campbells, but saw it as tributary to the Campbellian movement "because all the vital and permanent in the teachings of Stone, and much more, were found in the teachings of Campbell."

[9]See the "Parable of the Iron Bedstead," *Christian Baptist* (1826) 4:19.

result of the seven-league hurdle which some of his more scholastic followers attempted to make it. In the Preface to *The Christian System,* he wrote:

> We Americans owe our national privileges and our civil liberties to the Protestant reformers. They achieved not only an imperishable fame for themselves, but a rich legacy for their posterity. When we contrast the present state of these United States with Spanish America, and the condition of the English nation with that of Spain, Portugal, and Italy, we begin to appreciate how much we are indebted to the intelligence, faith, and courage of Martin Luther and his heroic associates in that glorious reformation.[10]

Ironically, Campbell attributes the ultimate failures of the Protestant Reformation to the "scholastic generation" of followers who controverted or prevented the original direction of the effort. He lamented the absence of a second generation of leaders to continue the great work of the sixteenth-century reformers:

> He [Luther] restored the Bible to the world A.D. 1534, and boldly defended its claims against the impious and arrogant pretensions of the haughty and tyrannical See of Rome. But unfortunately, at his death there was no Joshua to lead the people, who rallied under the banners of the Bible, out of the wilderness in which Luther died. His tenets were soon converted into a new state religion, and the spirit of reformation which he excited and inspired was soon quenched by the broils and feuds of the Protestant princes and the collisions of rival political interests, both on the continent and in the islands of Europe.[11]

Campbell's concern about the outcome of the Protestant Reformation became prophetic about the course his own reformation would follow. Ronald E. Osborne of the Christian Church (Disciples of Christ) has pointed this out:

---

[10]Alexander Campbell, *The Christian System,* vii. Although Campbell was consistently critical of the incomplete results of the Protestant Reformation, he was just as consistent in giving credit to the sixteenth-century reformers for the religious freedom and the privilege of individual thinking enjoyed by his own generation. See his address delivered to The Western Literary Institute and College of Professional Teachers in Cincinnati, Ohio, during October, 1836, in D. L. Talbott, ed., *Transactions of the Sixth Annual Meeting of the Western Literary Institute, College of Professional Teachers.* Held in Cincinnati, Ohio, October, 1836 (Cincinnati: Published by the Executive Committee, quoted in Humble, *Campbell and Controversy,* 123.

[11]Ibid.

While Campbell's "true Bibleism" brought emancipation to him and his contemporaries as they worked out their simple and reasonable exposition of biblical doctrine, it nevertheless turned to legalism and human tradition in the hands of their successors.[12]

It is clear that for both Thomas and Alexander Campbell the desire to establish a new beginning for the church based on apostolic practice and teaching did not utterly wipe out their sense of history. They were sufficiently grounded in a liberal education and in theological perspectives to recognize some historical continuity within the Body of Christ. In 1837, in his numerous debates, Alexander Campbell laced his arguments with numerous references to the history of ideas.[13] Sometimes these were used to demonstrate inconsistencies in his opponents' arguments. Sometimes he used them to underline his confidence in the rational process and in liberal learning.

George G. Beazley, Jr. summarizes the philosophy of history held by the earliest Restoration leaders:

> The early Disciple fathers tried to restore the church of the New Testament period. Often they failed to sense the inevitable effect of the seventeen centuries between their period and the first century. Enlightenment thought, in which the Campbells and Walter Scott were grounded, was highly ideational and had little sense of the organic nature of cultural history. However, the abyss between the world of most of the New Testament writers and that of Christians who have come later, particularly those who are post-Renaissance, lies in the understanding of the nature of the future.[14]

Beazley suggests that Alexander Campbell's view of eschatology, expressed in *The Millennial Harbinger,* was "predicated on a long continued history in which the doctrines of the 'ancient order of things' and the 'primitive gospel' would gradually conquer Christians' minds by their self-evident truths and a united church would preach the gospel to every creature."[15]

---

[12]Ronald E. Osborne, "Theology among the Disciples," in Beazley, ed., *The Christian Church (Disciples of Christ)*, 92.

[13]See Humble, *Campbell and Controversy,* chap. 3, 78-118. Campbell participated in debates with Robert Owen, the atheistic socialist, as well as with two Presbyterian ministers, with whom he debated about infant baptism, and with a Catholic priest.

[14]George G. Beazley, Jr., "A Look at the Future of the Christian Church (Disciples of Christ)," in Beazley, ed., *The Christian Church (Disciples of Christ)* (St. Louis: Bethany, 1973), 314.

[15]Ibid., 315.

Campbell's expectation of an evolutionary development of the Millennium in the United States contrasted with both contemporary premillennial and amillennial views held by orthodox Protestants. The projection of a future world built by God working through the restoration rested on an appreciation of God working in history. Forces which formed the mind-set and became a part of the fiber of the lives of the restoration leaders need to be considered. Some of these elements were evident; others were more subtle but had no less an impact on values, theological beliefs, and attitudes which developed in the Movement. In the area of aesthetic values, Protestant traditions had penetrated deeply and continued to exert influence, becoming normative for the Movement's leaders—in both worship and general artistic practice.

Those normative Protestant aesthetic values came especially from European Calvinism, the Irish and Scottish Presbyterianism of John Knox, and the influences of the free churches of the British Isles. From another direction, the cumulative effect of the Enlightenment, especially the thought of John Locke (1632-1704), clearly influenced the American Restoration Movement. Both the theology and aesthetic ethos of the Lutheran Reformation was fundamental for the Stone-Campbell Movement leaders, particularly those concepts of personal and religious freedom which the nineteenth-century reformers valued so highly. These influences will be examined in their turn.

The American Restoration Movement developed more directly from the Reformed faith as represented by the thought of John Calvin, John Knox, and the English and American Puritans. In polity, Irish and Scottish Presbyterianism predominated. Hence, the aesthetic values of Thomas and Alexander Campbell, Barton W. Stone, and Walter Scott were not shaped by the liturgy, architecture, poetry, or cultivation of spiritual music which characterized the Lutheran Reformation. None of the leading sixteenth-century Protestant reformers were opposed to art, as some have assumed, but there were different degrees of artistic affinity between Luther and Calvin.[16]

Luther personally corresponded with the famous German Renaissance painter and printmaker Albrecht Dürer and was also a warm friend and patron of the artist Lucas Cranach. Luther wrote:

> I do not hold that the Gospel should destroy all the arts, as certain superstitious folk believe. On the contrary, I would fain see all the arts, and especially that of music, serving Him who

---

[16]For example, G. G. Coulton, *Art and the Reformation* (Hamdon, Conn.: Archon Books, 1969), 407, states that Calvin "was far less inimical to art than is generally imagined."

hath created them and given them to us. . . . The Law of Moses forbade only the image of God; the crucifix is not forbidden.[17]

Luther resisted making an extreme break with traditional Catholic practice in the use of music, liturgy, and images, as was advocated by some other reformers. Luther retained the Latin mass in his earliest *Formulae Missal et Communinis* of 1523. Three years later his German mass included several elements from the liturgy of the Roman mass, with substitutions of German hymns and songs for some sections. Luther even left his hiding place in Eisenach's Wartburg Castle to counter the image-breaking and disorder perpetrated in the town of Wittenberg during his absence. Andreas Carlstadt, once a defender of Luther, had rejected all church music and religious images as distractions and had led the citizens of Wittenberg to destroy relics, images, and pictures.[18]

Luther's personal involvement in musical art was not confined strictly to church or liturgical use. He played the lute and the flute and sang the alto part in polyphonic music at his home. He even composed some melodies and motets, and continually stressed the importance of music to stir the hearts and elevate the minds of people. His reform of the liturgy allowed for creativity in music.

Luther stressed the use of vernacular language in chorales and hymns; he encouraged participation by the congregation in unison singing of the musical portions of the service. The organ was used only to provide intonation, for playing preludes, and for other non-sung portions of the liturgy.[19] By the eighteenth century, the German chorale had become central to both the vocal and instrumental parts of worship, so that the close tie between the worship of God and the composition of church music resulted—through Schutz, Buxtehude, and J. S. Bach—in some of the most powerful Protestant expression in the arts.

The Reformed tradition, that branch of the Protestant Reformation developed primarily by followers of John Calvin, has a direct relationship with the American Restoration Movement. Historically, this relationship may be traced through the Calvinist tradition in Scotland and Ireland, together with less direct roots in the Church of England, and through English and American Puritanism. Positive influences of Calvinism as well as negative reactions to it surface in Campbellian thought. Recent thinkers have found more residual Calvinism in the Restoration

---

[17]Ibid., 408.

[18]See A. G. Dickens, *Reformation and Society in Sixteenth-Century Europe* (London: Harcourt, Brace and World, 1966), 70. Dickens's work is widely regarded as authoritative. See also Roland H. Bainton, *Christendom*, 2 vols. (New York: Harper & Row, 1966), 2:25, and De Lamar Jensen, *Reformation Europe* (Lexington, Mass.: D. C. Heath, 1981), 55.

[19]See Gustave Reese, *Music in the Renaissance* (New York: Norton & Co., 1954), 673-74; Bainton, *Christendom*, 2:26.

Movement than the leaders of that movement want to admit. All four of the "original fathers"—Thomas and Alexander Campbell, Barton Stone, and Walter Scott—were reared in the Presbyterian Church. Although they each rejected rigid predestinarianism and insisted that Christ had died for all who did not reject the gospel, they each retained most of the basic elements of the Reformed faith.

The primary concern of this chapter relates to aesthetic attitudes found in European ideas that shaped the thinking of the American reformers of the Ohio Valley. However, several aspects of Reformed theology are important for any study of attitudes held by the Campbells and their colleagues.

John Calvin (1509-64) enjoyed the broad literary strength of his humanistic background. He studied in Paris, Orléans, and Bourges and he received a doctorate in law sometime before 1532. His *Commentary* on Seneca's *Two Books on Clemency* appeared in Paris in April of 1532. This *Commentary* has been seen as "the principal monument to young Calvin's humanistic attainments. . . . The book is to be thought of as an ambitious humanist contribution to political ethics."[20]

Calvin's sense of history reflected the perspective of his earlier studies in humanistic thought. His view of the church was less existential than that adopted by the stricter nineteenth-century American restorationists. In his study of Calvinism, McNeill suggests that

> Calvin repudiates the allegation that the Protestant position involves the necessity of affirming the true Church to have been long extinct. The Church has not ceased to be, and will continue to the end of time: but it has not always been visible, and it does not consist of an external organization.[21]

Calvin, in Book 4 of his great work, the *Institutes of the Christian Religion,* wrote:

> However, when we categorically deny to the papists the title of the church, we do not for this reason impugn the existence of churches among them. . . . To sum up, I call them churches to the extent that the Lord wonderfully preserves in them a remnant of his people, however woefully dispersed and scattered, and to the extent that some marks of the church remain—especially those marks whose effectiveness neither the devil's wiles nor human depravity can destroy. But on the other hand, because in them those marks have been erased to which we

---

[20]John T. McNeill, *The History and Character of Calvinism* (New York: Oxford University Press, 1954), 104.

[21]Ibid., 123.

should pay particular regard in this discourse, I say that every one of their congregations and their whole body lack the lawful form of the church.[22]

The idea of discontinuity in Western church history—an idea found in the most radical restorationist statements of the American Disciples—is not entirely unique, however. Calvin—whose thought provided the single most important Reformation source for the Campbells, Stone, and Scott—did sometimes suggest a break between his own religious practice and that of the Roman Catholic Church of the sixteenth century. William Bouwsma, in his recent biographical study of Calvin, refers to a quotation from Calvin's commentary on 2 Timothy which implies this discontinuity:

If we wish to be his disciples, we must unlearn everything we have learned apart from Christ. For example, our own pure instruction in the faith began with forgetting and rejecting the whole instruction of the papacy.[23]

Just as it was unrealistic for American Restorations to ignore the continuous history of the church, so it was for Calvin to believe he had completely broken from his past. William J. Bouwsma writes:

This was an illusion. Discontinuities, historical and biographical, are rarely as decisive as they seem to those involved; and Calvin's claim to have made so large a change reflected the limitations in his awareness of how far his understanding even of the gospel depended on inherited assumptions he could not easily, or ever shake off, if only because he was largely unconscious of them. The Reformation slogan *scriptura sola* was intrinsically naive; and Calvin's claim that Scripture was his "only guide," and acquiescence in its "plain doctrines" as his "constant rule of wisdom," could never have been more than an aspiration. He had "forgotten" only a fraction of what he had learned under the papacy.[24]

Calvin dealt with the apparent inconsistency of his simultaneous repudiation and acceptance of Roman Catholic tradition by distinguishing between the "visible" and "invisible" church. The invisible church,

---

[22]John Calvin, *Institutes of the Christian Religion*, ed. John T. McNeill, tr. Ford Lewis Battles (Philadelphia: Westminster Press, 1960), 2:3.12.

[23]John Calvin, *Commentary on 2 Timothy 3:14,* quoted in William J. Bouwsma, *John Calvin: A Sixteenth-Century Portrait* (New York: Oxford University Press, 1988), 98.

[24]See William J. Bouwsma, *John Calvin: A Sixteenth-Century Portrait* (New York: Oxford University Press, 1988), 98. Here Bouwsma cites Calvin's *Commentary on 2 Timothy 3:15.*

according to the Catechism of 1537, is limited to the elect,[25] but the visible deals with the practical problems of church polity and discipline.

Another doctrine that the Reformation anticipated, which is a fundamental doctrine of the nineteenth-century Restoration Movement, is the authority of the Bible as the Word of God. The Protestantism of the German-speaking cantons of Switzerland was based on the teachings of the Swiss humanist Huldrich Zwingli. Zwingli and his followers regarded the Bible not only as the proclamation of salvation, but also as a pattern for church organization. It provided authoritative and final direction for the church in doctrine, discipline, and worship.[26]

Calvin also related the authenticity of the Church of Christ to the integrity of the Word. Under the heading, "The Church is founded upon God's Word," he wrote of the empty external glitter that "blinds the eyes of the simple" and "ought not to move us a whit to grant that the Church exists where God's Word is not found."[27]

In the area of aesthetic practice, Calvin's well-known opposition to "hymns of human composure" did not at all represent a personal dislike for beauty or lack of a sensitive appreciation for the power of the arts. Using the Apostle Paul as his guide, Calvin taught that the only appropriate texts for singing or reciting were the psalms. He wrote a lengthy statement about this in his preface to the 1542 *Psalter,* which received its complete form, after several partial editions, in 1562.[28] The French vernacular was used for congregational singing of the psalms, a practice apparently cultivated with enthusiasm by Calvin's congregation at Strasbourg during the 1540s and later at Geneva:

> The 'little French church' was remarkable for the hearty congregational singing practiced in its worship. In 1545 a Walloon student in Strasbourg wrote to a friend in Antwerp that he had been unable to refrain from weeping for joy during the first days of his sojourn there when all, men and women, joined together in the psalmody.[29]

[25]Ibid.

[26]Ibid., 214.

[27]See Bainton, *Christendom,* 2:30-31; McNeil, *History and Character of Calvinism,* 73. Albert Henry Newman, a Baptist historian writing early during the twentieth century, says of the "biblical Anabaptists" in the sixteenth century: "Their adherence to the Scriptures, especially the New Testament, as the only and sufficient rule of faith and practice, their use of reasonably sound methods of Scripture interpretation, their freedom from chiliastic enthusiasm, their intense zeal for the spread of the gospel, and their readiness to suffer even unto death for their faith, commend them to us as worthy of admiration." *A Manual of Church History* (Philadelphia: American Baptist Publication Society, 1902), 168-69.

[28]Reese, *Music in the Renaissance,* 358-59.

[29]McNeill, *History and Character of Calvinism,* 147.

Like Luther, Calvin contributed to hymnody literature. Unlike Luther, he did so, not by writing original hymns, but by writing vernacular and metrical versions of biblical psalms.[30] In addition to his 1542 preface, Calvin added a section to the 1543 edition which extended the province of singing praises wider than just the house of worship:

> Here he has in mind the extension of psalm singing to 'houses' and 'fields'. He wants the human voice to become 'an organ of praise to God.' Music, he says, is the first gift of god [*sic*], or one of the first, for man's recreation and pleasure, and we ought carefully to avoid permitting it to serve dissoluteness and lasciviousness.[31]

That the Genevan reformers accepted aesthetic phenomena as worthwhile gifts of pleasure outside the specific context of teaching, learning, and worship is evident in Calvin's discussion of the effects of these phenomena on the senses:

> Let this be our principle: that the use of God's gifts is not wrongly directed to that end which the author himself created and destined them for us, since he created them for our good, not for our ruin. Accordingly, no one will hold to a straighter path than he who diligently looks to this end. Now if we ponder to what end God created food, we shall find that he meant not only to provide for necessity but also for delight and good cheer. Thus the purpose of clothing, apart from necessity, was comeliness and decency. In grasses, trees, and fruits, apart from their various uses, there is beauty of appearance and pleasantness of odor. . . . For if this were not true, the prophet would not have reckoned them among the benefits of God, "that wine gladdens the heart of man, that oil makes his face shine" [Ps. 104:15].[32]

The passage continues with a discussion of the pleasurable gifts of precious stones, colors, and flowers, showing that Calvin recognized the value of beauty. Simplicity in life and worship and the avoidance of ornamentation, however, were high priorities in the Calvinist order of values. Thus, while singing was prized in congregational worship and at home, to warm the heart, the poetic content should be psalms. Calvin believed that congregational psalm-singing should be unaccompanied because the singer should concentrate on the words of the psalm and

---

[30]John H. Leith, *An Introduction to the Reformed Tradition* (Atlanta: John Knox Press, 1977), 195.

[31]McNeill, *History and Character of Calvinism,* 149.

[32]Calvin, *Institutes* 3:10.2.

because organs were used for non-liturgical purposes in the sixteenth century.[33]

In his rejection of instrumental music for congregational worship, Calvin prefigured the position of the early American Restoration reformers. Similarly, too, divisive problems accompanied introduction of this idea, both in the sixteenth century and the mid-nineteenth century. On the other hand, Calvin echoed some of the same tensions which Saint Augustine had felt in his support for psalmody and his concern that it remain a practical function of teaching in the church:

> Yet we do not here condemn speaking and singing but rather strongly commend them, provided they are associated with the heart's affection. For thus do they exercise the mind in thinking of God and keep it attentive—unstable and variable as it is, and readily relaxed and diverted in different directions, unless it be supported by various helps. Moreover, since the glory of God ought, in a measure, to shine in the several parts of our bodies, it is especially fitting that the tongue has been assigned and destined for this task, both through singing and through speaking. For it was peculiarly created to tell and proclaim the praise of God.[34]

The sources of melodies for Calvin's *Psalter* were of less concern than those for the texts. Some psalm melodies were borrowed from the Lutherans, nearly half of them were drawn from secular songs, and about eighty-five were originally composed or arranged by Louis Bourgeois, a Genevan musician associated with the Reformation. Calvin's criteria for the musical content were "that it should be the equal of the text in majesty" and "appropriate to sing in the church (*propre a chanter en l'Eglise*)."[35]

Twentieth-century scholars differ concerning the question of polyphonic singing in the church. A number of significant sixteenth-century composers set melodies from the *Psalter* in parts, particularly after 1560.[36] In the preface to the Genevan edition of his 1565 collection of specific settings in four parts of the Genevan *Psalter,* by the famed composer Claude Goudimel, the composer stressed that the collection was intended for "home use rather than for the service"—important, in view of Calvin's insistence that music in the church be restricted to

---

[33]Leith, *Introduction to Reformed Tradition,* 201-2.

[34]Calvin, *Institutes* 3:20.31. Calvin even refers to Augustinian concerns in the next section of the work.

[35]Reese, *Music in the Renaissance,* 359-60.

[36]Including Louis Bourgeois, Claude Goudimel, Claude Le Jeune, and probably Hubert Waelrant.

monophony.[37] There is disagreement over whether Calvin actually opposed harmonization or whether he was simply so busy with other pastoral duties that he did not give much consideration to aesthetic matters.[38]

For students of the Stone-Campbell movement in America the parallels are obvious in the aesthetic of simplicity espoused by John Calvin and its echo in the worship practices of the American reform movement. Calvin's functional approach to a music ethos is reflected in his attitudes toward visual arts, architecture, and literature. His discussions of painting and sculpture in the *Institutes* revolve around the avoidance of idolatry, a practice Calvin clearly attributed to the Roman Catholic use of images. The major section is headed, "It is Unlawful to Attribute a Visible Form to God, and Generally Whoever Sets up Idols Revolts against the True God."[39] In the sixteenth century, Pope Gregory and the German Catholic theologian Johann von Eck had argued that pictures and images represent a powerful teaching device by the church. To refute this, Calvin concluded:

> If it were not true that whatever knowledge of God is sought from images is fallacious and counterfeit, the prophets would not so generally have condemned it.[40]

After a vigorous attack on art representative of Deity and the saints, Calvin did acknowledge that there was some use for sculpture and painting:

> And yet, I am not gripped by the superstition of thinking absolutely no images permissible. But because sculpture and painting are gifts of God, I seek a pure and legitimate use of each, lest those things which the Lord has conferred upon us for his glory and our good be not only polluted by perverse misuse but also turned to our destruction . . . it remains that only those things are to be sculptured or painted which the eyes are capable of seeing: let not God's majesty, which is far above the perception

---

[37]Reese, *Music in the Renaissance,* 502.

[38]Ibid. Reese writes that Calvin insisted that music in the church be restricted to monophony. However, Leith, *Introduction to Reformed Tradition,* 202, writes: "Music should be appropriate to the words and to worship, but the contention that he opposed four-part singing as such or its use in worship has been refuted by Doumergue. Calvin and Zwingli alike were guided in worship by biblical and theological principles, not by psychological or aesthetic considerations. Calvin, like Zwingli, appreciated music as the gift of God; but Calvin in particular was too occupied with his work to contribute much to music save in its use in the church."

[39]Calvin, *Institutes,* 1:11.1.

[40]Ibid., 1:11.5.

of the eyes, be debased through unseemly representations. Within this class some are histories and events, some are images and forms of bodies without any depicting of past events. The former have some use in teaching or admonition; as for the latter, I do not see what they can afford other than pleasure.[41]

The key word in this polemic is "use"—the ethical requirement of a utilitarian employment for teaching or preaching to justify the existence of art or music. Clearly, pleasure was considered an unworthy justification for the existence of art. This stance became normative for British and American Puritanism.

Leith says flatly that Calvin did not believe that the visual arts were effective instruments for communicating the gospel, nor did Calvin give much attention to the arts. Leith excuses him, however, by pointing out that he was an exceedingly busy person who did not have the time to pursue cultural activities. Calvin did believe that the visual arts were gifts of God and should be used "in pure and legitimate ways" for joy and pleasure.[42]

Calvin obviously believed that words were more effective than images. His humanist background gave him confidence in the power of words. He and the other reformers believed that reliance on images to communicate the faith had produced theological illiteracy and corrupted the gospel message. The reformers' preference for the logic of language and cognitive formulations of the gospel are clearly identifiable in the concepts of Alexander Campbell and his successors.

Reliance upon the Word of God (*sola scriptura*) was a cornerstone of the Protestant Reformation. That reliance is reaffirmed in the Stone-Campbell Movement, whose leaders believed that primacy of the Word over ecclesiastical tradition or authority is rooted in the New Testament. The declaration posited at the beginning of John's Gospel—that the Word was "in the beginning" and participated in creation, together with the identification of that Word as the Christ (John 1:14), who was made flesh and dwelt among us (John 1:3)—provides the framework for the ensuing Pauline emphasis on the Word throughout the New Testament. Paul describes the "sword of the Spirit" as the Word of God (Eph. 6:17), and urges Timothy to "preach the Word" (2 Tim. 4:2), and admonishes the young preacher also to continue in what he has learned—the "sacred writings which are able to instruct you for salvation through faith in Christ Jesus" (2 Tim. 3:14-15).

[41]Calvin, *Institutes,* 1:11.12.

[42]Leith, *Introduction to Reformed Tradition,* 191.

During the "scholastic" period of the Disciples movement, questions arose about the relationship between the Spirit and the Word, between Jesus Christ and the Word, and between the Bible and the Word. These same questions, of course, have been live issues from the Protestant Reformation until the present time.

It is difficult to pinpoint the central thrust of Calvin's own teaching about the Word of God. Even though he received a humanist education, his literary study of the Bible resulted in adopting the scriptures as his guide, authority, and arsenal. Calvin's emphasis on the Word of God is well known; but his followers have been hard pressed to identify the center of his thought or its dominant theme. Some see it in the sovereign majesty of God, others in the doctrine of election. Still others see his major topics as expressions of concern to "be an interpreter of the divine Book, the Word of God by which man obtains a knowledge of salvation."[43]

Calvinist emphasis is neatly summarized in the statement that Reformed theology has always been intensely biblical. Hence, the Church of Christ should not be bound by laws, commandments, or human traditions apart from the Word of God.[44]

Alexander Campbell's preaching and debating mirrored much of Calvin's theological approach, which has been described as "commentary upon scripture as a whole and . . . the way the church had read scripture in its theology and creeds." Campbell, like Calvin, emphasized his favorite books of the New Testament; but he, too, attempted to establish his theology upon the whole of scripture. Those who commented on Campbell's whole-part approach of applying all of scripture to an individual problem or difficult passage spoke of his "comprehensiveness" and use of the "overall picture." One can find the same criticisms of Calvin: that he failed to "distinguish adequately between the lights and shadows of scripture," by treating all scripture on the same level.[45]

Eschatology was another aspect of Alexander Campbell's thought in which we can see echoes of Calvin's thinking. Thus it would be worthwhile to examine Calvin's concepts about the nature of the Kingdom of God and the movement of God in human history. First, Calvin was militant in his repudiation of chiliasm (millenarianism), which he regarded as "too childish either to need or to be worth a repudiation."[46] Calvin's

---

[43]See McNeill, *History and Character of Calvinism,* 201-3. Also see I. John Hesselink, "Law and Gospel or Gospel and Law? Calvin's Understanding of the Relationship," *Calviniana: Ideas and Influence of Jean Calvin,* ed. R. V. Schnucker (Kirksville, Mo.: Sixteenth Century Publishers, 1988), 13-33.

[44]Leith, *Introduction to Reformed Tradition,* 97.

[45]Ibid., 99-100; Richardson, *Memoirs,* 2:451.

[46]Calvin, *Institutes,* 3:25.5.

highly developed sense of history is revealed in his discussion of the second petition of the Lord's prayer, "Thy Kingdom come," and proceeds to show how God sets up his Kingdom:

> God reigns where men, both by denial of themselves and by contempt of the world and of earthly life, pledge themselves to his righteousness in order to aspire to a heavenly life. Thus there are two parts to this Kingdom: first, that God by the power of his Spirit correct all the desires of the flesh which by squadrons was against him; second, that he shape all our thoughts in obedience to this rule.   . . . .
>
> Therefore God sets up his Kingdom by humbling the whole world, but in different ways. For he tames the wantonness of some, breaks the untamable pride of others.[47]

The theocratic city government of Geneva, administered by Calvin from 1541 until his death in 1564, reflected his belief that God moves in human history. Calvin sought not only the salvation of souls in Geneva, but a society that was reformed by the Word of God. John Knox is said to have remarked, "In other places, I confess Christ to be truly preached; but manners and religion to be so sincerely reformed, I have not seen in any other place."[48]

However, Calvin emphasized that the Kingdom's fullness would be delayed until the final coming of Christ when, as Paul teaches, "God will be all in all" (I Cor. 15:28), and he did not spend a great deal of time speculating on the nature or time of that final coming.

Even though Alexander Campbell entitled his religious journal *The Millennial Harbinger*, his eschatological ideas were similar to Calvin's. Campbell did not expect an imminent return of Christ; rather, he expected a long continuation of history, in which there would be time to restore the "ancient order of things," and the "primitive gospel" would gradually conquer Christians' minds by self-evident truths and a unified church would preach the gospel to every creature.[49]

More similarities between John Calvin and Alexander Campbell can be discovered. One that provides a lively ground for a comparison is in the aesthetic category of creative poetry. Both reformers made youthful attempts at verse, which were not continued into their later years except for providing material for Christian worship. Both demonstrated some propensity for aesthetic concerns, though both placed them under the

---

[47]Ibid., 3:20.42.

[48]Leith, *Introduction to Reformed Tradition*, 72-73.

[49]Beazley, "Future of the Christian Church (Disciples of Christ)," in *The Christian Church (Disciples of Christ)*, 315.

burden of religious utility. Calvin's appreciation of stylistic eloquence has been described by McNeill:

> While his thoughts flow, the words in which he clothes them are chosen and sifted with a trained sense of artistic fitness. We see in his writing both a scriptural simplicity and a Ciceronian eloquence.[50]

In describing Calvin's appreciation of both natural beauty and beautiful language, McNeill mentions the youthful poetry:

> Calvin confessed to Bucer's former secretary, Conrad Herbert . . . 'a natural propensity to poetry,' which, however, he had not followed since he was twenty-five, save for his *Epinicium* of 1540. . . . Calvin had not a high opinion of his own verses; and this judgment has not been seriously disputed even by warm admirers of his prose.[51]

Alexander Campbell, living within an ethos derived from the Reformed branch of the Christian Church, dedicated most of his poetic labors to Christian utility: creating and editing Christian hymnbooks. During his early years in the United States, he did contribute a series of essays and a number of "Sunday poems" to the Washington, Pennsylvania, *Reporter*. Robert Richardson, in his sympathetic biography of Campbell, includes a youthful poem by the future reformer, commenting kindly but realistically:

> These lines afford a fair specimen of his skill in versification, and while they betray the absence of that delicacy of ear which readily detects redundant or defective measure, they, at the same time, exhibit poetic fancy and feeling.[52]

Richardson realized that Alexander Campbell's true talents and interests were in the realm of the logical rather than aesthetic use of language. In this sense, at least, Campbell remained in the Calvinist heritage of the Protestant Reformation. Campbell's eloquence and facility with words was recognized in his own time. Some years after his debate with Campbell, Catholic Bishop John Purcell wrote:

> Now as for Mr. Campbell's standing in future ages, I think it is quite within the bounds of truth to say that not ecclesiastical history alone, but profane history, will place him on the same

---

[50]McNeill, *History and Character of Calvinism*, 232.
[51]Ibid.
[52]Richardson, *Memoirs*, 1:193.

pedestal with Luther and Calvin and Wesley, the peer of either of them. Had he lived in the early ages of Christendom and accomplished the wonderful amount of good will with which he is justly credited he would after death have been sanctified and canonized and "enrolled in the capital" along with St. Chrysosthom and St. Jerome as a father in the church, his name forever embalmed in its annals as a worthy successor of St. Peter and St. Paul.[53]

Although some have viewed Calvinism and Puritanism as a negative influence on philosophies of learning, education, culture, and the arts, others have seen the positive side of these traditions. Leith remarks, in his chapter "Culture and the Reformed Tradition,"

> The great Reformed theologians and churchmen did not origi-
> nally set out to enrich culture. Their work was the interpretation
> and application of the Word of God and leadership in the life of
> the Church. Yet in performing these functions with integrity and
> competence, they mightily shaped culture.[54]

The medium where the Yes-No tension of Calvinism most clearly influenced aesthetic attitudes of the Disciples fathers was the area of drama and theater. The uselessness of a Christian spending time with fiction and drama, with stories that never really happened at all, became for Alexander Campbell and his wife, Selina, a major reason for rejecting those forms. The tension between the winsomeness of artistic presentation and the untruth of a poem's content caused Plato (*ca.*427-*ca.* 347 B.C.) to suggest casting musicians and poets out of his ideal republic. The tension was faced again by Saint Augustine (354-430). Calvin's own use of the concept of the stage as the center of life, with his literal criticism of actual stage people, echoed the ancient tensions in the Protestant Reformation.

Saint Augustine, especially during his last years, called stage performances a "voluptuous madness," the love of the stage a "filthy scab." Medieval theologians decried the "lie" of fiction as from the Devil, "a liar from the beginning." Augustine reflected this "typical temper of the Middle Ages. . . [which] said in effect: Life is serious business; reflection should be committed to serious things; there is room neither in life nor in reflection for anything but the study of righteousness."[55]

---

[53]Humble, *Campbell and Controversy*, 156, citing an interview in *The Christian Evangelist*, December 1, 1898. Humble speculates that the interviewer was probably governor Ira D. Chase of Indiana, a Christian minister.

[54]Leith, *Introduction to Reformed Tradition*, 211.

[55]See Augustine, *Confessions*, 1:16, quoted in Katherine Gilbert and Helmut Kuhn, *A History of Aesthetics* (Bloomington: Indiana University Press, 1954), 121.

Augustine, however, realized the importance of dramatic presentation for the truth of the Gospel, and, in a desire that people should be enriched by classic literature, dialectically came to the position that poetic fiction contained a certain kind of metaphoric truth. Augustine's standard even required that the actor who represents another individual on stage must do so expertly and accurately, or else be guilty of true dishonesty. Artistic standards for actors and writers of fiction were therefore dictated by ethical as much as aesthetic considerations. And Augustine is credited by the rationale which defends "the willing suspension of unbelief" in theater and fiction, the unwritten pact between artist and audience which distinguishes between fiction and drama on the one hand, and lying and doctrinal heresy on the other.[56] Augustine's analogy of life as a play, or a play-within-a-play, provides a basis for understanding his conception of drama as an ontological condition of Christian redemption:

> His psychological interpretation of the redemption, when separated from the providential play-within-a-play in which he embedded it, is very suggestive to modern minds accustomed to thinking in materialistic, rather than in supernaturalistic, terms. And his notion of the gradual unfolding of Christian truth is congenial to our own conceptions.[57]

William Bouwsma points out that, for Calvin's age, the drama as life analogy is normative in a basic understanding of the human condition and that Calvin himself shared this vision of human existence:

> Rooted in the classics and the Bible, a dramatic vision of existence was as serious an element in the mentality of Calvin's contemporaries as their preoccupation with power. . . . He often described the universe as 'a glorious theater' in which, as spectators, we admire God's works. We can also watch it in the unfolding drama of historical existence, in which God wishes us 'to attend not only to the last hundred years or so but to the time since the creation of the world.'[58]

Calvin's heritage of Renaissance humanism was expressed by William Shakespeare in the bard's view that "all the world's a stage, and all the men and women merely players." (*As You Like It*, 2:7)

[56]Ibid., 124, 126.

[57]W. T. Jones, *A History of Western Philosophy* (New York: Harcourt, Brace and Co., 1952), 1: 390.

[58]Bouwsma, *Calvin: A Portrait*, 177.

Since men and women are also the actors in God's theater, Calvin saw his own career in dramatic terms. He spoke repeatedly of the "roles" which God had assigned to him in life. But Calvin, like Augustine long before him, and Alexander Campbell after him, was not entirely comfortable with the "honesty" and "deception inherent in the theater:"

> But although Calvin shared the theatrical perspective of his age, he was also uncomfortable with it. The ambiguity of 'play' suggests what troubled him. 'Play,' as with children, can express what is most authentic and spontaneous in human existence. But role playing, whether in society or on the stage, is different. In society we play roles that may require the true self to meet the expectations of others or to deceive them. Acting on the stage also involves the substitution of an artificial for an authentic self; it does not express the natural vitality and freedom of human beings but hides behind a mask, assumes a persona—another term borrowed from the theater.[59]

The concept of 'fantasy,' a term which later was to bother Selina Campbell greatly, also worried Calvin:

> The charge of 'fantasy' gives another clue to what troubled Calvin. He generally opposes 'new things,' and theatrical performances smacked of the presumption he associated with all human 'invention.' At times he suggests Plato. 'Poets have invented what pleases them,' he charged, 'and thus they have filled the world with the grossest and foulest errors. Since all theaters resound with these lying fictions, the minds of the crowd have been imbued with this sort of madness, for we know that human nature is always prone to vanity.'[60]

Calvin's century was one in which that greatest of playwrights, William Shakespeare, worked in Stratford in England. Inevitably, the *Zeitgeist* of the sixteenth century might produce in him those Platonic-Augustinian tensions about fantasy, fiction, and theater. However, for the nineteenth-century American Restoration Movement's leaders, the Puritan period—with its emphasis on the godliness of practicality and usefulness—had intervened. Besides this, life on the American frontier, where living involved a daily race with necessity, diminished those tensions, leaving the generally negative view towards fantasy and the stage.

[59]Ibid.
[60]Ibid., 178-79.

3

Old World Roots: The British Isles

This chapter enumerates influences beyond the sixteenth-century Calvinist Reformation which contributed to the cultural milieu in which Thomas and Alexander Campbell acquired their basic intellectual/religious perceptions. Some of these influences involve continued developments in religious reformation, including Calvinist, Anglican, Puritan, and Independent Church strains which surfaced in the experience of the Campbells. Others incorporate philosophical concepts from the English Enlightenment and rationalism which impacted the thinking of the future religious reformers. Both intellectual forces—religious doctrines and secular philosophy—contributed to the cultural *Zeitgeist* which influenced their views of the language, doctrine, and aesthetic effort, and the arts.

The Anglican Church had adopted various components of Calvinist doctrine from the period of its separation from Rome in 1534. By the time of Thomas Campbell's ministry in the Seceder Presbyterian Church of Ireland (1780s), it had moved from the predestinarian stance of Calvin to an Arminian view of free will. Many of the developing practices in episcopal polity involved the very "Romish" tendencies against which the Puritans and the Campbells reacted.[1]

The continuity in polity with the Catholic tradition cultivated by the episcopal leadership of the Anglican Church tended to preserve traditional emphasis on the fine arts. Imbibing ideas which emerged from Renaissance Humanism and the Counter-Reformation, the Anglican Church actively sustained its interest in church architecture, liturgy and liturgical music, the visual arts, and even clerical vestments and trappings.

On the other hand, the English Reformation produced those who propagated an enlarged and less man-shaped concept of God, who wished to restore primitive Christianity by reference to the documents, by developing fresh human responses and new codes of worship, and by doing away with sectarianism.

The influence of Calvinism upon the Church of England waxed and waned with the changes of leadership and of the political/religious climate that occurred between the sixteenth and early nineteenth cen-

---

[1]See A. G. Dickens, *Reformation and Society,* 187 ff. for a discussion of the Elizabethan period of the English Church.

turies. Calvinist practice was, however, more normative for the polity of English and American Puritans. Some Puritan characteristics developed as reactions against Anglican episcopacy. At the core of the earliest reactions were questions about clerical vestments and the Eucharist. John Hooper (d. 1555), bishop of Gloucester, was a Zwinglian Reformer whose scruples against vestments led to his martyrdom. John Knox preferred sitting at communion, but accepted the kneeling position in the interests of peace and charity. English Calvinist Puritans became more rigid about points of worship than had their predecessors such as John Calvin and Martin Bucer.[2]

The Church of England provided a broad umbrella for heterogeneous and even conflicting ideologies under the reign of Queen Elizabeth. On the one hand, the Reformed theology existed along with the worship prescribed by the *Book of Common Prayer,* with episcopal polity, and with divergent theologies such as Arminianism. On the other hand, the Puritan movement accommodated Reformed theology to its special concern for nurturing religious life and sought to gain recognition for presbyterian and congregational polities.[3]

The Puritan approach to language and thus to preaching was derived largely from the Calvinist tradition, especially the emphasis accorded to the power of the spoken word. Puritan preaching reflected the rejection of ornamental rhetoric and emphasized the power of the Word. Thus, a sharp line was drawn between episcopal aesthetics and the utilitarian use of words in the pursuit of truth later practiced by American Restoration Movement preachers. Alexander Campbell's preaching was evidently rich in metaphoric expressions—especially Biblical metaphors and parables—and the vocabulary which he brought into use was richer than that of many of his hearers, but the goal of his message remained the same as that of the Puritans: the accurate and forceful presentation of biblical truth. Richardson discussed Campbell as a preacher:

> Nothing indeed was more striking than his singular ability to interest his hearers in the subject of which he treated. With this his own mind was occupied, and, being free from all thoughts of self, there was in his addresses an entire absence of egotism, and nothing in his delivery to direct the attention from the theme on which he discoursed. . . . Without any gestures, either emphatic or descriptive, the speaker stood in the most natural and easy attitude, resting upon his innate powers of intellect and his complete mastery of the subject, impressing all with the sense of a superior presence and a mighty mind. His enun-

[2]See John T. McNeill, *History and Character of Calvinism,* 309-10.
[3]See Leith, *Introduction to Reformed Tradition,* 42.

ciation was distinct, his diction chaste and simple, his sentences clear and forcible. The intonations of his clear ringing voice were admirably adapted to the sentiment, while by his strong and bold emphasis upon important words he imparted to what he said a peculiar force and authority.[4]

Puritans also emphasized the power of the preached word. They disdained the rhetorical and ornate oratory of orthodox Anglicans, and developed what became known as Plain Style preaching.

Puritanism was a doubly important influence on the American Stone-Campbell Movement. It sent its leavening power through the Calvinistic Seceder Church in Scotland and Ireland where Thomas Campbell had been an active minister. It also had a strong effect on the American religious mind-set. More will be said in chapter four about the direct influences of Puritanism on Presbyterianism and American Protestantism in general.

Although Puritanism exerted a generally negative effect on art in Christian life, this effect should not be considered totally negative. The mixed attitude of Puritanism set some boundaries that may well have tempered tendencies that could have marred some of the greatest intellectual and spiritual achievements of Englishmen. Out of this mixed milieu came John Milton and Oliver Cromwell and John Bunyan, all sons of the Puritan tradition.

The Puritan approach to matters of church polity is readily discernible in some aspects of the American Restoration Movement. One concept, with roots in English Wycliffite and Lollard traditions of the fourteenth and fifteenth centuries, was the Puritan attitude toward authority of the scriptures in matters of church practice. The other concept, implicitly tied to the first and of Continental origin, was the practice of limiting praise of God in public worship to psalm-singing, usually unaccompanied by instruments. The second concept emerged as a matter of debate among various nineteenth-century Restoration Movement groups.

The principle of the sufficiency of the scriptures became the *terra firma* of Puritan polity and it shines through Thomas Campbell's *Declaration and Address*. In retrospect, it might appear that the motto of

---

[4]This description follows a description of one of Campbell's sermons reported by Dr. Herman Humphrey, former President of Amherst College. See Richardson, *Memoirs*, 2:583-84. Archibald McLean adds to this description: "Judge Riddle, speaking of his [Campbell's] preaching and the effect of it, said there was no appeal to passion, no effort at pathos, no figures of rhetoric; but a warm, kindling, heated, glowing, manly argument, silencing the will, captivating the judgment, and satisfying the reason." See Archibald McLean, *Alexander Campbell as a Preacher* (St. Louis: The Christian Publishing Co., 1908), 25.

the Washington Christian Association, "Where the scriptures speak, we speak, and where the scriptures are silent, we are silent" could have been acceptable to the Elizabethan Puritans. The application of this principle in worship has been basic for the American Disciples as well as the English Puritans.

In 1552 the Anglican Archbishop, Thomas Cranmer, took issue with objections to the new *Book of Common Prayer.* He wrote:

> They say that kneeling is not commanded in Scripture: and what is not commanded in Scripture is unlawful. There is the root of the errors of the sects! If that be true, take away the whole Book of Service, and let us have no more trouble in setting forth an order in religion, or indeed in common policy. If kneeling be not expressly enjoined in Holy Scripture, neither is standing nor sitting. Let them lie down on the ground, and eat their meat like Turks or Tartars.[5]

Acceptance of scripture as the norm for worship and for general church polity became the dominant factor in Thomas Campbell's 1809 document, which in turn became the initial charter for the Campbellian concept of restoration:

> Our desire, therefore, for ourselves and our brethren would be, that, rejecting human opinions and the inventions of men as of any authority, or as having any place in the Church of God, we might forever cease from further contentions about such things; returning to and holding fast by the original standard; taking the Divine word alone for our rule; the Holy Spirit for our teacher and guide, to lead us into all truth; and Christ alone, as exhibited in the word, for our salvation; that by so doing, we may be at peace among ourselves, follow peace with all men, and holiness, without which no man shall see the Lord.[6]

The principle of *sola scriptura* brought the Puritans into conflict with episcopacy in England in numerous dimensions. It is important to note that many of these conflicts involved matters relating to the *Book of Common Prayer* and thus the liturgy of the church, as well as questions about the visual appearance of church architecture and ornamentation and clerical dress. Many Episcopal bishops were Calvinists who were opposed to the *Book of Common Prayer,* and there was conflict between the strong puritan-presbyterian element in the Church of

---

[5]Ibid., 17. Henson's quotation is from Dixon, *History of the Church of England,* 111:476.

[6]Thomas Campbell, *Declaration and Address,* 73-74.

England and the "remnant of popery" represented by the high-church episcopal branch:

> Archbishop Parker was strongly opposed to cap, surplice, and wafer bread. Bishop Jewell called the ecclesiastical vestments the 'habits of the stage,' the 'relics of the Amosites,' and wished to see them 'exterminated by the roots.' Bishop Pilkington spoke of them as 'popish apparel,' which should have been left behind with popery, and is not 'becoming those that profess godliness.'[7]

The objectivity of the liturgy, with its collects and psalms for the church year, was rejected by sixteenth- and seventeenth-century Puritans, and was ultimately rejected by the free churches in America. Disciples of Christ, under the influence of Thomas and Alexander Campbell, also rejected the subjective approach utilized by some free Protestant theologies with a strong emphasis on personal experience. Rather, they opted for the Calvinist tradition of emphasis upon the preaching of the Word and its normative authority in the life of the church.

The Puritans had adopted the Genevan Calvinist approach to music in worship along the lines of their conservative theology. This policy prefigured the approach taken by the conservative wing of the Restoration Movement in its attitude toward church organs. However, Restoration attitudes towards song literature was not so conservative as the Puritan restriction to psalm-singing in church. The important place given to psalm-singing in church by the Puritans was heightened further by the publication of the Sternhold and Hopkins *Psalter*—a collection of the Psalms in English and in metrical verse—in 1562.

In 1583, John Whitgift, a Calvinist in theology, became Archbishop of Canterbury in 1583. In a letter to the Puritan Thomas Cartwright, of the University of Cambridge, Whitgift wrote: "Singing, I am sure you do not disallow, being used in all Reformed Churches, and an art allowed in Scriptures, and used in praising God by David." Cartwright's answer defines the parameters of Puritan thought in relation to singing in worship. He assumed that Whitgift

> will not defend the piping and organs, nor other singing than is used in the Reformed Churches, which is, in the singing of two psalms, one in the beginning and another in the ending, in a plain tune, easy both to be sung of those which have no art in

---

[7]Albert Henry Newman, *A Manual of Church History* (Chicago: American Baptist Publication Society, 1902), 270.

singing, and understanding those which, because they cannot read, cannot sing with the rest of the church.[8]

The English Puritans were more liberal in the use of musical instruments in worship than the Scottish Presbyterians who, in turn, more directly influenced the milieu in which Thomas Campbell acquired his theological foundation.

Lynn Hieronymus notes the similarity of the basis on which the Puritans and the early American Restorationist leaders rejected a prepared liturgy because (1) the liturgy is prepared by man and not directly out of the Word of God, and (2) the fervent belief in the local autonomy of each congregation negated the use of a liturgical pattern developed for all the churches of a group.[9] Hieronymus denies, however, that there is a direct historical relationship between the Disciples and the Puritans.

Admittedly, it is difficult to establish a direct connection between the theological foundations and the aesthetic mores of New England Puritanism and Disciples beginnings. However, it has been shown that the Puritan element was pervasive in the American development of almost all Protestant bodies except Lutherans, and this general permeation of evangelical religion by Puritan thought can be extended to the Presbyterian background of Thomas and Alexander Campbell. Von Ogden Vogt observes that

> The Puritans objected to material elements in the sacraments. They abolished not only holy water and ashes but also pictures and statues, not only shrines of the saints but organs and instruments of music and even the use of the ring in the marriage service. Presbyterian, Reformed, Baptist, and Congregational bodies were largely touched at the very beginning with the Puritan spirit.[10]

While the horizontal ties between American Puritanism and the Campbellian Restoration are somewhat tenuous, the seminal influence of Calvinism, through the Scottish Presbyterian Church and the Independent Churches, is quite clear. The re-emergence of characteristic Reformed concepts through the thought and polity of the Scotch-Irish Presbyterians who became leaders of the American movement are clearly distinguishable. Those who believe the Restoration Movement constituted a clean and existential break with history do not recognize this

---

[8]H. Henley Henson, *Puritanism in England* (New York: Burt Franklin), 18-19. Henson's quotation is from Whitgift, *Works*, iii.106, 7, P.S.

[9]Lynn Hieronymus, *What the Bible Says about Worship* (Joplin, Mo.: College Press Publishing Co., 1984), 166-67.

[10]Von Ogden Vogt, *Art and Religion* (Boston: Beacon Press, 1948), 39.

continuity. In theology, polity, and the aesthetics of both worship and private life, the antecedents and consequences are quite undeniable.

The character of Scottish and Irish Presbyterianism was influenced heavily by the preaching and activity of John Knox (1514-72). George Wishart (1513-46), who had studied in Geneva with the reformers, first brought Calvinistic theology to Scotland. Knox, while exiled in Germany and Geneva, became a strong supporter of Calvin's reformation. He was apparently associated with Wishart as early as 1546.[11] In 1560, the Scottish Parliament adopted a Reformed type of confession under Knox's leadership. Knox's work in both the theological and political arenas, together with his powerful preaching, helped steer Scotland toward the emergence of the Kirk as a part of the Reformed tradition. For at least a century, episcopacy in the royal tradition of England struggled with presbyterianism for ascendency; since 1689, the Church of Scotland has been consistently Presbyterian.[12]

Several aspects of Scottish Presbyterianism are found in principles of the American Restoration Movement. The democratic nature of the church prepared a mind-set for work on the American frontier. The established Reformed Church of Scotland permeated the life of the people. Like the Reformed tradition elsewhere, the Kirk emphasized an educated leadership. Those educated leaders became not only able spokesmen, but also faithful and devout ministers who were beloved and admired by the common folk. The Scottish Reformers not only established parish schools to educate their young, but they maintained well-run universities. Their strong social consciousness was manifested in their care of the poor and sick as well as in their stress upon the duties of the rich.[13]

The striking emphasis on building colleges which characterized all streams of the Stone-Campbell Movement emerged out of an emphasis its principal leaders had experienced in their respective Calvinist backgrounds. Their accompanying concern for the needs of suffering people also found consistent expression in the people-centered structures of Disciples churches in America.

Another Disciples tradition which shows a relationship to Scottish Reformation attitudes is emphasis on the Lord's Supper. Although the Lord's Supper is central in worship for Disciples, it does not have the same theological function it had for the Scottish Kirk.

Richard L. Greaves writes at length about the doctrine of the Lord's Supper in the Scottish Reformation. Knox accorded a central position to

[11]McNeill, *History and Character of Calvinism*, 294.

[12]Leith, *Introduction to Reformed Tradition*, 41.

[13]McNeill, *History and Character of Calvinism*, 307.

the communion service. Greaves notes James S. McEwen's statement, "None in the Reformed world made the sacrament basic for the Church itself, as Knox did," and further wrote, "Lord Percy earlier made the same point, regarding Knox's achievement as his making the Lord's Supper the central act of Christian worship and the Kirk of Scotland a Eucharistic Church."[14]

In Knox's theology, transubstantiation was repudiated, but the body and blood of Jesus Christ was joined with the faithful communicants in such a way that he became food for their souls through the power of the Holy Spirit. Knox saw the elements as sacramental signs of the body and blood of Christ. Alexander Campbell, on the other hand, did not view the Supper as a sacrament, but as an ordinance to be celebrated joyfully:

> But a sacrament, an annual sacrament, or a quarterly sacrament, is like the oath of a Roman soldier, from which it derives its name, often taken with reluctance, and kept with bad faith. It is as sad as a funeral parade. The knell of the parish bell that summons the mourners to the house of sorrow, and the tocsin that awakes the recollection of a sacramental morn, are heard with equal dismay and aversion. The seldomer they occur the better.[15]

The Scots continued the Genevan psalm-singing tradition and used the English Sternhold and Hopkins collection. The first Reformed Scottish *Psalter* was issued in 1564 with John Knox as editor. The collection included forty-two psalms from the English *Psalter* of 1562, but the preference for the greater metrical variety of the Genevan collection is apparent in the eighty-seven psalms from Geneva. The musical settings were all monophonic.[16]

During the eighteenth century, some of the same kind of ecclesiastical fragmentation occurred that later provoked Barton W. Stone, Thomas Campbell, and Alexander Campbell to establish a new religious reform movement. One was Erastianism—from the 1568 thesis of Erastus—which was the doctrine of holding secular magistrates responsible for discipline. It gradually came to mean that the state or the prince had supreme authority in ecclesiastical questions. Further fragmentation occurred when the Patronage Act, enacted under the reign of Queen Anne (1702-14), gave lay patrons the right to present ministers to par-

---

[14]Richard L. Greaves, *Theology and Revolution in the Scottish Reformation* (Grand Rapids: Christian University Press, 1980), 104, quoting James S. McEwen, *The Faith of John Knox* (Richmond, Va.: John Knox Press, 1961), 47, and Eustace Percy, *John Knox* (Richmond, Va.: John Knox Press, 1965), 56.

[15]Alexander Campbell, *Christian Baptist* 3 (1825): 4.

[16]Reese, *Music in the Renaissance,* 801.

ishes. This act of patronage was an affront to classic Presbyterianism, and resulted in a division between Burghers who accepted the Burghers' Oath and its consequent patronage, and the Anti-Burghers who would not accept the oath.[17]

McAllister and Tucker have chronicled the successive divisions of the Kirk:

> In 1795 a question arose among Burgher Presbyterians over the power of civil magistrates in religion. This had the effect of producing two parties, distinguished from each other by the terms 'Old Light' Burghers and 'New Light' Burghers. The same controversy spread among the Anti-Burghers . . . when Thomas Campbell joined the Seceder church as a youth, he had become affiliated with the Anti-Burgher sect of the Seceders. When in 1806 the Anti-Burghers divided, Campbell found himself a member and minister of the Old Light Anti-Burgher Seceder Presbyterian Church.[18]

These divisions—which came to be a heavy concern of Thomas Campbell during the early nineteenth century—extended to the Reformed Churches in Ireland, where Scottish political realities had no validity, and even to the New World. Efforts to unify American secessionist congregations of Burghers and Anti-Burghers in New York, New England, and Philadelphia remained incomplete because of resistance from Scotland.[19] In 1806, Thomas Campbell was involved in the unsuccessful attempt by Irish presbyteries to resolve the question. In 1820, thirteen years after Thomas Campbell had departed for America, the Scottish Burgher and Anti-Burgher synods reunited and held special exercises to rejoice over this warm reunion.[20]

In Ireland, the Reformed tradition was established by the Ulster Plantation, which was inaugurated in 1606 by England's King James I. The English Crown transplanted Scottish and English communities to northern Ireland in an effort to "domesticate" the rough Irish population. Many Scots Protestants settled in the north Irish counties of Down and Antrim. Later, French Huguenots and English Puritans came also, reinforcing the Calvinist character of the Church in these counties and tying its affairs closely to that of the Scottish Kirk. The famed Irish archbishop, James Ussher (1582-1656), was Calvinistic in his theology and held moderate views on church polity. In 1634 he defeated an attempt to make Irish doctrinal standards conform exactly to those of the English.

---

[17]McNeill, *History and Character of Calvinism*, 353-55.

[18]McAllister and Tucker, *Journey in Faith*, 99.

[19]McNeill, *History and Character of Calvinism*, 363.

[20]See Richardson, *Memoirs*, 1:56-57.

The ancestors of Thomas Campbell's mother were French Huguenots who arrived in Ireland following an initial move to Scotland. This migration occurred when Louis XIV revoked the Edict of Nantes in 1685. This Edict, enacted in 1598, had provided French Protestants a measure of toleration and freedom, but was disliked by the Roman Catholic clergy. When it was revoked, the Protestant Huguenots fled France by the thousands to escape persecution. Thomas Campbell's ancestors settled in the western part of Scotland. Thomas was born in County Down, one of the two counties that received the major implantation during the tenure of Bishop Ussher.[21]

Although the Scottish Presbyterians became prosperous in Ireland, they still felt the sting of English control over their political, economic, and religious life. The farmers among them also suffered from drought and crop failures. Thus the Ulster Scots, in 1717, began the great eighteenth-century migration to America. A conservative estimate indicates that by 1776 at least 250,000 Presbyterians from northern Ireland arrived in America, where they have been identified as Scots-Irish.[22] The migration continued with further waves well after 1776. Among those who followed were Thomas Campbell in 1807, and many of his Ulster neighbors, who settled in the Ohio Valley.

The religious tension in northern Ireland in the nineteenth century was felt by a youthful Thomas Campbell. Young Campbell abhorred the whole system of Romanism, with its superstitions, its ceremonies, its spirit, and its practical effects. Neither did he feel comfortable with the lordly and aristocratic Episcopalians who not only looked down on dissenters of all stripe, but generally did not practice personal piety. As he matured and began to examine the history of the Presbyterian Church, Thomas could more clearly see the prevalence of a party spirit among even the Reformed branch of Protestants. Later in the American Restoration Movement it became Thomas's labor of life to oppose and overthrow that divisive spirit, and to work for unity in the Christian Church.[23]

A look at the religious and cultural milieu of Campbell's Ireland provides insight into his reasons for later reacting to "popery," episcopacy, and many of the liturgical practices associated with those concepts. Some of the same motives which earlier had prompted the English Puritans to reject pleasure for its own sake, extravagances in architecture, ornamentation in the visual environment, and an elaborate church music also shaped the aesthetic values of the Campbells, father and son.

[21]Ibid., 1:21.

[22]Leith, *Introduction to Reformed Tradition*, 43.

[23]See Richardson, *Memoirs*, 1:50.

Paul Henry Lang, in his monumental work, *Music in Western Civilization,* remarks that, compared with Martin Luther, John Calvin "was not well disposed toward music; like the Church Fathers, he recognized that 'properly practiced it affords a recreation but it also leads to voluptuousness . . . and we have to take care that it does not furnish the occasion for dropping the reins to dissoluteness or for causing us to become effeminate in disorderly delights.'"[24]

Lang summarizes the influence of the sober conservatism of Calvinism on the arts—especially in the Puritan connection—and makes it clear that while the use of psalms in worship was encouraged, the cultivation of music, theater, and the visual arts outside that context was not considered a very high calling for Christians. Lang places the Reformed tradition in context at this point. After noting the sincerity of Calvin and Calvinists and recognizing that this system had an immense value in the history of Christian thought, he remarks,

> It is noteworthy, however, that the countries which accepted the doctrines of Calvinism— Scotland, where John Knox implanted them, some parts of Holland and Switzerland, and the New England states—did not excel in music once these doctrines became an essential factor in their life.[25]

The closing of the English theaters in the seventeenth century under Cromwell's Commonwealth was one of the more extreme reactions of the Puritans to the arts. It was under Cromwell's rigid rule that the great traditions of the English stage vanished. The fact that the American leaders of the Restoration Movement were adept in the use of language and the Word, but slow to use the arts in both the worship of the church and the education of the human spirit does not make their views radically different from the Reformed theology out of which they emerged.

George Beazley, Jr. summarizes the kinship of the Disciples' tradition with Calvinism, and especially with the Puritan expression of the Reformation, in terms of aesthetic attitudes:

> Unfortunately, the Disciples shared with the Reformed tradition a suspicion of the arts. Not only did they want a place of worship stripped of superfluous ornamentation which might distract men's and women's minds from the proclamation of the Word of God, but most of them felt that the reading of novels was not conducive to the strict morality which they had set for themselves. Though, like the Puritans, they may have subconsciously

---

[24]Paul Henry Lang, *Music in Western Civilization* (New York: W. W. Norton and Co., 1941), 257.

[25]Ibid.

reveled in the literary concreteness of the Scriptural books, and though they may have savored beauty of language there and in the sermon, they would have felt that its purpose was to instruct, inform, and give the plan for man's salvation, not to be enjoyed as sensuous and imaginative pleasure. They did not have either the Anglican or the Lutheran pleasure in the esthetic quality of worship or their feel for the necessity of beautiful and graphic language in worship. Fortunately many present day Disciples have recognized and corrected this deprivation in their classic heritage, though even now the sense of artistic excellence would be less than in either the Lutheran or the Anglican tradition.[26]

Another major source of religious influence on Thomas and Alexander Campbell for their reforming activity in America is found in the broad category of Independent churches—reformers from the British Isles who eschewed Roman Catholic, Episcopal, and Presbyterian organizational structures. These groups emphasized plain but forceful preaching as well as the Arminian doctrine of freedom of the will, and are best exemplified by John Wesley (1703-91) and George Whitefield (1714-76). Other Independents from Great Britain and the Continent embodied various kinds of "Restorationist" groups. McAllister and Tucker list some distinguishing features of these groups:

> Their common idea was that the existing churches were cluttered with human additions to divine revelation; that the creeds were too complicated and speculative; that worship was too formal and the clergy too eager for worldly advantage. They stressed the independence of the local congregation and the importance of lay leaders. There is no indication that church unity played a part in the program of these groups.[27]

About the Independents in general, however, Richardson speaks approvingly: The concept of the right of every member to judge for himself as to the meaning of scripture resulted in repudiation of any authority claimed by presbyteries, synods, assemblies, conventions, or other church courts. It also manifested a tolerant spirit which was manifested when the Independents came to power in England.[28]

---

[26]George G. Beazley, Jr., "Who are the Disciples," *The Christian Church (Disciples of Christ),* esp. 65-66, for an excellent discussion of this subject. Beazley recognizes the lacuna and applauds efforts to remedy the situation.

[27]McAllister and Tucker, *Journey in Faith,* 93-94.

[28]Richardson, *Memoirs,* 1:65.

An Independent movement which had a major effect on the Disciples movement was that led by John Glas (1695-1773). Though with a different interpretation from that of Alexander Campbell, Glas distinguished between the Old and New Testaments with the purpose of restoring "primitive New Testament practices."[29] Glas was aided by his son-in-law, Robert Sandeman, who upheld the basic Reformation doctrine of justification by faith. Sandeman's understanding of faith, however, was limited to its intellectual content, a point of view that is close to Alexander Campbell's 1825 definition of faith:

> Now faith is neither more nor less than the belief of some testimony. This is what, in all ages, and amongst all people, is called faith. Faith without testimony is impossible; and nothing more nor less than testimony believed constitutes faith.[30]

Sandeman's migration to America, his step in founding a church in Danbury, Connecticut in 1763, and that church's ultimate affiliation with the Disciples movement about 1840 all underline the importance of the Glas-Sandeman connection to the American Stone-Campbell Movement.

At Rich Hill, the final Old World home of the Campbells, there was an Independent church pastored by a minister named Gibson, who became a friend of Thomas Campbell. The Campbells often attended the Independent meeting house for the evening services and thus heard a wide variety of traveling preachers. Richardson described this congregation:

> The Independents of Rich Hill, though in connection with those of Scotland, were Haldanean in sentiment, and did not adopt all the views of Glas or Sandeman. They attended weekly to the Lord's Supper, contributions, etc., but were opposed to going to theatres or such places of public amusements; to the doctrine of community of goods; feet washing, etc., as advocated by Sandeman. They were also, in a good measure, free from the dogmatic and bitter controversial spirit so characteristic of Sandeman and his followers.[31]

The Haldane brothers, James Alexander (1768-1851) and Robert (1764-1842), were wealthy laymen who worried about the formalism and sterility of the established church. They broke away from the

---

[29]McAllister and Tucker, *Journey in Faith,* 94. It would seem that Glas anticipated Alexander Campbell's famous 1816 sermon on the Law.

[30]Alexander Campbell, *Christian Baptist* 2 (1825): 64.

[31]Richardson, *Memoirs,* 1:71.

Reformed Scottish Kirk in 1799, after which they invested themselves and their fortune in promoting an evangelistic revival in Scotland. Through study of the scripture, the Haldanes came to believe that the only scriptural form of baptism was immersion, and they no longer baptized infants. Not only was this view adopted by the Campbells, but so was the Haldanes' position regarding church organization and practice. Also, Walter Scott associated himself with a Haldane congregation when he first arrived in Pittsburgh. Thus the Haldanes influenced not only religious thought in Scotland and Ireland, but on the American frontier as well.[32]

Alexander Campbell had an unexpected opportunity to observe the work and teaching of the Haldanes. Upon sailing with his family from Londonderry for America in October, 1808, the ship *Hibernia* on which they were traveling was dashed in a storm on a sunken rock and had to be abandoned. After seeing the family and most of their possessions safely to shore, Alexander and his mother considered the question of where they should winter until a more favorable season for sailing would return. The question was easily resolved, for Alexander had an ardent desire to attend the university where his father had been educated, and so the family proceeded at once to Glasgow.[33]

The year at Glasgow opened both academic and spiritual opportunities for Alexander Campbell. The spiritual blessings included the opportunity of knowing Greville Ewing, Independent minister, part-time teacher, and editor of an Independent religious journal. Ewing frequently included young Campbell in meetings at his home where the opportunity was presented to meet numerous reforming preachers with various shades of idependent convictions. Through Ewing, Campbell became very interested in the views of the Haldanes. Richardson indicates that it was chiefly through this interest that Campbell changed his religious views.[34]

The university course of study elected by Alexander for the term included Greek, Logic and Belles Lettres, and Experimental Philosophy, as well as supplementary studies in French and the Greek New Testament. He translated Homer's *Iliad*, Sophocles' *Oedipus Tyrannus,* wrote essays, and even composed some original poetry.[35] To help defray his expenses, he drew upon his previous experience as a schoolmaster to teach private classes in Latin, English, and arithmetic. He maintained a strict schedule of scripture reading and personal devotions.

[32]See McAllister and Tucker, *Journey in Faith,* 95.

[33]See Richardson, *Memoirs*, 1:114.

[34]Ibid., 1:188.

[35]Ibid., 1:132.

Clearly, this unexpected year of study affected the future of Alexander Campbell's life—in personal values, breadth of outlook, deep belief in formal education, and passion for Christian unity. In addition to his exposure to academic life and learning at the university level, there was another major factor that has affected the strong bent of the Disciples Restoration Movement toward the establishment and operation of colleges and universities, and toward unity. The additional bonus of his friendship with Greville Ewing and, through him, a closer look at the work of the Haldane brothers and other Independent reformers, increased the value of the year that was given him through the original disaster of the wreck of the *Hibernia*.

Another major source of attitudes for Thomas and Alexander Campbell was what Dwight Stevenson has called "The English Enlightenment."[36] Richardson wrote that John Locke, the Scottish philosopher, held a particularly high level of interest for Alexander in his youthful academic studies. Locke's *Essay Concerning Toleration* impressed him deeply and seems to have fixed his ideas of religious and civil liberty. Under the direction of his father, Alexander studied Locke's *Essay Concerning Human Understanding*.[37]

That the spirit and content of Locke's writings supplemented Alexander Campbell's study of the Bible and his fellowship with both Calvinist and Puritan preaching seems evident in various appraisals of his theological and aesthetic views. Alger Morton Fitch, in his study of Alexander Campbell's preaching, notes that the writings of John Locke on toleration, human understanding, and Christianity's reasonableness lodged in Alexander's thinking.[38] Ronald Osborne, in a reference to Campbell's continued interest in cosmopolitan reading, mentions that Campbell imported books from Britain throughout his life and attained remarkable erudition. Alexander addressed the religious and political issues of America in terms of Lockean philosophy and Scottish thought rather than in terms of eighteenth-century Continental theology.[39]

Ralph G. Wilburn notes that in addition to the Protestant understanding of the Bible in the principle of *sola scriptura*, the American Restoration fathers were influenced by the appeal to experience, derived from

[36] Dwight E. Stevenson, *Disciple Preaching in the First Generation* (Forrest F. Reed Lectures for 1969, Nashville: The Disciples of Christ Historical Society, 1969), 27.

[37] Richardson, *Memoirs*, 1:33-34.

[38] Alger Morton Fitch, *Alexander Campbell, Preacher of Reform and Reformer of Preaching* (Austin, Texas: Sweet Publishing Co., 1970), 85.

[39] Ronald Osborne, "Theology among the Disciples," in *The Christian Church (Disciples of Christ)*, ed. Beazley, 85.

the rationalism of the Enlightenment.[40] Beazley concludes that the Disciples have a heritage which is an American blend of Lockean philosophy and of a serious biblical authoritarianism.[41]

John Locke (1632-1704) was the son of a man with Puritan tendencies and was raised with a strong sense of moral principles. Locke's method was:

> empirical rather than rationalistic; he relied on analytic observation; and his conclusions were held in a tentative spirit. But to him skepticism was not an end in itself; it was a prelude to a more scientific philosophy. He wanted to destroy the idols of his time, to bring about intellectual clarity, to remove confusion, and to contribute to the flowering of the sciences.[42]

The congenial relationship between Locke's *Essay Concerning Toleration* and the basic concepts of American democracy provides a backdrop for the development of the Stone-Campbell Movement as a typically American phenomenon. The *Essay Concerning Human Understanding* provided an epistemological basis for the early Restoration Movement and some of its concepts are quite recognizable in developing Restoration thought. Locke denied vigorously the existence of innate ideas, a position which undercuts the Calvinistic teaching of original sin. He taught two basic means of receiving ideas, through *sensation* and *reflection*. He accepted the concept of divine revelation, but insisted upon the basic principle that rationalistic Disciples have depended upon from their first generation:

> . . . faith can never convince us of anything that contradicts our knowledge. Because, though faith be founded on the testimony of God (who cannot lie) revealing any proposition to us; yet we cannot have an assurance of the truth of its being a divine revelation greater than our own knowledge: since the whole strength of the certainty depends upon our knowledge that God revealed it. . . .[43]

---

[40]Ralph Wilburn, "Disciple Thought in Protestant Perspective: an Interpretation" in *The Reconstruction of Theology*, ed. Ralph Wilburn (St. Louis: Bethany Press, 1963), 313.

[41]Beazley, "Future of the Christian Church," 73.

[42]Frederick Mayer, *A History of Modern Philosophy*, vol. 2 (New York: American Book Co., 1951), 176, 177. Locke flourished after the English statesman, scientist, and man of letters, Francis Bacon (1521-1626). Bacon conceived a plan for the reform of knowledge which included the method of inquiry based on induction. He stated the need to contemplate "things as they are, without superstition or imposture, error, or confusion," and he was instrumental in giving powerful impetus to the development of seventeenth-century science.

[43]See John Locke, *An Essay Concerning Human Understanding* (New York: Dutton, 1978), esp. secs. 1:2, 2:1, 4:18.

Alexander Campbell responded with Christian reasonableness to the challenge for debate by Robert Owen, the atheist socialist, through the pages of the *Christian Baptist*. In 1828, he wrote:

Now, be it known to Mr. Owen, and all whom it may concern, that I, relying on the author, the reasonableness, and the excellence of the Christian religion, will engage to meet Mr. Owen at any time within one year from this date, at any place equidistant from New Harmony and Bethany. . . .[44]

During the debate with Owen,[45] Campbell referred to the Lockean epistemology in denying the "laws of human nature" asserted by his opponent. Alexander Campbell took the position of Locke, David Hume (1711-1776), and R. V. G. Mirabeau (1749-1791): that all our original ideas are the results of sensation and reflection. He did not believe that man could have any idea the archetype of which did not exist in nature.

In the same debate, Campbell, in one sentence, credited the Protestant Reformers, one of the greatest Puritan poets, and the philosopher John Locke with establishing the free society enjoyed in the West:

The Reformation from Popery gave the first shock to the despotism of Europe. The labors of the Reformers—and the more recent labors of Milton the poet, and Locke the philosopher, have done more to issue in the free institutions of Europe and America, than the labors of all the sceptics from Celsus to my friend Mr. Owen.[46]

The teachings of Locke on freedom, perception, revelation, and other issues vital to both the young American government and the infant Restoration Movement were doubtless crucial. However, there were other implications of his teaching that may have been counterproductive to the proclamation of a joyous and spiritual Christianity. Robert Richardson mentions the problem in the discussion of disagreements about the work and office of the Holy Spirit.[47] In a "Dialogue on the Holy Spirit," Alexander Campbell had, indeed,

applied his reasonings specially to the case of conversion, and had stated in it that while the Holy Spirit operated upon sinners by the demonstrations and evidences of the gospel, he took up

---

[44]Alexander Campbell, *Christian Baptist* 5 (1828): 443.

[45]See Richardson, *Memoirs*, 2:273 for a discussion of this debate.

[46]"Campbell-Owen Debate," 2, 5, quoted in Bill J. Humble, *Campbell and Controversy* (Joplin, Mo.: College Press Publishing Co., 1986), 124.

[47]See Richardson, *Memoirs*, 2:355. Richardson was himself critical of the most extreme presentation of the "Word alone" theory in a rationalistic context for the conversion of sinners.

his abode in the saints. 'The Spirit of God,' said he, 'the author of these proofs, by them opens men's minds to hear, to obey the gospel.'[48]

Richardson identified the dilemma faced by Campbell: the opponents on one side accused him of denying the "operations of the Holy Spirit," and on the other "some of those who were professed advocates of the Reformation were led to construct a word-alone theory which virtually dispensed with the great promise of the gospel—the gift of the Holy Spirit to believers."[49] Richardson also attempted to identify the source of their rationalistic denial of the Holy Spirit's work:

> Taking Locke's philosophy as the basis of their system, and carrying his "Essay on the Human Understanding" along with the Bible in their saddlebags, they denied to its Creator any access to the human soul except by "words and arguments," while they conceded to the author of evil a direct approach, and had more to say in their discourses about "the laws of human nature" than about the gospel of Christ.[50]

The nature of the Holy Spirit's work in conversion and in the church has remained a lively question throughout the history and through the divisions of Disciples since Campbell's "Dialogue." The issue has a new relevance in the current period of questions over charismatic gifts. The question of the juxtaposition between attitudes toward the Holy Spirit's work in the believer and toward aesthetic experiences is one which might yield some interesting conclusions.

In the case of John Locke, and most of his contemporary thinkers, the emphasis upon rationalistic perception did coincide with a basic lack of interest in the arts. It is an interesting fact of history that the period of Neo-Classicism in the visual arts and literature, as well as the Classical period in the history of Western art and music, occurred during the late seventeenth and eighteenth centuries, a period that overlaps the latter stages of the Enlightenment. The arts of this period emphasized form, symmetry, and rational control of artistic components, and seem to have a great deal in common with philosophy. Gilbert and Kuhn, in their *History of Esthetics*, explain why this potentially compatible marriage did not take place:

> It is true that the philosophy of the seventeenth century paralleled the rising Neo-Classicism in art. But philosophers on the

---

[48]Ibid., 2:355.

[49]Ibid. Richardson perhaps reflected an anti-Lockean, pro-spiritual attitude here.

[50]Ibid., 2:356.

whole turned against the Aristotelian spirit from which art drew its fresh inspiration. Their Greek philosopher was Democritus rather than Aristotle or Plato. They applied reason to politics, psychology, optics, physics, to general method and metaphysics, and in this their kinship was with Copernicus and Galileo, Kepler and Newton.[51]

Getting down to individual cases, John Locke was "the most grudging of all in his references to the work of wit and fancy." In the *Essay Concerning Human Understanding,* Locke attacks the use of wit and eloquence in the art of rhetoric as devices primarily used for purposes of deception:

> I confess, in discourses where we seek rather pleasure and delight than information and improvement, such ornaments as are borrowed from them can scarce pass for faults. But yet, if we would speak of things as they are, we must allow that all the art of rhetoric, besides order and clearness, all the artificial and figurative application of words eloquence hath invented, are for nothing else but to insinuate wrong *ideas,* move the passions and thereby mislead the judgment, and so indeed are perfect cheat. . . .[52]

Thus the Puritanism of Locke's background passed into his "secular" approach to philosophy, and quite directly entered the mainstream of the thinking of the Disciples fathers. A recapitulation of the basic European thrust of aesthetic ideas which impacted Thomas and Alexander Campbell—as well as Walter Scott, Barton W. Stone, and the other primary leaders—does not promise great emphasis on poetry or painting. The Calvinist Reformation, tempered by English Puritanism, British Independent theology, and Lockean philosophy, did not provide a hopeful background for a faith expressed through the arts. Yet, John Milton, John Bunyan, various psalm-book writers, and a few other prophets of a less rational and more affective approach to Christian faith appeared through the maze of words and theology, and the possibility of another side existed in the hearts of the Restoration Movement reformers. The next chapter will consider influences they encountered on the western side of the Atlantic.

---

[51]Katherine Gilbert and Helmut Kuhn, *A History of Esthetics* (Bloomington: Indiana University Press, 1954), 202.

[52]Locke, *Essays Concerning Human Understanding* 3:3:34.

Plate 3
ALEXANDER AND SELINA CAMPBELL
Courtesy Disciples of Christ Historical Society

4

The Parable of the Sower: American Soil

The New World, entered by Thomas Campbell in 1807 and his family in 1809, was undergoing a period of rapid social change and political ferment. The geographical size of the young nation had doubled in 1803, when President Thomas Jefferson's administration negotiated the purchase of the Louisiana Territory from France for $5 million. This transaction was also an indirect result of the Napoleonic wars in Europe and the international jockeying for strategic position and money by European powers. The purchase helped to permanently redistribute political power in the United States from the New England Federalists to the Republicans, whose power emanated primarily from the West.

The *Brutus,* on which Thomas Campbell sailed in April, 1807 left Londonderry for Philadelphia only two months before British-American tensions climaxed in an attack by the British man-of-war *Leopard* on the American ship *Chesapeake.* The *Chesapeake* was a casualty of the French and English War, in which the young American nation suffered as a neutral country while endeavoring to maintain her commercial and shipping interests in a belligerent climate.

On August 4, 1809, the *Latonia,* an American vessel from New York, sailed with Thomas Campbell's family from Greenock, Scotland. Tension on the Atlantic was no less than it had been when Thomas had sailed two years earlier; only in June, 1809 had President Madison signed a proclamation to restore the interrupted commercial intercourse with England.[1]

The Campbells arrived in the United States at a time when hundreds of Europeans were traveling to America as tourists. Later, many of those travelers published reports of their visits. Those reports in most cases reflected their authors' national political and social biases; nevertheless, they are valuable for study of the cultural and aesthetic mores of the people who forged the Restoration Movement on American soil.

Augustus John Foster, English Minister to the United States just before the War of 1812, collected his old notes during the 1830s and gave what he felt was a rare balanced account among the numerous travelogues which were published in Europe. Foster noted that some trav-

---

[1]The renewal of shipping between the two countries was disrupted more than once. The deteriorating relations of the United States with both France and England culminated in the War of 1812 between Britain and the United States.

elers had reported their visits in glowing terms and others had expressed abuse and contempt of the United States, all based on biased views. He acknowledged, even then, that the United States was too large an area to be described in a general travelogue, and he endeavored to make descriptions by states or regions.[2]

The most famous of these Old World travelers was the Frenchman Alexis de Tocqueville, who visited America between 1831 and 1832, originally to study the American penal system. Tocqueville reported, however, in a much broader fashion on his visits. His journal is a standard reference source for study of early American institutions.

His visit to America occurred some twenty years after the founding of the Washington Christian Association and the publication of Thomas Campbell's *Declaration and Address*. Tocqueville's diaries were interesting to Americans because they reflected a time when the young nation was becoming a new world with new social structures, at the same time that reform had begun in England. It has been observed that Tocqueville lives in today's world, not because we have rediscovered him, but because the problems he observed have become our problems.[3] A frequent theme sounded by Tocqueville was the Jeffersonian concern that a responsible electorate must be supported by an effective educational system. Writing in his journal nine years before the founding of Bethany College by Restoration leaders, Tocqueville sounded an alarm for the future cultural and political life of the Republic:

> Why, as civilization spreads, do outstanding men become fewer? Why, when attainments are the lot of all, do great intellectual talents become rarer? Why, when there are no longer lower classes, are there no more upper classes? Why, when knowledge of how to rule reaches the masses, is there a lack of great abilities in the direction of society? America clearly poses these questions. But who can answer them?[4]

Alexander Campbell echoed a similar zeal for education in a democracy when he appealed to his friends to join in the venture of Bethany College:

> Men, and not brick and mortar, make colleges, and these colleges make men. These men make books, and these books make the living world in which we individually live, and move, and

---

[2]Sir Augustus John Foster, *Jeffersonian America: Notes on the United States of America Collected in the Years 1805-6-7 and 11-12* (reprint; Westport, Conn.: Greenwood Press, 1980), 3, 6.

[3]See J. P. Mayer's "Introduction" to Alexis de Tocqueville, *Journey to America*, tr. George Laurence, ed. J. P. Mayer (Westport, Conn.: Greenwood Press, 1954), x.

[4]Tocqueville, *Journey to America*, 161.

have our being. How all-important, then, that our colleges should understand and teach the true philosophy of man! They create the men that furnish the teachers of men—the men that fill the pulpit, the legislative halls, the senators, the judges, and the governors of the earth. Do we expect to fill these high stations by merely voting or praying for men? Or shall we choose empirics, charlatans, mountebanks, and every pretender to eminent claims upon the suffrages of the people? Forbid it, reason, conscience, and Heaven![5]

Campbell's concern for sound intellectual preparation for leaders of both the nation and the Church ultimately resulted in many colleges, universities, seminaries, and Bible colleges founded and supported by the various branches of the Restoration Movement.[6]

In the broadest sense, the Restoration Movement must be viewed as a Christian response to the wider cultural and societal questions posed in Tocqueville's journal. While Walter Scott's *Gospel Restored* emphasized the primary importance of individual conversion in the Christian relationship to God, Alexander Campbell worked throughout his career to sustain the parallel importance of Christian and social institutions as part of Christian responsibility to God and man. One of the fragmenting issues within the Restoration Movement has been the juxtaposition of a personal relationship with Christ, on the one hand, and response to social issues as expression of Christlike living, on the other. It is to the credit of the early nineteenth-century reformers that they were usually willing to complement each other's understanding rather than to divide into legalistic self-righteous sectarianism.

Tocqueville took note of the rationalistic and intellectual inclinations of the American populace—a tendency that was reflected in the Restoration leaders' strong emphasis on cognition over feelings and the affective aspects of knowledge. Under a list of "Reasons for the social state and present government in America," Tocqueville included "Their origin: Excellent point of departure. Intimate mixture of religion and liberty. Cold and rationalistic race."[7]

---

[5]Alexander Campbell, quoted in Perry E. Gresham, "Alexander Campbell, Schoolmaster," *The Sage of Bethany, A Pioneer in Broadcloth*, ed. Perry E. Gresham (St. Louis: Bethany Press, 1960), 22.

[6]Some of the colleges affiliated with the Christian Church (Disciples of Christ) are accredited by the National Association of Schools of Music and the National Association of Schools of Art and Design. Some affiliated with the Church of Christ are accredited by the National Association of Schools of Music. Most of the colleges related to the independent Churches of Christ are Bible colleges and may not have sought accreditation.

[7]Tocqueville, *Journey to America*, 184.

During his journey to Canada, Tocqueville was constrained to compare Canadian life with that of the United States. He concluded that Americans were superior in knowledge, reasoning, and "the mercantile spirit" but the French Canadians possessed a greater sensibility and superior qualities of the heart—"theirs is a life of the heart, the others of the head."[8]

Tocqueville's observations were based on only a short visit. However, the Frenchman may have described both the strength and the internal flaw that became pervasive in the American Restoration Movement, which developed a tradition dependent upon logical biblical exegesis, debate, education, and intellectual growth. Like its Scottish ancestry and a great deal of American thought, Restorationism is lacking in the warmth of poetry, art, human sensitivity, and ultimately, the overt demonstration of Christlike love.

Prince Maximilian of Germany also visited North America, from 1832 to 1834. He published a report of his travels, with illustrations by the artist Carl Bodmer, in Koblenz, Germany, during 1841. Maximilian traveled from Boston through New York, Pennsylvania, Ohio, Indiana, and Saint Louis to the western part of the United States. He visited the Ohio Valley when the primary activities of the Campbells and their colleagues were under way there.

In Philadelphia, Maximilian saw "many churches . . . of various religious denominations, mostly without external ornamentation, in a very simple style, constructed of brick." He acknowledged the youthfulness of the country in comparison with European cities with the explanation that the United States lacked the history of ancient Europe, and so had no Gothic cathedrals or imposing monuments to instruct or inspire a tourist. In his listing of noteworthy buildings of the city, Maximilian mentioned the statehouse, the university, and the Bank of Pennsylvania, all designed by Benjamin Latrobe. He was greatly pleased by the German Moravian town of Bethlehem, in both its design and its comparative cleanliness—although not by the home-made wine, which proved to be a "very sour drink."[9]

The German prince was not favorably impressed with Pittsburgh (where several of the Restoration Movement leaders had been active for nearly a decade) because of the heavy gray smoke which covered the city. A visit to Economy, where the colony leader George Rapp officiated over religious and civic matters, was a pleasant interlude in his travels.

---

[8]Ibid., 192.

[9]Maximilian, Prinz zu Wied, *Reise in das innere Nordamerika*, Band I, (Koblenz: sonderausgabe der Rhenania Buchhandlung, n.d.), 35, 42. Translation by D. Jorgenson. Maximilian acknowledged that "In the Lancaster area near York one can obtain much better wine."

This settlement had one hundred houses, originally quickly built of wood, but by then replaced with brick houses. Maximilian noted that the church was "roomy and simple, out of brick, with a high tower and a gored clock."[10]

Maximilian and Bodmer attended a Sunday service in the German colony. The prince's description of that visit provides an interesting view of a Sunday morning service:

> Since it was Sunday, people gathered at nine o'clock in the church, which had neither chancel nor organ. The men sat at the right side of the preacher, the women on the left, the older people in front, with the young people moved to the rear. The family of Herr Rapp had the first place.
>
> When the church had assembled, the elder Rapp entered with a quick step, sat down at an elevated table, and began a song, which was sung in what seemed to be a quick tempo. After a standing prayer, he preached in clever and (for country people) very graphic pictures, with fiery gesticulations over a passage of the Bible. After the sermon, another stanza was sung, Rapp said a prayer which the congregation repeated while sitting. The word, 'Amen' was repeated at that time by the entire congregation. Then the women left first, with the men following last.[11]

The simplicity of the worship service at Economy reflected the colony's emphasis on fundamentals, and had aspects of the equally simple worship of the Restoration pioneers, whether or not any actual historical connection could be made.

Another valuable report of travel in the New World during the first part of the nineteenth century is that of Benjamin Henry Latrobe, architect, engineer, naturalist, and artist. Latrobe was born in England in 1764, emigrated in 1795, and lived in the United States until his death in 1820. His travel account draws upon his European perspective, his education in Moravian institutions in England and Germany, and his "buying into" the American scene after settling in the United States. His own drawings, pen and ink sketches, and watercolors greatly enrich his travel diaries.

Latrobe is remembered as an engineer whose work contributed to the application of steam and mechanical power to construction problems, including the erection of the Philadelphia waterworks from 1799-1801. His architectural heritage includes work on the United

[10]Ibid., 82.
[11]Ibid., 83.

Plate 4

View on the New Turnpike Road from Chambersburg to Bedford

BENJAMIN HENRY LATROBE

Courtesy Museum and Library of Maryland History

States Capitol Building from 1803 until 1811, and a second term from 1815 to 1817 after the Capitol was burned by British troops in 1814. Other buildings which added to his fame were the Bank of Pennsylvania (1798-1801), and his architectural masterpiece, the Roman Catholic Cathedral of Baltimore, known as the first American monument to the Greek revival.[12]

Latrobe used the common modes of American transportation—horseback, stagecoach, wagon, sailing ship, and river steamboat—while exploring the young nation, just as Alexander Campbell did in his tireless travels to support the American Reformation. Latrobe wanted to avoid the lack of balance in the reports of other Europeans. He loudly criticized the "traveling bookmakers" who only looked superficially at the country and made their reports through the medium of their own habits. Like Maximilian, Latrobe was a naturalist and his sketches reflect a careful and scientific accuracy.

It has been observed that Latrobe's conceptual view of science was Baconian: experimental, empirical, descriptive, and lacking hypothesis. Baconianism dominated not only British science, but in the early nineteenth century it was the "unquestioned orthodoxy in American science."[13] This was the same philosophy that Robert Richardson brought a few years later to the Bethany College science curriculum.

There are three stylistic strands which have been identified in Latrobe's architectural work, and which, due to the broad audience for his public buildings, made a rather wide impact on the American experience. These strands have been labeled the Picturesque, the Neoclassical, and the Sublime. The Picturesque was an eighteenth-century British concept through which the criteria for judging landscape paintings are attributed to other arts and to nature. Latrobe's own "Essay on Landscape" outlines his description of the Picturesque, a tradition which might relate his ideal to some of the work of Joshua Reynolds, Thomas Gainsborough, and especially the Reverend William Gilpin.[14]

Latrobe's roots in neoclassicism include not only references to the Greek classics, books he probably brought with him from London, but the neoclassic values of grace, order, symmetry, and a "purification" of nature filtered through the artist's organizational structure. His architectural renderings are closest to the Classical tradition; his nonprofessional sketches are nearer to the Picturesque.

---

[12]Edward C. Carter II, John C. Van Horne, and Charles E. Brownell, eds., *Latrobe's View of America, 1795-1820* (New Haven: Yale University Press, for the Maryland Historical Society, 1985), 6-7.

[13]Ibid., 13.

[14]Ibid., 18-19.

76

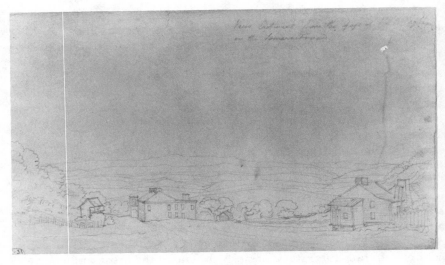

Plate 5

View Eastward from the Gap of the Allegheny on the Somerset Road

BENJAMIN HENRY LATROBE

Courtesy Museum and Library of Maryland History

Sublimity, especially in the tradition of British aesthetics and in the work of the German philosopher Immanuel Kant, refers to awesome, huge, enormous, and sometimes fear-inspiring experiences.[15] Latrobe found such natural phenomena as Niagara Falls and the Hudson River Palisades to be Sublime; more than once he painted a storm at sea in the Sublime tradition.

One of the most cogent philosophical thrusts the work of Latrobe provided for American mores was the proposition that fancy and imagination—through the Picturesque and Sublime traditions—have a legitimate and important place in the balanced intellectual life of a people. The cultivation of the classical tradition also suggests that structure, order, and form have a vital role in ordering ideas, along with the truth of the content presented.

Concomitantly, Alexander Campbell combined the Classical traditions of structure, order, and form with the Sublime and Picturesque traditions of fancy and imagination. His preaching demonstrated his knowledge of Bible language, with its beauty and grace of expression. He skillfully delivered Bible themes, thoughts, terms, and facts with a beauty that deeply impressed his hearers.

Just as Latrobe aesthetically painted what he saw, so Campbell aesthetically presented Bible truths. He consistently used metaphor, simile, and analogy to illustrate scriptural truths or to defend an argument.[16]

Latrobe's sketches and journalistic descriptions included the route traveled by the Campbells on their original route to Washington County from New York, as well as the area around Washington City, Pennsylvania and Wheeling, Virginia, where they invested most of their lives. The route from the East to Washington County and the overnight inns along the way are described in some detail by Richardson in his *Memoirs of Alexander Campbell*. Richardson's eye for aesthetic beauty, ready to record the nuance of Nature's beautiful colors and shapes, provides the reader one of his most eloquent descriptions. His writing displays a nineteenth-century gentleman's deference to women as the more receptive sex to aesthetic Sublimity. Describing central Pennsylvania, he wrote:

---

[15]This description is from Gilbert and Kuhn, *History of Esthetics* (Bloomington: Indiana University Press, 1954), 322.

[16]See Archibald McLean, *Alexander Campbell as a Preacher* (St. Louis: The Christian Publishing Co., 1973), 33-34. The "Bible themes by Bible names" credo enunciated by the *Declaration and Address* and the Restoration founders suggests a literalism which is not entirely representative of their real concept. In spite of the trend in the second generation of Disciples, sometimes called the Scholastics, toward a literal legalism, the first generation appreciated the possibilities of knowing and feeling in more than a mathematical and logical dimension.

Nothing, however, was fitted to afford more delight, especially to the females of the party, than the rich colors with which autumn had tinged many of the forest trees. Here the bright golden hue of the hickory, and the beautiful orange tints of the maple, were contrasting with the dark green of the unchanging pine. Here the scarlet oak (Quercus coccinea) and the brilliantly tinted Tupelo, shone resplendent amidst surrounding verdure, and the ampelopsis, or American ivy, covered closely with its digitate leaves of crimson the lofty trunks of decaying trees. Thus their slow and toilsome progress over the numerous and lofty ridges of the Alleghenies and across the intervening valleys was cheered and enlivened by the strangeness and the beauty of the objects which presented themselves along the route. Birds of gay and varied plumage, which had been unknown amidst the solitude and silence of the primeval forest, flitted from tree to tree along the borders of the cultivated districts. The active squirrel mounted to the topmost branches in quest of nuts; various wild animals were suddenly started from the thickets along the way; and sometimes, amid the deeper recesses of the mountains, might still be seen in the distance, a few timid deer, hastening to the security of their accustomed haunts.[17]

Richardson's dual interests in science (he was by profession a medical doctor) and in the aesthetics of natural beauty may well be compared with Latrobe's concerns as naturalist and artist. Latrobe's verbal description is more banal, but a description of his pencil and watercolor sketch of a scene of the turnpike between Chambersburg and Bedford, Pennsylvania, provides another dimension of this thought:

The road, which formerly was carried along the slope of the rocky mountain on the right, is now made, by blowing down the road, to run close to the Bank of the Juniata for a very considerable distance. The rocky [mountain] is a red argillaceous schist regularly crystalized in rhomboital parallelopipedous. The distant mountain is called the Warrior's mountain. The Juniata passes through it beyond the village of Bloody run [*sic*].

The view was taken when the country was covered with snow. Jany 22[d], 1820 [*sic*]. On the rocks the sun had however melted it and left them almost bare.[18]

---

[17]Richardson, *Memoirs*, 1:212.
[18]Latrobe, *Sketchbook X*, quoted in Carter et al., *Latrobe's View* 372.

Latrobe made a sketch of the White Horse Inn between Somerset and Bedford in Pennsylvania which complements Richardson's bland description of such an inn used by Thomas Campbell's family as they traveled west toward Washington County. Richardson, writing in 1868, commented almost nostalgically that

> At this period, hotels of this character could be found every ten or twenty miles, but since the establishment of railroads and the tunneling of the mountains, their glory has departed and they are now 'few and far between,' and doing but little business, since passengers can travel at their ease, seated on the soft plush or velvet cushions of luxurious cars, and over as great a distance in an hour as could be accomplished by the old road-wagon in a day.[19]

The American cultural environment that hosted the young Restoration Movement around 1810-40 was beset by polarities. On the one hand was the urban environment of the eastern cities which imbibed the European or "cultivated" tradition. On the other, was the western frontier and the South, where the "vernacular" tradition was fostered by folk artists and amateurs whose first callings were in more utilitarian pursuits than art and literature. There seems to have been a middle ground between these two poles found in the emerging city-towns west of Philadelphia. In these new city-towns, some contact was maintained with the urbane and wealthy eastern seaboard cities; and yet one could feel some of the western resentment or envy of those "down East" centers of culture. Serious artistic work was disdained by men of the in-between towns and the frontier. Men with the frontier pioneering spirit thought of art, especially music, as the province of women or immigrant "professors." Cultivation of land and money, not the mind and spirit, seemed to be most important.[20] The work ethos of early American Puritanism prevailed on the developing frontier and in the new towns.

The slow beginnings of the cultivated tradition in American musical life can be contrasted with that of Europe. Early New England attitudes have been compared with those of the Old World:

> The very ideology of many colonists was totally incompatible with the aristocratic public cultivation of the secular arts. While the New England Puritans were engaged in such rudimentary musical disputations as whether the Bible sanctioned the reading or the singing of the psalms, and the organ in King's

[19]Richardson, *Memoirs*, 1:213-14.

[20]See H. Wiley Hitchcock, *Music in the United States, A Historical Introduction* (Englewood Cliffs, N. J.: Prentice-Hall, 1969), 45.

Chapel was threateningly characterized as an 'infernal box of whistles with the devil inside,' Bach and Handel were composing their masterpieces for church and concert stage. While Boston's 'tanner-composer' William Billings (1746-1800) was composing his 'fugueing pieces' and compiling the *Psalm Singer,* Haydn and Mozart were laying the foundation for the modern symphony, and Beethoven was beginning his sensational career as pianist and composer in glittering Vienna, the literal hub of the musical world.[21]

Alexander Campbell arrived in the New World thirty-three years before the establishment of the first permanent American symphony orchestra. The New York Philharmonic Symphony Society made its initial appearance December 7, 1842, in the five-hundred-seat Apollo Rooms on Broadway Street near Canal Street. This was the only major orchestra to be established until after Campbell's death in 1866; the New York Symphony Society was established in 1878, and the Boston Symphony provided the second American city with an orchestra upon its establishment in 1881.[22]

In addition to the centers of urban musical activity in Boston, New York, and Philadelphia, a few isolated pockets of musical excellence appeared in some of the German communities of Pennsylvania and the Carolinas. Of these, the richest and most sophisticated musical culture was created by the Moravians who first reached America about 1732. Bethlehem, Pennsylvania became an important Moravian center in 1741. For the Moravians, music was an essential part of religious life. Sacred music—anthems, arias, motets, chorales—was arranged for instrumentalists, soloists, and choirs. Weddings, christenings, funerals, and other religious occasions were observed with music, especially by brass ensembles.[23]

During the first half of the nineteenth century, "serious" American musicians were turning from England to Germany as the source of musical studies and traditions. Thomas Hastings (1784-1872) compiled numerous collections of church music, and turned increasingly to the "science, genius, and taste" of "German musik." He is reputed to have written about six hundred hymn texts and composed a thousand hymn tunes, including a melody for Augustus M. Toplady's hymn, "Rock of Ages." Lowell Mason (1792-1872) influenced American musical life and the public school teaching of music as decidedly as any American musi-

---

[21]John H. Mueller, *The American Symphony Orchestra* (Bloomington: Indiana University Press, 1951), 17.

[22]Ibid., 37. The New York Symphony Society was merged with the New York Philharmonic in 1928.

[23]Hitchcock, *Music in the United States,* 17.

cian. Mason was taught by a German musician during residence in Savannah, and contributed both choral works and some twelve hundred hymn tunes. Louis Moreau Gottschalk (1829-69) is described as "without question the most colorful personality, the most articulate intelligence, the most talented performer, and the most provocative composer among the mid-nineteenth-century pianists . . . ." Gottschalk studied in Paris, rather than in Germany, and displayed some of the same romantic traits which helped shape Europe's great pianist-composers—Chopin and Liszt—into legendary names in their own times. Upon his return to America, Gottschalk became a traveling virtuoso and has been seen as America's first matinee idol.[24]

For most Disciples of the early nineteenth century, the vernacular tradition of American music was more important than the cultivated branch in the formation of both congregational worship and musical aesthetics. The vernacular aspect of Yankee music resulted from the combination of folk songs and revival hymns with "fugueing tunes" and anthems composed by quasi-educated men from the northeastern cities. These pieces became the rural music of the South and the American frontier. There they were joined with several other kinds of religious music and became the basis for the vernacular music tradition that has lived on into the twentieth century.[25]

The shape note hymn books of the South and West later became important in the development of a hymnody for Disciples, particularly during the period when no organs were used to supply a harmonic basis for the congregational singing. For the non-instrumental Churches of Christ, this tradition has continued well into the last half of the twentieth century.[26]

The prevailing work ethos affected development of the arts in the young country in different ways. Both cultured and vernacular strains can be found not only in music but also painting, sculpture, architecture, and literature of the nineteenth century. The polarity of the cultured and vernacular seems widest in the literature of music. At the end of the eighteenth century there seems to have been a relative homogeneity of musical practice, but in the early nineteenth century the gulf began to widen. Hitchcock made the following comparison:

---

[24]Ibid., 55-56, 57, 73, 74.

[25]Ibid., 92.

[26]One representative hymnal used by Churches of Christ from 1937 until 1986, *Great Songs of the Church*, was available in both shaped and round note editions. This was the case with numerous hymnals used by the non-instrumental churches of the Restoration Movement.

. . . as the nineteenth century unfolds we can distinguish with
increasing clarity two bodies of American music: cultivated and
vernacular traditions become visible; an eventually profound
schism in American musical culture begins to open up. On the
one hand this continues a vernacular tradition of utilitarian and
entertainment music, essentially unconcerned with artistic or
philosophical idealism; a music based on established or newly
diffused American raw materials; a 'popular' in the largest sense,
broadly based, widespread, naive, and unselfconscious. On the
other hand there grows a cultivated tradition of fine-art music
significantly concerned with moral, artistic, or cultural idealism; a music almost exclusively based on continental European
raw materials and models, looked to rather self-consciously; an
essentially transatlantic music of the pretenders to gentility;
hopefully sophisticated and by no means widespread throughout all segments of the populace.[27]

John Mueller examined the "lag" of American musical art behind its
sister cultural endeavors:

In contrast to the state of music, the achievements of the new
world in the realm of the other arts and sciences, after all, were
not so rudimentary. In painting, Copley, Peale, West, Turnbull,
and Gilbert Stuart had permanently enriched their field before
the nineteenth century was well begun. In sculpture, Thomas
Crawford, Horatio Greenough, and Hiram Powers had achieved
an international reputation before the middle of the century.[28]

Painters such as John Singleton Copley (1738-1815), Charles
Wilson Peale (1741-1827), Benjamin West (1730-1813), and his
student Gilbert Stuart (1755-1828) had gained international fame.
During the period when the Washington Christian Association and the
Brush Run Church were founded, the heroic style of painting—with its
heavy emphasis on genre, landscape, and anecdotal painting—was
developed in a Romantic style by Thomas Cole (1801-48), Frederic
Church (1826-1900), George Catlin (1796-1872),[29] and the Missouri
artist-politician George Caleb Bingham (1811-79).

Before the development of the camera, portraiture was a major
source of activity and income for artists—and a respectably practical
activity among all kinds of people of note. Thomas and Alexander Camp-

---

[27]Hitchcock, *Music in the United States,* 44.

[28]Mueller, *American Symphony Orchestra,* 17-18.

[29]Catlin, born in Pennsylvania, devoted himself to a study of American Indians.
Between 1829-38 he executed a series of Indian portraits and sketches; he wrote *Life
Among the Indians* (1867) and other works about native Americans.

bell and most of the other leaders of the Restoration Movement were among those whose likenesses were recorded by artists of that period.[30]

Sculpture, like music, enjoyed the activity of craftsmen and artists from both the cultured and vernacular streams. The "cultured" development has been connected to the same needs which motivated portraiture:

> An American school of sculptors, distinct from the native folk carving tradition, came into existence in the interval between the Revolutionary War and the Civil War. This development was largely the result of the surge of patriotic sentiment that followed the successful struggle for independence. A desire for commemorative portraits made itself felt almost immediately after the Revolution, with figures of George Washington, the revered revolutionary hero, most in demand. Since there seemed to be no native artists of sufficient prestige to undertake monumental sculptures, the first major commissions went to Europeans.[31]

The necessity at the turn of the century to commission Jean-Antoine Houdon from France to create a full-length statue of General Washington, and to turn to other European artists for the sculpture needs of the young republic, was alleviated well before the Civil War, when many young American sculptors were studying in Europe and carrying out large and lucrative commissions.

The vernacular tradition of sculpture was developed by those now considered to be craftsmen of high quality. They were the many wood carvers who created wood carvings for ships and buildings and who are now admired for their great skill. These craftsmen did not set out to be "artists," but their technical and expressive abilities are now recognized as a genre of art.

In architecture, the work of Benjamin Latrobe, mentioned earlier in this chapter, was part of the cultured tradition, the Classic revival. Between 1785 and 1810, this movement was oriented more toward Roman than Greek antiquity. The resulting American architecture is called the Federal style. After 1810, the Classic strain derived more specifically from ancient Greece, and is called Greek Revival.

---

[30]Numerous portraits of the "Restoration fathers" are extant at the Disciples of Christ Historical Library in Nashville, Tennessee, at the Campbell mansion in Bethany, West Virginia, and at various colleges and universities related to the three primary streams of the Restoration Movement.

[31]See David M. Mendelowitz, *History of American Art*, (New York: Holt, Rinehart and Winston, 1970).

Analogous to the vernacular tradition was the valuable work of the woodcutters. The simple architecture created by divergent religious groups such as the Shakers, the Quakers, and rural/frontier religious groups became known as some of the most creative and beautiful buildings to grace the American continent. Although the Romantic impulses of the nineteenth century include a return to an elaborate Gothic style and even some Romanesque churches, the vernacular tradition prevailed among the leaders of the young Disciples churches. Relative cost, of course, was a decisive factor in the construction of most of their worship buildings.[32]

In literature, the "polite" traditions of the United States of the first third of the nineteenth century were closely related to those of its English parent. The values with which poetry, essays, and fiction were judged were values redirected by the American outlook, but closely tied to contemporary critical evaluations emanating from the mother country.[33]

The Scottish "common sense" school of philosophy was well represented in the critical journals read by literate Americans. In the area of aesthetics, the chief spokesman for this school was Thomas Reid (1710-96). Reid was critical of John Locke's aesthetic views, and complained that contemporary philosophers "resolve all our perceptions into mere feelings or sensations in the person that perceives, without anything corresponding to those feelings in the external object."[34]

Charvat emphasizes the dependence of the American cultural mind upon the British Isles, especially upon Scotland:

> It is more accurate to say that it was culturally allied with Scotland. In America the most popular foreign periodicals were the *Edinburgh* and *Quarterly* reviews and Campbell's *New Monthly Magazine.* All three were run by Scots who had been brought up in the same philosophical and critical tradition. The philosophical background was the Scotch "common sense" school; the critical and aesthetic tradition was that of Karnes, Blair, and Alison, the "psychological" aestheticians. Now the interesting thing is that this philosophy and this aesthetics were just as popular in America as they were in Scotland.[35]

---

[32]See chap. 7 of this book.

[33]See William Charvat, *The Origins of American Critical Thought, 1810-1835* (New York: A. S. Barnes, 1961), 27, "In the final analysis, all the 'sources' of a national culture are indigenous, since a nation always chooses those foreign 'influences' which are congenial to its own temperament. But America is a child of the Old World, and in the first quarter of the century it was still very close to its parents."

[34]Gilbert and Kuhn, *History of Esthetics,* 252.

[35]Charvat, *Origins of Critical Thought,* 29.

In 1783, Reverend Hugh Blair published his *Lectures On Rhetoric and Belles Lettres* in Britain. They were published in many complete and abridged editions in the United States, in both small towns as well as larger cities. Numerous American professors were indebted to Blair's ideas during the first half of the nineteenth century, including the noted Edward Tyrell Channing of Harvard and John Quincy Adams, who lectured at Harvard from 1806 until 1809. Blair's *Rhetoric* was used at Yale from 1785, and later at most of the major academic institutions in the American northeast. Some of Blair's doctrines also penetrated American thinking through their incorporation into William Wordsworth's work.[36]

Another area of special interest in considering the Romantic appreciation for nature enjoyed by the young Alexander Campbell is Blair's doctrine of sublimity, a concept which was particularly useful to poets of the Romantic era. Blair wrote, "In all good writing the sublime lies in the thought, not in the words; when the thought is noble the language will be dignified." Here, too, Sublime did not mean only elegant, but was based on vastness, awfulness, or solemnity.[37]

Since Glasgow University was partially staffed by teachers of the Common Sense school, it may be assumed that Alexander Campbell, during his year of study there, had been thoroughly introduced to this system of thought. His later exultation in the experience of sublimity—excited by nature rather than through art—was described by Richardson in the narrative of young Campbell's initial trip through the Pennsylvania mountains:

All nature around him seemed to sympathize with his emotions. The balmy air, fresh from the wild mountain slopes, the new varieties of birds, which from almost every tree seemed, to his fancy, to chant their evening song in praise of the freedom of their native woods, the approaching shades of evening, veiling the distant landscape in a gentle haze,—all seemed to speak of liberty, security and peace. He was far from being an enthusiast, but, on this occasion, all the bright hopes and glowing fancies of his youthful nature seem to have been aroused. Keenly susceptible as he was to impressions of grandeur, and tending still, in the habitual workings of his mind to religious thought, as he

---

[36]Charvat suggests that Wordsworth may have been successful because his own philosophy was built on Scottish philosophy and criticism. He was initially influenced not only by Hugh Blair, but by the writers Francis Hutchison, David Hartley, Lord Kames, Sir Joshua Reynolds, William Shenstone, Archibald Alison, and Erasmus Darwin. See ibid., 30-31, 71; and Arthur Beatty, *William Wordsworth, His Doctrines and Art in their Historical Relations* (Madison: University of Wisconsin Press, 1962), 38.

[37]Charvat, *Origins of Critical Thought*, 46.

ranged through the deep, untrodden glades, or paused beneath
the canopy of verdure which the wild vine had woven as the roof
upon the spreading warp of branching oaks, his heart over-
flowed with gratitude and reverence.[38]

Charvat acknowledged the danger of over-generalization for the
twenty-five-year period about which he wrote, and provided six
"denominators" in American criticism which dominated the period
when Disciples institutions were in their formative stage. Some of these
principles reflect the Scottish background discussed above; others,
through Puritan and other American influences, are quite indigenous to
the New World:

1. The critic thought of himself as the watchdog of society.

2. Literature must not condone rebellion of any kind against
   the existing social and economic order.

3. Literature must not contain anything derogatory, implicitly
   or explicitly, to religious ideals and moral standards.

4. Literature should be optimistic; it should not condone philosophical pessimism or skepticism.

5. Literature should deal with the intelligible, not the mystical
   or obscure.

6. Literature should be social in point of view, not
   egocentric.[39]

The moralistic tone of these critical principles reflects the heavy
influence of religious institutions and clergymen on the "cultivated" tradition of the eastern cities. These principles were internalized with
varying degrees of urgency by individuals living on the frontier in their
vernacular folk arts.

Most of the principles are directly reflected in the writings and the
positions taken by the Campbells, Walter Scott, Robert Richardson,
William Pendleton, and other leaders of the Restoration Movement who
were involved in literary pursuits. Some of Alexander Campbell's earliest American essays were written for the Washington, Pennsylvania
Reporter and were comments on "social ills." Richardson notes that
"Alexander . . . felt strongly disposed to urge the need of a social as
well as of a religious reformation."[40] Borrowing the feminine name Clarinda, he continued this series several months from May 1810, changing

---

[38]Richardson, *Memoirs*, 1:207.

[39]Charvat, *Origins of Critical Thought*, 7-23.

[40]Richardson, *Memoirs*, 1:283.

to the pseudonymn Bonus Homo for the later and most controversial installments of the column.

The optimism demanded by the fourth principle, that literature should not condone pessimism or skepticism, seems to have motivated Campbell throughout his American years. His narrative of an evening walk in the Pennsylvania mountains concluded with a summary of the young immigrant's thoughts about his newly adopted country. After discovering that most citizens left their doors unbarred at night, Campbell speculated about the reasons:

> In attempting to account for this, to him, unwonted security, his experience in the Old World led him to refer it, in a large measure, to the absence of Catholicism; and, after his devotions, he gradually fell into slumber amidst grateful reflections upon the goodness of Providence in bringing him to a land under the benign influence of the free institutions, the equal rights, the educational advantages, and the moral and religious elevation secured to all in a purely Protestant community.[41]

Richardson wrote astutely that "he soon learned too, by personal experience, that sectarian bigotry and clerical intolerance had changed their climate, and not their spirit, in crossing the Atlantic, and that no government or party or people is exempt from those errors and moral delinquencies which belong to a common humanity."[42]

Nevertheless, his confidence and optimism in America remained high throughout his life, despite the deep hurt and disappointment occasioned by the Civil War. The prospectus of his mature periodical, the *Millennial Harbinger,* implicitly suggests the choice of title:

> This work shall be devoted to the destruction of Sectarianism, Infidelity, and AntiChristian doctrine and practice. It shall have for its object the development, and introduction of that political and religious order of that society called THE MILLENNIUM, which will be the consummation of that ultimate amelioration of society proposed in the Christian Scriptures.[43]

Campbell's position regarding the millennium was not chiliastic, but might be considered socially post-millennial. The hope that the United States—about which he often wrote in most appreciative terms—might be the environment which could provide opportunity for a social/religious evolution leading to the return of Christ seems to have

---

[41]Ibid., 1:210.

[42]Ibid., 1: 211.

[43]Alexander Campbell, *Millennial Harbinger,* (1830), 1.

been a constant hope during many years of his editorial labors.[44] McAllister and Tucker comment:

> The choice of a name for the new paper should not be taken to suggest that Campbell expected an imminent return of Christ from the clouds of heaven. Indeed, he believed that ultimately Christ would reign on earth, but he doubted that any person was in a position to prophesy as to times or seasons. The millennium, in his judgment, would be realized gradually rather than by a cataclysmic event. Through his journal Campbell hoped to work for a reformation essential to the establishment of the kingdom. In this sense it was a harbinger of the millennium.[45]

The poetry of early nineteenth-century America was subjected to the cardinal tests of literature given earlier in this chapter, just as was prose literature. The "moral test" in particular was important. Technically, poetic diction was the chief preoccupation of the critics until 1815. This concern related to the popular understanding of semantic references, not far divorced from the "Bible things by Bible words" emphasis of Thomas Campbell's *Declaration and Address*. The developing Romantic movement was aided by William Wordsworth's doctrines in broadening its view to include more tolerance in the understanding of "poetic language." The accompanying Romantic balance of imagination and reason, mystery and warmth in art, the love of nature, and dependence upon symbolism all found expression both in the poetry cultivated by 1810 America and inner tensions of Disciples thought. Interestingly, poetry, among members of the religious community, was accepted more readily than prose fiction—the novel, the romance in Nathaniel Hawthorne's sense, or short stories.

---

[44]Herbert Spencer (1820-1903) gave a non-theistic and naturalistic twist to a parallel optimistic view in his theory of social evolution. "Evolution, then, under its primary aspect, is a change from a less coherent form to a more coherent form, consequent on the dissipation of motion and integration of matter. This is the universal process through which sensible existences, individually and as a whole, pass during the ascending half of their histories. This proves to be a character displayed in the earliest changes which the universe is supposed to have undergone, and in those latest changes which we trace in societies and the products of social life." See Herbert Spencer, *First Principles* (New York: Appleton, Century-Crofts, n.d.), chap. 14. While Campbell's societal improvement was to be climaxed with the Second Coming of Jesus Christ and the ultimate optimistic millennial hope, Spencer's ascending period of evolution was to be followed by a period of dissolution, tending to move the temporary optimistic hope into an ultimate expectation of doomsday. See also John H. Hopkins, "The idea of progress in nineteenth century Disciples preaching" (Lexington, Ky.: Lexington Theological Seminary, unpublished B.D. thesis, 1961).

[45]McAllister and Tucker, *Journey in Faith*, 145. That Barton W. Stone, Walter Scott, and other Restoration fathers did hold a more chiliastic view has been shown by E. L. Jorgenson in *Faith of our Fathers*, (Louisville: Word and Work Publishers, n.d.), 48, 147.

While he was a student at Glasgow University, Alexander Campbell took a class under Professor Jardine in Logic and Belles Lettres. Jardine, a former teacher of Alexander's father, had also taught the Scottish poet Thomas Campbell (1777-1824).

During his studies, Alexander read "Life and Poems" of James Hay Beattie and Johnson's "Lives of the Poets," and he made personal copies of extracts from Johnson. Richardson reports that he wrote a number of juvenile poems during this period, but "these . . . do not possess sufficient merit for publication, nor did he himself ever esteem them worthy of it."[46] Richardson, writing in the 1870s, provided a rather typical Romantic description of the poetic process:

> The true poet must possess, by nature, the most delicate perceptions of beauty and of harmony, and that vivid imagination to which these are allied, and which not only creates, but gives unity and life and action to its productions, so as to make 'things that are not' seem 'things that are.'[47]

The Romantic impulse to create poetry, particularly in the face of the awesome aspects of nature which the Scottish critics called the sublime, surfaced from time to time in Campbell's experience. On board the *Latonia,* twelve days on the Atlantic en route to New York, he was

> filled with the loftiest conceptions of the Divine Majesty, he contemplated with awe the sublime displays of power exhibited in its boundless extent, its innumerable tenantry, its mighty waves and howling tempests, and, in the midst of his feelings in . . . [a] poem entitled, 'The Ocean.'[48]

The activity of Campbell as hymn writer, hymnal editor, and translator during his mature life suggests the enduring validity poetry and its study held for him. The index for the *Millennial Harbinger* lists approximately 150 references to poems or articles on poets and poetry for the forty years of the journal's existence. Most of the poems carry religious or subjective titles and were penned by people relatively unknown in the world of poetic art. Lord Byron's "Destruction of Sennacherib," some hymns by William Cowper, and a few verses by the Christian poet John Greenleaf Whittier, are among the most notable items. The inclusion of poetry penned by members of the Disciples fellowship suggests the continued acceptance of the medium as a valid literary vehicle for Christian expression. Vachel Lindsay's later attempt to relate his Disciples-oriented Christianity with poetic expression echoes the more rudimen-

---

[46]Richardson, *Memoirs,* 1:131-32.

[47]Ibid., 1:134.

[48]Ibid., 1:201-2.

tary sallies of the early Restoration pioneers into the realm of metaphor, symbol, and the non-literal use of the written word.

The essay, in the hands of Campbell, Richardson, and other editors of nineteenth-century religious journals addressed to Christian Churches and the Disciples, became a powerful engine for the dissemination of Restoration principles. Alexander Campbell used it in the interest of religion, education, and social reformation, and the breadth of subjects addressed in the *Harbinger* from the initial issue of 1830 until the closing number of 1870 demonstrates not only his command of the Bible and his primary cause of religious reformation, but a cognizance of the social and political issues that characterized the period.

During the early nineteenth century, most American Christians, as well as literary critics, considered the art of fiction less acceptable than poetry or the essay. Reputable critical journals ignored fiction except to occasionally attack it. Since the novel did not have respect as a literary form, there was no defined body of rules by which it could be measured. This changed, however, in 1815, after the publication of Sir Walter Scott's *Waverly*, the first of a series of enormously popular historic-romantic novels.

The first principle of literary criticism—relating to moral responsibility—was considered binding for fiction as well as poetry. Dr. Samuel Miller, a member of the Scottish Common Sense school, wrote of eighteenth-century novels that "To fill the mind with unreal and delusive pictures of life, is, in the end, to beguile it from sober duty, and to cheat it of substantial enjoyment."[49] In 1811, the Philadelphia *Mirror of Taste and Dramatic Censor* published a condemnation of novels which illustrates the dilemma assigned to them by contemporary thought:

> Nineteen in twenty of these books so called are positively mischievous. . . . If a novel be so perfectly natural as to give a true picture of life, it does no more for us than is already done to our hands in the ordinary incidents of the day. . . . If, on the other hand, it presents an untrue picture of life, it imparts false and exaggerated notions which are sure to corrupt the heart.[50]

The "willing suspension of disbelief," so vital to drama and fiction, was not an easy condition of mind for a society so strongly influenced by Puritan thought. It is important to note the tensions related to the power of the literal and clear word. First, it was a semantic reference which was unambiguous, and was susceptible to the powerful logical process of which Alexander Campbell ultimately became a master. Second, Campbell experienced a competing attraction toward the

[49]Charvat, *Origins of Critical Thought*, 137-38.
[50]Quoted in ibid., 138.

poetic, the musical, the quality of relationship with both God and man interpreted by the language of the Psalms and the Apocalypse. Richardson, highly conscious of this cleavage of values within Campbell's mind, attempted to deal with the question at some length:

> That he himself possessed a good degree of the imaginative faculty is unquestionable; but in him the understanding and the judgment largely predominated, and his imagination displayed itself, not in poetic creations, but in the far-reaching grasp by which, as an orator, he seized upon principles, facts, illustrations and analogies, and so modified and combined them as to render them all tributary to his main design. It was in the choice of arguments, in unexpected applications of familiar facts, in comprehensive generalizations, widening the horizon of human thought and revealing new and striking relations, that this faculty manifested itself; subservient always, however, to the proof of some logical proposition or to the development of some important truth. His deficiency in the musical faculty, as well as the preponderance of the reasoning powers and of the practical understanding, would, doubtless, have inhibited the attainment of any poetic distinction.[51]

In the progress of Campbell's career, the tension in which he was able to hold the poetic-logical tendencies in his life may well have helped generate the genius that made him a natural leader of the American Restoration Movement. It is important to realize, however, that for those who followed him, the literal and slavish imitation of the cognitive and logical part of his heritage has sometimes resulted in a loveless legalism. The other extreme has been the late nineteenth-century application of the lyrical and imaginative, coupled with a true 'Campbellian' social consciousness, amplified to the point of a break with historic Christianity and the creation of a liberalism which failed to acknowledge the scriptural norms upon which the Movement was generated.

Osborne points out that Alexander Campbell's doctrine of God was "orthodox," a doctrine which incidentally brought him into some dialogue with fellow reformer Barton W. Stone who always had difficulty with the doctrine of the Trinity as a scriptural concept.[52] In a parallel assessment, it might be noted that in matters of literary criticism, Campbell also accepted the mores of American thought, measured by the six principles enumerated by Charvat. There was one notable exception, proposition number 3: Literature must not contain anything derogatory, implicitly or explicitly, to religious ideals and moral standards.

[51]Ibid., 1:134.
[52]Osborne in Beazley, ed., *The Christian Church*, 89.

During the entire seven years that *The Christian Baptist* was published, Campbell fearlessly breached the polite acceptance of this credo
by using reason, ridicule, biblical authority, and sometimes even caustic
wit to call attention to the abuses of institutionalized Christian clergy.
For this he was criticized (see many letters to the editor from 1827 until
1830), both to his face and behind his back. He received letters from
his friends chiding him for his lack of Christian grace,[53] and from opponents who objected to both the substance and the style of his message.[54]

The editor's own rationale from the perspective of two intervening
years is given in the *Millennial Harbinger* of 1831:

> In a word, and without a figure, he regarded the so-called Chris-
> tian community as having lost all healthy excitability; and his
> first volume of the 'Christian Baptist,' the 'most uncharitable,'
> the severe, sarcastic, and ironical he ever wrote, was an experi-
> ment to ascertain whether society could be moved by fear or
> rage—whether it could be made to feel at all the decisive symp-
> toms of the moral malady which was consuming the last spark
> of moral life and motion. It operated favorably upon the whole,
> though very unfavorably to the reputation of its author as
> respected his 'Christian spirit.'[55]

Apparently, Campbell's violation of the "do-not-touch" understanding regarding religious institutions did not hinder circulation of his
journal.[56] Nevertheless, it may be argued that the tone adopted for a temporary and specific project by Campbell remained a general weapon in
the hands of some of his followers, who assumed that it was an appropriate tool for the presentation of the Gospel in all times and seasons.

In the early 1800s, American frontier life was lived in a time of great
social ferment. There was a general decline in morality and spiritual
values—so much so that some could believe that "it was still doubtful
in the year 1800 whether Christianity would succeed in becoming a universal world religion."[57] It was in this kind of environment that the young
American religious reformation would be nurtured.

---

[53]See the critical letter from Robert Semple, *Christian Baptist* 4:85.

[54]Richardson, *Memoirs*, 1:283.

[55]*Millennial Harbinger* (1831): 19-20.

[56]See Gary L. Lee, "Background of the *Christian Baptist*" in *Alexander Campbell, The
Christian Baptist* (Joplin, Mo.: College Press Publishing Co., 1983), 21.

[57]See Max Ward Randall, *The Great Awakenings and the Restoration Movement*
(Joplin, Mo.: College Press Publishing Co., 1983), 13. Randall quotes James DeForest
Murch in a very dismal assessment of the time: "The period under consideration was one
of the lowest eras spiritually in the history of America," 14.

Randall lists numerous factors that contributed to the "American dark age" of which he wrote:

1. The revolution, with the collapse of the earlier governmental certainties.

2. The moral breakdown which routinely accompanies major wars.

3. Rationalist humanism and skepticism from Europe antagonistic to Christian belief.

4. Widespread renunciation of Christianity as superstition with a great decline in Biblical study, worship, and general religious life.

5. The stampede for the frontier, resulting in erosions of family solidarity.

6. Breakdown in social conduct resulting from isolation on the frontier.

7. "French infidelity which flooded the new nation." This was fortified by the political alliance with France during the Revolution.[58]

Randall underlines the desperation of the American spiritual condition, especially in the West:

The Revolution brought political freedom and independence for the thirteen states, but the land was ravaged and the people impoverished. Every denomination underwent severe trials. Houses of worship were burned or otherwise destroyed. Preachers and priests were driven from their homes and parrishes [*sic*]. Some were killed and many beaten, imprisoned or otherwise prosecuted. Congregations were rent, never to come together again. . . . Some felt that the Church was too far gone to be revived. . . . Towns in Kentucky were named after infidels. Logan County, Kentucky, was so populated with criminals that they controlled the county.[59]

Of the two separate beginning movements that resulted in a united church during the early 1830s, that stream led by Barton W. Stone was nearest the basic rudiments of the frontier. Walter Scott later perfected the style and content of his message so that it was admirably adapted for

[58]Ibid., 14-18.
[59]Ibid., 18.

frontier utility, but Stone began his reformation during the Second Great Awakening in the backwoods of Kentucky:

> Barton W. Stone (1772-1844) struggled with the difficult issues with which a rigid Calvinism confronted a man of the frontier. Educated in a log college in the western mountains of North Carolina, he resisted the harshness of prevailing doctrines of predestination and atonement and never found orthodox trinitarianism fully credible. Tenacious in his insistence on his own intellectual integrity, he nevertheless manifested an ironic and catholic spirit which sought union among all who would "take the Bible as the only sure guide to heaven."[60]

Stone's experience among people living in rudimentary conditions no doubt was an important factor in his original impulse to dedicate his life to Christian unity. Perhaps this experience also caused him to tolerate a wider degree of diversity than his brethren from the more "cultivated" tradition of northern Virginia could accept.

The 1800 census listed nine-tenths of the slightly more than five million Americans east of the Alleghenies. More than half of the other one-tenth were in Kentucky and Tennessee. Only fifty-one thousand people lived in the Northwest Territory—later Ohio, Indiana, Illinois, Michigan, and Wisconsin. The increase from 1800 until 1840 in this area was multiplied sixty times in one generation.[61] These statistics provide a background for a perception of the intense social ferment and the educational-cultural contrasts confronted by those who were endeavoring to reform the church and propagate the Gospel to the thousands of unchurched individuals on the western side of the country.

The centrality of Disciples activity in the West and thus the rural areas of the United States has clearly had a moderating effect on the vernacular/"cultured" tradition balance of the churches. In a 1973 statistical profile of Disciples, Howard E. Dentler recognized this fact:

> All of this is to say that perhaps where Disciples were located and how they distributed themselves with relationship to urban or rural settings is more important to the understanding of the nature of their members and of their policies than the exact number in the movement. Up to the last ten years Disciples were not a predominantly urban movement, though they have had significant congregations in urban centers. The pattern of concen-

[60]Osborne, in Beazley, ed., *The Christian Church*, 84.

[61]Winfred E. Garrison, "Pioneer in Broadcloth" in Perry E. Gresham, ed., *The Sage of Bethany, Pioneer in Broadcloth* (St. Louis: Bethany Press, 1960), 48-49.

tration in the Mississippi Valley area, and in the small villages, was set during the age of expansion.[62]

In an attempt to portray some of the dualistic dimensions of Alexander Campbell's personality and attitudes, Winfred Garrison has described him as a "pioneer in broadcloth." Broadcloth was the heavy and lustrous woolen fabric from which merchant tailors made the black, skirted coats of gentlemen, especially of preachers, politicians, and of any who claimed gentility.[63] Juxtaposing this term with the noun "pioneer," Garrison grasped the enigma that surrounded Alexander Campbell in his adopted environment:

> The central idea, then, is that Alexander Campbell was a man who had characteristics of mind and personality that were in contrast with the frontier environment in which he did his pioneering work. But the matter is not quite that simple. He had, in fact, two sets of characteristics, so that the contrast was partly within himself. The world of Alexander Campbell also had contrasts within itself so that his total environment included a wide gamut ranging from the crudities of the American frontier to the cultivated and scholarly circles which formed the background of his very early years and the burgeoning and blossoming American culture which, intermittently at least, provided the setting for his life and work during his middle and later years. If this seems to complicate to the point of confusion what appeared to start out as a simple contrast between a cultured gentleman and a tough neighborhood, it is safer to risk a little confusion than to avoid it by oversimplification of what was not, after all, a very simple situation.[64]

Tragically, the heirs of the Stone-Campbell Movement appear to have both a diminishing interest and an increasing difficulty in communicating and experiencing Christian fellowship with each other. This chapter has explored some of the American cultural environment and intellectual and religious roots of the movement which contained within themselves numerous tautologies. Chapter 5 will explore another area of the Disciples religious heritage which has affected their theology and their aesthetics since 1809.

---

[62]Howard E. Dentler, "Statistical Profile of the Christian Church (Disciples of Christ)," *The Christian Church,* 309.

[63]Garrison, "Pioneer in Broadcloth," 46.

[64]Ibid.

Plate 6
WALTER SCOTT
Courtesy Disciples of Christ Historical Society

5

Sin and Redemption: Reformation Theology, American Understandings, and Restoration Ethos

One way a Christian movement may be viewed in a scriptural context is to examine its approach to the biblical understanding of sin and redemption. Some Bible students differentiate between physical evil (natural disorder or disaster) and moral evil (sin). Both, from a biblical perspective, originated with human sin (Gen. 3). Sin and redemption of the individual is the primary focus of the Christian Gospel. As foretold by the messianic prophets, the redemptive act of God in Christ, centered in the cross, focuses on the problem of personal sin. Matthew quotes the messenger who reassured Joseph concerning the divine nature of Mary's expected child: "she will bear a son, and you shall call his name Jesus, for he will save his people from their sins." (Matt. 1:21)

The Apostle Paul was deeply conscious of the grace of forgiveness extended to his own soul. His letters provide a clear basis for understanding God's grace through his Son:

> Therefore, since we are justified by faith, we have peace with God through our Lord Jesus Christ. Through him we have obtained access to this grace in which we stand, and we rejoice in our hope of sharing the glory of God. (Rom. 5:1-2)

The Old Testament anticipates the Gospel chronicle in its expression of the deep craving for redemption from personal sin by the sweet fulfillment of God's forgiving grace, and in its poetic description of the process. The heavy weight of unconfessed and unforgiven sin was poetically described by King David in a penitential psalm when Nathan the prophet came to him after he had gone in to Bathsheba:

> Have mercy on me, O God, according to
> thy steadfast love;
> according to thy abundant mercy
> blot out my transgressions.
> Wash me thoroughly from my iniquity,
> and cleanse me from my sin! (Ps. 51:1-2)

This psalm is a personal confession of sin as an individual act of evil which caused heartfelt guilt. The poet makes the rather startling declaration that his sin—apparently against both Bathsheba and her murdered husband—is really sin against God himself:

> For I know my transgressions,
>   and my sin is ever before me.
> Against thee, thee only, have I sinned,
>   and done that which is evil in thy sight.   . . .

(Ps. 51:3-4a)

The richness of the fifty-first Psalm and other penitential psalms was felt by a leading composer of the sixteenth century, Orlando di Lasso (1532-94). Lasso, a polyphonic master, may have been at his best when he composed sacred motets with texts from "those psalms that treat of the passionate struggle of man with himself and his God."[1] Lasso composed over two thousand works, including music for the seven penitential psalms. The sense of drama in the relationship between human sin and God's forgiveness was understood by Lasso. An understanding of the Christian gospel provides a purpose for deep commitment—and thus for art.

This experience—the deep cognizance of personal sin with the dramatic perception of justification through the grace of God—may partially explain the generative power of Lutheranism in preaching, art, and music. Luther's personal struggle with salvation—his consciousness of sin and the impossibility of escaping the consequences of that sin through his own acts of righteousness—is well known. Luther became an Augustinian monk, intensely studied the scriptures, and struggled to experience God's grace. Once, while traveling (and preoccupied by the death of a close friend), a violent thunderstorm overtook him. He then and there vowed a life of celibacy and dedication if he should escape death.

Even after he entered the cloistered life, however, Luther found little serenity. His study of the scriptures only increased the terror he felt due to his sins. The Church's doctrine of salvation became a message of rejection rather than of hope, for he so keenly felt his own unworthiness before God, the righteous judge. He would pray for hours on end, and he wearied his confessor by seeking absolution for every remembered sin. His despair was almost beyond expression. In such a condition, Luther encountered the Apostle Paul's quotation of Habakkuk: "The just shall live by faith" (Rom. 1:17).

---

[1] Gustave Reese, *Music in the Renaissance* (New York: Norton and Co., 1954), 506.

A major insight into the principle of justification was gained by Luther in a tower room at the University of Wittenberg in what has been called Luther's *Turmerlebnis* or Tower Experience. There he fully understood that "the righteousness of God" was to be understood through the mercy of God and that "the just shall live by faith." Later, Luther would write of this experience, "Now I felt exactly as though I had been born again, and I believed that I had entered Paradise through widely opened doors."[2] Luther's profound experience in which he found peace of mind from his spiritual torment was the basis for the great Protestant Reformation. The focus of the Reformation upon *sola fide* (faith alone) and *sola gratia* (grace alone) created a drama of salvation in the spirit of Luther's favorite Pauline epistles, those to the Romans and the Galatians.

As the Reformation which he initiated progressed, Luther worked actively to build an educational system. He wrote profusely, producing Bible commentaries, tracts, catechisms, a liturgy, and even a great many expressive hymns.

The second great leader of the Reformation was John Calvin, whose followers developed what is known as the Reformed or Calvinist branch of the Reformation. Traditionally, the Reformed branch has not been as friendly to the arts nor as aesthetically perceptive as some other Protestants. Calvin tolerated visual art but did not give it the prominence as did other Protestants. On the other hand, Luther clearly stated, "I do not hold that the Gospel should destroy all the arts, as certain superstitious folk believe. On the contrary, I would fain see all the arts, and especially that of music, serving Him who hath created them and given them unto us. . . ."[3]

The great individualist and colorist Matthias Grünewald (c. 1480-1528), who assimilated some of the compositional elements of Dürer and Cranach the Elder, was unique in his expressive power and the visionary revelation of spiritual drama. His master work, the great Isenheim Altarpiece, was created shortly before the beginning of the Lutheran Reformation (c. 1510-15). It contains a central crucifixion panel and its most remarkable features are the spectacular effects of light and color and the expression of intense pain which he was able to depict.[4] Helen Gardner has written:

[2] *Opera Luther,* 2d ed., 7 vols., ed. H. Schmidt (Frankfurt am Main, 1865—), 1:22-23.

[3] G. G. Coulton, *Art and the Reformation* (Hamden, Conn.: Archon Books, 1969), 408.

[4] The altarpiece is currently in the Musee Unterlinden in Colmar, France.

No other artist has produced such an image of the dreadful ugliness of pain. The sharp, angular shapes of anguish appear in the figures of the swooning Virgin and St. John, and in the shrill delirium of the Magdalene . . . when we turn from the Good Friday of the *Crucifixion* to the Easter Sunday of the *Resurrection*, an inner panel of the Isenheim Altarpiece, the mood changes from disaster to triumph.[5]

Grünewald used an array of expressionist devices to convey terror and anguish. The use of light and shadow, silhouette and unusual color could portray powerful images rather than beautiful ones. Thus he has presented one of the most graphic representations in history of the suffering Christ. It does not represent Lutheranism inasmuch as it was created during the time Martin Luther was searching for grace, but it does represent the general *Zeitgeist.*

The stark drama of Christ's redeeming sacrifice presented by this master artist of the Renaissance was created during the same time that Martin Luther was searching deeply for grace. Grünewald's altarpiece represents a mood of the *Zeitgeist,* and also suggests that the artist was himself receptive to God's grace and faith.

Albrecht Dürer (1471-1528), the best known artist of northern Europe during his lifetime, was well known to Luther, who corresponded with him. Dürer never officially broke with Catholicism, but his letters and diaries contain expressions of the Lutheran faith.[6] Dürer lived in Nürnberg, one of the leading cities of the Lutheran Reformation, where he witnessed both the spiritual power and, at times, the breakdown in morality in the radically altered official power structures occasioned by the Reformation.

In her biography of Dürer, Mary M. K. Heaton is cautious in assuming the Lutheran proclivities of the Nürnberg artist:

Dürer himself, though sympathizing strongly with the Reformers, does not appear to have been moved to any open rebellion against the Church of Rome. He still, as we saw in his journal, paid a father confessor, and probably attended the services of the Church, though he denounced much of her doctrine as iniquitous. It is probable, however, that had he lived he would have come forward more boldly in favour of reform, for the eloquent persuasive Melancthon, who held Dürer in very high estimation, had great influence over him in his later years, and would doubt-

[5]See Helen Gardner, *Art Through the Ages* (New York: Harcourt, Brace and World, 1970), 534.

[6]Coulton, *Art and Reformation*, 409 n.

less have moved him more and more toward the adoption of the new faith. Dürer's regard for Luther, also, and belief in the efficacy of his teaching, we have seen called forth in his journal by the news of that 'godly man's' captivity.[7]

Heaton notes that late in his life, Dürer produced very few traditional representations of the Catholic Church,[8] and she mentions a Holy Family which is not a "Virgin picture" in the Roman Catholic sense at all. Coulton supports further the Reformation impulse in Dürer's later years:

> . . . in 1514 he was still orthodox; in 1520 we find him on Luther's side, and intending to engrave his portrait 'for a lasting remembrance of a Christian man who helped me out of great distress,' though he never took any formal step to break with the Church. . . . He took his stand upon the Bible: 'All worldly rulers in these dangerous times should give good heed that they receive not human misguidance for the Word of God, for God will have nothing added to His Word nor taken away from it.'[9]

One of Dürer's late works illustrates his evolving style together with his increasing acceptance of Protestant theology. He painted two panels of the *Four Apostles* and presented them to the Nürnberg city fathers, without commission, in 1526. Gardner describes the panels:

> The work has been called Dürer's religious and political testament, in which he expresses his sympathies for the Protestant cause and warns against the dangerous times, when religion, truth, justice, and the virtues all seemed to be threatened. The four apostles— John and Peter on one panel, Mark and Paul on the other—stand on guard for the city. Quotations from each of their books in the German of Luther's translation of the New Testament are written on the frames. They warn against the coming of perilous times and the preaching of false prophets who will distort the Word of God. The figures of the apostles summarize Dürer's whole craft and learning.[10]

Among artists who were Luther's contemporaries, Lucas Cranach the Elder most specifically professed an overt Reformation theology. He was not only a follower of Luther, but a friend as well. His paintings are con-

[7]Mary Margaret K. Heaton, *The Life of Albrecht Dürer of Nürnberg* (Portland, Me.: Longwood Press, 1881; reprinted 1977), 347.

[8]Ibid.

[9]Coulton, *Art and Reformation,* 119.

[10]Gardner, *Art Through the Ages,* 538-39.

sidered to be outstandingly representative of German Protestant painting. Cranach was influenced by Dürer's woodcuts, an influence which led to an active rivalry at a later period.

About 1505 Cranach was appointed to the prestigious position of court painter to Luther's later supporter, Elector Frederick the Wise of Coburg. In addition, he worked in the printing business for a time. With his fellow workers, the goldsmith Christian Döring and the printer Johann Rhau-Grunenberg, Cranach helped finance Luther's September Testament of 1522, a partial translation of the Bible. Cranach also contributed the woodcuts for this early printed work.[11]

In terms of Cranach's specific relationship to both Martin Luther and the Protestant faith, Schade says:

> Lucas Cranach the Elder was close to Luther and Melancthon, although it is hardly possible to tell from the sources whether it was in his capacity as a friend, counselor and confidant of the princes or as a painter. He made his first portrait of Luther in 1520, in the two versions we have already discussed. In the spring of 1521 he was already at work on the Passional Christi et Antichristi, the first and most outspoken pamphlet of the Reformation to use pictures as weapons.[12]

Cranach's stark presentations of Christian scenes are sometimes reminiscent of Dürer's. His dramatic representation of Christian narratives emphasizes the Lutheran understanding of salvation and justification. In addition, the power of his illustrations both supported the circulation of Luther's published works and helped underwrite the costs of their publication.

The artist who most fully embodied the Lutheran gospel evangel in his work, however, was a musician rather than a painter, and was born 139 years after Luther's death: Johann Sebastian Bach (1685-1750). Albert Schweitzer discusses Bach's Christian spirituality and his Lutheranism. In a discussion of the problems of performing or understanding Bach's works, Schweitzer writes:

> He had put all his devotion into them, and God at any rate certainly understood them. The S. D. G. (*Soli Deo Gloria*, 'To God alone be praise') and the J. J. (*Jesu juva*, 'Help me, Jesus!') with which he garnishes his scores, are for him no formulas, but the Credo that runs through all his work. Music is an act of worship with Bach. His artistic activity and his personality are both based

---

[11]Werner Schade, *Cranach, a Family of Master Painters*, tr. Helen Sebba (New York: Putnam's Sons, 1980), 43.

[12]Ibid., 71-72.

on his piety. . . . All great art, even secular, is in itself religious in his eyes; for him the tones do not perish, but ascend to God like praise too deep for utterance.[13]

Bach's affinity for using music to express the Gospel was prepared by Martin Luther himself. It has been observed that if Luther had chosen music as a career instead of the more important work he had to do, he may well have ranked with the great musicians of his time. Theodore Hoelty-Nickel writes that

> because of his remarkable gift of music, supported by excellent training in both theory and applied music, and especially because of his great love of music, which remained with him all of his life, he used this special—you might say this additional— gift of God for the purpose of implementing his work, preaching the gospel through his hymns, and finding an honored place for music in the liturgy of the church.[14]

Bach's religious commitment had in place the needed forms for the expression of his credo. The Lutheran chorale (an appropriate vehicle for the re-establishment of congregational singing), the Lutheran motet, the cantata, the various organ forms, and the Passions had been established by Luther, his musical colleague, Johann Walther, and their successors. Other composers, such as Dietrich Buxtehude, Johann Kuhnau, and G. P. Telemann developed them into refined vehicles of Christian expression. Lutheran worship design and Lutheran theology provided an ideal framework for the body of Bach's great labors. It is true that some of the poetry which Bach set to music displays Pietistic tendencies, but other evidence indicates that Bach's views were strictly Lutheran.[15]

In Bach's art, the settings of church chorales, chorale preludes, church cantatas, and motets were vehicles for the expression of the Lutheran theology of salvation by grace. Even the secular forms—the instrumental and keyboard works, the secular cantatas, and the songs— provide an opportunity for the expression of belief in a teleological creation given by the power and love of God. But the Passions and the

[13]Albert Schweitzer, *J. S. Bach*, vol. 1, tr. Ernest Newman (Boston: Bruce Humphries, 1905; reprinted 1962), 166-67.

[14]Theodore Hoelty-Nickel, "Luther and Music," in *Luther and Culture*, vol. 4, Martin Luther Lectures (Decorah, Iowa: Luther College Press, 1960), 148. Luther's personal genius, which created or rearranged approximately thirty-six hymns and several hymnbooks, is unique among Christian reformers. While John Calvin and Alexander Campbell added to the psalm and hymn literature available for their respective movements, neither enjoyed great musical ability, and their primary interest seems to have been avoiding the theological errors of existing hymns more than exulting in the musical outpouring of the spirit.

[15]See Schweitzer, *Bach*, 168.

B-minor Mass may, of all his work, best illustrate both the ultimate musical expression in any medium and the maximum commitment of a Christian artist. For the Lutheran scholar Jaroslav Pelikan, the last Bach composition, "Vor deinen Thron tret' ich hiermit, (And now I step before thy throne)" (BWV 668) approaches the power of the major choral works as a symbol of approaching the very throne of the Lord:

> Artists have had to limit themselves because they were finite and because the matters they described were finite too. But Christian artists have felt able to claim that they were not dealing only with the finite and the temporal. Like Bach, they have stood before the throne of earthly kings; but Bach's last composition . . . has become a mythic symbol of how they have also stepped before the eternal throne itself. . . . The antiphons in Bach's setting of the 'Sanctus' for the *Mass in B Minor* have seemed to many hearers not only to fill the earth and the heavens with the glory of God, as the words 'Pleni sunt coeli et terra gloria ejus [Heaven and earth are full of thy glory]' declare, but to go beyond their periphery into the very presence of the Almighty. Bach's artistry in the Mass has indeed bespoken a boundless freedom.[16]

The burden of human sin with the absolute joy of its forgiveness and personal justification in Christ constitutes the greatest drama of Christianity, and thus of the artists who lived in a context of Lutheran theology. The fact of the new birth and the radical change it produces in the Christian's relationship to God are fundamental to a Lutheran understanding of Christian faith. The art of Johann Sebastian Bach reinforces and interprets this understanding as clearly as art has ever proclaimed a religious message. Gerardus Van der Leeuw wrote:

> Thus Johann Sebastian Bach performed the awesome miracle of combining his service to the congregation with his service to art, the liturgical structure of his work with its aesthetic structure. The artist is priest, is himself a theologian. A miracle was developed by him. Here art has become in truth a holy action.[17]

The Lutheran Reformation—its theology, the openness of its leaders for the ministry of the arts, and perhaps the timing of its occurrence in

---

[16]Jaroslav Pelikan, *Bach among the Theologians* (Philadelphia: Fortress Press, 1986), 122.

[17]Gerardus Van der Leeuw, *Sacred and Profane Beauty: The Holy in Art*, tr. David E. Green (New York: Holt, Reinhart and Winston, 1963), 242. In this paragraph, Van der Leeuw seems to have anticipated the title of Pelikan's work, *Bach Among the Theologians*.

history—generated masterpieces of creative art which spoke of the great redemptive themes of Christianity. It is a powerful model for the way in which a religious movement can both inspire and make use of aesthetic means for the expression of Christian grace, along with the earlier great art forms of Roman Catholic theology and worship.

While the Disciples Restoration Movement has not produced an artistic spokesperson as eloquent as Bach or Cranach or Dürer, one Disciple, Robert Richardson, may have come close to providing a poetic interpretation of the faith as understood by the followers of Barton W. Stone and Alexander Campbell.[18]

Catholic and Lutheran Christianity provide valuable models of the way theology and aesthetic attitudes can reinforce each other. The Stone-Campbell Movement, however, has no direct lineage from those traditions, but finds its historic ancestry in the other principal branch of the Protestant Reformation. Since almost all the leaders of the American movement came directly from Reformed (Calvinist) churches, Reformed uses of art provide more direct clues to the experiences and attitudes brought by restoration leaders to their movement.

The Reformed churches were blessed by individuals who were able to speak with power on a favorite Calvinist theme: the process and growth of the Christian life in a disciple's pilgrimage to the eternal. John Milton, John Bunyan, and Rembrandt van Rijn are among the strongest voices of literature and art who lived within the Calvinist tradition.

Milton (1608-1674) was an "irregular" Calvinist and Puritan, who lived at the high water mark of English Puritanism. He ultimately broke with the Presbyterians but struggled alongside the Puritans in the battle for freedom of speech, press, and religion. Milton has been called the "bard of Calvinism unbound," but even though he visited Italy to study the learning of the Renaissance, he remained a Puritan in his beliefs about God's dealing with mankind. *Paradise Lost,* his masterpiece, became the great Christian epic about the fall and redemption. Milton's great drama has been important in English culture for at least three hundred years. It has been observed that

> Today there is still some confusion in popular Christianity between the imagery of Milton and the Bible. Milton did not write systematic theology, and yet he combined the critical powers of reflections and observations with the power of image and metaphor so that the Ninth Book of *Paradise Lost* uncovers the nature of temptation, evil, and human pride in ways that no systematic theology can.[19]

[18]See chap. 9 of this book.

[19]Leith, *Introduction to Reformed Tradition,*196.

Book Twelve of *Paradise Lost,* the concluding section, sings a summary of Christ's redemptive work on earth, His resurrection and triumph, and the ongoing responsibility of His disciples on earth. The dominant Calvinist theme of God's sovereignty is also hymned in this apostrophe to grace:

. . . the stars of morn shall see him rise
Out of his grace, fresh as the dawning light,
Thy ransom paid, which man from death redeems,
His death for man, as many as offered life
Neglect not, and the benefit embrace
By faith not void of works: this godlike act
Annuls thy doom, the death thou shouldst have died,
In sin forever lost from life; this act
Shall bruise the head of Satan, crush his strength
Defeating sin and death, his two main arms,
And fix far deeper in his head their stings
Than temporal death shall bruise the victor's heel,
Or theirs whom he redeems, a death like sleep,
A gentle wafting to immortal life.[20]

Another Christian masterpiece is the work of the nonconformist preacher, John Bunyan (1628-88), which is nearer the vernacular tradition of seventeenth-century England than the poems of Milton. Bunyan's most famous work, the allegory *Pilgrim's Progress,* has been called

a work of genius. No one could have been taught to write it in the schools. It is the product of a remarkable Christian imagination and of the wisdom of Christian experience. Behind it is the 'bruised conscience' that knows the terror of life without God, the vision of human existence as it came from God, and the transformation of fallen and disordered lives by the grace of God. *Pilgrim's Progress* is parabolic theology. It tells the story of ordinary human experience in such a way that the reader moves from those experiences that he knows to the grace of God that illumines and transforms those experiences. . . . As a work of Christian imagination, *Pilgrim's Progress* has never been surpassed.[21]

---

[20]John Milton, "Paradise Lost," in *Paradise Lost and other Poems*, ed. Maurice Kelley (Roslyn, N.Y.: Walter J. Black, 1943), 380. David McWhirter's Index to the *Millennial Harbinger* includes five references to John Milton.

[21]Leith, *Introduction to Reformed Tradition*, 195.

While the Reformed tradition has not, on the whole, produced great art, one exception is the work of that great seventeenth-century master painter, Rembrandt van Rijn (1606-69). The relationship of this great Dutch painter with the Calvinist Reformation is much less clear than that of Bach with Lutheranism. Rembrandt did have close contacts with the Mennonites and there are strong reasons for believing he admired the simplicity of the Mennonite lifestyle. Nevertheless, the facts of his life indicate his firm foothold in the Calvinist Reformed tradition. He was born in a Reformed community to parents who had been married in a Reformed church. He also was married in a Reformed church to a woman from a a strict Reformed family whose brother-in-law was a Reformed theologian; and his son was baptized in the Reformed church.

Rembrandt was not an orthodox Calvinist, but he was too much of a Calvinist to directly represent God the father as so many artists before him had done. Along with the Calvinist emphasis on the sovereignty of God, some of the major religious emphases of Rembrandt's art have been described:

> His art is profoundly an act of the Incarnation. The world has been created by God and is good because it proceeds from the hand of God and is irradiated by the presence of God. In this, he does not differ in principle from many another artist, such as his predecessors in Flanders of the fifteenth century. His concern is rather with the entry of the divine into history, the intersection of the timeless with time.[22]

Rembrandt was a willing servant of the Lord, whose many paintings, etchings, drawings, and prints include biblical subjects. Of the works of this master of light and shadow, about eight hundred and fifty survive: one hundred and sixty paintings, eighty etchings, and over six hundred drawings.

With the strong emphasis on the investiture of humanity in the Son of God as proclaimed in the Gospel message, Rembrandt, Calvin-like, emphasized themes with high moral choices: pain, the problem of evil and redemption, the daily grind of human existence. Even though he is famous for his use of light and shadow, Rembrandt's expression of the Christian drama did not turn on the brilliant color and sharp demarcation of Grünewald, nor did he depict heavenly tumult, the triumph of the Church, or even the awesomeness of heaven and hell.[23] Rather,

---

[22]John W. Dixon, *Nature and Grace in Art* (Chapel Hill: University of North Carolina Press, 1964), 164.

[23]Ibid., 585.

Rembrandt made painting a method for probing the states of the human soul, both in portraiture and in his uniquely personal and authentic illustration of the scriptures. The abolition of religious art by the Reformed Church of Holland did not prevent him from making a series of religious paintings and prints that synopsize the Bible from a single point of view—that of a believing Christian, a poet of the spiritual, convinced that its message must be interpreted in human terms for human beings.[24]

Rembrandt powerfully expressed the humanity and humility of Jesus. This specific emphasis is applied in his *Return of the Prodigal Son* where the weeping son crouches before the forgiving father in deep contrition, while the father embraces him. In the soft shadows, three figures note the lesson of mercy. This scene is wholly determined by Rembrandt's inward vision of its meaning.

For Lutherans, the drama of their message, in both visual and musical arts, led to a study of the joyous meaning of personal salvation from sin and justification with God. Reformed art seems more preoccupied—in keeping with the Genevan experiment and its theocratic attempt to make society the Kingdom of God—with the vicissitudes of the Christian pilgrimage, morality, and the ongoing relationship with God enjoyed by those who are called to be Christ's disciples. Both concerns turn on major biblical and theological Christian principles, and thus have motivated response by artists as well as theologians.

The thesis advanced here is that the drama of both the Lutheran and Calvinist Reformations is occupied with events, desires, and faith about matters that made major differences in the lives of those touched by reformation movements. Specifically, Lutheran theology and Lutheran art touched the American Restoration Movement only indirectly; the Calvinist Reformation, on the other hand, was a direct antecedent to the American Disciples Movement, and generated both continuity and reaction. This brief review of artistic responses to European reformation movements is designed to study the relationship between the works of those who happened to be artists and the power of the gospel which was the primary preoccupation of their lives. Later in this chapter, the approach to evil and forgiveness, with the resulting ethos generated in the church, will be studied in the context of nineteenth-century Disciples theology.

It is clear that the burden of sin—both in the heavy load carried by the individual seeking God's initial forgiveness and justification, and the ongoing problem of evil encountered by Christians in *The Pilgrim's Progress*—is a primary concern of Christian history. Consideration will

---

[24]Gardner, *Art Through the Ages*, 584.

be given at this point to the way in which American thinkers have dealt with the question, from the perspective of both the New England Puritans and the nineteenth-century Transcendentalists.

New England Puritanism has been a formative factor in the theology, the work ethic, and the aesthetics of the American continent throughout the history of the United States. Multitudes of historians have examined the impact of this movement on every aspect of American life and culture, and all have concluded that Puritanism has had an enormous influence in America.

Although the Restoration Movement may be seen, in some dimensions, as a reaction against Calvinism, including its Puritan manifestations, there were at least two direct channels through which it reached the Disciples leaders. Chapter 3 dealt with the direct impact of English Puritanism on the life and ministry of Thomas Campbell, a Presbyterian Seceder. Max Ward Randall has documented the influence of the Great Awakening on Samuel Davies, who in turn became known to Rice Haggard. Haggard was a colleague of Barton W. Stone in the "first of the two 'main' streams of the Reformation of the early nineteenth century [which] took for itself the name 'Christian' at Cane Ridge, Kentucky."[25]

For the purposes of this study, the period of the Great Awakening will be considered because of its relationship to the Second Awakening, and thus to the activities of Stone (1772-1844). The thought and preaching of Jonathan Edwards (1703-58), who was active during the Great Awakening, have been normative for the way many Americans have perceived the questions of sin and redemption, and in the relationship of "heart religion" to aesthetic attitudes. Edwards's thought may be contrasted with that of the "liberals" of his age—churches and leaders who held Socinian and Arminian beliefs in contrast with the stricter Calvinism of the Puritan congregations.

In 1629, the Massachusetts Bay Colony was established. While other colonies of the young country possessed some Puritan elements, the congregationalism of this New England colony has come to represent Puritan thought and the generating power of its dissemination in the New World. The colony underwent various stages of "purity" in its history through the seventeenth century. Several platforms and associations punctuated political and spiritual high points and values and, at other times, the erosion of those same values.

Jonathan Edwards was born during a period when spirituality was at a relatively low ebb. Edwards's grandfather, Solomon Stoddard, was pastor of a church at Northampton, Massachusetts. Stoddard adhered to the Half-Way Covenant of 1662, which decreed that the children of

---

[25]Max Ward Randall, *The Great Awakening and the Restoration Movement* (Joplin, Mo.: College Press Publishing Company, 1983), 72, 87-92.

morally upright, orthodox, baptized parents should be permitted baptism but not admitted to the Lord's Supper, even if their parents had not made a personal confession and were not full members of the church. This Half-Way Covenant generated heavy controversy for some time.[26] The issue of controlled attendance to communion is interesting to the Disciples historian because the issue also arose during the early years of the Restoration Movement.

As the grandchildren of the so-called half-way covenanters were presented for baptism, the church became more and more lax about who could be baptized and who could partake of the Lord's Supper. About 1700, Stoddard maintained that

'the Lord's Supper was instituted to be a means of regeneration,' and was accustomed to urge all, without discrimination, to participate in the ordinance. Thus the distinction between the church and the world was well-nigh obliterated. In many communities, without any religious awakening whatever, almost all the young people of the congregation would come forward at appointed times and in a formal way own the covenant.[27]

Jonathan Edwards described the distressing state of religious sensitivity in Northampton that existed during his two-year tenure between 1728 and 1731 as his grandfather's assistant pastor.

The greater part seemed to be at that time very insensible of the things of religion. Just after my grandfather's death, it seemed to be a time of extraordinary dullness in religion; licentiousness for some years greatly prevailed among the youth of the town. They were addicted to night-walking, and frequenting the tavern; and lewd practices without any regard to order in the families they belonged to.[28]

The spiritual malaise of the colonies beyond Massachusetts has been ascribed to Deism, "Socinianized Arminianism," skepticism, and "indifferentism," which were all prevalent. Preaching in the New World, as in England, had lost much of its fervor. Most church members were living a worldly life while feeling a false security.

---

[26]Albert Henry Newman, *A Manual of Church History*, vol. 2 (Chicago: American Baptist Publication Society, 1945), 669.

[27]Ibid., 670.

[28]Jonathan Edwards, "A Faithful Narrative of the Surprising Work of God," in *Jonathan Edwards on Evangelism*, ed. Carl J. C. Wolf (Westport, Conn.: Greenwood Press, 1981), 18.

This backdrop for the Great Awakening resembled the social and spiritual circumstances which also preceded the Second Great Awakening on the Kentucky frontier—circumstances described as the "American dark age" in chapter 4. The Great Awakening began in a tentative way in two or three "harvest" periods of Stoddard's ministry, but the strong winds of revival became insistent and powerful at the end of 1733. Interestingly, the phenomenon began with young people. It was intensified by the untimely deaths of individuals in the county, coupled with the dying exhortations of one of those individuals for her acquaintances to receive God's mercy.

Edwards, firm in his Augustinian and Calvinist beliefs of predestination and *sola fide,* strangely attributed the people's new spiritual concern to the spread of Arminianism. Many New Englanders felt that as Arminianism flourished, God might withdraw from their midst and remove the opportunity for salvation.[29]

In his "Faithful Narrative" of the Great Awakening, Edwards described the conversions:[30]

> These awakenings, when they first seized upon persons, have had two effects: one was that they have brought them immediately to quit their sinful practices and dread their former vices; the other that it put them on earnest application to the means of salvation, reading, prayer, meditation, the ordinances of God's house, and private conference. Their cry was, 'what shall we do to be saved?'[31]

Despite criticism and the wide rift that developed between ministers of the Awakening and the conservative clergy (including most of the educated ministers at Harvard and Yale Colleges), the influence of the Great Awakening in New England was vast. A large number of ministers admitted that they had been performing the functions of their office as unconverted men. In New England, between twenty-five and fifty thousand people were converted, and probably a similar number in the middle and southern colonies. The vast number of conversions coupled with a natural increase in the population and the great wave of immigration between 1734 and 1760 resulted in a dramatic increase in new Congregational, Baptist, and Presbyterian ministers and churches. Even so, there were churches in Pennsylvania, Delaware, and New Jersey that were without ministers.[32] Thus the great number of Presbyterian

---

[29]Newman, *Manual of Church History,* 2: 674.

[30]Edwards's narrative reminds this author of Stone's defense for the spiritual exercises in which he participated at Cane Ridge. Edwards, like Stone after him, was criticized by conservative clergy for his part in the movement.

[31]Edwards, "Faithful Narrative," in Wolf, *Edwards on Evangelism,* 24.

[32]Newman, *Manual of Church History,* 676.

Churches in the Chartiers Presbytery (where Thomas Campbell was at first eagerly received because of the great shortage of ministers) grew out of the Great Awakening of the eighteenth century.

The specific aspects of Edwards's theology that are important to the theme of this chapter relate, on the one hand, to his concept of sin and salvation and, on the other, to his emphasis on the heart—an emphasis which led to a definite empathy for aesthetics.

The best-known utterance of Edwards is his sermon, "Sinners in the Hands of an Angry God," delivered at Enfield, Massachusetts in July, 1741. Edwards's thought has been misjudged because the sermon has been read too narrowly and in isolation from his other sermons and pamphlets. In Wolf's compendium of Edwards's evangelism, "Sinners in the Hands of an Angry God" appears only two pages after the "Treatise on Grace," an essay which helps to place the first sermon in a more balanced context. In the "Treatise on Grace," Edwards wrote:

(a) We are abundantly taught in the Scripture that divine love is the sum of all duty, Rom. 13:8, 1 Tim. 1:5.

(b) The apostle speaks of divine love as that which is the essence of all Christianity in the thirteenth chapter of the First Epistle to the Corinthians.

That love to God and a Christian love to men are thus but one in their root and foundation-principle in the heart is confirmed by several passsages in the First Epistle of John, 3:16-17, 4:20-21, 5:1-2. Divine love, as it has God for its object, may thus be described. It is the soul's relish of the supreme excellency of the divine nature, including the heart to God as the chief good.[33]

True to the Calvinist strain in his heritage, Edwards placed great emphasis upon the full sovereignty of God, and thus reverence for Him in worship and in life. The Reformation heritage of *sola fide* and *sola gratia* was maintained as a defense against the "liberalism" of Arminianism, and the problem of sin and evil in the world were taken as fundamental to the understanding of Christian salvation. The Lutheran and Calvinist cornerstone of justification by faith alone was the principle which Edwards advocated. His preaching generated a good deal of tension in his hearers, but in the view of Edwards himself, the abuse he suffered for preaching this doctrine was countered by the fact that, in the autumn of 1734, "God's work wonderfully broke forth amongst us,

---

[33]Jonathan Edwards, "The Treatise on Grace," in Wolf, *Edwards on Evangelism*, 119.

and souls began to flock to Christ, as the Savior in whose righteousness alone they hoped to be justified."[34]

Edwards's concept of evil and of sin was diametrically opposed to the trivialization of sin which was expressed through the rising tide of liberalism. Edwards's belief in original sin was also opposed to the doctrine of free will which would be espoused by most of the Disciples reformers half a century later. The power of his witness, however, consists at least partially in the fact that he recognized the propensity of men for moral evil and the utter alienation from God which resulted. Simonson describes Edwards's understanding of evil, with the consequent necessity of human redemption.

The Augustinian view of original sin was held by many of Edwards's contemporaries and immediate predecessors, but the radical assertion of the doctrine with its logical results required a bold and highly-motivated preacher in eighteenth-century New England. The doctrine of original sin had no affinity with the growing optimism of liberalism, the gospel of mankind's human perfectibility.[35] The grand drama of salvation was no less radical within Edwards's understanding of sin and redemption. The joyous celebration of redemption by Luther, Bach, and Calvin are echoed by this preacher of *sola fide*:

> Edwards's goal, like that of his Calvinist forebearers [*sic*], was salvation—the ultimate deliverance from the demonic power of evil, sin, and death. Justification *sola fide* was the acquittal of sin; salvation was the new freedom from sin, the resurrection bringing a new being and a new heart.[36]

The necessity for a sermon to include a very explicit, even graphic, description of hell was to bring sinners to the joyous release from sin and struggle into the light of justification and salvation. Edwards was a master at stirring his hearers' imagination to make the terrors of hell more real than could any preacher of a traditional sermon.

The drama of damnation and release through the grace of Christ enacted in this transaction became a matter of the heart, and thus entered the realm of the aesthetic—a development which the logical fathers of the Restoration Movement would probably have resisted stoutly. Edwards is often called a preacher of the heart. The Great Awakening

---

[34]Harold P. Simonson, *Jonathan Edwards: Theologian of the Heart* (Grand Rapids: Eerdmans, 1974), 41.

[35]Nor would it be compatible with an upward-spiraling social evolution such as that outlined by Herbert Spencer during the nineteenth century. Even the moderate post-millennialism of Alexander Campbell would have been rejected in the understanding of evil held by Jonathan Edwards.

[36]Simonson, *Jonathan Edwards,* 44.

owed a great deal to his ability to verbally draw graphic images and to involve his hearers in the ancient dialogue between heaven and hell.

Much of the drama of damnation and release through grace of the Great Awakening continued into the Second Great Awakening and became, among the Disciples, a part of the discussion concerning sin, grace, and the law. In the decade prior to the Civil War, some of the editor-bishops of the proliferating Disciples journals were beginning to express new ideas on the relationship between those three doctrines. They were moving toward a more conservative legalistic stance which eventually would cast a pall over aesthetic development in the movement. This struggle over the relationship between sin, grace, and law was mirrored at the same time in Hawthorne's *Scarlet Letter* of 1850.

Hawthorne, whose grandfather had presided over a witches' trial in 1692, was deeply conscious of his Puritan heritage. Many scholars have studied Hawthorne's struggle with his heritage,[37] and they point out that although he rejected Calvinist orthodoxy, he also rejected unitarianism. His estimate of the problem of evil in the world was similar to that of the Protestant Reformation leaders. Hawthorne viewed the Puritan religious system as hard, cold, and confined. He believed that it was only the fervent faith of firm believers that redeemed them at all. He condemned Puritans for denying civil liberty to other religious groups, and turned his back on the rigid restrictive, prejudical religion of his ancestors.[38]

Despite his rejection of the Calvinist orthodoxy, which he called "a lump of coal," Hawthorne retained an understanding of evil that respected the reality of the spiritual/moral questions posed by this understanding. In contrast with transcendental liberalism, which he termed "a feather" because it tended to trivialize sin as a temporary obstacle to be overcome in humanity's march toward a better world, Hawthorne dealt in a Christian style with the question of justification.

In *The Scarlet Letter,* the final act of confession by the guilty clergyman retains a legalistic hangover from an earlier American era. Hawthorne's Reverend Dimmesdale does not receive forgiveness and justification *sola fide*, and the Reformation doctrine of the grace of God as taught by Jonathan Edwards is not fully accepted by the author. Yet, for-

---

[37]Joseph Schwartz, "Three Aspects of Hawthorne's Puritanism," in *Twentieth Century Interpretations of The Scarlet Letter*, ed. John C. Green (Englewood Cliffs, N.J.: Prentice-Hall, 1968), 34. Schwartz notes: "It began when James Russell Lowell called him a 'Puritan Tieck,' and when Herman Melville, his sometime friend, seeing more deeply into his own personality than into Hawthorne's, found his appeal in 'blackness, ten times more black . . . than Calvinistic sense of Inner Depravity and Original Sin, from whose visitations, in some shape or other, no deeply thinking mind is always and wholly free.'" (Ludwig Tieck (1773-1853), a German Romantic writer from Jena, often featured the fantastic satire, grotesqueness, stories from the Middle Ages, and references to art and music in his novels.)

[38]Ibid., 47.

giveness through confession of sin and God's mercy, after the agony of guilt which ultimately led to confession, is claimed by Hawthorne:

'Hester,' said the clergyman, 'farewell.' 'Shall we not meet again?' whispered she, bending her face down close to his. 'Shall we not spend our immortal life together? Surely, surely, we have ransomed one another, with all this woe! Thou lookest far into eternity, with those bright dying eyes! Then tell me what thou seest?'

'Hush, Hester, hush!' said he, with tremulous solemnity. 'The law we broke!—the sin here so awfully revealed!—let these alone be in thy thoughts! I fear! I fear! It may be, that, when we forgot our God,—when we violated our reverence each for the other's soul,—it was thenceforth vain to hope that we could meet hereafter, in an everlasting and pure reunion. God knows: and He is merciful! He hath proved His mercy, most of all, in my afflictions. By giving me this burning torture to bear upon my breast! By sending yonder dock and terrible old man, to keep the torture always at red-heat! By bringing me hither, to die this death of triumphant ignominy before the people! Had either of these agonies been wanting, I had been lost forever! Praised be his name! His will be done! Farewell!'[39]

Hawthorne's Mr. Dimmesdale is a graphic reflection of Edwards's doctrine that personal suffering through a sense of guilt is sometimes necessary to bring about a true conversion. In his essay, "Judging Persons' Experiences," Edwards wrote:

That it be because their slate appears terrible on the account of those things, wherein its dreadfulness indeed consists; and that their concern be solid, not operating very much by pangs and sudden passions, freaks and frights, and a capriciousness of mind.

That they be convinced of sins of heart and life: that their pretenses of sin of heart be not without reflection of their wicked practices; and also that they are not only convinced of sin of practice, but sin of heart.[40]

[39]Nathaniel Hawthorne, *The Scarlet Letter*, 2d ed., ed. Scully Bradley, et al. (New York: Norton, 1979), 181.

[40]Jonathan Edwards, "Judging Persons' Experiences," in Wolf, *Edwards on Evangelism*, 121.

Agnes McNeill Donohue has titled her intriguing study of Hawthorne *Calvin's Ironic Stepchild*. She explores the much-debated ambiguity of Hawthorne, and gives special attention to the endings of his novels and tales. Donohue suggests that some clarity can be obtained by perceiving the consistent ironic mode, which motivates Hawthorne to leave his characters with the possibility of alternate choices. She writes, "But the black flower of Calvin's doctrine of total depravity—of man's necessary yet culpable sinning—stimulated Hawthorne's imagination as no Emersonian Rhodora could."[41]

Basing her summary on a perceptive analysis of all the major works, Donohue concludes:

> Hawthorne's works, before his European hegira, are prodigies of a Calvinist-ordained ironic mode that conditions his narrative voice, determines the aesthetic distance between himself, his characters, and his readers, prescribes his concept of character, orders his ritualistic structure, controls his murky atmosphere and settings, enjoins his symbolism, and decrees his theme. Most particularly, the Calvinist dogmas of total depravity, predestination, reprobation, and denial of freedom of the will infuse his works. Beneath the deceptive lambency and lucidity of Hawthorne's style boils a brutal, barbarous, dooming underview of man's moral nature. Yet this partially submerged, damnatory Calvinism that betrayed Hawthorne into irony proved the healthiest climate for producing the dramatic tension of his art. It dictated the iron necessity for his characters to reenact the Fall from Eden, which Hawthorne could spy on from his chary nineteenth-century remove, his uneasy survival amidst the mouldering remnant of the American Dream.[42]

Hawthorne lived with his family in Concord, Massachusetts, in the "Old Manse" for three and a half years; his neighbors included Henry David Thoreau and Ralph Waldo Emerson. Those friendships were important to him for more than twenty years. Although Hawthorne rejected their transcendentalism, he valued their insights and the opportunity to carry on frequent conversations with them. In Hawthorne the Puritan had become the artist.[43]

---

[41]Agnes McNeill Donohue, *Hawthorne, Calvin's Ironic Stepchild* (Kent, Ohio: Kent State University Press, 1985), ix, 36-37.

[42]Ibid., 338-39.

[43]Lloyd Morris, *The Rebellious Puritan: Portrait of Mr. Hawthorne* (New York: Harcourt, Brace & Co., 1927), 4.

Ralph Waldo Emerson would probably have viewed Hawthorne's writings as incessantly preoccupied with sin and evil, with the loneliness of the human soul. In his mature years, Emerson, the Trancendentalist, had no such "dark side" to his perception of evil. Some of his readers "disturbed by his undeviating optimism, feel that he ignores the problem of evil in the world."[44]

Emerson's transcendental stance is described clearly in his essay, "The Over-Soul," an essay which diverges sharply from a biblical view of ontology. Rooted in a philosophical framework not unlike the neo-Platonic thinker, Plotinus, Emerson's over-soul relates to the Eternal One. The over-arching relationship of humanity to all elements of life and nature provides a rationale for reincarnation and for the brotherhood of all creatures in a vision typical of the Romantic century:

> That Unity, that Over-Soul, within which every man's particular being is contained and made one with all other; that common heart of which all sincere conversation is the worship to which all right action is submission; that overpowering reality which confutes our tricks and talents and constrains everyone to pass for what he is and to speak from his character and not from his tongue, and which evermore tends to pass into our thought and hand and become wisdom and virtue and power and beauty. We live in succession, in division, in pacts, in particular. Meantime within man is the soul of the whole; the wise silence; the universal beauty, to which every pact and particle is equally related; the eternal ONE.[45]

Another of Emerson's essays, "Self Reliance," sharply differs from the Reformation (and the New Testament) in its description of good and evil:

> Whoso would be a man must be a nonconformist. He who would gather immortal palms must not be hindered by the name of goodness, but must explore if it be goodness. Nothing is at last sacred but the integrity of your own mind. . . . I remember an answer which when quite young I was prompted to make to a valued advisor who was wont to importune me with the dear doctrines of the church. On my saying, 'what have I to do with the sacredness of traditions, if I live wholly from within?' my friend suggested, 'But these impulses may be from below, not from above.' I replied, 'They do not seem to me to be such; but

---

[44]Ralph Waldo Emerson, *The Best of Ralph Waldo Emerson*, ed. Gordon S. Haight (Roslyn, N.Y.: Walter J. Black, 1949), xiv.

[45]Emerson, "The Over-Soul," in ibid.

if I am the Devil's child, I will live then from the Devil.' No law can be sacred to me but that of my own nature.[46]

In the world of Ralph Waldo Emerson, transcendental thought was closely tied to philosophical idealism, religious Unitarianism, and nineteenth-century Romanticism. Its easy optimism, which did not acknowledge the metaphysical reality of evil, anticipated in numerous ways the evolutionary expectations of religious liberalism which entered the Disciples stream late during the same century. It is of special relevance to note that the Reformation understanding of the enormity of the problem of evil led, in the Puritan framework, to a sense of repentance, confession, and justification. This concept is similar to the understanding held by Martin Luther in his discovery of *sola fide* and *sola gratia*. The drama of the encounter between sinners and their Savior led to both personal commitment and celebration of their salvation through art.

And in that same world of Hawthorne and Emerson, the leaders of the Restoration Movement worked out their views on sin and justification with a result far different from that of the Great Awakening and the Transcendentalists. Of the two principal branches which eventually combined to create the Christian Churches-Churches of Christ, the branch led by Stone in Kentucky began the earliest. The personal spiritual pilgrimage of Stone contrasts with the path to salvation preached by the followers of Jonathan Edwards. The very predestinarian doctrine of the Puritan evangelists, which failed to provide release to convicted sinners, became the source of Stone's burden. The common element of Edwards's theology and that of Stone was a genuine concern for the dreadfulness of evil.

Stone, a native of Maryland, entered an academy in Guilford, North Carolina in 1790, when he was eighteen years old. There he met other students who were seriously engaged in Bible study and worship. In his autobiography, he reported that their daily walk evinced to him their sincere piety and happiness.[47] Far from receiving comfort from the example of those pious students, Stone lamented:

This was a source of uneasiness to my mind, and frequently brought me to serious reflection. I labored to banish these serious thoughts, believing that religion would impede my progress in learning. . . . I therefore associated with that part of the students who made light of divine things, and joined with them

---

[46]Emerson, "Self-Reliance," ibid., 123.

[47]*Barton W. Stone, The Biography of Barton W. Stone. Written by Himself*, with additions and reflections by Elder John Rogers (Cincinnati: J. A. and U. P. James, 1847; reprinted Joplin, Mo.: College Press Publishing Co., 1986), 7.

in their jests at the pious. For this my conscience severely upbraided me when alone, and made me so unhappy that I could neither enjoy the company of the pious nor of the impious.[48]

Later in the year, Stone attended, with his school roommate, an evangelistic meeting conducted by the great Presbyterian preacher, James McGready. McGready figured heavily in the Second Great Awakening a few years later, especially in Logan County, Kentucky. Logan County, near the southern border of the state, had the reputation of being a refuge for horse thieves, highway robbers, escaped murderers, and other criminals. Besides McGready, William Hodge, and other preachers of Methodist, Baptist, and Presbyterian persuasion conducted camp meetings throughout the area. Often preachers of all three denominations would preach at the same meeting. In 1801, Stone attended a camp meeting in Logan County. He was astonished to see people "get religion" in the meeting. McAllister and Tucker describe the scene of the revival:

> Stone carefully observed the physical demonstrations that accompanied the conversion experience. A number of the affected fell to the ground, as if dead, and lay motionless for several hours before regaining full consciousness. As they shouted with joy for their deliverance from the devil, others were caught up in the frenzy and praised God for the gift of salvation. Although Stone saw much in Logan County which he regarded as fanaticism, he became convinced that on balance the good far outweighed the bad.[49]

Stone's earnest concern for both the salvation of sinners and the unity of Christians, coupled with his great speaking ability, influenced both the Western Awakening and the Restoration Movement. The concern of McGready—the belief that the problems of evangelism and salvation from sin were compounded by the sectarian divisiveness of Christians—became a concern for Stone. The later Stone reforms would maintain emphasis on the relationship between evangelism and salvation. Stone's focus was: "that they may all be one; even as thou, Father, art in me, and I in thee, that they also may be in us, so that the world may believe that thou hast sent me." (John 17:21)

That year, however, Stone heard a more traditional Calvinist sermon from McGready. He described the preacher and the result:

> He [McGready] rose and looked around on the assembly. His person was not prepossessing, nor his appearance interesting, except his remarkable gravity, and small piercing eyes. His

---

[48]Ibid.

[49]McAllister and Tucker, *Journey in Faith,* 71.

coarse tremulous voice excited in me the idea of something unearthly. His gestures were *sui generis,* the perfect reverse of elegance. Everything appeared by him forgotten, but the salvation of souls. Such earnestness—such zeal—such powerful persuasion, enforced by the joys of heaven and miseries of hell, I had never witnessed before. My mind was chained by him, and followed him closely in his rounds of heaven, earth, and hell, with feelings indescribable. His concluding remarks were addressed to the sinner to flee the wrath to come without delay. Never before had I comparatively felt the force of truth. Such was my excitement, that had I been standing, I should probably have sunk to the floor under the impression.[50]

McGready and his Calvinism produced terror in young Stone but not hope. Struggling with the desire to follow Christ and escape his burden of guilt, Stone took into account the need to wait for the sovereignty of God while he kept "striving to obtain saving faith—sometimes desponding, and almost despairing of ever getting it."

Stone's account of his conversion may not be as dramatic as those of other great reforming leaders, nor may it square with Edwards's understanding of agonizing over inherent sin; thus it is important to note that Stone also understood the power of sin and the greatness of justification in Christ as well as the others.

He did not come to his mature view of baptism for the remission of sins and Christian atonement until about 1804; he even acknowledged, concerning baptism, that "into the spirit of the doctrine I was never fully led, until it was revived by Brother Alexander Campbell, some years afterward."[51]

Stone was so impressed with the revival meeting in Logan County that he resolved to bring it back to Bourbon County, where he was assigned to the churches at Cane Ridge and Concord. He was successful, and the Cane Ridge revival exceeded the Logan County event in magnitude and intensity, lasting about six days. Stone's description of the Cane Ridge meetings provide a graphic picture of the intense activity:

The roads were literally crowded with wagons, carriages, horsemen, and footmen, moving to the solemn camp. The sight was affecting. It was judged by military men on the ground, that there were between twenty and thirty thousand collected. Four or five preachers were frequently speaking at the same time, in different parts of the encampment, without confusion. The Methodist

[50]Ibid., 8.
[51]Ibid., 11.

and Baptist preachers aided in the work, and all appeared cordially united in it—of one mind and one soul, and the salvation of sinners seemed to be the object of all. We all engaged in singing the same songs of praise—all united in prayer, and all preached the same things—free salvation urged upon all by faith and repentance. . . . The numbers converted, will be known only in eternity.[52]

Stone's ensuing labors for unity, his leadership of the growing group of people called simply "Christian," and his burden for Christian unity, were all deeply affected by his experience in this Second Great Awakening. Max Ward Randall emphasizes that "it was Stone's conviction through his life, though he did come to question some aspects of revival . . . that the phenomenon of Logan County and Cane Ridge was the work of God."[53] The issue of the operation of the Holy Spirit in conversion became one of the more obvious differences between Stone and Alexander Campbell, but even Campbell's biographer acknowledged that great good resulted from the meetings which resulted in church growth and increased religious fervor.[54]

The belief that "Christ came into the world to save sinners" (1 Tim. 1:15), and in the reality of sin, from which men and women require redemption, were major factors in the passion that Stone carried for unity of the church. While he rejected the Calvinist doctrine of predestination, he shared with the Protestant reformers and with Puritans like Jonathan Edwards a deep sense of faith in the grace of God and justification by faith. He did not consider evil inconsequential; on the contrary, he invested his life in what he considered the symbiotic goals of evangelizing and unifying the people of God.

Finally, it is important to examine the views of Alexander Campbell concerning sin and justification in relation to the concepts held by Stone and the leaders of the Protestant Reformation. The *Millennial Harbinger,* throughout its forty years of existence, reflected a strong interest in the problems of evil and redemption. The index of the *Harbinger* includes fifteen entries on the subject of "Justification," seventy-three on "Salvation," and twenty-five on "Sin." *The Christian System,* Campbell's compendium of Christian doctrine, includes articles on "Regeneration," "Remission of Sins," "Repentance," "Sacrifice for Sin," "Sin-Offering," "Pardon," and, of course, articles relating to the Restoration Movement understanding of baptism.

---

[52]Stone and Rogers, *[Auto]biography of Stone,* 135.

[53]Randall, *Great Awakening and Restoration Movement,* 51.

[54]Richardson, *Memoirs,* 2:193.

Although the total proportion of attention given to the classic Reformation question of evil and forgiveness may be less than that of some earlier journals, the *Harbinger* reflects a maturing interest in the matters of sin and justification over preoccupation with church structure, Christian logic, and dialectical argument, which are predominant in *The Christian Baptist*.

Like Luther, Edwards, and Stone, Alexander Campbell was able to report a youthful struggle with personal doubts and concerns for his own salvation before he experienced the healing grace of forgiven guilt. His biographer, Richardson, narrated the events:

> As his convictions deepened, he underwent much conflict of mind, and experienced great concern in regard to his own salvation, so that he lost for a time his usual vivacity, and sought, in lonely walks in fields and by prayer in secluded spots, to obtain such evidences of Divine acceptance as his pious acquaintances were accustomed to consider requisite; it being universally held by the Seceders that 'an assured persuasion of the truth of God's promise in the Gospel, with respect to one's self in particular, is implied in the very nature of saving faith.'[55]

The agony of conviction experienced by the teenaged Alexander Campbell was, in many respects, similar to that of Stone after the experience of hearing the sermon by James McGready. Richardson provides an account in Campbell's own words:

> From the time that I could read the Scriptures, I became convinced that Jesus was the Son of God. I was also fully persuaded that I was a sinner, and must obtain pardon through the merits of Christ or be lost forever. This caused me great distress of soul, and I had much exercise of mind under the awakenings of a guilty conscience. Finally, after many strugglings, I was enabled to put my trust in the Saviour, and to feel my reliance on him as the only Saviour of sinners. From the moment I was able to feel this reliance on the Lord Jesus Christ, I obtained and enjoyed peace of mind. It never entered my head to investigate the subjects of baptism or the doctrines of the creed.[56]

Other matters often occupied Campbell's editorial labors, but entries in the *Millennial Harbinger* bear witness to his continuing belief in the centrality of justification. His burden for the salvation of sinners and his estimate of evil as the enemy of humanity came across as major

---

[55]Richardson, *Memoirs*, 1:48-49.

[56]Ibid., 1:49.

concerns in an 1831 "Review of Archippus, No. III:" "The question of *justification* is a question which all confess to be worthy of the most serious, solemn, and profound investigation."[57]

The question of justification for sin in Campbell's writings, however, is characteristically considered in the context of larger meanings of faith. This context emphasizes the discovery that the response of faith includes obedience through baptism by immersion. For example, Campbell replied to two Baptist elders in an 1843 *Harbinger* article, "The Design of Baptism:"

> When a sinner is declared to be justified by faith without works, it is not equivalent to saying, a sinner is justified by faith without baptism; for baptism, as respects the subject of it, is no where in scripture called a work. . . . But again, no truly enlightened Christian regards the phrase 'being justified by faith,' as indicative of justification by the mere abstract act of believing, without action, passion, or volition. Such a metaphysical faith is not that active instrumental cause of a sinner's justification described by Paul as 'the substance of things hoped for and the evidence of things not seen.'[58]

Campbell referred to the Protestant thought of his time as Platonic, or "Papalism," or "both combined," in the emphasis given to conceptual faith alone. His estimate of the epistle of James was higher than that held by Martin Luther, who called it "an epistle of straw:"

> Faith, indeed, is always the principle and the instrument by which a sinner is justified; but the positive declaration of justification is always in consequence of the obedience of faith. Hence, James represents faith as never *perfected* till it works obedience. To advocate justification by faith alone, or by the bare belief of the base truth, or by a faith yet inoperative, is to plead an imperfect faith as the reason or the occasion of remission of sins.[59]

Campbell objected that *sola fide* was not a New Testament expression at all, and that faith, to be consistent with New Testament teaching, must be an operative faith. Two entire pages of entries under "Baptism" in the index to the *Harbinger* infer the emphasis that Walter Scott developed in the "Restored Gospel," and a primary interest of the Disciples reformers in the "restoration of the Ancient Gospel." While both Camp-

---

[57]Alexander Campbell, *Millennial Harbinger* (1831): 226.
[58]Alexander Campbell, *Millennial Harbinger* (1843): 197.
[59]Ibid., 198.

bell and Stone shared a burden for the salvation of men and women, the primary inception of the Kentucky *Christians* and the Stone movement grew out of the Second Great Awakening. Randall suggests that Campbell's first paper, *The Christian Baptist,* "in its first years . . . said little about the planting or growth of churches."[60] Garrett lists several references to news in the *Baptist* about evangelistic successes, but summarizes, "A few other references to evangelists at work may be found in the pages of *The Christian Baptist,* prior to 1829, but they are not many."[61] The appointment of Walter Scott as Evangelist for the Mahoning Baptist Association in 1826 rapidly impacted the numbers and the emphasis of the movement led by Campbell.

Many of the converts to the "Reformers'" position were drawn from other Christian groups, and this tended to diminish the new movement's basic emphasis on sin and redemption and move it toward major emphasis upon complete obedience to Christ and the scriptures. The Campbells' fervor for unity became focused on restoration of a biblical framework for the church as the vehicle for that unity. The result was a lessened enthusiasm for salvation and the horror of evil seen in a Pauline-Reformation perspective.[62]

George Beazley has characterized the differing ethos of the Stone and Campbell movements regarding their respective relationships to evangelism and their concepts of sin. The differences have endured throughout the history of the combined Restoration Movement, reflecting the Romantic century and the "heart religion" of Stone which retained at least the spirit of Jonathan Edwards, on the one hand, and the cooler, logical drive toward ecclesiastical purity in the spirit of John Locke on the other:

> The revivalist movement in America, in which Stone's Christians were born, and which dominated the 1866-1917 period of Disciples life, was a religious expression of that orientation in the arts and philosophy which is known as Romanticism. It was a mixed gift. On the one hand, revivalism tended to exalt individualism to the point where corporate life in the church became secondary. It also tended to emphasize emotionalism and subjectivity to the point where rational thought about Christian

---

[60]Randall, *Great Awakening and Restoration Movement,* 284.

[61]Leroy Garrett quotes John Williams's *Life of Elder John Smith* in a report from "Raccoon John Smith" that he had *baptized* seven hundred sinners and *capsized* fifteen hundred Baptists. See Garrett, *Stone-Campbell Movement,* 277.

[62]Beazley observes that the Disciples' isolation from Lutheranism "has made it difficult for [them] to appreciate Lutheran position such as '*sola gratia,*'" and that "many Disciples discovered the doctrine of grace in Tillich rather than in Luther." See Beazley, "Future of the Christian Church," 64-65.

faith was depreciated, where objectivity and sacramental life was lost, and where only the feelings of the worshiper were important in baptism or during the eucharist. In the earliest period, the Stone movement was caught up in this warm concern for the world, and these characteristics were not unknown in Walter Scott's preaching. But the strong rationalism and biblicism of the Disciples kept them from surrendering to the revivalism to quite the degree that the Methodists and Baptists (who were not so much children of the Enlightenment) did.[63]

The next section of this book examines some of the aesthetic results of the theological roots outlined in this chapter.

[63]Ibid., 76-77.

Plate 7
THOMAS CAMPBELL
Courtesy Disciples of Christ Historical Society

6

Toward Restoration:
The Movement Emerges

The decision in 1811 by the Washington Christian Association leaders to organize into a church was a veritable Rubicon for its members. Thomas Campbell was reluctant to take the first irrevocable step over that line; but he was fully convinced that because of hostile feelings among the parties of the association, it must be done. It was time for the Washington Christian Association to become an independent church so that the members could practice the church ordinances and enjoy the privileges of a church relationship.

Several conditions prompted this change in attitude for Thomas Campbell. First, to properly administer baptism and the Lord's Supper, the congregation would have to become an organized church. Then, too, Thomas's son Alexander would soon require ordination, a function of a church. And, not much progress had been made in drawing Christian people to the Association concept of union, as Thomas had dreamed. Thus, Thomas felt it was his duty to organize an independent community of believers.

The formation of a church required a specific polity to govern what had been an eclectic group when it was originally formed into the Washington Christian Association. Some students of the Stone-Campbell Movement believe that this was the event which moved the center of gravity from an emphasis on unity of Christians to a central concern of restoring the New Testament church.

The shift was more gradual, however, than this interpretation might suggest: the concept of unity through restoration had been at least suggested in the "Declaration and Address," and the gradual emergence of doctrinal polity in the newly founded church was actually somewhat evolutionary. Leroy Garrett considers the two leading concepts of the Movement in his history: unity and restoration. These concepts are, at the least, in tension with each other; at worst, outright contradictory and a source of faction within the Movement. Garrett correctly observes that

> The restoration motif is viewed as possibly contradictory to the unity plea in that it calls for an exact or detailed recovery of primitive Christianity in doctrine, worship, and organization,

127

which, if insisted upon, calls for a uniformity that is at variance with the principles laid down by Thomas Campbell.[1]

Another doctrinal discovery tended to move the new congregation away from its Calvinist origins. The Campbells and other leaders of the Brush Run Church had reached the conclusion that baptism was for believers only and that immersion was the only true and scriptural form of Christian obedience. The practice was initiated when Thomas Campbell acknowledged that immersion was the New Testament form of baptism, and agreed to baptize two former members of the Washington Christian Association by immersion in the Buffalo Creek, not far from the Brush Run meeting house, on July 4, 1811.[2]

Both Thomas and Alexander had considered the issue of scriptural baptism on other occasions, but had recognized the implications for problems in Christian unity and were reluctant to act upon their emerging understanding of the scriptures. About June 1811, Alexander decided that he had let this matter "slip" long enough and that he wished "to think and let think on these matters."[3]

About a year later, the question of infant baptism became personal and urgent for Alexander. He had married Margaret Brown in March, 1811. When their first child—a daughter—was born the next year, the matter of the baby's baptism arose. The growing conviction that infant baptism was without divine authority led to another question: "May we omit *believers' baptism,* which all admit to be divinely commanded?" The logical sum of their dilemma was articulated by Richardson, who asked the question which has ever since been a point of departure for the heirs of the Campbell tradition: "If the baptism of infants be without warrant, it is invalid, and they who receive it are, in point of fact, still unbaptized."

The result of Alexander Campbell's rethinking about believers' baptism led, on June 12, 1812, to the immersion of Thomas and Alexander Campbell, their wives, Alexander's sister Dorothea, and one couple from the Brush Run fellowship. Elder Matthias Luce, a Baptist minister, baptized each of the seven upon a simple confession of Christ. The meeting was not so simple, however. Thomas and Alexander felt constrained to speak about the reasons for their action, and the meeting lasted about seven hours! One young man had to leave the meeting to attend a muster of volunteers for the War of 1812. After reporting for muster he returned in time to hear the last hour of preaching and witness the baptisms![4]

---

[1]Garrett, *Stone-Campbell Movement,* 156-57.

[2]Richardson, *Memoirs,* 1:372.

[3]Ibid., 1:392.

[4]Ibid., 1: 397-98.

The rejection by Thomas and Alexander of paedobaptism and sprinkling raised fundamental questions that have impacted the Restoration Movement down to the present. The thinking that precipitated their obedience to the call for adult immersion tends to annul their acceptance as Christians of those who have not shared such a baptismal experience. Campbell's debates with several Presbyterian preachers helped to crystallize his thoughts about believers' immersion and conformity to the "primitive pattern," or the Restoration concept. Bill J. Humble places these positions in perspective in his book about Alexander Campbell's debates:

> Thomas Campbell's original dream had been the unity of all believers in Christ, but his son's debates shattered this vision. The Restoration Movement had now become an independent religious body, still advocating a return to the Christianity of the first century, but presenting to the religious world for its acceptance a specific body of doctrines which had been tested in public debate and which the Christians sincerely believed was the embodiment of first century Christianity.[5]

Questions relevant to both theological and cultural aspects of the Restoration Movement were cracks appearing in its framework even before Alexander Campbell's death. These kinds of questions have continued to provoke controversy, both among and within the groups decended from the Stone-Campbell tradition. Some of these implicit questions are:

1. After his baptism by Matthias Luce in the Brush Run Creek, did Alexander Campbell believe that he had never truly been a Christian until that day, June 12, 1812?
2. Alexander Campbell was ordained by the Brush Run Church nearly six months before his baptism by immersion. His certificate was signed by his father, Thomas Campbell, as senior minister and by four deacons of the congregation. If he was not a Christian until his baptism by immersion, and since he clearly believed in the importance of ordination by a local congregation, how is it that he was not reordained after his baptism?
3. Thomas Campbell, upon his arrival in the United States, was found by the Synod of North America to be a Seceder Presbyterian minister in good standing.[6] His licensure and ordination were by the Seceder Presbyterian Church in his native Ireland. After his baptism in 1812,

[5]Humble, *Campbell and Controversy*, (Joplin, Mo.: College Press Publishing Co., 1986), 281.

[6]William Herbert Hanna, *Thomas Campbell: Seceder and Christian Union Advocate* (Joplin, Mo.: College Press Publishing Co., n.d.), 28.

he continued preaching without any suggestion that he needed a new ordination. Did he consider himself to have been a Christian when he was ordained, and those who ordained him Christians?

These and similar questions have been at the core of disagreement between the "exclusive" and "inclusive" heirs of the Campbells' understanding of immersion. The questions above are not definitively answered in the early writings of Alexander Campbell—especially not in his essays on "The Ancient Gospel" which appeared in *The Christian Baptist.* The irenic spirit which Thomas maintained throughout his life suggests that his implicit answers to those questions would demonstrate an inclusive stance. At the same time, however, he held firmly to his belief that adult immersion constituted Christian baptism in the spirit of Acts 2:38, which is a key scripture for the Disciples.

Still, during the seven years *The Christian Baptist* was published (1823-30) Thomas often referred to people in other denominational situations as "brother," or who are implicitly considered to be Christians in his argument. The March 6, 1826, issue contains a letter from a "German Baptist" or "Dunkard" of Indiana who believed in trine (triple) immersion amd foot washing, and who was not convinced of the efficacy of celebrating the Lord's Supper weekly. Campbell's reply reveals an attitude more liberal than much of his other writing in that publication:

Dear Brother—

For such I recognize you, notwithstanding the varieties of opinion which you express on some topics, on which we might never express or agree. But if we should not, as not unity of opinion, but unity of faith, is the only true bond of Christian union, I will esteem and love you, as I do every man, of whatever name, who believes sincerely that Jesus is the Messiah and hopes in his salvation.[7]

In an essay of 1825, on the subject of "Christian Union," Campbell implied that Christians were scattered among all denominations. The very call made for the "unity of all Christians," the primary substance of the "Declaration and Address" of Thomas Campbell, and an ongoing concern for the reform movement, all bear witness to the fact that there *are* Christians in various divided situations who need to be reunited. Campbell wrote:

Reader, attend to what I am about to write. I address all denominations of Christians, not with a design to oppose or defend one

---

[7]Alexander Campbell, *Christian Baptist*, (rprt. Joplin, Mo.: College Press Publishing), 3:223.

sect more than another, or to pull down one system and build up another; but to show the error of all and to point out an infallible remedy. . . . Disunion among Christians is their disgrace and a perpetual reproach and dishonor to the Lord Jesus Christ.[8]

Several years later, Campbell was challenged to address unequivocally the matter of "Christians among the Sects." A lady from Lunenburg, Virginia, wrote the famous editor on July 8, 1837, expressing some shock that Campbell had found Christians in "all Protestant parties":

> Dear brother Campbell—
> I was much surprised to-day, while reading the Harbinger, to see that you recognize the Protestant parties as Christian. You say, you 'find in all Protestant parties Christians.'[9]

Expressing her desire to do the right thing about the issue, the Lunenburg lady asked a series of pointed questions:

> Will you be so good as to let me know how any one becomes a Christian? What act of yours gave you the name of Christian? At what time had Paul the name of Christ called upon him? At what time did Cornelius have Christ named on him? Is it not through this name we obtain eternal life? Does the name of Christ or Christian belong to any but those who believe the *gospel,* repent, and are buried by baptism into the death of Christ?[10]

Thomas Campbell's answer in the *Millennial Harbinger* required three full pages of large-type print. It was published one month before the first installment of a series of essays on the problems of "opinionism" in the Church—i.e., the propagation of personal *opinion* vis-à-vis the sharing of scriptural *facts*. This distinction was a normative concept for the Campbells from the time of the "Declaration and Address" throughout their lives, and answering the Lunenburg query with a personal opinion obviously had distasteful aspects for the *Harbinger* editor. In reply to a critical letter about his answer to the "Lunenburg Question," Campbell noted in the November 1837 issue:

> We gave it as our *opinion* that there were Christians among the Protestant sects; an opinion, indeed, which we have always expressed when called upon.[11]

---

[8]Ibid., 2:162.
[9]*Millennial Harbinger* (1837): 411.
[10]Ibid.
[11]Ibid., 506.

To reinforce the fact that he was dealing in an area where he felt opinion prevailed, Campbell continued:

> Now the nice point of opinion on which some brethren differ, is this: Can a person who simply, not perversely, *mistakes* the outward baptism, have the inward? . . . To which I answer, that, in my opinion, *it is possible*. Farther than this I do not affirm.[12]

Previous or subsequent statements by Alexander Campbell regarding baptism by immersion have been ambiguous to some, but his answer to the Lunenburg letter and his later statements in defense of that answer are not ambiguous at all. It is clear that he could not bring himself to believe that he was not a disciple of Christ before his immersion in 1812, nor could he accept the fact that his father's Christianity and ordination were not valid before that time. He also made clear his belief that each person is responsible for the understanding that he has the opportunity to acquire. In that sense, he would have been disobedient to Christ to refuse immersion after being convinced it was the scriptural mode of baptism.

Campbell's "opinion" is based partly upon deductive logic, and partly upon his understanding of scripture:

> In reply to this conscientious sister, I observe that if there be no Christians in the Protestant sects, there are certainly none among the Romanists, none among the Jews, Turks, Pagans; and therefore no Christians in the world except ourselves, or such of us as keep, or strive to keep, all the commandments of Jesus. Therefore, for many centuries there has been no church of Christ, no Christians in the world; and the promises concerning the everlasting kingdom of Messiah have failed, and the gates of hell have prevailed against his church! This cannot be; and therefore there are Christians among the sects.[13]

Moving from the generalized logic of history and Christ's promises for his church to the specific issue of individuals, Campbell continued:

---

[12]Ibid., 507. With such a beginning, there was great potential for diversity in attitude by second-generation Disciples. The dialogue continues to the present over such issues as relationships between Restoration tradition churches and other Christian groups, acceptance of members who were baptized as infants or who have non-immersion baptism, and participation in international ecumenical movements. On one side are arrayed some Churches of Christ and Christian Churches which retain an exclusivist position apart from the rest of Christendom. On the other are the Christian Churches (Disciples of Christ), many of which practice "open membership" and support, denominationally, the Consultation on Church Unity (COCU) and the World Council of Churches.

[13]Ibid., 411.

But who is a Christian? I answer, every one that believes in his heart that Jesus of Nazareth is the Messiah, the Son of God; repents of his sins, and obeys him in all things according to his measure of knowledge of his will.[14]

The numerous critical letters the *Harbinger* editor received about his response to the Lunenburg letter suggest that as early as 1837, many of Campbell's fellow Disciples had outdone their leaders in exclusive orthodoxy! The November issue of the journal makes it plain that Campbell felt compelled to defend his liberal attitude against critics on one side, while trying to avoid giving too much comfort to the "sectarians" on the other side who were defending paedobaptism. Staunchly remaining with his principles, however, he got to the essence of the question concerning "who is a Christian" in the following statement:

My high regard for these correspondents, however, calls for a few remarks on these sentences, as farther explanatory of our views. We cheerfully agree with them, as well as with our sister of Lunenburg, that the term *Christian* was given first to immersed believers and to none else; but we do not think that it was given to them because they were immersed, but because they had put on Christ. . . . [15]

The delicate position in which Campbell found himself at this juncture of the Restoration Movement was not an easy one. Having only recently become independent from the Baptist church, he was faced with problems of establishing a new fellowship with a clear ecclesiastical polity. He was also confronted by a new sectarianism which emphasized "form of doctrine" over Christian spirituality, potentially endangering the entire structure with legalism. The care he endeavored to use in walking a line inoffensive to his right-wing brethren and still asserting a basic scriptural position is evident in yet another response made in the December 1837 *Harbinger*:

Judging from numerous letters received at this office, my reply to the sister from Lunenburg has given some pain to our brethren, and some pleasure to our sectarian friends. . . . Some of our brethren seem to think that we have neutralized much that has been said on the importance of baptism for remission, and disarmed them of much of their artillery against the ignorance, error, and indifference of the times upon the whole subject of Christian duty and Christian privilege.[16]

[14]Ibid.
[15]Ibid.
[16]Ibid., 561.

With a sardonic note of satisfaction that his correspondents are at least not "Campbellites,"—judging from the severity of their criticism—Campbell noted that he wished neither to "dogmatize" nor to "contend for the opinion itself." The response this time required over seven pages—more than the original reply to the Lunenburg letter—and very carefully defended against three concerns: (1) the charge of inconsistency, (2) sectarian application of his opinion, and (3) his reasons for having delivered the opinion at the time it was given.[17]

An interesting new revelation surfaced in his third commentary on the Lunenburg letter and comments on his critics: the rather frank admission that "scholasticism" was already operative in the Disciples fellowship, manifested by a spirit of exclusive negativism rather than the original spirit of loving unity which had characterized the old Washington Christian Association:

> But we had still more urgent reasons than the difficulties of this sister to express such an opinion:—some of our brethren were too much addicted to denouncing the sects and representing them *en masse* as wholly aliens from the possibility of salvation—as wholly antichristian and corrupt. Now as the Lord says of Babylon, "Come out of her, *my people,*" I felt constrained to rebuke them over the shoulders of this inquisitive lady. These very zealous brethren gave a countenance to the popular clamor that we make baptism a saviour, or a passport to heaven, disparaging all the private and social virtues of the professing public. Now as they were propounding opinions to others, I intended to bring them to the proper medium by propounding an opinion to them in terms as strong and as pungent as their own.[18]

Because Campbell, in response to his critics, seemed to backpedal from the primary thrust of his answer to the famous Lunenburg letter, some contemporary scholars of the movement expressed the belief that it did not represent his most mature thought. His steadfastness in defending his answer, as well as criticizing in turn the attitudes of his brethren who had grown rigid about forms over meaning, certifies the fact that his response represented a studied intent. Subsequent essays, including those of his brother-in-law, Archibald McKeever (who wrote under the pen name Christianos), continued to attest that "the man whose heart is bowed to the Divine will is accepted."[19]

[17]Ibid.

[18]Ibid., 564-65.

[19]Garrett, *Stone-Campbell Movement*, 581.

Concerning Campbell's ultimate attitude about fellowship, Garrett writes that after Christianos' essays in the years 1838-40, "he realized, perhaps as never before, that a large and respectable part of the community he had helped create was more conservative and exclusivistic than himself. Moderation was the only answer, even if by equivocation, a tool he sometimes used." Garrett acknowledges that "Campbell obviously did some retrenching during the three-year controversy. His unambiguous stand in the Lunenburg letter in behalf of the unimmersed believer was not now unambiguous. It is not that he had changed his mind, but that he had a unity movement on his hands that had reactionary elements stronger than he had supposed, and he did not want it to blow up in his face through internal disputes."[20]

Intellectually, both in mode and faith, the logic of the rationalistic roots beneath the Restoration concept became a powerful counter-force against the unity spirit introduced by Thomas Campbell. Garrett sees in the "Christians-in-the-Sects" argument the roots of the Churches of Christ, the heirs of the consistently rationalistic element in the Disciples fellowship of the 1840s.[21]

In one sense, Campbell fell victim to his own success as editor of *The Christian Baptist*. The first issues of Volume I beginning August 3, 1823 carried articles supporting one of the editor's views concerning the clergymen of the period.[22] The essays over the evils of the established Protestant clergy did not serve to build a spirit of kindness between the reformers and other churches, and the fearless spirit of truth-seeking at all costs not only cut a straight line across all religious questions, but sometimes displayed the writer's penchant for sarcasm. Some theology students of the Hamilton Seminary in New York reprimanded the spirit of the paper:

> We admit that there may be much in the church at the present day that is reprehensible. But what way is most likely to effect a change? Is it by a confirmed course of ridicule and sarcasm, or by a dignified, argumentative, and candid exposition of error, and a mild and persuasive invitation to amendment?[23]

Campbell's reply showed little inclination toward repentance for the hardhitting aspects of his paper, and he even asked that his attitude not be termed "sarcastic:"

---

[20]Ibid., 584, 585.

[21]Ibid.

[22]A. Campbell, "The Origin of the 'Christian Clergy,' splendid Meeting Houses, and Fixed Salaries, Exhibited from Ecclesiastical History," *The Christian Baptist*, 1 no. 1 (1823): 8.

[23]*The Christian Baptist* 4, no. 2 (1826): 284.

You must not call this sarcasm nor raillery; for I assure you I
doubt not but your pious souls have been sorely grieved with
the impious spirit of "The Christian Baptist;" for it never has
looked with a benign aspect either upon the professors of theological schools, nor their disciples. It has never flattered their
pious efforts in making Christian bishops for Christian congregations by means of a system of speculation, and a few rules for
collecting sermons, or manufacturing those of ancient times
down to the present taste and fashion.[24]

Campbell's teaching on the place of immersion in the process of
regeneration was articulate and consistent in both the *Baptist* and the
Harbinger. In an article on the subject, he wrote:

Thus we find that when the gospel was announced on Pentecost,
and when Peter opened the kingdom of heaven to the Jews, he
commanded them to be immersed for the remission of sins. This
is quite sufficient, if we had not another word on the subject. I
say it is quite sufficient to shew that the forgiveness of sins and
Christian immersion were, in their first proclamations by the
holy apostles, inseparably connected together. Peter, to whom
was committed the keys, opened the kingdom of heaven in this
manner, and made repentance, or reformation, and immersion,
equally necessary to forgiveness.[25]

The tension faced by Campbell and the Disciples between the doctrine of baptism for the remission of sins and the question of Christians
in other groups presaged long-range problems to be considered by future
Disciples. In spite of Alexander Campbell's heavy reliance on logical
argument and the rational process, he was capable of tolerating at least
a minimum of intellectual ambiguity. Confronted by the concerns of
Jesus (John 17) and by the Apostle Paul (I Corinthians) for Christian
unity on the one hand, and with a categorical scriptural mandate for the
immersion of adult believers on the other, Campbell managed to live
with the apparently opposing principles in tension. Garrett suggests that
he "preserved the Movement through appeasement," and that "moderation was the only answer, even if by equivocation, a tool he sometimes
used."[26]

While some of the "scholastic" heirs of Campbell have seen compromise and moderation as tools of Satan and a denial of the scriptural basis
on which the Church of Christ must find itself, their brethren in the

[24]Ibid., 235.

[25]Ibid., 5, no. 7 (1828): 416-17.

[26]Garrett, *Stone-Campbell Movement*, 585, 584.

liberal wing have found that scriptural literalism is not a basic part of their faith, and thus have not experienced great tension in espousing "open membership" to all who call themselves Christians.

A third way was described by another twentieth-century thinker of the Stone-Campbell Movement. Under the title, "Harmonizing the Scriptures," R. H. Boll wrote in the spirit of Alexander Campbell's mediation:

> There is another vicious principle of Bible interpretation constantly adopted by theorists. It lies in the "harmonizing" of apparently conflicting texts. Here is a passage making a statement; over there is another which seems to declare the opposite. Now for those who simply believe God's word it is not difficult to see that there must be a higher harmony between the two which does violence to neither, and that we are at liberty to believe and preach both these passages just as they stand—and that whether or not we are able to perceive the tie that unites them. But with the theorist it is otherwise. One of these passages is for him, the other against him. One of them, therefore, is accepted at what it says and strongly emphasized; the other has to be knocked out of commission. . . . Thank God that a Christian need not learn the serpentine arts which those who have a theory to defend are obliged to practice.[27]

Questions such as the polarity between election and free will seem not to have generated great controversy within the Movement—a rather surprising fact, since the inception of the Movement constituted, to a great extent, a rejection of the Calvinist doctrine of predestination. Campbell did devote many pages of the *Harbinger* to the matter of the influence of the Holy Spirit in regeneration, over which Disciples doctrine broke sharply with its Calvinist roots. The lack of toleration for unresolved conflicts, however, led to the question about whether the true Church of Christ had indeed existed between the first century or two and 1809.[28] Campbell argued in his original response to the Lunenburg letter that Christ's promise guaranteed the Church's existence throughout that period, and that the Stone-Campbell Movement did not constitute a resurrection from the dead.

[27]R. H. Boll, "Harmonizing the Scriptures" in *Truth and Grace*, ed. J. W. Shepherd (Cincinnati: F. L.Rowe, 1917), 115.

[28]In a reply to a letter of "Sister Susan" of Virginia written in 1835 about the question of re-baptism, Campbell wrote: "For my part, although I have been reluctantly constrained to think that the remnant, according to the election of grace, in this age of apostacy, is, indeed, small, yet I thank God that his promise has not failed—that even at this present time there is an election—a remnant—and that this remnant did not commence either in 1827, 1823, or in 1809." *Millennial Harbinger* (1835): 418.

The matter of tolerance for ambiguity relates also to the existence of art in a religious community. Art ministers to qualities of feeling which are not categorical, whereas dialectical debate relies on a cognitive, rationalistic argument. The critics of Campbell's response to the Lunenburg letter reflected their distaste for ambiguity and a preference for vocal music which utilized the language of poetry over the inexact message of non-vocal music. Implicit in their criticism was a distaste for visual art, and even for fiction based on "non-fact" or Augustine's "willing suspension of disbelief."

The reformers' 1812 adoption of baptism by immersion inevitably estranged them even further than they already were from their former Presbyterian brethren. The same development, however, seemingly made for more natural fellowship with the Baptists, even though the similarity in mode of baptism clouded many deeper disagreements between the Baptists and the "reformers." Richardson noted the gulf between the two groups:

> The practice of immersion indeed, instead of sprinkling, seemed to constitute the only important difference between the Baptists and other sects; and although the Brush Run members had adopted immersion, and were hence reputed to be Baptists, they felt there was a wide difference between them and the Baptist communities in regard to the great principles of religious liberty and progress, as well as to the necessity of returning to the faith and practice of the primitive Churches. In their conformity to these, they had advanced far beyond the Baptist stand-point, even before the adoption of immersion, which, with the simple baptismal confession they had chosen, did not bring them to the position held by the Baptists, but, in reality, had placed them still farther in advance.[29]

However, Mathias Luce and a few other Baptist preachers who knew of the Brush Run Church urged the leaders to consider uniting with the Redstone Baptist Association of that region. The Campbells did not have high regard for most Baptist preachers, but highly regarded Baptist people in general. The Brush Run congregation decided in the fall of 1813 to make an overture to the Redstone Association. The proposal included several pages of remonstrances against human creeds and the reservation that members "be allowed to teach and preach whatever we learned from the Holy Scriptures, regardless of any creed or formula in Christendom."[30]

---

[29]Richardson, *Memoirs*, 1:437.
[30]*Millennial Harbinger* (1848): 276.

The Campbells preached regularly on the enlarged circuits available to them through their association with the Baptists. Alexander was also involved in the rigors of farm work along with speaking, writing, and advocating the cause of reform, and in 1818 he inaugurated his first venture into operating an educational institution when he opened the Buffalo Seminary. He had long been aware of the value of "cultivated minds" in the work of the gospel, and had often expressed his preference for learning and culture as a background for an active ministry. In the 1848 article referred to above, Campbell wrote his earliest negative impressions of the Baptist clergy associated with the Redstone Association:

> Indeed, the ministry of some sects is generally in the aggregate the worse portion of them. It was certainly so in the Redstone Association thirty years ago. They were little men in a big office. The office did not fit them. They had a wrong idea, too, of what was wanting. They seemed to think that a change of apparel—a black coat instead of a drab—a broad rim on their hat instead of a narrow one—a prolongation of the face, and a factitious gravity—a longer and a more emphatic pronunciation of certain words, rather than scriptural knowledge, humility, spirituality, zeal, and Christian affection, with great devotion and great philanthropy, were the grand desiderata.[31]

He complained that those preachers had "but one, two, or, at most, three sermons; and these were either delivered in one uniform style and order, or minced down into one medley by way of variety." The young reformer sided with the educated clergy of other groups in thinking of the Baptist ministers generally as "illiterate and uncouth men, without either learning or academic accomplishments, or polish."[32] Baptists in general, however, merited more respect:

> I confess, however, that I was better pleased with the Baptist people than with any other community. They read the Bible, and seemed to care but little for any thing else in religion than "*conversion*" and "*Bible* doctrine."[33]

Campbell's personal predicament was one of his many replays of the ancient Platonic tension: a love for poetry countered by the conviction that ethically much great poetry was unacceptable in the ideal republic. Alexander Campbell enjoyed the European background of his youth,

---

[31]Ibid. (1848): 345.
[32]Ibid.
[33]Ibid. (1848): 346.

including the year at Glasgow University, as well as the educational standards of the Presbyterian Seceder clergy of which his father had been a member. Against his aesthetic and intellectual predilection, however, he espoused a doctrine of only "speaking where the Bible speaks."[34] The Buffalo Seminary was an attempt to address the need for better education and better-equipped preachers.

Alexander's background in operating his father's academy in Ireland made him well-prepared for teaching in northern Virginia. He subjected the full house of young pupils to a strong curriculum as well as definitive discipline. The enrollment was quite cosmopolitan, including scholars from Pittsburgh, Pennsylvania, Ohio, and from communities in northern Virginia. The results of this initial venture into American education had mixed results, however. The motives of many of the students resulted more from the academic ambitions of well-to-do parents for their sons than to religious instruction, which was the school's principal *raison d'etre*. Students were turned away because available places were oversubscribed, so that the final result was hardly satisfactory to the Academy's founder. Campbell was disappointed that so few of the students were inclined to enter the ministry, but instead used their good classical education as a foundation for law or medical studies.[35]

Alexander visited the various Baptist churches of the Redstone Association, made some longer speaking and discussion tours, and worked as Director of the Buffalo Academy. These activities helped him become increasingly convinced that the authority of the written word was needed to further the reformation which he and his father represented. During 1820, he debated with John Walker, a Seceder Presbyterian minister of Mount Pleasant, Ohio, over the question of baptism. Campbell published the debate and found that publication to be well received and in wide demand. The inauguration of *The Christian Baptist* on August 3, 1823, followed circulation of a prospectus for the paper in the spring of that year. The magazine was bold in its attack on the clergy and frequently contained sarcastic, iconoclastic articles. Thomas Campbell was distressed over his son's harsh policy and tried to encourage him to be milder in his writing. Eventually, in 1830, Alexander discontinued *The Christian Baptist,* and began circulating a milder journal, the *Millennial Harbinger.*[36]

---

[34]One consequence of this for the Restoration Movement was a consistent effort—even by dissenting branches—to develop and maintain liberal arts colleges with a concurrent reluctance to develop "professional" theological seminaries. Another may have been the vigor with which leaders of the Movement castigated the evils of clericalism and the ecclesiastical trappings of clergy.

[35]Ibid., 1:492.

[36]McAllister and Tucker, *Journey in Faith,* 123, 127-28.

Evangelism and church growth did not seem to be primary concerns of the reformers during the earlier years of their efforts. Instead, they were preoccupied with developing doctrine and polity, and especially with restoring "the ancient order of things." Their primary fellowship in 1827 was a small circle of churches in the Mahoning Baptist Association. In that year, Walter Scott was appointed an evangelist for the Mahoning Baptist Association with remarkable results for the reformers' cause.[37]

Evangelistic emphasis was more characteristic of the Kentucky Christians, led by Barton W. Stone, than with the "Reformed Baptists" associated with the Campbells. In the years before Walter Scott was sent out, the churches of the Mahoning Association did well to hold their own or to see some modest growth.[38] In fact, without the preaching of Scott on the Western Reserve or Stone's "Christian" movement, the Campbells' dream of a biblically based Christian union would have soon died on the rapidly changing frontier.[39] Scott's particular contribution to "the ancient order of things" was "the Gospel restored." He became intensely effective in evangelizing for the Mahoning Association on the Western Reserve.[40] At the 1828 Associational meeting, after one year of his work, more than one thousand additions were reported.[41] Scott's remarkable ability to communicate with frontier people was partly based upon the simple logic of his presentation.

George Beazley's view of the Scott Gospel reflects, perhaps, his own relatively liberal orientation in his ascription of the formula to "Lockean psychology":

> Scott's view of the church as (at least in the visible form) a gathered social contract community of Christians saved by their faith, confession and obedience to Christ in baptism was an ecclesiological expression of John Locke's *Second Essay on Civil Government*. As one Disciples historian is fond of saying, John Locke is to classic Disciples theology as Aristotle is to Thomas Aquinas.[42]

---

[37]A. Dale Fiers, "Structure—Past, Present, and Future" in Beazley, ed., *The Christian Church (Disciples of Christ)*, 141. Fiers suggests that at that time the movement came into being as a movement for evangelism and for Christian unity on the frontier of the United States.

[38]Garrett, *Stone-Campbell Movement*, 220.

[39]McAllister and Tucker, *Journey in Faith*, 133.

[40]See chapter 2 of this book.

[41]McAllister and Tucker, 133.

[42]George G. Beazley, Jr.,"Who are the Disciples?" in Beazley, ed., *The Christian Church (Disciples of Christ)*, 24-25.

Walt Yancey, writing from a contemporary Church of Christ perspective, notes the greater spirituality of Walter Scott's perspective compared with many modern "Restorationist" presentations. He points out that the evolution of Scott's five or six points—half of which were human initiative and half of which were God's responses—has evolved into a totally humanistic presentation: (1) hear, (2) believe, (3) repent, (4) confess, and (5) be baptized.[43] From a reformation viewpoint the original Scott formula appears synergistic; the contemporary version, however, is entirely human-centered and thus makes conversion a totally humanistic phenomenon.

The Disciples' vigorous evangelization and proselytizing efforts on the Western Reserve and the work of the Stone-oriented Christians in the Mid-South and West exacerbated tensions between Disciples/Christians and Baptists. There were numerous differences within the Disciples group. Some of them related to the reformers' emphasis on the oneness of the church, the Baptist use of confessions of faith, the use of the word "Baptist" as a sectarian name, the purpose of baptism, the distinction made by Baptists between clergy and "laity," the reformers' sharp distinction between Old and New Testaments, as well as other misunderstandings.[44] Compounding the misunderstandings and making communication difficult were problems related to educational, cultural, and even aesthetic mores.

The separation process extended over several years, but moved inexorably toward finality so that by 1830 it was nearly complete. During the same year, Alexander Campbell discontinued publication of *The Christian Baptist* and launched the new, more irenic *Millennial Harbiner*:

> On balance *The Millennial Harbinger* was more constructive and less iconoclastic than *The Christian Baptist*. The responsibility of leading a separate religious movement altered Campbell's point of view more than he was willing to admit. A more positive approach is evident in the second number of *The Millennial Harbinger*. Although Campbell suggested that he and his readers should continue to oppose the abuses of the age, he cautioned: 'We must not run into the opposite extreme; or in our haste to get out of Babylon, we must not run past Jerusalem.' The reformer had begun to be tamed.[45]

---

[43]Walt Yancey, *Endangered Heritage: An Evaluation of Church of Christ Doctrine* (Joplin, Mo.: College Press Publishing Co., 1987), 51.

[44]McAllister and Tucker, *Journey in Faith*, 144-41.

[45]Ibid., 146.

One of the greatest achievements by the leaders of both the Stone Movement and the Campbell Movement was their consolidation. It would seem to be a most natural result of the unity plea, which had characterized both groups from their inception, that they should demonstrate their doctrine in practice. A candid appraisal of the obstacles to the consummation of such a union, however, underlines the miracle of its having occurred at all. The union represented the only major marriage of the heirs of the Restoration Movement. It stands as a sharp, happy contrast to the more familiar stories of disfellowshipping, separation, and broken relationships within the Movement. Richardson observed that the successful evangelistic efforts of the Stone-oriented "Christian Connection" on the Western Reserve made the churches of the Mahoning Association aware of the importance of evangelization.[46]

It was during one of Campbell's speaking tours that he and Barton W. Stone met each other in 1824. Richardson recorded the meeting with approval:

> While at Georgetown he formed the acquaintance of Barton W. Stone, already noted as well for his eminent Christian virtues as for his efforts to effect in Kentucky a religious reformation almost identical in its leading principles and aims with that in which Mr. Campbell was himself engaged. The two laborers in the same great field formed at once a warm, personal attachment to each other, which continued through life, and tended greatly to promote a subsequent union between the two yet distinct bands of reformers.[47]

During 1827, however, a serious disagreement occurred between the two men when Stone, editor of *The Christian Messenger,* wrote to the editor of *The Christian Baptist,* taking him gently but firmly to task over comments concerning John 1:1. Stone's anti-trinitarian views, as well as his unorthodox beliefs about the pre-existence of Christ, surfaced clearly in his letter. Campbell's reply maintained a brotherly stance, but he scolded Stone for his challenge to what Campbell had expressed as only "opinions," which were not pressed on the reader as anything more than that.[48]

A later exchange, aired in both Stone's *Christian Messenger* and Campbell's *Millennial Harbinger,* concerned uniting the Christians and the Disciples:

---

[46]Richardson, *Memoirs,* 2:204-5.

[47]Ibid., 2:118.

[48]See *The Christian Baptist* 5 (1827): 379.

Stone opened the correspondence by stating flatly that no reason existed to prevent union as far as the Christians were concerned. In essence the Reformed Baptists—as he called them—had accepted the doctrine taught by the Christians for a number of years. Stone's candor upset Campbell. Other antisectarian reformers were pioneers clearing forests and burning brush, Campbell replied, but only he and his followers had restored the ancient gospel. Stone was unwilling to concede the point. In his next letter he noted Campbell's 'plain denial' of the Christians' claim to priority and then observed: 'I am aware of the deceptibility of the human mind, and of its strong propensity to make for ourselves *a great name.*' Campbell was infuriated. Writing in the last issue of the *Millennial Harbinger* of 1831, he observed that Stone 'has a little of the *man* as well as of the Christian about him.' 'I solicited a free, candid and affectionate correspondence on any points of difference,' he continued. 'But in asking for bread I did not expect a *stone.*'[49]

Had the union of the Christians and the Disciples depended only on good feelings between Stone and Campbell, it doubtless would not have occurred—at least at this time. Both groups had other leaders, however, including John T. Johnson and "Raccoon" John Smith for the Disciples, who were able to proceed toward union. A four-day conference at Georgetown, Kentucky on December 25, 1831 was followed by a larger meeting at the Hill Street Christian Church in Lexington, Kentucky on January 1, 1832. The chief spokesmen at these conferences were Stone and Smith.

The union of churches in Georgetown, Lexington, and later in Paris, Kentucky led to the union of the two groups throughout the state. Their differences diminished and, in most cases, good will prevailed. Richardson acknowledged the reservations voiced by Alexander Campbell at first, however:

> He thought sufficient time had not perhaps been allowed for a thorough comprehension of the principles of the Reformation, and dreaded lest these should in any wise be overruled or lost sight of in so sudden and unceremonious an arrangement. His misgivings, however, proved to be entirely groundless. . . . All were united upon the Bible alone, and with the most fraternal feelings strove together for the faith and institutions of the gospel.[50]

[49]McAllister and Tucker, *Journey of Faith,* 140-41.
[50]Richardson, *Memoirs,* 2:387.

In summary, of the Movement's primary leaders, Alexander Campbell supported the union, but Barton W. Stone was the active, moving force behind accomplishing it.[51]

Stone's ultimate feelings for Alexander Campbell are made clear in his autobiography written late in his life:

> I will not say there are no faults in brother Campbell; but these are fewer, perhaps, in him, than any man I know on earth; and over these few my love would throw a veil, and hide them from view forever. I am constrained, and willingly constrained to acknowledge him the greatest promoter of this reformation of any man living. The Lord reward him![52]

Stone defended his actions to promote the union of the Christians and the Disciples, saying that he viewed it as the noblest act of his life.[53]

Garrett estimates that the combined numbers of the two groups in 1832 was between twenty and thirty thousand, of whom at least eight thousand represented Stone's Christian Connection. The differences in polity, doctrine, and style of the two streams presented some problems in the continued task of uniting the churches, none of which assumed any ecclesiastical authority to promote the alliance. Because the differences relate, in some cases quite directly, to the primary purpose of this book, Garrett's summary of those differences is given here:

1. The most notable difference was in evangelism, both in theory and practice. The Christians were zealous and emotional, even to the point of using the mourner's bench, which was then so common, and they had numerous evangelists. The Disciples, who did not have a single itinerant preacher in the field at the time of union, had neglected evangelism. Too, they were more rational in their

---

[51]McAllister and Tucker, *Journey of Faith*, 152. A notice in the *Millennial Harbinger* of January 1832 contain Campbell's comment over a headline from a Virginia publication, "Campbellites Uniting with Arians." The author accused the "Campbellites" of Georgetown, Kentucky, of uniting with an Arian congregation. The author clearly referred to the Stone-oriented *Christians* as the "Arians" in the drama, since Barton W. Stone was frequently accused of Arianism because of his opposition to Calvinist trinitarian doctrine. Campbell, in this article written soon after the incident, defended the union: "I can vouch for the fact, that in the case alluded to those stigmatized 'Campbellites' have surrendered nothing, not a single truth that they either believed or taught; and they who have united with us from all parties have met us upon the ancient gospel and the ancient order of things." Alexander Campbell, "Campbellites United with the Arians," *Millennial Harbinger* (January 1832): 36.

[52]Stone, *Biography*, 76.

[53]McAllister and Tucker, 145. That Barton W. Stone, Walter Scott, and other Restoration fathers did hold a more chiliastic view has been shown by E. L. Jorgenson in *Faith of our Fathers* (Louisville: Word and Work Publishers, n.d.), 48, 147.

approach, far less emotional, and the thought of a mourner's bench really turned them off.

2. While they were both immersionists, the Christians did not emphasize it like the Disciples did, believing that one can be saved without being immersed and that it is not necessary to Christian communion. Like Campbell, Stone taught baptism for the remission of sins, but he did not press the point and admitted to an inconsistency in application.

3. The Christians had an ordained ministry and a higher concept of the ministerial office, and insisted that only the ordained may baptize and preside over the Lord's Supper. The Disciples were actually anticlerical and believed in the priesthood of all believers in the sense that any believer may baptize and serve Communion.

4. Those in the Stone movement were adamant in wearing the name Christian, believing this to be a divinely-appointed name, while the Campbell followers preferred Disciples, Campbell himself concluding that "Christian" was given in derision by outsiders and not divinely given at all. In the five years following the union the name Christian was more widely used, but eventually the name Disciples prevailed, though both names have always been used in identifying both the church and the members.

5. From the very first Sunday at Brush Run the Disciples served the Supper every first day, influenced as they were by Scottish reformers. The Christians observed it on an irregular basis up to the time of the union.

6. The Christians had a broader view of the ministry of the Holy Spirit, both in the conversion of the sinner and in the life of the believer, while the Disciples were inclined to relate the Spirit's influence to the scriptures and the preaching of the Word.

7. While both were unity conscious, the idea of uniting all men in Christ was more predominant with the Christians, while the Disciples were more concerned for a restoration of the ancient order. This difference caused Richardson to think of the Stone people as preachers and the Campbell folk as teachers.[54]

Several of these characteristic differences have a direct bearing on the relationship of theology to aesthetics. Implicit in them is the Disciples' heavy reliance on the process of logic and the short shrift accorded to the importance of feelings. The varying approaches to the evangelistic process, the place of the Lord's Supper, understanding the work of the Holy Spirit, and the preoccupation of the Stone Christians with oneness in Christ affected the future of the movement in both cultural and aes-

---

[54]Garrett, *Stone-Campbell Movement*, 282-83.

thetic ways as well as in the potential for Christian unity. Some of those attitudes and their expressions in academic structures, public worship, and personal values will be explored more fully in the next three chapters.

148

Plate 8
DR. ROBERT RICHARDSON
Courtesy Disciples of Christ Historical Society

7

Education, Culture, and Restoration

The Stone-Campbell Movement enjoyed its first numerical successes in the rural areas of Kentucky in the wake of revivalist sentiment following the Second Great Awakening, and through the simple gospel presentations of Walter Scott in the Western Reserve of Ohio. In light of the frontier, and sometimes the backwoods locations of many early Christian and Disciples churches, the emphasis placed upon liberal education by the first-generation leaders is enigmatic. The remarkable ability of leaders like Walter Scott, "Raccoon" John Smith, and especially Alexander Campbell to live with a foot in each of two very different worlds gave the Movement its characteristic appeal to folks of varied cultures.

Chapter 4 refers to the contrast between the "vernacular" tradition of the pioneering and rural peoples of the West, and the "cultured" tradition of social life and the arts which was pursued by a growing nucleus of people in the eastern cities during the early nineteenth century. Winfred Garrison's term, "pioneer in broadcloth," catches the essence of Alexander Campbell's versatility in moving with grace between the two worlds. Describing the contrasts between the frontier and the academic-cultured circles in which Campbell labored, Garrison writes:

> This was the kind of diversified and changing environment in which our hero lived and did his work. He could do it as successfully as he did because he himself had the two kinds of contrasting qualities. This was the reason he could make such an impact on the society of his time. He could speak to the condition of all its levels because he had all these levels within his own personality.[1]

Eva Jane Wrather, biographer of Alexander Campbell and student of Disciples history, suggests that her subject, like Jefferson and Franklin, embodied the Renaissance concept of the "whole man." Campbell

> . . . was the true 'citizen of the world'—equally at home in a frontier log cabin or a mansion on Tidewater Virginia; equally at

---

[1]Winfred Garrison "Pioneer in Broadcloth" in Perry E. Gresham, ed., *The Sage of Bethany, Pioneer in Broadcloth* (St. Louis: Bethany Press, 1960), 53.

ease with an awkward college freshman or a lady-in-waiting at the court of Queen Victoria.[2]

Ronald E. Osborne presents a picture of the four primary leaders of the Restoration Movement—Thomas and Alexander Campbell, Barton W. Stone, and Walter Scott:

> Educationally, these men secured for themselves what was available to the determined student, but none of them had the advantage of postgraduate studies, none possessed a doctorate, none had the opportunity for sustained intellectual work offered by a university professorship. Yet three of them studied in Scottish universities and the other in one of the better frontier colleges. All of them labored as preachers, teachers, editors, and authors. And Alexander Campbell possessed a mind of magnitude and power which commanded the respect of the leading citizens of his time.[3]

Alexander Campbell's experience operating the Buffalo Seminary is discussed in chapter 6. His evolving philosophy of education was emphasized during the first years of the *Millennial Harbinger's* publication. In fact, the "prospectus" of the first issue included questions about education among its primary concerns. Campbell noted 'the inadequacy of all the present systems of education, literary and moral, to develope [*sic*] the powers of the human mind, and to prepare man for rational and social happiness.'[4]

The context for the emergence of the Disciples' approach to education must be considered against the experiences of Thomas and Alexander Campbell and Walter Scott in European private education, and the contrasting struggles in the United States for the development of a universal system of public education. Horace Mann was born only eight years later than Alexander Campbell, and the period of his battle for standards in the Massachusetts State Board of Education was occurring at the same time that Campbell's essays in the *Harbinger* were pointing to the establishment of Bethany College, and Walter Scott was serving his one year as president of the first collegiate institution associated with the Restoration Movement. Just before the American Civil War, Mann served

---

[2]Eva Jane Wrather, "Alexander Campbell and the Judgment of History" in Gresham, ed. *Sage of Bethany*, 166.

[3]Ronald E. Osborne, "Theology Among the Disciples" in Beazley, ed., *The Christian Church*, 83.

[4]*Millennial Harbinger* (1830) 1:1.

six years as president of a college in a neighboring state to Campbell's Bethany, and, ironically, was able to demonstrate the co-educational situation Campbell had talked about but had been unable to realize in fact.[5]

Some of Campbell's *Harbinger* essays during the 1830s related to issues which continued to claim his attention many years, such as the Lockean denial of innate ideas in newborn children, the superiority of practice over theory, and the awesome importance of Christian education in the family. Using one of his heroes of science as a beginning point, he opened an article of April 1835:

> Newton entered life without a single idea: so have all the men of all ages of time. Man has capacity or susceptibility from the hand of his Creator; no more. He is, therefore, passive before he can be active. He receives impressions before he makes them. That something we call *mind,* acts not till acted upon through the medium of sense. The animal frame, the five senses, like the five mechanical powers, are but the machinery through which and by which the mind acts, and is acted upon. The material universe enters the soul, or acts upon the mind only by the medium of sense; and no other universe can enter the soul but through the material universe. So that the Great Spirit operates upon the human mind through the material universe.[6]

This essay illustrates a second area where John Locke's epistemology served the Disciples fathers well. The first was in Locke's differentiation between *faith* and *opinion,* a familiar pair of terms in Alexander Campbell's essays. One is reminded of young Campbell's study of Locke under his father's tutelage. In "No Innate Principles in the Mind," Alexander would have read:

> It is an established opinion amongst some men that there are in the *understanding* certain innate principles, some primary notions . . . , characters, as it were, stamped upon the mind of man, which the soul receives in its very first being and brings into the world with it. It would be sufficient to convince unprejudiced readers of the falseness of this supposition, if I should only show (as I hope I shall in the following parts of this discourse) how men, barely by the use of their natural faculties,

---

[5]For an interesting discussion of the parallels seen in the Disciples' movement for universal education and Horace Mann's efforts in Massachusetts, see Harold E. Fey, "The Christian Church (Disciples of Christ) and Higher Education" in Beazley, ed., *The Christian Church*, 218-19.

[6]*Millennial Harbinger* (1835) 6:152.

152 Theology & Aesthetics in Stone-Campbell Movement

may attain to all the knowledge they have, without the help of any innate impressions, and may arrive at certainty without any such original notions or principles.[7]

Campbell's application of the principle is the realization that "the moment of birth is the entrance into the school of nature—that God has, by the first impression of the attributes of things upon the new-born infant compelled it to begin to learn." [8] He acknowledged that Francis Bacon's *Novum Organum* was the modern discovery of the empirical method, and said, "Nature's school is a school of arts and sciences."[9]

In the next essay on education, which appeared one month later on page 225 of the May 1835 *Harbinger*, he championed the cause of women's education in a bold, modern mode:

> Mothers are of necessity and of right the first teachers. How important, then, that they themselves have been well educated. On them physically, intellectually, morally, chiefly depend the destinies of the whole race. On this account females deserve, demand, and are worthy to receive as good an education as the males. . . .

Campbell's logical demand for equal educational opportunity for women was not to be met in his own college until many years after its founding. Despite the strong arguments advanced in the 1835 *Harbinger,* it was left for Oberlin College and then Antioch College with its president, Horace Mann, to provide a much earlier higher education opportunity for females in the United States in 1852.

An interesting aspect of Campbell's beliefs about education—especially in light of the charter curriculum of Bethany College in the early 1840s—relates to his preference for modern humanities studies over classical learning. Campbell agreed with Thomas Smith Grimke of South Carolina, who loudly denounced Classical Greek and Roman studies and demanded more emphasis on current affairs.[10] Campbell preferred modern literature to the classics, which related to his almost Dewey-like preference for the instrumental value of learning over the possible intrinsic value of knowledge.

A "new series" of articles on education was begun in August 1832, which introduced the two interrelated questions into a general discussion of reform in education:

---

[7]John Locke, *An Essay Concerning Human Understanding*, ed. John W. Yolton (New York: Dutton, 1978), 9.

[8]*Millennial Harbinger* (1835) 6:153.

[9]Ibid.

[10]See Perry E. Gresham, "Alexander Campbell, Schoolmaster" in Gresham, ed., *Sage of Bethany*, 18.

But the systems of education call for a reformation as radical and extensive as the popular systems of government and religion. In most of our common schools years are squandered in learning little else than an irrational way of 'reading, writing, and ciphering,' with some of the technicalities of grammar and geography. A mere smattering in words, without the knowledge of anything in nature, society, or religion, is the reward of the literary toils of our children in our common schools during the time allotted to their education.[11]

Relating the needed reform to collegiate education, the *Harbinger* editor suggested that since teachers are educated in colleges, higher education must be the first target for American educational reform. This provided the platform for a critique of the traditional college curriculum:

The first error in magnitude, because the most pernicious in its consequences, which many wise men have labored to reform, and which must be reformed before any very beneficial change can be introduced, is the value placed upon the science and learning of Greece and Rome. Since the revival of literature in the kingdoms once composing the Western Roman Empire, ever since the year of Grace 1500, classic literature and classic antiquity, the natural, political, moral, and social philosophy of Greece and Rome, which never at any time exerted a salutary influence upon those communities, have so bewitched and infatuated the literati of the West, that all our literary institutions have been as enslaved to the idolatry of Grecian and Roman models as were the Catholic laity to the See of Rome in the long dark night of papistical supremacy.[12]

The rationale for allowing modern learning to supersede the classics was not based, in Campbell's argument, entirely upon his post-Renaissance favorites such as Newton and Bacon. The utility of learning should be the basis of judgment for the comparative worth of the disciplines offered students. That worth clearly depends not upon eloquence of style, design, or grandeur of concept, but Plato-like, the writer sought the public good and moral philosophy—political science and ethical values—as the norm by which a curriculum should be judged:

Even those who have acquired a taste for those productions, who admire them as prodigies of "intellectual power and literary

---

[11]*Millennial Harbinger* (1832) 3:408-9.
[12]Ibid.

excellence," and prize them as the only perfect models of good taste, wit, and eloquence, indispensable to a good and elegant education, are at a loss to show any solid and lasting good conferred by them upon their contemporaries or upon posterity. In all their efforts to institute a system of moral philosophy they failed, and failing here they left behind them no monument of public good achieved for the great family of man.[13]

Campbell was even more specific about the negative values engendered by classical literature in an essay entitled, "Christian Scheme of Education" published in the August 1834 *Harbinger.*

In the 1835 journal, another series of "Essays on Education" developed further a criticism of the strong hold of Aristotelianism on medieval scholasticism, together with an appreciation for the developing light of learning after Copernicus, Galileo, Kepler, Luther, and especially Bacon. The *Millennial Harbinger* essays and various printed addresses for the Western Literary Institute and College of Professional Teachers at Cincinnati, the female institute at Steubenville, Ohio, and for numerous other academic situations demonstrate a remarkable breadth of interest, study, and a reflection of Campbell's dualism. That dualism allowed for an appreciation of both the written Word of God in the Bible and God's revelation in nature. To the College of Teachers he spoke at length about problems in epistemology and psychology, and complained about the perennial difficulties in attaining empirical, objective measurement of matters of the mind. He expressed some hope that such an empirical approach might be attained through the momentarily popular "science" of phrenology.[14] But the most significant aspect of his philosophy of education—the chief concern of all earthly objects, as he described it in 1838[15]—was his comprehensive plan for a total educational system which he first introduced in a series of essays during 1839. The four "schools" that he believed were essential to the development of man were, in his plan, the family, the elementary school, the college, and the church.[16] That which secured all the components of his educational philosophy was a concern for moral education, a theme which became the repeated ritornello of his academic structure.

The first successful effort by leaders of the Stone-Campbell Movement to create an institution of higher education was not Campbell's doing, despite his editorial labors toward developing a philosophy of

---

[13]Ibid., 410.

[14]*Millennial Harbinger* (1836) Extra: 579-604.

[15]*Millennial Harbinger* (1838) 2:92.

[16]*Millennial Harbinger* (1839) 5:234.

education. Instead, Bacon College was established by a splinter group from Georgetown College in Kentucky when a Restoration-oriented professor of mathematics and civil engineering was excluded from the Baptist institution. The new college was organized at Georgetown, Kentucky, November 10, 1836. Classes began on November 14, and a charter was secured from the Kentucky legislature on February 23, 1837. The school's name was carefully chosen as a tribute to the scientific method of Sir Francis Bacon.[17]

Walter Scott was called to be the first president of the new Christian college. With a degree from the University of Edinburgh and years of experience in conducting academies, Scott had more formal preparation and experience for academic leadership than the founding presidents of many other American frontier colleges. He had also served as a trustee of Miami University in Oxford, Ohio, having been appointed to that position by the Ohio state legislature in 1834. Though he consented to accept the presidency only on a temporary basis, he was active in recruiting students, at which he seems to have been quite successful, and in raising money. He was also involved in the teaching program of the college, with direct classroom responsibility for "moral and mental sciences, belles lettres, etc."[18]

Scott's inaugural address, which was probably delivered in February 1837, outlined four fundamental areas of the curriculum. Like Campbell's plan for a complete educational system from childhood through adulthood, Scott's curriculum was proposed for elementary, secondary, and college level studies. The four primary curricular areas reflect Scott's strong dependence upon Bacon's inductive method, his own experience as a flautist and music student in Scotland, his hearty interest in an academic system to be designed for his dynamic adopted country, and ultimately his highest religious values. The four areas outlined in Scott's address, as listed by his biographer, are (1) Nature (2) Art (useful, ornamental, and fine arts), (3) Society, and (4) Religion.[19]

Alexander Campbell's interest in the Bacon College project reflected, at best, mixed emotions. Printed in the May 1836 *Millennial Harbinger* was an open letter from two Jacksonville, Illinois proponents of the project to the "brethren of the Reformation." The letter proposed a meeting to be held six months after the March date of the letter to discuss the possibility of establishing a Christian college. The letter noted that the Catholics, Baptists, Presbyterians, Methodists, and others

[17]Dwight E. Stevenson, *The Voice of the Golden Oracle* (Joplin, Mo.: College Press, n.d.), 164.

[18]Ibid.

[19]Ibid.

had established colleges and asked "shall there not be a Christian college?"[20]

Editor Campbell appended his remarks to the announcement and included a summary of his educational philosophy. His first point was a Lockean concept that children born into the world bring "nothing but capacities—no ideas or knowledge of any sort whatever; and are, therefore, to be educated." Another item repeats his often-stated complaint that classic mythology had displaced modern science and sacred literature. His characteristic concern about the evils of schools of theology occupied one entire rubric. After providing a list of items about which "our brethren have already attained," Campbell specifically expressed his belief that a thorough knowledge of God's work in the history of the world, together with study of geography, chronology, and Ancient languages, would equip a person to correctly interpret "all the manners, customs, and remote allusions found in the two Testaments."[21] Alexander Campbell was unequivocal in his support of the study of the sciences and the social sciences. A strong statement of God's action in history, and the characteristic support by Restoration groups for liberal education reflect a consistent acceptance of these principles by most strains of the Disciples heritage.

Having articulated his belief in liberal arts education, however, Campbell dragged his feet as graciously as he could in endorsing the proposed early meeting for the purpose of designing what would become Bacon College. His expressed concern was whether any colleges related to the reform movement would maintain high quality in both academic and religious dimensions. It is possible that the *Harbinger* editor anticipated a problem which has been a peculiarly American dilemma—not only in the Stone-Campbell tradition, but with most religious groups: the enormous challenge of maintaining Christian institutions of higher education which support free inquiry and high quality studies in the arts and sciences on the one hand, and the unabashed maintenance of Christian values, instruction, and campus morality on the other.

McAllister and Tucker suggest that Campbell's apparent coolness toward the planning meeting may have been related to his own hopes for inaugurating a Christian college:

> From Bethany, Alexander Campbell kept a watchful eye on the developments in higher education in Kentucky. The opening of Bacon College was duly announced in The Millennial Harbinger but Campbell was not altogether pleased. He had given much

[20]See *Millennial Harbinger* (1836) 5:199.
[21]Ibid., 201-2.

thought to developing a college himself and had lectured extensively on the subject of education.[22]

Campbell's concerns about an appropriate Christian college are expressed in several questions at the end of his "Remarks" in the May 1836 *Harbinger*:

> Can we have literary institutions, or one or more colleges that could separate the chaff from the wheat of true science; and that could make all true learning and sound philosophy subservient to the gospel—to true religion and sound morality, without any partialities, affections, or antipathies as respects any particular sect, party, or interest—a purely LITERARY and MORAL institution?[23]

The practical suggestion Campbell provided was to recommend that more time be given to consider the larger questions he had posed so that the matter could be more "calmly and dispassionately, and profoundly considered:"

> . . . I fear . . . that the time mentioned in the preceding letter is too immediate for the intelligent action of the great community to which the matter is submitted. Two or three months, however, may be added without any real detriment; and it is much better to have the matter well examined before any expression of our views be required.[24]

In any case, the new school opened in November 1836 with more than 130 students. Walter Scott resigned the presidency after the first year, as he had planned to do, and was succeeded by D. S. Burnett. Scott's tenure as president provided him opportunity to appear on the 1837 fall program at the College of Teachers in Cincinnati. There he associated with William Holmes McGuffy, who was born near Bethany and who was the editor of *McGuffy's Eclectic Readers*. He was also in the company of Joseph Ray, whose arithmetic textbooks were standard fare in many American schools for half a century.[25]

---

[22]McAllister and Tucker, *Journey in Faith*, 163.
[23]*Millennial Harbinger* (1836) 5:202.
[24]Ibid.
[25]Stevenson, *Voice of the Golden Oracle*, 165.

Bacon College was formally endorsed by the editor of the *Millennial Harbinger* in December 1837, after it had enrolled 203 students. Eight faculty members were listed in his article, along with seventeen members of the board of trustees. Academic areas included civil engineering and drawing, a field which was popular in the West due to the demand for surveyors on the expanding frontiers. Campbell finally spoke quite generously for the school in his commendation:

> Its learned and talented faculty, its freedom from sectarian influence, and its plan of adopting its course of instruction to the genius of the age, have given it even at this early day a very high standing with the community.[26]

Campbell acknowledged that he had been "backward" by not endorsing the school earlier, but explained that before he could do so he had to ascertain the views and designs, prospects, means, etc., but most of all the discipline and moral culture which would prevail at Bacon College. His academic credo—the one which was evident later in the founding of his own Bethany College—is given in the following words:

> I give my vote for learning and science and for high attainments in all branches of useful knowledge, but I would not give *morality* for them all; and therefore I have resolved never to speak in favor of any literary institution, from a common school to a University, however superior their literary eminence, that does not first of all, and above all, exercise a sovereign and supreme guardianship over the morals of its students and wards, and endeavor to make *good* rather than *great* men. Colleges without this are no blessing to any country. So I think.[27]

Bacon College moved to Harrodsburg, Kentucky in 1839, was discontinued in 1850, was restored as Kentucky University in 1858, moved to Lexington in 1865, where as heir to the property of Transylvania University, it presently stands as Transylvania College.[28]

By 1839, it seems Alexander Campbell was satisfied that Bacon College was solidly established and that the growing fellowship of the combined Stone-Campbell Movement could support both Bacon and the comprehensive educational institution he had envisioned for a long time. In the October 1837 *Harbinger* the long-awaited announcement of "A New Institution" appeared, subtitled "Plan of a Literary, Moral, and

[26]*Millennial Harbinger* (1837) 1:571.

[27]Ibid.

[28]This chronology was obtained from Stevenson, *Voice of the Golden Oracle*, 165.

Religious School; or the Union of Four Institutions in One—The Combination of the Family, the Primary School, the College, and the Church in One Great System of Education." The opening lines of the announcement reveal the high place the scheme occupied in Campbell's value system:

> I am about to divulge to this community, to philanthropists, to lovers of good order, to the Disciples of Christ a favorite scheme deeply impressed upon my mind; long cherished, and in the establishment and supervision of it, it is probable, *if the Lord will,* I shall close my earthly projects.[29]

The curriculum of the new school was somewhat short in the matter of the arts; but Campbell's concept of the proper setting for his new school included an emphasis upon a pastoral location, not only to escape urban sin and distraction, but for the aesthetic qualities such a setting could provide a complete learning experience:

> In the first place, the location must be rural—in the country, detached from all external society; not convenient to any town or place of rendezvous—in the midst of forests, fields, and gardens—salubrious air, pure water—diversified scenery of hills and valleys, limpid brooks, and meandering streams of rapid flowing water. Such is the spot which I have selected.[30]

Numerous notices in the 1840 *Millennial Harbinger* updated the planning activities for the opening of Campbell's hoped-for inclusive educational institution. A series of four essays on the "New Institution" provided the editor opportunity to speak more about the ideal location alluded to above. The comprehensive plan included training for young children, young college-age students, and even a normal school for the training of teachers. Campbell acknowledged the need of children for physical exercise, but criticized organized competitive sports which would have young people "romping over the turf in violent efforts for mastery in frivolous *pastimes* . . . which rather corrupt than improve both their morals and their taste." He prescribed rather "fishing, fowling, and hunting, when free from violent efforts or circumstances of danger . . . as well as swimming, riding, and walking." Agriculture was commended for the study and practice of students, because it, "next to religion and morality, and the art of reading and writing, ought to be taught in all its branches. . . ."[31]

---

[29]*Millennial Harbinger* (1837) 3:132.
[30]Ibid.
[31]*Millennial Harbinger* (1841) 3:132.

Campbell's credo that moral education is the cornerstone of all excellent education was reinforced in his third essay with a quotation from a writer named De Fellenburg. Campbell underlines the piece with this summary:

> An immoral man is uneducated. The blasphemer, the profane swearers, the liar, the calumniator, the duellist, the braggadocia, the peculator, etc. etc. are vulgar, barbarous, and uneducated persons.[32]

The fourth essay in the series, which appeared in the May *Harbinger,* emphasized the great need of both Church and State for the type of institution described, outlined some of the physical needs of the projected school, and launched a fervent appeal for funding from those able to underwrite the plan:

> But buildings upon a large scale are necessary even to a commencement. Places are already engaged before we have dug the first spadeful of earth. We wish to lose no time unnecessarily in commencing and propose the present year to make the preparation for erecting the college proper, the Steward's Inn, and the great Family Mansion. We are then obliged to make our *first appeal* to the wealthy and philanthropic portion of the community, that those among them who may be desirous to promote the good of their contemporaries and posterity for generations to come, may have an opportunity of consecrating a portion of that abundance which God, the source of all wealth and prosperity, may have entrusted to their stewardship.[33]

The November 1841 *Harbinger* contains the "proceedings" of the first two meetings—held in May and September—of the Bethany College Board of Trustees. The roster of trustees appointed by the end of the second meeting seems remarkably cosmopolitan for the era, including men from six or seven states. Thomas Campbell was elected Chairman of the Board, Alexander Campbell was elected President of the College, and Robert Richardson served as a regular member of the Board. This situation later proved to be a problem for Dr. Richardson, since he was also on the first faculty member of the new college.

---

[32] *Millennial Harbinger* (1841) 4:158. A peculator is one who steals or misappropriates money or property entrusted to one's care; an embezzler.

[33] *Millennial Harbinger* (1841) 5:220.

By this time Alexander Campbell was concerned about the slow response to his early appeal for funds. Not only did he provide the land for the school from his farm, but he also undertook building the Steward's Inn at his own expense. His worries are clearly reflected in his November report on the progress of support for a new school:

> Unless our friends are very prompt in rendering assistance, these two buildings cannot possibly be raised next season, and we cannot go into operation so soon. . . . If the Lord opens the hearts of his people, to be as liberal as he is kind to them, we will succeed: otherwise, this useful enterprise will flag. But this is what I cannot yet begin to think.[34]

Frequent references to the college during 1841 emphasize a discovery which was gradually being made by Alexander Campbell: that his pleas to the young brotherhood for support for his comprehensive educational structure were not productive. His articles reflect difficulty in securing sufficient financial support for the establishment and operation of the excellent institution he had conceived. The Disciples were conceptually very interested in liberal arts education—a trait which has remained constant throughout their history.[35] Campbell reflected this interest when he wrote, "popular education is dependent on liberal education, as lakes and rivers are dependent on oceans and seas for their periodical and full supplies."[36]

On the other hand, organizing and retaining sufficient support for education has, unfortunately, also characterized Disciples history. During Campbell's time, the Disciples demonstrated little understanding of what it took, both academically and financially, to erect and maintain an educational institution.[37]

In his June 1841 *Harbinger* report on the second annual meeting of the Board, held in May, Campbell complained:

> We sometimes wonder at the tardiness and hesitancy with which many persons approach to aid such an undertaking as this; persons, too, on whom God has bestowed ample means of building up such an institution without real sacrifice. . . .

---

[34] *Millennial Harbinger* (1841) 10:510.

[35] It is interesting that the Christian churches (Disciples of Christ) and the non-instrumental Churches of Christ have retained their early Restoration Movement emphasis on the liberal arts Christian college. The Christian churches-Churches of Christ, perhaps in reaction to Disciples liberalism, and in the model of J. W. McGarvey at the College of the Bible, have deviated from the historic Campbellite concept by preferring Bible colleges.

[36] *Millennial Harbinger* (1841) 6:272.

[37] See McAllister and Tucker, *Journey in Faith*, 165, where this fact is also noted.

Simpleton that I was, I expected some hundred or two sons of consolation, real philanthropists, to step forward and subscribe each his 1000 dollars, and say, 'Go on with this great system of human improvement; and if this is not enough, call on us again.'[38]

Then, in somewhat uncharacteristic desperation, he wrote, "We must have help."[39]

Later in the year the new college president solicited donations of books for the library, furniture, scientific apparatus and furniture, as well as cash. In the same issue a correspondent, Daniel Orange, commended Campbell for his excellent plans for the college at Bethany, and commiserated with him his fund-raising dilemma. Orange pointed out, however, that "from the situation of money matters in this country at this time," he felt it would not be possible to raise the needed funds." Orange wondered, in his letter, why the Bethany board failed to go to England where their money-raising efforts might have been more successful![40]

Disappointed or not, Campbell and his board pushed ahead from their appointment in 1840 until the projected opening of the college in November 1841. Campbell contributed ten thousand dollars of his own money, built a boarding house called the Steward's Inn, and worked tirelessly to raise funds and recruit students. A charter was given by the Virginia Legislature in 1840, and a basic faculty was announced in the August 1841, *Harbinger*. Five professors were named with their teaching disciplines, and with the promise that a professor of English literature would be named before the academic term began in November.

The list of disciplines to be included in the college curriculum provides a strong commentary on the academic values held by the leaders, and especially by President Campbell. The list also reflects the basic curricular design of the institutions Campbell considered to be worthy models. Those models included the "eastern college of Virginia," Thomas Jefferson's admired university at Charlottesville. Some interesting comparisons may also be made with Campbell's own one-year experience at the University of Glasgow. His American experience and the changing times contributed to a heavier emphasis upon Baconian empirical science at Bethany, more emphasis upon the useful and pragmatic,

---

[38]*Millennial Harbinger* (1841) 6:272, 273.
[39]Ibid., 6:273.
[40]*Millennial Harbinger* (1841) 7:330, 332.

and his belief in moral and religious education clearly provided the core of the curricular structure.[41]

Professors and their disciplines announced in the *Harbinger* were: Mr. A. F. Ross, late Professor of New Athens College, Ohio, Professor of Ancient Languages and Ancient History; Mr. Charles Stuart, of Kentucky, Professor of Algebra and General Mathematics; Dr. R. Richardson, Professor of Chemistry, Geology, and the kindred sciences; and Mr. W. K. Pendleton, of the University of Virginia, Professor of Natural Philosophy and such of the Natural Sciences as come not in the course of Dr. R. Richardson. The announcement was also made that "besides a general superintendency of the Institution, to the President will be assigned Mental Philosophy, Evidences of Christianity, Morals and Political Economy."[42] Mr. W. W. Eaton, of St. John's, New Brunswick, was appointed to the sixth chair in English literature during the special October meeting of the board.[43]

Two months before the official opening of Bethany College, Alexander Campbell provided an address to be read for an education convention at Clarksburg, Virginia. The written speech provides several significant keys to the author's thoughts about the subject. He had been invited to address the convention, but the press of his schedule at the time prevented him from being present in person. Not only does the address outline his beliefs concerning the purposes of education, but it highlights some of the regional resentment held by Virginians in the West against the superior cultural, educational, and financial resources controlled by the Eastern Establishment. Campbell had served in a convention during the year 1829 to rewrite the state constitution of Virginia, a situation in which he had hoped to help end slavery in Virginia. He was active in the proceedings, but experienced for the first time the power of the wealthy landowners of the eastern part of the state and doubtless witnessed the contrast in the interests of West and East that

---

[41]Harold E. Fey, "The Christian Church (Disciples of Christ) and Higher Education" in Beazley, ed., *The Christian Church*, 218, reminds his readers that the early aims of the founders of Harvard were not greatly different from the motivations of the Bethany College planners: "Puritans launched Harvard, America's first college, in 1636. It was patterned after Emmanuel College of Cambridge University and had as its mottoes 'Christo et Ecclesiae' and 'In Christi Gloriam.' Its famous statement of purpose reflects the religious aims of Harvard, which were shared by each of the early American schools. . . . The courses of study were cast in the Ancient mold of liberal education, so they served to form leaders in other fields as well as in the ministry. All programs were religious in tone and classical in orientation. They emphasized religion but also Greek and Latin languages and literature, philosophy, mathematics and science.

[42]*Millennial Harbinger* (1841) 6:377-78.

[43]*Millennial Harbinger* (1842) 1:34.

finally resulted in the establishment of West Virginia as a separate state in 1863.[44]

The old regional competition was, therefore, still a factor in Campbell's ambitions for his new school. Remembering his disappointment in the convention twelve years earlier, he lamented:

> Judge, fellow citizens, of my disappointment and mortification to see a resolution, as I supposed every way honorable to the Old Dominion, replete with blessings to the state, nailed to the table by a mere parliamentary maneuver—by those, too, who had not courage to vote against it, or formally to oppose it.[45]

With that point of reference, Campbell placed in perspective the education question:

> There are many of us in the West who will be satisfied with nothing short of a wise and just provision for all. We will not allow that it is either just or honorable that Eastern Virginia should have all the University and College powers, and that West Virginia should have only Common Schools. Shall we of the West be satisfied that the Legislature of Virginia shall bestow $450,000 on one Eastern University, and put us off with an annual pittance for common schools! Let it only do half as much for two or three Western Colleges as it has done for an Eastern one, and then we of the West will begin to think that we are not regarded as step-children.[46]

The Bethany College founders attempted to closely approximate the programs of the University of Virginia, from curriculum to auxiliary enterprises, which reflects not only Campbell's admiration for Thomas Jefferson and his academic design, but the East-West competition in the large state of Virginia. The attempt to match even non-academic quality is illustrated in a note from the board minutes of May 1841, when, on motion of Dr. Robert Richardson, it was "unanimously resolved, that the Bill of Fare for the Steward's Inn shall be the same as that of the University of Virginia."[47]

The opening of Bethany College took place on November 2, 1841. Approximately one hundred students were enrolled for the first term, and Campbell was able to report that 128 were entered in the spring term, less seven who had been dismissed for various academic and per-

---

[44]See McAllister and Tucker, *Journey in Faith*, 129.

[45]"An Address" in *Millennial Harbinger* (1841) 10:451.

[46]Ibid., 449.

[47]*Millennial Harbinger* (1841) 6:270.

sonal reasons. The opening day was dominated by a series of extended addresses by faculty members on subjects related to their respective academic disciplines. From those addresses, and from the curricular areas listed above, it is clear that Alexander Campbell already was experiencing some of the frustrations of academic administration. The college's curricular patterns and faculty convictions overruled some of his personal philosophical ideas. Even though he had supported T. S. Grimke's attack against devotion to the Greek and Roman classics, he now found himself to be the leader of an institution where those classics constituted the humanities core of a liberal education.

A. F. Ross, Professor of Languages and Ancient History, delivered an address to the assembled students and faculty which seems to have been a defense of his discipline from the very criticism his new college president had earlier articulated:

> . . . notwithstanding the dictates of all experience, there are those who object to the study of the ancient classics, and it becomes him who would be their advocate to illustrate their importance and utility.[48]

The word "utility" in the title of Ross's lecture is a key to the Bethany curricular concept as conceived by Campbell, and Ross doubtless felt called upon to demonstrate that his discipline had pragmatic uses in order to justify its prominent place in the curriculum. A statement on page 12 of the 1843-1844 *Catalog of Bethany College* specifies this Campbellite—and to a great extent the Disciples—aspect of college learning:

> In order to insure to the students of this institution that general and practical knowledge which may fit them for the duties of life, popular lectures are delivered to the whole class upon such subjects or are intimately connected with the happiness and well-being of individuals and of society.

It was against this framework of philosophical logic, a theology that "speaks where the Bible speaks and is silent where the Bible is silent," and an American pragmatism which measured all learning on a scale of utility rather than for its intrinsic or terminal worth, that A. F. Ross had to justify his Department of Classics. It also formed the environment for future instruction in the arts, poetry, and fiction.

---

[48]A. F. Ross, "The Importance and Utility of the Study of the Ancient Classics," *Introductory Addresses Delivered at the Organization of Bethany College* (Bethany, Va.: A. Campbell, 1841), 4.

Walter Scott had also contended for practical knowledge in the Baconian sense, even to the adoption of Francis Bacon's name for the Kentucky college. Scott had also enjoyed the experience of high quality musical performance as a flautist and was a talented singer.[49] Not surprisingly, the Bacon curricular proposal contained the fine arts in the same general category with the "useful arts" of agriculture, mechanics, manufacturing, trade, engineering, and building. The "ornamental" and fine arts at Bacon College were to include writing, drawing, etching, music, painting, sculpture, engraving, and architecture.[50]

Although Alexander Campbell's addresses on the subject of education frequently included references to the "ornamental arts," such references were usually made at the level of the elementary school. In his September 1841 written address to the convention at Clarksburg, he had listed seven essential arts in education: thinking, speaking, reading, singing, writing, calculating, and bookkeeping. Later in the address, music was listed as an important science to be taught—as Aristotle might have agreed, not to a "correct" or professional level—but important in the hierarchy of elementary studies. Hymn singing was practiced at Bethany College, but there is no reference to the formal study of music or any of the other fine and lively arts.

A. F. Ross undertook the practical defense of classical language study by listing in some detail the benefits he felt such studies provided for intellectual growth. These included development of memory, the faculty of associating ideas, practice in precision, and the permanence of language meanings. For Ross, exercise in stretching memory was to be found in vocabulary learning, grammar, and judgment in sentence structure.[51]

Ross then turned to the argument of "the *associating faculty*," the "faculty by which we recognize relations, the operation of which has been termed comparing. . . . " In this psychological concept Ross showed his own dependence upon the Scottish "Associationist" philosophers, especially the ever-useful John Locke and his *Essay on Human Understanding,* together with Hume, Reid, and the Common Sense School. In the study of ancient languages, Ross contended that "a simultaneous and vigorous exercise of all the most important faculties of the human mind is continually required. . . ." He argued that "precision" was also to be gained from the study of Latin and Greek. With the Bethany

[49]Stevenson, *Voice of the Golden Oracle,* 20.

[50]Ibid., 166.

[51] Ross, in introducing this category, anticipated Campbell's later address, delivered at the Union Literary Society of Washington College. See Alexander Campbell, "The Philosophy of Memory and of Commemorative Institutions," *Millennial Harbinger* (1841) 12:558-76.

emphasis upon the natural sciences and empirical knowledge, and with Campbell's great capacity for detail exemplified in his debates, this argument must have been appreciated by the faculty. The very "permanence of meaning" which is characteristic of only a "dead language" was, in Mr. Ross's argument, a valuable tool for the development of scientific language, and certainly important for the trustworthy and unchanging message of the New Testament scriptures.[52]

Ross thus established the practicality of the mental set which might be undergirded by study of ancient languages. He then boldly turned to the point of controversy, the moral content of the classics. Doubtless conscious of the earlier pronouncements of President Campbell, he argued, concerning the "influence on the moral faculty" of classical literature:

> We are aware that this head had been a favorite topic of declamation with the opponents of classical literature. Their influence has been represented as demoralizing, and their principles as altogether unfit to be imbibed by the youth of a Christian community.[53]

Ross argued that the classics illustrate human virtue in concrete terms in a much more convincing manner than modern literature can or most moralists do, Ross began his arguments with "*First*. The classics illustrate the universality of moral distinctions and the supremacy of conscience." He acknowledged the inferior religious understanding of the Ancient Greek and Roman authors, and added, "Granting that in the classics some passages are obscene—granting some are immoral. . . still we must contend that in the sentiments of the classics there is a vast preponderance in favor of virtue."[54] Ross continued:

> Though immersed in the darkness of a grovelling and absurd superstition—though worshipping abominable gods, still that immortal principle which God has implanted in the human mind ever recognized the eternal distinctions of right and wrong.[55]

---

[52]Ross, "Importance and Utility of Ancient Classics," 4-11.

[53]Ibid., 14.

[54]Ibid., 16. Ross here anticipated a later discussion between Campbell, Dr. Robert Richardson, and Tolbert Fanning of the Tennessee Disciples which almost precipitated a religious division over the question of "natural theology."

[55]Ibid. See Garrett, *Stone-Campbell Movement*, 316-20 for a discussion of differing understandings of Rom. 1:19-20 and the term "natural theology" during the developmental phase of Disciples theology in the nineteenth century.

In his *second place,* Ross contended that study of the classics "strengthens the discriminating power of the moral faculty by exercise." He became eloquent in developing this idea:

> Literature is never better employed than in bearing testimony to exalted deeds out of the history of the species, and in thus giving an eternity of fame to sublime manifestations of virtue.[56]

Grasping at least a token from the aesthetic aspect of ancient literature, Ross said that characters from the classics

> have come down to us recorded in history and in song, adorned with the most exalted virtues of the species, and with their frailties and imperfections worn off by the attrition of ages. Virtue thus embalmed in the works of genius, and associated with all the splendors of poetry and fiction, receives, if possible, a more divine beauty and loveliness from this connection with the productions of the gifted spirits of our race, and is thus attended by every circumstance which can give it a lodgment in the human heart.[57]

That Ross had been able to exert major influence on the curriculum seems evident from a perusal of an early Bethany catalog. A two-year "scientific course" provided basic skills courses in English grammar and mathematics up to trigonometry. The introductory courses included physiology, zoology, botany, chemistry, and geology. The *raison d'etre* of the college, moral philosophy, was offered in a course during the second year, and like Bacon College, Bethany provided its students with a practical course in surveying. The four-year college course, however, reflected the heavier demands of classical learning typical of the great colleges of the period. True to the high regard for Locke and Bacon, the empirical sciences were well-represented, but the curriculum for the first three years contained about twenty courses in Greek and Roman subjects, an assignment which must have taxed greatly the one-man faculty in the area.

In his opening address, Dr. Robert Richardson, Professor of Chemistry, Geology, and the kindred sciences, attempted a liberal comprehensiveness in a Renaissance spirit. The doctor—who played the violin, wrote eloquent essays, and deeply embraced the Restoration Movement as represented by Alexander Campbell—displayed a spirit of sensitivity, irenic inclusiveness with his estranged brethren, and a comprehensive

---

[56]Ross, "Importance and Utility of Ancient Classics," 20.
[57]Ibid.

world view which must have given Bethany a large part of its liberal stance in academics.

He opened his address with a reference to the *Zeitgeist* of his age compared with that of earlier periods, and referred to the Genesis account of Jabal's agriculture, Jubal's music, and Tubal-Cain's engineering prowess. All of these areas he considered valid for contemporary study, and his discussion of the development of literature and science during the Renaissance linked the two in a symbiotic relationship. Like his colleagues, he took time to express appreciation for the work of Francis Bacon, whom he enthusiastically called "the Luther of science."[58]

W. K. Pendleton, Professor of Natural Philosophy, Astronomy, and Natural History, later became a co-editor with Campbell of the *Millennial Harbinger* and was twice Campbell's son-in-law. Ultimately, he succeeded his father-in-law as President of Bethany College. His University of Virginia background must have made him an attractive faculty member to the board of Bethany. His address defines "natural philosophy" as the discipline of physics, or "that science which teaches us the laws that govern every phenomena [*sic*] of Nature."[59]

In harmony with his colleagues, Pendleton credited Francis Bacon with the establishment of empirical science on a sound basis, although his organization of scientific phenomena tends to utilize a deductive logical framework. His taxonomy of the "natural order of things" suggests the chronological precedence of art before science, and the implicit inferiority of artistic thinking compared with science:

> There is indeed nothing, we may safely assert, now known and valued in the arts, that has not been discovered or applied and perfected by science. It is true, that in the natural order of things, the Arts must have preceded Science, because the natural wants and craving of man would prompt him, first to seek their gratification, by whatever means his own or the experience of others might suggest;—but his inventions and discoveries would stop with his necessities, and his knowledge be at best, but empirical.
>
> Such was the limit of Art, during the dark ages, and from this point, began the influence of Science, and its march has been and is still onward.[60]

---

[58]Robert Richardson, "General Introductory Discourse," *Introductory Addresses: Bethany College*, 36.

[59]W. K. Pendleton, "An Address," *Introductory Addresses: Bethany College*, 82.

[60]Ibid., 53.

Pendleton's developing role as a primary leader in the religious, journalistic, and academic aspects of the Restoration Movement was an indication that his attitude toward the arts was normative for his circle. It therefore becomes easy to understand why the early Bethany College catalog had little to offer in the way of creative literature, poetry, art, music, and the visual arts. On the other hand, Pendleton was able to encompass the motivation for studying the physical sciences within a teleology that undergirded the familiar theme of studying both the Creator and moral virtue.

The president's primary teaching discipline bore the nineteenth-century term, "Mental Philosophy." The subject of mental philosophy, as viewed by Campbell, shares the problem of subjectivity with modern psychology, although Campbell viewed the subject as a history of epistemology in a philosophical context. With the customary homage to Bacon, he proceeds to attack the formidable problems of applying empirical observation to the study of the human mind. By postulating that mind is active and matter passive, a rejection of Platonic pure form, Campbell reasoned to a First Cause of all things. This argument had been used in his debate with the socialist unbeliever Robert Owen in 1829.

In a significant part of his address, Campbell dealt with the perennial problem of the existence of evil and the justice of God. In rejecting philosophy as a source of knowledge for morality and justice, Campbell sustained the need of biblical truth for both. He acknowledges, however, that human logic can be useful in the areas of teaching and reasoning. The Scottish Common Sense School comes in for credit in the area of teaching.

Several aspects of the Bethany concept strike a modern critic as being remarkably progressive. Similar to the problem-solving instrumentalism that John Dewey would later develop, emphasis was laid upon the *process* of learning more than the ultimate content. Alexander Campbell wrote:

> With us education has primary regard to the formation of habits, more than to the acquisition of knowledge; more in teaching a person the use of himself than in teaching him to use the labors of others. We define education to be *the development and improvement of the physical, intellectual and moral powers of man, with a reference to his whole destiny in the Universe of God.*[61]

---

[61]Alexander Campbell, "Introductory Lecture," *Introductory Addresses: Bethany College*, 82.

The flexibility advertised by the college catalog described an arrangement later developed by the Montessori advocates and others during the late nineteenth century. A statement on page 11 of the 1843-1844 *Catalog of Bethany College* stated:

> The arrangements of the institution are such that students are not restricted to a fixed routine of classes requiring attendance at College a certain number of years, without regard to age or proficiency. On the contrary, the classes are arranged with a strict regard to the proficiency of each student, so that there are no barriers in the way of the most rapid progress, and those who are possessed of superior natural capacity, or greater maturity of mind, will not be delayed in their course by an arbitrary restriction to the progress of a particular class.

Another dimension of Campbell's great educational vision that was transmitted through academic life at Bethany College was the thrust for American teacher education. Campbell's motivations were clearly broader than merely providing intellectual fortification for the young church of the Restoration Movement. It included a burden for the improvement of the public educational program of his adopted country. The Bethany catalog statement quoted above included a section introducing a plan for a teachers' college:

> It is part of the plan of the Institution, to add to the Departments now organized, as soon as sufficient endowment can be obtained, a Normal School, or school for teachers, in which young men will be systematically and practically fitted for the business of teaching upon the most approved principles and by the most improved methods.

Although the normal school did not materialize in the form projected, Bethany produced many teachers for both its sister colleges and for public colleges and schools. Eventually, a Department of Education was added to the college and teacher education became a regular discipline along with the liberal arts. Numerous future college presidents and college founders were graduated from the Bethany program.[62]

---

[62]One of those graduates was Joseph Baldwin (1826-1899), class of 1852. After military service in the Civil War, Baldwin became the founding president of the North Missouri Normal School and Commercial College in 1867. That institution has now grown into Northeast Missouri State University (where this author is employed). In 1881, Baldwin became the president of the Sam Houston Normal Institute at Huntsville, Texas; in 1891 he began teaching at the University of Texas, Austin.

In spite of Campbell's difficulties in raising money for the school, the July 1842 issue of the *Harbinger* carried an optimistic report of the buildings planned or already available for the opening of the college in November:

> It is but two years since the first brick was molded for the erection of Bethany College. During this time a College Proper, four stories, 83 by 45; a Steward's Inn, equal to 107 feet by 36, 4 stories—have been completed; and one wing of a Mansion House, 73 feet by 24, two stories, will be completed about the 1st of September.[63]

Campbell spoke also of his hopes for fall, which included rooms for 150 to 160 students, and his joy was clear also in announcing the "incipient College Library and considerable Chemical and Philosophical Apparatus." A question about the college's admission policy was also on his mind. A serious problem had occurred during the first academic year when it was discovered that many students who had been recruited were not intellectually or morally mature enough to profit by the Bethany concept. Campbell announced that the college could accommodate "some forty or fifty students more than the present applicants" for the coming year.[64]

The admissions problem was discussed by Campbell in May 1843, in relation to one of his primary hopes: that young men interested in preaching could be educated at Bethany. The lack of such candidates was reminiscent of the earlier lack of young men who were interested in preaching at the Buffalo Seminary.

> I know not how to express my surprise that the churches seem to take so little interest in raising up well qualified young men to plead the cause of Bible Christianity. Does any one doubt the expediency of cultivating the best minds of those devoted to the greatest and best of all causes![65]

Campbell, admitting his disappointment, continued:

> I did, indeed, expect that the brethren would furnish us with abundant material, that when we, at the expense of much self-denial and oppressive toils, propose our services in this great work, we should not have so little of this kind of labor to perform.

[63]*Millennial Harbinger* (1842) 7:319.
[64]Ibid., 320.
[65]*Millennial Harbinger* (1843) 5:217.

Send us, brethren, a few scores or hundreds of noble spirits—or, allow us to select a few for you—and be liberal; and the Lord being with us, and blessing our labors, you will hear to all eternity the grateful songs of many ransomed sons and daughters saved by your Christian liberality.[66]

Further news reports of the college during the year suggest that there had been some discipline problems. In June, Campbell reported that two students had been expelled and nine dismissed only for the balance of the session. Campbell, in fact, promised:

Our days of experimenting close with the present session. On the arrival of a new student, besides his good testimonials, care will be taken soon to ascertain his character. . . .[67]

The process of moving toward "select admission" continued in the next session and has been subsequently a process of relative importance throughout the institution's history.[68]

Campbell endured the hardships and struggles of giving birth and nurture to a new academic institution. In August 1846, he was at last able to provide an upbeat report on the progress and prospects of his school:

We have just finished one of the most agreeable and prosperous sessions we have yet experienced in our infant institution. We report 128 students in our catalogue for the session just ended, and with all propriety we may say, that, in the present condition of society, we could hardly expect to see a more orderly, circumspect, and industrious class of young men assembled from fifteen States of this Union, than those who have composed the classes of Bethany College during the last year.[69]

The president expressed his belief that Bethany was unique among academic institutions in the attention given to religious and moral teaching with an absence of "sectarian bias, in its emphasis upon human physiology and on study of human anatomy."[70] The familiar question of why "Christian philanthropists" failed to rally fully for the school's support continued to worry him, as it has baffled other leaders of church-related colleges between Campbell's time and the present.

[66]Ibid., 219.

[67]*Millennial Harbinger* (1843) 6:279.

[68]*Millennial Harbinger* (1844) 10:472.

[69]*Millennial Harbinger* (1846) 443-44.

[70]Ibid., 444.

Comments on creative work in the arts by students of Bethany College were few during the first years of the school's life. A few poems, including one by a student on the occasion of a funeral service for a fellow student, reflect more of the vernacular tradition discussed in chapter 4 of this book than the level of verse which might have been created by students in a creative writing class. Musical experiences described by available references speak of hymn singing, but not of music in the "polite tradition" of America's eastern cities. Painting and sculpture do not figure in the curriculum, except as by-products of classical studies, and a selection from a *Young Ladies' Guide* printed in the 1848 *Harbinger* suggests at least nominal agreement with the article's claim that the danger of reading fiction is great for young people, especially for young females![71]

A Bethany College education clearly emphasized logic, science, and classical learning over the development of the imaginative and creative faculties or the cultivation of sensitivities to aesthetic phenomena. On the one hand, it is tempting to speculate that this hierarchy of studies is the academic counterpoint to a religious philosophy which denounced mourners' benches, revivalism and emotionalism in preaching, and even seemed somewhat backward about developing a doctrine of the Holy Spirit. This conclusion, however, would not be entirely correct. Colleges of other religious backgrounds and the emerging state universities shared with the Bethany founders a curricular philosophy which was very similar to that of President Campbell's school, except for the influence of the Bible and, in the eastern schools, less emphasis on practical subjects such as surveying.

Campbell himself often published pieces by other men, to which he gave apparent editorial assent, which advocated training of the imaginative faculty and experience in the arts. Among these was an article entitled, "What is Education?" by W. C. Channing in the 1840 *Millennial Harbinger*. Defining education in terms of unfolding his intellectual faculties, training his moral conscience, and building his sense of citizenship, Channing betrayed his modernity of vision in anticipating the claims of modern liberal arts education: "The great end of education is not to train a man to get a living."[72] Added to all the other purposes, Channing remarked,

> Again, to educate a man is to cultivate his imagination and taste, to awaken his sensibility to the beauties of art, to give him the capacity of enjoying the writings of men of genius, to prepare him for the innocent and refined pleasures of literature.[73]

[71]*Millennial Harbinger* (1848) 5:274.

[72]*Millennial Harbinger* (1840) 9:430.

[73]Ibid., 431.

During the years since its founding, Bethany College has developed modest programs in the arts and literature. There are venerable American institutions which have retained the European and ultimately the Aristotelian view of the separation between the study *of* art and the study *about* art. Thus, while Harvard University has confined its academic program in the arts primarily to literature study, art history, musicology, and aesthetics, Yale has developed a School of Art and a School of Music where creation and performance are cultivated as in an art institute or a music conservatory.

Frederick Mayer, in a discussion of Aristotle's views on the relationship between gentlemen and the arts, says:

> Aristotle's main ideal in art was not professionalism. He would not have encouraged our modern trend, in which child prodigies and virtuosos are developed. The primary element in art, he maintained, is an appreciation and understanding of life. Furthermore, he felt that esthetic pleasure varies according to education and social status.[74]

Besides the viewpoint of Aristotelian classicism, the Puritan work ethic and doctrine of pleasure, considered in chapters 3 and 4, probably were operational in the original academic omission of pleasure-giving arts as part of a respectable academic offering at Bethany. The much-admired philosophers of the seventeenth century, such as Francis Bacon and John Locke, were freely utilized by the faculty in undergirding empirical knowledge. They held short shrift for the arts in their respective world views, so it should not be too surprising that the north Virginia college of the Restoration Movement did not find much room for them in its curriculum.

The extent to which the central higher education institution of the Restoration Movement impacted attitudes of the churches and their members will be considered in the following chapters. If it is true that music, fiction, art, and drama were not officially a part of Bethany's offerings, it is also true that individuals such as Walter Scott at Bacon College and Robert Richardson at Bethany loved and participated in the arts, and hymn singing in worship was a joy to Thomas and Alexander Campbell.

---

[74]Frederick Mayer, *A History of Ancient and Medieval Philosophy*, vol. 1 (New York: American Book Co., 1950), 190.

The Restoration Movement was not destined to be entirely devoid of aesthetic pleasure, creative activity, or even emotional preaching.[75]

[75]Some Bethany students must have owned and practiced on musical instruments, because an obscure item in the college's by-laws, published in 1842, states: "The use of musical instruments is interdicted before dinner, after 10 o'clock at night, and on Lord's Days. See *Millennial Harbinger* (1842) 1:30.

8

Aesthetics and the Reformers:
Public Worship

The previous chapter may convey the message that the arts and aesthetic experience in general were not important to the founder and first faculty members of the Bethany College. These men were children of their time and place, and they emphasized empirical knowledge, whether in science or religion. They conformed to their heritage, which included Scottish Calvinism, English and American Puritanism, eighteenth-century rationalism, and not least, frontier American emphasis on practicality. The members of the Stone-Campbell Movement seemed to be less friendly to the realm of emotions influenced by the arts than other, equally educated Protestant Christians. The unfriendliness might be credited to the Disciples' high view of logic and empirical knowledge, as well as the categorical doctrine of speaking where the Bible speaks and remaining silent in areas of biblical silence. The approach to scriptural silence did provide a creative area of ambiguity in the thought of Alexander Campbell and in his spiritual descendants—an area hospitable to artistic endeavor.

The gradual shift from emphasis on Christian unity to emphasis on a New Testament restoration pattern reduced the pioneers' willingness to imagine, to allow emotions any part in the religious experience, and thus encouraged intellectual uniformity among the leaders of the group.[1] Doctrinal positions included less emphasis upon the Holy Spirit in conversion and emphasized correctness of doctrine almost as much as forgiveness of sin. These tendencies helped de-personalize an emotional, personal experience with Jesus Christ for people seeking "the true way." Symbolic of the gradual exorcism of feelings that might have produced art was the removal of the mourner's bench from Barton W. Stone's Kentucky Christian churches.

These first-generation reformers were not devoid of a capacity for deep emotions, or of willingness to express feelings about some situations. For example, Alexander Campbell included a sensitive short essay

---

[1]Harold L. Lunger, *The Political Ethics of Alexander Campbell* (St. Louis: Bethany Press, 1954), 57, suggests that the change in emphasis on reformation to emphasis on restoration occurred among the reformers about 1830, a date which represents the first year of publication of the *Millennial Harbinger*, and shortly before the union of the Kentucky "Christians" and the Campbell-oriented "Disciples."

in the May 1847 *Millennial Harbinger* by an unidentified author on the subject of "Tears."

The approach taken by the Bethany leaders of the Restoration Movement to the area of non-cognitive knowledge and emotional expression is most fully recorded in the arena of preaching. The specific consideration of the effective human presentation of the gospel focuses on Campbell's own style of preaching and on the medieval Augustinian tension between play on the emotions and the objective content of the message.

Similarities between the American Restoration Movement and Saint Augustine's *Confessions* seemed valid to Alexander Campbell when he printed an extended quotation in an 1833 *Harbinger Extra* on the subject of Regeneration. He emphasized the necessity for preachers to be living demonstrations of the "new man" in Christ while they "seek out arguments to convince and allure them." With an implicit reference to eloquence, the editor added, "we must show them in our speech and behavior that we believe what we preach."[2]

A quotation from Saint Augustine (A.D. 354-430) emphasizes Campbell's familiar theme—the importance for the preacher to know the scripture. Augustine spoke of the manner of presentation used by the proclaimer of God's Truth:

> Some, however, in their way of doing it, are blunt, frigid, inelegant, others, ingenious, ornate, vehement. Now he who engages in the business of which I am treating, must be able to speak and dispute with wisdom, even if he cannot do so with eloquence, in order that he may profit his audience; although he will profit them less, in this case, than if he could combine wisdom and eloquence together.[3]

Continuing in a vein that mirrored Plato's concern about eloquent poets who confused their readers with charmingly presented passages of misinformation and thereby created a dangerous situation for the state, Augustine observed that

> He who abounds in eloquence without wisdom, is certainly so much the more to be avoided, from the very fact that the hearer is delighted with what it is useless to hear, and thinks what is said, to be true, because it is spoken with eloquence.[4]

---

[2]*Millennial Harbinger, Extra* (1833) 6:382.

[3]Augustine, from the *biblical Repository*, 574, translated by O. A. Taylor in *Millennial Harbinger* (1833) 6:383.

[4]Ibid.

The ancient tension between absolute and cognitive truth, with a practical dedication to matters of serious import, on the one hand, and an appreciation for beauty, joy, and life beyond "bread alone" on the other, was mentioned briefly in chapter 1. In a discussion of early Christianity's approach to art, Gilbert and Kuhn provide some reasons for the estrangement between the medieval church and the arts:

> The vices which the men of the Middle Ages linked with art: hypocrisy, sensuality, violence, seemed to them the more dangerous, as they had in earlier times to Plato, because of the accompanying seductive charm. 'Poets are pernicious, for because of the sweetness of their modulations, souls fall from grace,' said Lactantius. Art appeared to the churchman in the guise of a Siren engaged in drawing men off from the narrow way of righteousness; and in proportion to its power to attract was the obligation heavier to make no terms.[5]

Referring to Saint Augustine's treatise, *On the Fitting and the Beautiful,* Gilbert and Kuhn refer to a state of mind that anticipates by several hundred years the American Puritans, and to some extent that of Alexander Campbell himself:

> It said in effect: Life is earnest business; reflection should be committed to serious things; there is room neither in life nor in reflection for anything but the study of righteousness.[6]

Alexander Campbell's agreement with the sentiments of Christians in Augustine's age is borne out by both his preaching and his teaching about preaching. A series of essays on the Ministerial Character in the 1845 *Harbinger* began with a plea for gravity on the part of the minister. After quoting Saint Paul's commission to preach with gravity, urging deacons to be grave, and exhorting parents to raise children with all gravity, Campbell asks:

> What, then, is *gravity?* It is just the opposite of *levity. Grave,* etymologically, intimates *weight;* while *levity* indicates *lightness, or the want of weight.*[7]

---

[5]Gilbert and Kuhn, *A History of Esthetics*, 123.
[6]Ibid., 124.
[7]*Millennial Harbinger* (1945) 1:15.

Leaning on traditional male chauvinism introduced by the classic Greek philosophers, amplified by the neo-classical authors Addison and Pope, and retained in the all-male shape of the Bethany College student body, Campbell continued: "Addison contrasts gravity with vivacity. 'As vivacity is the gift of women, gravity (says he) is that of men.'" So Pope in his version of Homer's *Odyssey*—

> Hear me, my friends, who this good banquet grace,
> 'Tis sweet to play the fool in time and place;
> And wine can of the wise their wits beguile,
> Make the sage frolic, and the serious smile;
> The *grave* in merry measures frisk about,
> And many a long-repented word bring out.
>   Pope's Homer Od. 1ib-14[8]

In his study of Campbell's preaching style and content, Alger Morton Fitch, Jr. contrasts Campbell's and "Raccoon" John Smith's use of humor in the pulpit and during serious conversation. Campbell felt that ministering to souls without gravity would be like a physician giving a dying man an amusing tale rather than sympathy. Campbell loved "Raccoon" John Smith, but was always uneasy when John was tempted to joke in the pulpit.[9]

An article in the January 1835 *Harbinger* delineates two of the editor's personal concerns about some of the preaching being carried out in the young movement:

> There are two things so superlatively uncomely, that they must excite universal disgust. To see a young man who cannot do more than parse a common sentence of the King's English, mount the stand and lampoon all the Rabbis and Doctors, all the commentators and critics of a thousand years, as a set of fools or knaves—as a pack of dunces or mercenary imposters—is infinitely more nauseating than lobelia itself, and shockingly repulsive to all the finer feelings of our nature. Again, to see a person, young or old, appear in the garb of a preacher of righteousness, with the Living oracles in his hand, addressing us in the name of Jesus Christ, with the flippancy of a comedian, courting smiles instead of wooing souls to Jesus Christ, acting the religious mountebank, full of levity, displaying wit and seeking the reputation of a smart fellow in the presence of God—is the climax

---

[8]Ibid.

[9]Fitch, *Alexander Campbell, Preacher of Reform and Reformer of Preaching*, 50.

of irreverence as respects God, and inhumanity as respects man.[10]

If aesthetic sensitivity includes appropriateness in language and demeanor, then Campbell's concerns for preaching were based partly upon aesthetic premises, including his characteristic concern for the preacher's use of language. Overt humor was not included in his repertoire of appropriate devices for pulpit communication. This is underlined by Campbell's quotation from William Cowper which rebukes the use of levity when dealing with spiritual matters:

> He that negotiates between God and man,
> As God's ambassador, the grand concerns
> of judgment and of mercy, should beware
> Of lightness in his speech. 'Tis pitiful
> To court a grin, when you should woo a soul:
> To break a jest, when pity would inspire
> Pathetic exhortation; and t'address
> The skittish fancy with facetious tales,
> When sent with God's commission to the heart!
> Task-Book ii[11]

Alexander Campbell's charisma as a preacher within the framework of his high understanding of the Christian messenger's role remains a rather strange phenomenon. Comments by contemporaries who heard him speak document broadly his captivating pulpit power. Robert Richardson, his first and still most comprehensive biographer, describes several instances of Campbell's preaching when some of his listeners were completely under the power of the speaker's message. Archibald McLean published a small booklet on the subject, *Alexander Campbell as a Preacher,* in 1908.[12] Dwight Stevenson's 1969 book, *Disciples Preaching in the First Generation,* includes numerous references to the preaching of both Campbell and Stone.[13]

McLean related an incident which demonstrated Campbell's power to move audiences:

---

[10]*Millennial Harbinger* (1835) 1:135.

[11]Ibid., 136.

[12]Archibald McLean, *Alexander Campbell as Preacher* (St. Louis: Christian Publishing Co., 1908; reprinted Nashville: Reed & Co., 1973). McLean arrived at Bethany College in 1870, four years after Campbell's death, and ultimately became fourth president of Bethany.

[13]Dwight E. Stevenson, *Disciples Preaching in the First Generation* (Nashville: Disciples of Christ Historical Society, 1969).

He convinced his auditors; he did more than that—he stirred them. On one occasion it is said, when he was addressing one of the most intelligent audiences that ever assembled in Kentucky, quite a number of highly gifted and educated men rose unconsciously to their feet and leaned forward towards the speaker, as if fearing to lose a single word that fell from his lips; and what made the case more remarkable was that many of them were public advocates of the views he was assailing, as being, in his judgment, contrary to the Word of God; yet such were the force, clearness and eloquence that he brought to his task, that even those who differed from him could not but pay this high tribute to his admirable powers of close thought, and of lofty and brilliant expression.[14]

Campbell's characteristic emphasis on the power of logical language suggests that he was much more interested in the message than the medium, or that, indeed, the content of the message contributed most to an appropriate preaching medium. Richardson refers to this relationship between the message and Campbell's presentation:

At his bidding, the facts of scripture seemed to acquire new force and meaning; a connected train of scriptural truths and illustrations opened up unexpected and lofty views of the Divine plan of redemption; while, ascending to higher planes of thought, he left far behind him the controversies and difficulties of all human systems, as the eagle soaring aloft in the sunlight leaves far below him the stormy clouds that darken the mountain's brow or overspread the valley with gloom and desolation.[15]

Richardson also relates an incident told by "Raccoon" John Smith to a friend of Campbell's. Having ridden thirty miles to hear Campbell preach in Kentucky, Smith acknowledged the great amount of light the preacher had focused on the scriptures, but complained of having come so far to hear a thirty-minute sermon. His friend told him that the sermon had taken two hours and thirty minutes. Smith, on learning the duration of the lesson, retorted, "Two hours of my time are gone and I know not how, though *wide awake*.[16]

---

[14]McLean, *Campbell as Preacher*, 28.

[15]Richardson, *Memoirs*, 2:106.

[16]Ibid., 110.

Richardson describes how Alexander Campbell leaned upon the power of internal content to convey his message, and thus eschewed theatrical support:

> Without any gestures, either emphatic or descriptive, the speaker stood in the most natural and easy attitude, resting upon his innate powers of intellect and his complete mastery of the subject, impressing all with the sense of a superior presence and a mighty mind. His enunciation was distinct, his diction chaste and simple, his sentences clear and forcible. The intonations of his clear and ringing voice were admirably adapted to the sentiment, while by his strong and bold emphasis upon important words he imparted to what he said a peculiar force and authority. . . . His power was thus derived, not from graceful action, gesture, nor from flowery language, nor elaborate or glowing description, nor merely from logical argumentation, but from his singular faculty of stating and connecting facts. . . .[17]

Campbell believed the message was much more than the vehicle. His success in communicating that message without theatrical or other extrinsic support may have reinforced his belief that logical and cognitive content is much superior to emotional means of carrying the evangel. The logical extension of that credo is seen in the reformers' emerging attitudes toward other art forms related to preaching and corporate worship, such as architecture, music, worship forms, painting, sculpture, and literature.

In an 1838 commencement address at New Athens College in Ohio, Campbell briefly defined art in the context of general education. He first defined literature as "the knowledge of letters" and science as "the accurate and certain knowledge of some particular subject." He then proceeded to his derivative definition of art: "the application of science, or the rules of some particular practice or calling, or the practice itself." In his short summary, he said:

> Literature is the knowledge of the signs of thought; science, the knowledge of the things of thought: and art, the application of these signs and things to the numerous and various ends of individual and social life.[18]

Utility was Campbell's criterion for evaluating his three components of the liberal education. He acknowledged the advantages which accrue to the man of literature, but concluded:

---

[17]Richardson, *Memoirs*, 2: 584.
[18]*Millennial Harbinger* (1838) 11:505.

. . . Still we must plead that such a person is greatly inferior to
the man of science in point of really useful and practical knowledge, as he who can only name a horse in ten languages is greatly
inferior in the knowledge of that useful and noble animal to the
keeper of a livery stable, who can only name the animal in his
vernacular. Believe me, young gentlemen, a man with one language and many sciences, or even useful arts, is much more
likely (for he is better prepared) to be a valuable and useful
member of society, than he who has many languages and only
one or two sciences.[19]

It would be another century before the American educator John Dewey
would propound a similar philosophy of instrumentalism. The possibility of intrinsic value in literature and the arts is not an option in the
system outlined by the *Harbinger* editor, and the concept of *art pour
l'art* (art for the sake of art) would have received short shrift in the 1841
Bethany College program.

In the next section of his lecture, Campbell asked the primary question of traditional aesthetics: What is art? He supplied his own answer:
Utility.

And what is *art?* Art is the application of science; or it is the rules
of some particular practice or calling, or it is the practice itself.
. . . Thus we naturally associate science and art, theory and
practice, faith and obedience, as correlate terms—as mutually
implying each other; especially the latter as presupposing the
former: for art without science, practice without theory, and
obedience without faith, would be as anomalous and unnatural
as an effect without a cause, fruit without blossoms, or a child
without a parent.[20]

A primary element of twentieth-century thinking about the arts—
already operative in Romantic Europe of 1838—includes an epistemology of art. Concepts of creativity engendered by arts teachers are based,
at least partially, on the possibilities of divergent thinking opened
through doing art. The Restoration fathers—and many of their
contemporaries—placed heavy emphasis upon convergent and rational
thought. It was difficult for them to consider aesthetic thought and the
terminal value of art. Thus, theological development and especially
divergence in "matters of opinion" became very difficult.

[19]Ibid., 505-6.
[20]Ibid., 43.

It is suggested here that the drive to conform or divide experienced by second-generation Disciples was, to at least a modest extent, related to this epistemological limitation. Thomas Campbell had endeavored to provide for both convergent and divergent thought when he discriminated between "faith" and "opinion." As the Movement developed, the room available for divergent "opinion" gradually diminished until very little space was left for alternative beliefs within the Restoration Movement. The inevitable cracks in the Movement's unity occurred when that space was exhausted.

An interesting facet of Campbell's thought relates science to faith. His eagerness to consider all knowledge, including the Bible, in the light of empirical understanding places him in a more liberal intellectual position than many of his spiritual descendents.

The remainder of this chapter will discuss early Disciples practices and beliefs affecting aesthetic attitudes in corporate church life. Chapter 9 will consider affinities of individual Disciples for the arts. The literature of the early Restoration Movement supports this separation, as do some twentieth-century views by members of the non-instrumental Churches of Christ.[21] Some of the pronouncements by the Restoration fathers tend to lump multiple "innovations" into one sentence. Nevertheless, to the extent feasible, the following discussion will give separate consideration to various aspects of art and architecture relating to worship.

.   .   .

Two important but separate principles were the bases for Campbell's preference for simple church architecture. One was the ethically based belief that money should be spent on the fundamental needs of evangelism, help for suffering humanity, and practical Christian work instead of for ornate worship buildings. Campbell's fiscal attitudes accommodated a belief that his personal largesse should be used for the benefit of Bethany College and other Disciples institutions. His basic conservatism about money might have done justice to his Scottish background. His excellent management of the farm and his press enabled him to accumulate substantial fiscal worth, and his concerns for the Lord's money were doubtless related to attitudes about his own.

---

[21]J. L. Addams, a Church of Christ minister, delineated this distinction in a 1950s tract "Why We Sing" (Louisville: Word and Work, n.d.): "No friend, we don't have anything against instrumental music. We like it and enjoy it, just as any other normal people. We excel in it and teach it to our children. But we don't find its use mentioned in the New Testament as pertaining to the church. . . ." Kenneth C. Hanson, *The Hymnology and the Hymns of the Restoration Movement*, unpublished B.D. thesis, Christian Theological Seminary, Indianapolis, 1951), 57 explains: "The [anti-organ brethren] contended that artistic accomplishment was one thing, but worship was quite another."

Campbell's second principle derived from the rural American preference for simplicity shared by many of his countrymen. This preference may seem inconsistent from a twentieth-century perspective because his nineteenth-century rhetoric often seems overly ornate, heavy-footed, and anything but direct and simple. In visual and musical art, however, the fondness for naturalism, functional practicality, and almost *Bauhaus*-like honesty generally prevailed. Part of this taste doubtless was a positive preference for the integrity and honesty of classical simplicity. Even more to the point, however, is Campbell's revulsion for "Popery." The concern of Campbell and many other Protestant leaders about Catholic power is reflected in a report borrowed from the 1835 *New York Observer:*

> Popery is more dangerous and more formidable than any power in the United States, on the ground that, through its *despotic organization,* it can concentrate its efforts for any purpose, with complete effect, and that organization being wholly under foreign control, it can have no real sympathy with anything American.[22]

In the same *Harbinger* issue, Campbell wrote that three unclean spirits were becoming more threatening each day: the papacy, infidelity, and sectarianism.[23] Ornate liturgies, church music, and other religious trappings were a reflection of the "Mother of Harlots" which were manifested, in turn, by the Protestant sectarian descendants of the Roman Catholic Church.

Richardson described the 1832 erection of meeting houses in Virginia. In harmony with the Disciples' functional understanding of things, the term "meeting house" is used instead of "church building" or more elaborate descriptive words.

> These were plain, substantial buildings, conveniently arranged, and without any of those expensive and unnecessary ornaments in which vanity and pride so often expend the wealth which ought to be devoted to charitable and religious use. Such, indeed, has in general been the character of the meeting-houses built by the Reformers. Mr. Campbell himself, who was extremely simple in all his tastes and habits, was opposed to everything which savored of show or ostentation in house, dress or equipage.[24]

---

[22]"Popery," in *Millennial Harbinger* (1835) 7: 116.

[23]Ibid., 140.

[24]Richardson, *Memoirs*, 2:364.

The ethical dimension of Alexander Campbell's objection to elaborate and expensive houses of worship is stated in a rather sarcastic article entitled "Turning out the Apostles," written about Saint Paul's Church in New York City. Campbell observes that the apostles would have found themselves unwelcome also in "the St. Paul's, the St. Peter's, the St. John's, and the Christ's Churches of English and Roman episcopacy," as well as in the "religious theatres of the Scarlet Lady." Campbell based his antagonism on the charge of misuse of funds. He would have preferred that the thousands of dollars squandered on the pomp and adornment of those edifices should have been used to feed, clothe, and educate those who lived in "the sordid huts of cheerless poverty."[25]

Not only the buildings, but their accoutrements of luxury, came in for this morally-based criticism of church stewardship:

> Pulpits built of mahogany, cushioned and crimsoned in all the gorgeousness of unblushing pride, like inner temples, costing from two or three thousand dollars, environ the object of their adoration—encircle the golden altar on which they present their weekly oblations to that god who delights in a splendid house—in the ornaments of crimson and scarlet—in gold and silver—in the melodies of organs, and the sounds of unbelieving and unsanctified choristers, more than in the incense of a grateful heart, 'whose fragrance smells to heaven.'[26]

Certainly aesthetic taste as well as prudent use of the Lord's money in the face of great human and evangelistic needs were major considerations for the Campbellians. Another consideration was the spiritual question of pride. Campbell did not want to see any congregation puffed up with pride over its meeting-house. Commenting on a letter from the Richmond, Virginia area about several new buildings under construc-

---

[25] *Millennial Harbinger* (1834) 1:17. Campbell's concerns about the cost of church edifices in the face of human and evangelistic needs finds echo in the twentieth century. During the social revolution of the late 1960s, a member of the Board of Directors of the Board of Church Extension, Christian Churches (Disciples of Christ), addressed the exigencies of 1969: "These changed conditions include, in my thinking, not merely the runaway interest rates and skyrocketing building cost which have made church building almost impossible; not merely the 'renewal' emphasis of the past decade which has poured contempt upon the 'edifice complex' and made traditional church building seem virtually immoral; not merely the sudden discovery that the quiet shift of rural population to urban centers has generated a revolution which makes church building look futile. These are three of the most obvious components of a synergism which adds up to a total that is more than the sum of the parts." (See J. J. Van Boskirk to Board of Church Extension, quoted in Lani L. Olson, *Building A Witness: 100 Years of Church Extension* [Indianapolis: Board of Church Extension of Disciples of Christ, 1983], 69-70.)

[26] *Millennial Harbinger* (1834) 1:17.

tion, the *Harbinger* editor dealt with several facets of the cost and structure question:

> It is most devoutly to be wished that all who plead for reformation would carry out their principles in the plainness, convenience, and cheapness of the buildings which they erect for the assemblies of Chrisitans. No greater satire could be inscribed on marble against the religion of Jesus Christ, than are many of the houses called churches, whenever the people have the means of gratifying the spirit which is in them.[27]

Campbell was involved in the latter phases of the reformers' relationship with the Baptists. He spoke partly from within and partly as an outside observer in his critical comments in the *Christian Baptist* about emerging Baptist attitudes toward church buildings:

> There is no difference between Baptists and other sects in this particular. Opulent communities amongst them have stately edifices, with lofty steeple and ponderous bells. There are some Baptist cathedrals on which more than 40,000 dollars have been expended for the sake of proving that the Baptists would be as respectable as any other sect if they had it in their power.[28]

Campbell suggested that the Quakers approached his own concept of simplicity closer than any other American group, and he laid down criteria of convenience and durability as the desired essentials for Disciples in the construction of their meeting houses.

Campbell was not completely an iconoclast on the question of houses for worship. In the *Harbinger* and personally he urged Christian congregations to build convenient and comfortable houses for public worship. In 1853 he gave a fairly cautious assent to support the plea of a small band of Restoration-oriented Christians in Washington, D.C. for a respectable church building in the national capital. By 1853 his assent had grown to a vigorous proposal of support.[29] The building, he felt, should be the "largest meeting house in Washington City," and he offered to be one of a hundred or three hundred brethren to buy stock in the project.[30]

The early nineteenth-century concept of functionalism was predominate in Campbell's view of both theology and architecture. This viewpoint is central to the most complete specifications for a worship

---

[27]"Building Houses for Christian Worship," *Millennial Harbinger* (1832) 1:7.

[28]Richardson, *Memoirs*, 2:365.

[29]*Millennial Harbinger* (1853) 1:53.

[30]*Millennial Harbinger* (1853) 6:355-56.

meeting house he has left. The description is in "Meeting Houses" in the 1834 *Millennial Harbinger*. The article begins with his customary themes of the misuse of money and the serving of religious vanity and pride. This time, however, he attempts to show the other side: the need for local congregations to provide "convenient and comfortable houses for the public worship of Christian congregations, and for the accommodation of those who may be induced to visit their assemblies. Places of meeting, he continues, "are just as necessary as paper and ink for the spread of truth," and he levies a challenge to those who refused to support the construction of church houses, because "some of us Disciples are as fearful of spending money in this way as of committing sacrilege. . . . It is false logic to refuse the God of heaven the honor of a place of meeting for his praise, because Pagans have reared temples to idols."[31]

Campbell's description of a proper meeting house begins with references to both functional appropriateness and aesthetic taste:

> The point, however, is the mode or style in which Christian synagogues should be erected. There appears to be no taste in this business. Stately synagogues, with tall steeples, lofty pulpits, and magnificent galleries, are a satire upon the Christian profession. A Christian meeting-house ought to be humble, commodious, and free from all the splendor of this vain and sinful world.[34]

The house proposed by Campbell addresses problems of acoustics and of the sight lines available to the audience. The visual accessibility of the communion table reinforces the centrality of the Lord's Supper in the weekly services of the Disciples:

> It should be a one story house, without steeple, galleries, or pulpit. The floor should be an inclined plane, descending from the entrance one foot in every eight or ten. The Lord's table and the seats for the elders of the congregation should be at the remote end, opposite to the entrance, and consequently on the lowest part of the floor, visible to every eye in the house. To those acquainted with the philosophy of sound it would be unnecessary to say anything on the superior ease of speaking and of hearing in a house so fashioned; nor is it necessary to say that the facility of seeing the speakers would be equal to the facility of speaking and hearing. These are matters most important.[33]

---

[31]"Meeting Houses" in *Millennial Harbinger* (1834) 1:7,8.

[34]Ibid.

[33]Ibid.

During a tour of eastern Virginia in 1838, Campbell spoke again about Christian meeting houses after observing that the church of Charlottesville "has a good and comfortable meeting house, which may be visited without doing penance, as is too generally required in Eastern Virginia, and in all the South, so far as I have witnessed."[34] Again, Campbell was constrained to contrast the pitiable condition of many of the buildings used by the young Restoration Movement with the "princely" homes inhabited by many of the church's members:

> Meeting-houses do not generally resemble *Bethels,* or else the Lord keeps the poorest houses in the country. For my part, I cannot associate the idea of a flourishing spiritual temple, and that of an open, leaky, tottering, windowless, stoveless, wooden tabernacle as its residence. . . . Those splendid, rich, and gorgeous things, called Temples and Cathedrals, fitted up in all the vanity and pride of life, are not a keener satire on the meek and lowly Jesus, than are these dilapidated, cheerless, cold, and ruined places, called Christian meeting-houses, which one sees too often in those regions.[35]

Some construction details are suggested in addition to the 1834 specifications, including the observation that pulpit and speaker should be at the lowest end of the building for acoustics, visibility, and the best air! The ceiling, in contrast with Gothic construction and vaulted roofs, "ought never to be very high." If the ceiling did not incline parallel with the floor, it should not be over twelve to sixteen feet high. Campbell asked for "no galleries, of course," and asked that the windows be large for ventilation. He especially wanted the stove to be well removed from the speaker, remembering an occasion when he felt a stove "red as Nebuchadnezzar's furnace," became ill with a cold as a result, and ultimately failed to meet several scheduled appointments![36]

The symbolism Campbell required in church buildings featured the preaching of the Word, in the central place accorded the speaker, and the Lord's Supper with the equal visibility accorded the communion table. This slight deference to architectural symbolism underlines the primary emphasis of the Disciples on the Lord's Supper, an event they observed weekly. Traditional architectural symbolism represented by flying buttresses, vaulted ceilings, soaring towers with the cross, and internal art works were firmly rejected in the Campbellian box-like church auditorium. Campbell especially wanted the worshipping con-

---

[34] *Millennial Harbinger* (1839) 2:55
[35] Ibid.
[36] Ibid., 55-57.

gregation to be comfortable, a factor which is even more relevant for his day when one considers the length of most sermons.

The old church building at Bethany does not conform to all the specifications Campbell laid down for an ideal meeting-house, but it probably represents as close a period model of that ideal that is currently in existence (see pl. 10).

The austere architectural restrictions which Campbell prescribed for Disciples meeting houses did not, for him, apply to other types of institutions. In an article complimenting the good and comfortable but simply-designed meeting house at Charlottesville, Virginia, the author also mentioned the "splendid institution," the University of Virginia:

> Its localities are well selected: and its architectural designs, execution, and general taste reflect great credit on the distinguished mind of its illustrious founder. All the Grecian orders—the Corinthian, the Doric, the Ionic, the Tuscan, appear to be in good keeping with one another, and with the whole plan and its spacious accommodations; and are, upon the whole, the best specimen of good style and taste that we have seen in the United States.[37]

A disastrous fire which was discovered early in the morning of December 10, 1857, burned the primary academic building of Bethany College, as well as the library and teaching equipment. While students and faculty improvised to keep the school in operation, President Campbell and the Board of Trustees met four days later and made plans to raise fifty thousand dollars for a new building. President Campbell, now 69 years old, was sent back on the road to help raise money for a much-improved replacement for the building and equipment lost in the fire.[38]

A notice in the 1858 *Harbinger* announced Bethany's aspirations for an enlarged replacement building. The Gothic symbolism that was rejected in the building of church meeting houses held great meaning for the college president, since Bethany had, for him, taken on meaning as a central institution for the growing brotherhood:

> The friends have, every where, expressed the desire that our new building may reflect the liberality and spirit of our people, and we have accordingly spared no pain to project everything upon the most approved models of architectural taste and convenience. The Gothic has been adopted as the style most fitly expressive of the *aspiring* nature of the Christian's aims and

[37] Ibid., 57.

[38] Richardson, *Memoirs,* 2: 632-33.

OLD MAIN
Bethany, West Virginia

Plate 9

The Tower of Old Main (pen and ink)

BARBARA FIERS JOYCE

hopes, and every care is being taken to adapt the planes and proportions to the present wants and growing prospects of Bethany
College.[39]

During the arduous process of raising financial support for the new
building, the *Harbinger* provided a cheerful progress report in the
March issue. An editorial from the *Cincinnati Gazette* was subjoined to
the report, with a description of the architectural drawings. The *Gazette*
was complimentary in its praise, calling it "one of the most imposing
college buildings in the United States," and noted that "the exterior
design is calculated to make it show to the best advantage, and the inte-
rior arrangement embraces some new and desirable features." After providing some of the generous dimensions of the building which would
come to be the famous Old Main, the *Gazette* continued:

> The style of architecture is the Collegiate Gothic, and the irreg-
> ular outline, with the tower and the finials give a very pleasing
> effect. The walls are to be of brick, laid in the very best manner,
> and the roofs are to be covered with the best description of Penn-
> sylvania slate. The doors and window sills, lintels and hoods,
> steps, flagging, cornices, wall and tower coping, roof crotchets,
> finials, gargoyle blocks, and all outside moulded and orna-
> mented work, are to be of free-stone. The interior wood work is
> to be of white pine, and all the carpenter work, as well as every
> other department is to be done in the best manner.[40]

Bethany College represented education of the "whole man" and—at
least for its founding president—the institutional center of the Restoration Movement. Thus, it called forth the best artistic and architectural
beauty and symbolism which could be furnished. On the other hand,
meeting houses for congregations were not designed with such embel-
lishments of metaphoric significance, but only with functional and comfortable facilities for preaching and the Lord's Supper. The
architecturally significant larger church buildings, built by Restoration
Movement congregations at a somewhat later time, are descended less
from the basic worship houses of the first generation than from the quite

---

[39]*Millennial Harbinger* (1858) 7:417.

[40]*Millennial Harbinger* (1859) 2:161-62. The tower spire was planned to be 120
feet high, a surprising fact in the face of Campbell's crusade against the "stately synagogues
with tall steeples" erected by many metropolitan churches.

different collegiate tradition and Bethany's Old Main.[41] The simple and aesthetically honed lines of the small, simple meeting houses, however, contributed a share of influence to the wonderful church houses of the late nineteenth century—churches which were planned more in the American vernacular tradition—which dotted the middle-American rural areas and small towns.

The *reductio ad absurdum* of the Disciples' practical functionalism focused on at least one plan developed somewhat before 1920. Popularly called "domed boxes," the churches of the "Akron Plan" were an institutional effort to make Restoration Movement churches flexible and practical halls suitable for worship, education, and the social functions carried out by congregations. Lani L. Olson writes:

> For about thirty years, the most popular architectural plan and the one recommended by the Board [of Church Extension] was the Akron Plan of George Kramer. Built by hundreds of Disciples congregations, it was also copied by other denominations. Named after the Ohio town in which it was first built, the Akron plan stressed mass meetings. The sanctuary was a square auditorium full of semi-circular pews facing a pulpit in the corner; the floor was often bowled and sloped toward the pulpit. Sunday School was held in a one-room unit separated from the auditorium with large rolling wooden curtains. The Lord's Table, when it existed, was off to one side; the preacher and the choir were to be the focus of the masses present.[42]

The Akron Plan nearly sacrificed the equal centrality Alexander Campbell had offered the pulpit and the Lord's Table, but after World War II, the churches of all branches of the Movement tended to feature a more balanced architecture which highlighted both preaching and the Lord's Supper.

The apparent dichotomy between the simple meeting houses preferred by the Movement's founders and the "imposing" and "grand" appearance of Bethany's collegiate architecture clearly occurred to Campbell's second wife, Selina, as she wrote her *Home Life and Reminiscences of Alexander Campbell* after his death. Reinforcing the belief in simplicity earlier voiced by her husband, she wrote:

[41]The church building of the Disciples in Springfield, Illinois, where Vachel Lindsay worshiped was modeled after the ruins of Melrose Abbey, forty miles from Edinburgh, Scotland. The Gothic style Illinois building was dedicated in 1912. See Charles Foster McElroy, *Ministers of First Christian Church (Disciples of Christ), Springfield, Illinois, 1833-1962* (Springfield: Bethany Press, 1961); also see chapter 10 of this book.

[42]Olson, *Building a Witness*, 36.

I am not an admirer of decorations in the house of worship. I think stained windows and frescoed ceilings are not in keeping with the simplicity of the gospel and its teaching, and the humility taught by its Founder, the lowly Son of God.

It is plead that the Jewish Temple was grand, was gorgeous, etc. etc. But it was typical, and not to be followed or initiated by the Christian church![43]

In the same paragraph, Selina Campbell rhapsodized the beauty of the central Bethany College building:

No college building in these United States presents a more beautiful and imposing appearance than does the Gothic structure of Bethany College, on the lovely eminence on which it is situated, with Buffalo Creek meandering through meandering meadows.

After contrasting the grandeur of the college building with the appropriate style of church meeting houses, she continued:

But I was going to remark, that the chapel attached to Bethany College, in which they hold their commencement exhibitions, is quite a grand structure. It is well seated, and the beautiful windows of stained glass, on which the names of the donors are inscribed, add to its beauty and magnificence in appearance[44] [see pl. 12].

At this point in the narrative, Selina Campbell noticed the contrast between her eulogy to Bethany's Old Main and the simplicity preferred for the church meeting house. Consequently, she mused, "I presume such decorations are allowable in a college building, if anywhere."[45]

No rationale for the difference in philosophy between a proper church structure and academic architecture is provided by Selina in her *Reminiscences,* or her husband in his original *Harbinger* notices of the college building's creation. The difference seems to be assumed.

The hymnody of the Disciples evolved in much the same way as their buildings for worship: out of a preference for simplicity in structure and style but with a high regard for theological soundness in the poetry. Early Disciples hymn books were collections of hymn poetry without accom-

---

[43]Selina H. Campbell, *Home Life and Reminiscences of Alexander Campbell* (St. Louis: John Burns, 1882), 443.

[44]Ibid.

[45]Ibid., 444.

panying notation. In this respect they resembled the Bay Psalm Book—the first book printed in the United States, in 1640 in Cambridge, Massachusetts—and many hymnals of that period. The primitive level of congregational singing was a matter of concern for some church leaders. Walter Scott's 1833 editorial in his journal, *The Evangelist,* reflects his background of artist-level musicianship as a flutist and singer in Scotland:

> It is a fact that we can no more obey the command to sing unless we are at first taught to sing, than we can obey the command to read unless we are taught to read. Let us then try to fix the heart of God's young people by encouraging them to study sacred music; and of course to love the exercise of singing psalms, hymns, and spiritual songs, as they are commanded by the Holy Spirit.[46]

Scott's concern for the singing in the Movement's churches only reflects a long-standing concern by earlier American church leaders. Thomas Symmes, a Puritan minister of New England, had delivered a sermon on "The Reasonableness of Regular Singing" in 1720. In the sermon, he asked whether it would not greatly promote singing of psalms if singing schools were promoted. He even advocated that people unskilled in singing could hire an instructor and meet for an hour or two, two or three times a week, to learn to sing.[47]

One hundred years later Scott was still advocating Symmes's approach to the problem of poor singing in the churches. Kenneth C. Hanson, in an essay about early Disciples hymnody, observes:

> Mr. Scott realized the pitiable state of affairs in regard to sacred music in the churches and made an earnest effort to improve the situation. He made himself heard through the writing of several articles in *The Evangelist.* He urged the churches to adopt the singing school as an excellent method of improving the singing in the churches. His opinion was that the young people especially would benefit from the establishment of singing schools.

---

[46]Ibid. The ambiguity felt by pioneer Disciples (and probably by their successors) between a preference for simplicity in church architecture from a moral/religious standpoint, and a desire to worship in beauty from aesthetic desire, was experienced by American Puritans long before 1809. Nathaniel Hawthorne, a nineteenth-century Puritan, experienced feelings somewhat similar to those of Selina Campbell. Agnes McNeill Donohue, *Hawthorne, Calvin's Ironic Stepchild,* 33, explains: "Hawthorne had a difficult time when he first went to England. After not having been inside a church since he was a boy in Salem—and then in the bare Presbyterian meeting house—he felt guilty about his newly acquired taste for churches and magnificent cathedrals. He went to look, not to worship. . . . But what disturbed Hawthorne most was his awestruck admiration for the glories of the windows and the 'images' themselves."

[47]Walter Scott in *The Evangelist* (August 1833) 6:191-92.

OLD MEETINGHOUSE
Bethany, West Virginia

Plate 10

The Old Bethany Church (pen and ink)

BARBARA FIERS JOYCE

To further this idea, he took the lead in this matter and organized such a school in his church at Carthage, Ohio.[48]

Southern Harmony and Musical Companion, compiled by William Walker and Benjamin Franklin White, and the 1844 *Sacred Harp* published by B. F. White, were frequently used by singing schools in the Ohio and Missouri Valley areas.[49]

White used the *Sacred Harp* in his own singing schools, mostly in Georgia, and the book was directly instrumental in the uneven evolution of hymnody in Disciples churches. Based on a four-note, four-syllable musical system, using the syllables Me Fa Sol La, a major scale was sung by mutating the four syllables to accommodate the intervals of major and minor scales. *Sacred Harp* was expanded several times by White and in the revisions issued since his death in 1879. The 1971 version contains 563 pages with 531 songs. Origins of many of the songs are out of early American experience; others are translated into English from various European languages. Many exhibit typical vernacular tension between poetic and musical rhythms, and reflect their primitive beginnings from the folk religious experience of untutored poets and musicians. The honest settings of the *Sacred Harp* have become a basic factor of religious musical experience in American history, and were used by pioneering Disciples musicians as well as most other Protestant groups on the American frontier.[50]

When Alexander Campbell prepared to issue one of several hymnals which he published late in 1827, he wrote an article in the *Christian Baptist* providing direction for the aspects of hymnody that the author considered most important:

> Psalm and hymn singing, like every other part of Christian worship, has been corrupted by sectarianism. . . . He that sings them [hymns] in the spirit of the sect, pays homage to the idol of a party, but worships not the God of the whole earth.[51]

Like all of Campbell's hymnbooks, the one referred to in the *Christian Baptist* did not provide musical notation, a matter of conviction on the part of its compiler/author. When J. B. Ferguson proposed bringing out

---

[48]Kenneth Christian Hanson, *The Hymnology and Hymnals of the Restoration Movement,* unpublished B.D. thesis, (Indianapolis: Christian Theological Seminary, 1951), 14.

[49]Cited in Hitchcock, *Music in the United States: An Introduction* (Englewood Cliffs, N.J.: Prentice Hall, 1969), 8.

[50]See *The Original Sacred Harp* (Cullman, Ala.: Sacred Harp Publishing Co., 1971), 5.

[51]*Christian Baptist* (1827): 5:395.

one of the *Harbinger's* later books, published in 1848, with complete musical notation, Campbell objected strenuously:

> True, I have no faith in making new or old hymnbooks, with music on every alternate page, or on every page, for church or family service. I hold that learning to sing the praises of God, or learning the music, and praising God, are two distinct operations of the human mind, and never can be properly associated.[52]

Hymnbooks with musical notation were, for Campbell, an innovation as dangerous to the warm, simple worship of the Disciples as organs, singing choirs, and praying stools: Fill your churches, brethren, with organs—with singing choirs—and your pews with "Christian hymns and appropriate music," and you will become as cold and as fashionable as Bostonians and New Englanders, and may sing *farewell* to revivals, and Christian warmth, and Christian ardor, and everything that looks like living, zealous, active, and soul-redeeming Christianity. I have much to say on this desecration of Christian worship. We shall, I fear, need velvet cushions, or praying stools for our knees, and a few downy pillows for our pews, that we may take a comfortable nap during "divine service at the chapel."[53]

The emotional objection to notation in hymnals appears to be based upon two principles, the first a psychological belief that reading notes during worship would distract the average worshipper from considering deeply the spiritual sense of the poetry, and the second, more important, belief that notation symbolized the "trappings" of "popery" which were antithetical to the simple model of worship the reformers espoused. It is interesting to note that, after Campbell's death, deep and divisive arguments were to come after over organs, choirs, and other formal devices of worship, but the notation question was not important in the history of the Restoration Movement after Campbell.

In 1838 Walter Scott also brought out a new hymnal for the Disciples. Scott's penchant for organization emerged with the division of the book in three sections: "The Church Department," "The Gospel Department," and "Miscellany." Dwight Stevenson notes that "the Edinburgh musician cropped out in the editor of this hymnal; he insisted that sacred music ought to be good music."[54] Scott, steering a careful course between his musical convictions and the respect he held for Alexander Campbell's feelings, did not include notation in his new hymnal, but suggested that "the music of Mason's *Sacred Harp* has been set to the

---

[52]*Millennial Harbinger,* (1848): 12:711.

[53]Ibid.

[54]Ibid.

hymn book; so that to obtain tunes it is only necessary for the brethren to possess themselves of that incomparable work."[55]

The publishing entrepreneurs of Disciples were busy with hymnbooks almost from the beginning of their heavy preoccupation with the printing press. Barton W. Stone and J. T. Johnson published a book for the Christians oriented primarily toward their movement, while Campbell began marketing hymnbooks from Bethany in 1828 for the Disciples. In a move toward solidarity of the combined brotherhood, Campbell, Scott, Stone, and Johnson combined efforts in 1834 to provide a single book for all. Five hymns by Alexander Campbell appeared in the publication. Late in his life Campbell donated his financial interest in the hymnal to the American Christian Missionary Society.

The forum where the principle, "where the Bible speaks, we speak; where the Bible is silent, we are silent" received its most telling test was in the area of worship. Campbell, Stone, and Scott preferred not only external simplicity in buildings designed for Christian worship, but they also consistently preferred simplicity in corporate worship.

As patterns of worship evolved in the growing Disciples churches, two general areas of disagreement began to grow, and ultimately resulted in a separation between the Disciples during the latter half of the nineteenth century. The first area, involving each local congregation, focused on such matters as music, both vocal and instrumental, whether or not to use liturgies in a free church, the pattern for the order of worship, and the accoutrements of clerical dress and the furniture of worship. The other primary arena for religious controversy included the problems involved in organizing churches beyond the local congregation for missions, benevolent work, and even a rudimentary ecclesiastical structure.

Richardson summarized Alexander Campbell's preference for simplicity in worship:

> . . . he loved to see the utmost simplicity in the order and worship of the house of God. He delighted in the public reading of the scriptures, the plain and earnest exhortations of the brotherhood, and in solemn psalms and hymns of praise. He had no relish for anything formal or artificial, such as the repetitions in fugue tunes or the establishment of singing choirs. As to the use of musical instruments in worship, he was utterly opposed to it, and took occasion on a later period to remark in regard to it that it was well adapted to churches 'founded on the Jewish pattern of things' and practicing infant sprinkling.[56]

---

[55]Stevenson, *The Golden Oracle*, 175.

[56]Richardson, *Memoirs*, 2:658n.

Some years earlier Campbell had written of congregational freedom in the order of worship, suggesting that uniform laws of order were a heritage from "popery." Richardson places freedom in the order of worship in the category of biblical silence:

> As to a rigid observance of a particular order of worship, after remarking that "the patriarchal age was the infancy, the Jewish age the minority and the Christian age the manhood of the religious world, and that in the latter condition persons are allowed to have a judgment of their own and to exercise it," he deprecates any attempt to prescribe positive rules in matters of mere expediency.[57]

During 1836, a *Harbinger* editorial commented on an article by Francis W. Emmons of Iowa which had been published in the *Christian Preacher,* edited by D. S. Burnett of Cincinnati. Emmons had contended that the order of events listed in Acts 2:42 is "the order in which they should be attended to in the church on the Lord's day." Emmons entitled his article, "The ancient order of things in the public worship of the Christian Congregation." The expression, "ancient order," was regularly used by Alexander Campbell to express the concept of restoration of the apostolic church. Robert Richardson of the *Harbinger* was given the task of responding to Emmons's proposition that the order of items of worship is a divinely given mandate. Richardson, known for his irenic and fraternal approach to religious differences, concludes that churches of Christ do not have such a law, because (1) each congregation can "mind the same things" without necessarily arranging them in the *same order*; (2) God may be worshipped "in spirit and *in truth*" without a precise order of exercises; and (3) worship exercises *do not stand to each other in the relation of cause and effect.*[58] Richardson characteristically concluded in a conciliatory spirit, within the philosophy of the Restoration principle: in opinions, liberty, but not liberty to bind them upon other Christians.

Emmons, in his second letter to Richardson, agreed that "In the New Testament, we have no *iron bedsteads,* by which to lengthen or shorten any man, and no cards or fetters, but those of wisdom, benevolence, and love." Further, he said, "In the New Testament, its simplicity is not impaired by unnecessary bye-laws, nor its 'liberty' abridged by rigid forms. Hence, the minutae relating even to its important institutions, were left to the judgment of those who administer them. . . ."[59]

---

[57]Ibid., 2:224.

[58]Ibid.

[59]F. W. Emmons, "Reply to Letter I on Order and the Church," *Millennial Harbinger*, 9. 7:421.

Alexander Campbell had offered an Extra edition of the *Harbinger* on the subject of order in October, 1835. He related the teleological order of God's larger creation to the church, and emphasized the importance in Paul's words, of doing all things "in decency and order:"

> Because we have forms without the thing signified, "the form of godliness without the power," some object to all forms as of no value. This is an error. We may have the form of religion without the power, but we cannot have the power without the form.[60]

Campbell often manifested his strong belief in the dignity of worship, the proper decorum of leaders and worshippers, and his appreciation for biblical forms of worship.

In 1838, however, Campbell felt called upon to intervene in the continued discussion between F. W. Emmons and Robert Richardson. After analyzing Emmons's arguments that Luke describes the worship of the Jerusalem church, Campbell responded, "This is a pure assumption," and continued:

> It [the assumption concerning Luke] would give to the Christian worship a liturgy, a ritual form like the Jewish, wholly incompatible with the genius of Christ's religion, and would make its meaning and utility to depend essentially upon arrangement. This, to my mind, would be an intolerable idea, and hostile to the spirit and scope of the evangelical economy.[61]

When he summarized his arguments in favor of simplicity and congregational autonomy in matters of order of worship, Campbell became quite elegant in pressing his case. He asked, "Why should we tie up ourselves to formularies of worship when the Lord has left us free as to the time of day or night when, the house or place where, the meeting shall be held?"[62]

The strongest early Disciples essay against ritualism in the Christian Church is a piece by James Challen of Cincinnati published in the April 1845 *Millennial Harbinger,* apparently with the approbation of the editor for its content. Entitled "The Liturgy," the article begins with a plea for simplicity in Christian worship:

> In nothing is the worship prescribed by the New Institution more distinguished than for its simplicity and spirituality; and

---

[60]Alexander Campbell, "Extra on Order," *Millennial Harbinger* (1835) 8:192.

[61]*Millennial Harbinger*, 2.6:247.

[62]*Millennial Harbinger,* New Series, 2.6:249.

in this respect it presents a striking contrast with the Jewish worship. . . .[63]

Challen argued that the liturgy was developed in an age which was distinguished only for its ignorance and degeneracy. With some historical confusion about details, he speaks of the fourth-century period as a time of religious pomp and spiritual ignorance:

> This was . . . the age for splendid churches, erected for the worship of Him, who, while on the earth, had not where to lay his head. Organs, adopted from the theatre, and choirs which worshipped God by proxy, came also into use; the music of which, so soft and sweet, so chaste and grand, that none but the initiated could take a part in it.[64]

He continued his lament about the professionalism of "worship by proxy," and summarized with a warning that those who loved ritual and liturgy should look on it with great suspicion because of the age and circumstances which gave it birth.

The most notorious and long-standing disagreement about public worship between the heirs of Stone and Campbell has been over the use of music in the church. The earliest references to the problem in the *Millennial Harbinger* show Alexander Campbell's concern about "robed choirs" and the general formalities of liturgically oriented "worship by proxy," along with negative references to the use of musical instruments in worship. The controversy proved to be one of the major issues which divided the brotherhood—a brotherhood originally designed to promote Christian unity. The second generation of Disciples leaders was faced with questions about the use of instruments in the worship service. These questions usually revolved around the use of the Greek word *psallo* as used in Philippians 5 and Colossians 3 vis-à-vis the question of scriptural silence. It was perennially debated whether these passages suggest singing with no reference to instruments, or whether the word implied literal plucking of the strings of the harp (or kithara). Those who took the conservative path in regard to the "silence" of the scriptures—especially in regard to things as vital as the worship of God—held that instruments in worship were not a human choice and thus were not allowable.

Russell N. Squire, a member of the conservative Church of Christ wing of the Restoration Movement, contends that the "silence" doctrine comes from a misunderstanding of the Bible. Squire suggests that the

[63]James Challen, "The Liturgy," *Millennial Harbinger*, 2.4:159.
[64]Ibid., 160.

heritage of John Locke's epistemology has encouraged nineteenth-century Restorationists to regard the Bible as a "book of command, requirement, prohibition, authorization, [and] silence."[65]

> This thinking depended upon holding that the Bible is a closed, final, and complete revelation proscribing any further communication from God to man; it allowed for no further guidance from prayer and did not contemplate there may be biblical provision for later implementing of 'biblical silence' through answer to prayer. But other views, based on the Parable of the Talents, hold that there really is no place where the Bible is 'silent.'[66]

Others took the more "liberal" route ("progressive" as they saw themselves, but "digressive" to their brethren who took the conservative approach!). These "liberals" raised the question to a more fundamental level: did the silence of the scriptures as spoken of by Thomas Campbell in the *Declaration and Address* mean that the church should adjust in areas where there was no clear "thus saith the Lord," or did it mean that nothing was to be done? Interestingly, Campbell's negative approach to instrumental music was not based on the "silence of the scriptures" doctrine used by the second generation. Rather, Campbell's rejection of instrumental music was based on what might be termed his spiritual aesthetic: the lack of appropriateness of instrumental music in the simple worship style he felt was most effective for addressing God.

Campbell appreciation for the importance of congregational singing is beyond question; he wrote enough of psalmody and standards for both hymns and hymnals to prove this. His publication of various hymnals was of business as well as religious concern to him, and represented one area where the illicit copying of his work by others, even within the framework of the Restoration Movement, was a thorn in his side.[67] In 1851, he quoted from an article by "G." that described the strong powers of music upon human beings. Campbell alludes to the article as though it were drawn from the book of Psalms, although there is no direct reference to Psalms in the published section. The response to "G.'s" article focuses Campbell's campaign against the denominations and the "Jewish

---

[65]Russell N. Squire, *Where is the Bible Silent?* (Los Angeles: Southland Press, 1973), 64.

[66]Ibid.

[67]See "Psalmody--No. I" in *Millennial Harbinger* (1851) 4.1.10:576. Campbell was concerned about the use of Silas Leonard's *The Christian Psalmist* for the secular purposes of singing schools, and complains about Leonard "borrowing" material from his own book without permission.

pattern of things," and is reminiscent of his famous 1816 *Sermon on the Law:*

> The argument drawn from the Psalms in favor of instrumental music, is exceedingly apposite to the Roman Catholic, English Protestant, and Scotch Presbyterian churches, and even to the Methodist communities. Their churches having all the world in them—that is, all the fleshy propensity of all the communicants, and being founded on the Jewish pattern of things—baptism being given to all born into the world of these politico-ecclesiastic communities—I wonder not, then, that an organ, a fiddle, or a Jews-harp, should be requisite to stir up their carnal hearts, and work into ecstasy their animal souls, else 'hosannahs languish on their tongues, and their devotions die.' And that all persons who have no spiritual discernment, taste, or relish for their spiritual meditations, consolations and sympathies of renewed hearts, should call for such aid, is but natural.[68]

Campbell's satire—somewhat in the style of the feisty old *Christian Baptist*—manifests his belief that Christian worship is simple, plain, basically unadorned, and given in the spirit of primitive Christianity. Thus, his emphasis on spiritual taste in this much-quoted excerpt:

> Pure water from the flinty rock has no attractions for the mere topper or wine-bibber. A little alcohol, or genuine Cognac brandy, or good old Madeira, is essential to the beverage to make it truly refreshing. So to those who have no real devotions or spirituality in them, and whose animal nature flags under the oppression of church service, I think with Mr. G., that instrumental music would be not only a desideratum, but an essential prerequisite to fire up their souls to even animal devotion. But I presume, to all spiritually-minded Christians, such aids would be as a cow-bell at a concert.[69]

Numerous factors contributed to shaping the Restoration leaders' attitudes toward worship. The chemistry that formed feelings and ideas about hymns, congregational singing, choirs, and instrumental music is difficult to analyze. Although later generations of Disciples tended to depend upon one primary tenet when discussing choirs and instrumental music—the silence of the scriptures. That is unfortunate, for the

[68]*Millennial Harbinger,* 4.1.10:581-82.
[69]Ibid., 582.

understandings and feelings of Alexander Campbell and his fellow reformers cannot be accurately understood in terms as simple as that. The Disciples' heritage has been traced in detail in chapters 2 and 5. Latent European and American Calvinism, British religious thought, American Puritanism, and the reaction of the reformers against clericalism and "popery" all went into shaping Restorationist thought. The concept of the "Ancient Gospel" suggested a simplicity of worship which was easily supported by American rural primitivism. Thus, the concept of "spiritual aesthetics" was not doubt a larger part Campbell's thought than simply the "scriptural silence" advocated by second-generation conservative Disciples.

Campbell's spiritual aesthetics influenced his personality. Throughout his career he was verbally assaulted by editors, preachers, and even some of his earliest colleagues who questioned his character, motives, beliefs, and the direction of his theology.[70] Through all of the misrepresentation and attacks, Campbell demonstrated the love of Christ and the overriding Christian grace of forgiveness.

However, human frailty may have influenced some of Campbell's personal doctrinal positions which became increasingly crystallized as the years progressed. His greatest area of vulnerability and sensitivity concerned his favorite publications. Numerous remarks are printed by him about the lack of editorial courtesy given him in other publications. He occasionally became defensive about both the *Christian Baptist* and the *Millennial Harbinger*.

As mentioned earlier, Campbell was consistently opposed to the use of sacred poetry for "singing schools." When Silas Leonard, A. D. Filmore, Joseph Rhodes, Jr., and Alexander Hall published *The Christian Psalmist* in 1847, Campbell acceded to giving a brotherly notice of the event in the *Harbinger* but registered his personal disapproval of such a book with notes which could be used in a singing school. He wrote:

> I would prefer to have an organ, or a fashionable choir as a means
> of my worship than the words of a hymn set to the notes of a tune
> on which to fix my eyes while engaged in the worship of God.[71]

In 1849, Campbell had further occasion to object to the violation of "good taste, good sense, and good morals" by the "desecration" of the *Christian Hymn Book* by Silas Leonard:

---

[70]For example, a story of bitterness and passive persecution related by Richardson, *Memoirs*, 1:430, underlines the state of feelings held about Alexander Campbell by many people who should have honored their relationships as fellow Christians.

[71]*Millennial Harbinger* (1847): 179.

To prevent the desecration of our psalms, hymns, and spiritual songs, by setting them to music, for singing schools; and to prevent the substitution of fine musical performances for the praise of Zion, in the assemblies of the saints, I objected to a project got up by a 'brother S. W. Leonard,' lately of Jeffersonville, Indiana, of making out of our present Hymn Book, "a school book, a note book, a hymn book, and a church book."[72]

The dialogue between Leonard, an active evangelist and song leader, and Campbell became quite personal in their exchange of opinions occasioned by use of the book. Leonard cancelled his subscription to the *Harbinger* in the process. Campbell then printed a letter from a Disciple from Jeffersonville which was viciously critical of Leonard:

If the church at Jeffersonville is any worse off than he is, God help it. I suppose a more lifeless, light, chaffy, cold-hearted professor cannot be found, than friend Leonard. He is a preacher of the dryest and most indifferent kind, I ever heard in my life.[73]

Campbell admitted his personal involvement in this and other affairs, and concluded by writing: "The spirit of the *Christian Baptist* has been groaning within me, for some months past. It cannot be suppressed much longer, unless there appear a spirit of reformation."[74] With this warning, the editor of both *Harbinger* and *Hymnbook* acknowledged his personal emotional involvement in the Leonard controversy.

The abiding heat of this involvement was sustained into 1851, when Campbell's essay, "Psalmody—No. I," was published. Campbell was clearly upset with the continued discourtesies and even copyright violations carried on by "friend Leonard." The desecration included a "performance" in worship by three or four singers in front of the congregation:

During my tour through Indiana, last winter, the only special mortification I had to encounter was the frequent desecration of the Lord's day and of Christian worship by Mr. Leonard's Christian Psalmist, and the almost universal lack, in certain districts, of Christian psalmody or Christian praise. I have frequently seen some three or four persons, with a "Christian Psalmist" in their hands, *performing* all the praise, in that branch of social worship in the Christian church, in singing-school style, while all eyes and all ears seemed to be engrossed in the observance

---

[72] *Millennial Harbinger* (1849): 224.
[73] Anonymous letter, *Millennial Harbinger* (1849): 227.
[74] *Millennial Harbinger* (1849): 228.

of an ecclesiastico-theatrical devotion. My soul sickened at the sight and the sound on sundry memorable occasions.[75]

Beyond the complaint of "performances" in church instigated by "Mr." Leonard's Psalmist, Campbell proceeded to the cause of his complaint:

> Whereas this 'Brother Leonard,' good man, seizes, in defiance of both courtesy and law, my copy-right compositions and emandations, both of which are as much my property as my coat or my house, according to the seal of the United States and Christian law. Yet he boasts of selling 82,000 copies of these emandations, and while pocketing the reward of my labor, calumniates me into the bargain![76]

From the viewpoint of aesthetic criticism, Campbell quotes another editor's concern that the "doggerel" in Leonard's book will pervert the taste of the rising generation. "Coarseness and clumsiness of expression" are dangerous in song because they are "learned and conned by rote" and sung many times. Campbell concluded the piece with one more piece of irony: "So reads the first chapter on the best hymn-book in the English language."[77]

It is difficult to ascertain how much Campbell's negative experience with the singing school methods contributed to his views of music in the praise of God. He certainly felt that congregational singing was vital to Christian worship, that the exercise should give the singer joy, and that the participation could not be delegated to individuals or choirs which would do the exercise by proxy for the congregation. He believed the singers' single-minded concentration should be on the words—and that those words should be doctrinally sound and acceptable as good poetry. He was clear in his preference that worship should not be sullied by an organ or other instrument. Even so, he reported of his own participation in the services of churches that used instruments, an action which clearly demonstrates his categorical refusal to separate from other Christians for this reason alone. Since churches of the Stone-Campbell Movement did not generally adopt the organ (or melodeon) during his active life as editor, he was not as militant about the question as the next generation of Restoration editors on either side of the question.

---

[75]*Millennial Harbinger* (1851): 577.

[76]Ibid., 577-78.

[77]Ibid., 581.

Although Campbell did not directly apply the scriptural silence argument to the musical elements of worship, he was formidably opposed to everything which he related to "popery"—liturgy, formality, clerical trappings and vestments, cultivated music by choirs and organs, and highly adorned meeting houses. He advocated dignity and reverence by worshippers, participation by all Christians, hymnody of excellent theological and poetic content, and in all things, "decency and order." The all-encompassing yearning for unity was based on the return to the "Ancient Order." During the years after Campbell's death, some of the unifying concepts would be crystallized into grounds for separation, when the original plea for unity became drowned in the din of competing voices proclaiming the finality of their respective positions, even at the price of Christian love and fellowship.

9

Aesthetics and the Reformers:
Art and Life

The search for the "Ancient Order" motivated the Restoration leaders to advocate extreme simplicity in public worship, and resulted in a simple worship style. Absent was ornamentation in meeting houses; congregational hymnody was unsullied by choirs, instruments—or in Alexander Campbell's case, even hymnbooks with musical notation!

The low profile of the arts in Christian worship cannot be ascribed to a mere lack of feeling or imagination by the reformers. Their concern was to resist "popery," and "worship by proxy," or any extrinsic element that could hinder a purely spiritual proclamation of the gospel or corporate praise of God. In their personal lives and in their homes many of the reformers demonstrated aesthetic sensitivity and appreciation for art—elements which gave their first-generation Movement a creative flavor. For some, this sensitivity to aesthetic value coincided with a deep appreciation for the work of the Holy Spirit in Christian life. Their view of the scripture included high regard for authority and inspiration and rejected narrow legalism and a selective, "prooftext" approach to preaching.

Robert Richardson was among the prominent first-generation leaders who complimented his deep spirituality with a grasp of the arts and a sensitivity toward people. Between 1847 and 1850 he published "Communings in the Sanctuary," a series of sixteen pieces of spiritual and devotional thought to edify the Disciples. Richardson's biographer, Dwight Stevenson, writes, "Possibly Richardson was the only man among the polemical and didactic Reformers who spoke and wrote devotionally."[1] Stevenson suggests that Richardson considered worship of God as a cultivated art. Although he concurred with Campbell and others in his critique of lavish facilities, he did believe the physical environment should be planned so as to encourage a spirit of worship:

> Though we may indeed dispence [sic] with the 'long-drawn aisle and fretted vault,' the clustered pillars, the gorgeous tapestry, the carving, and the gilding which merely gratify a love of worldly splendor, surely a decent respect for the service of the

[1]Dwight E. Stevenson, *Home to Bethphage* (St. Louis: Christian Board of Publication, 1949), 164.

211

house of God should induce a careful attention to every means calculated to favor devotional feeling, and to sanctify those rites whose mysterious import claims the undivided attention of the soul![2]

Richardson was raised in an Episcopal church environment in Pittsburgh, and had also had experience in a Presbyterian community. No doubt his background accounted for his discomfort from the lack of reverence in many Disciples congregations. His "communing," therefore, continued in a search for some of the external causes:

How often may we justly impute to the absence of such aids, that want of reverence which is so conspicuous! How often are those wandering thoughts, those restless glances, those distracted feelings which are so readily marked, occasioned by those unpropitious arrangements by which the things and thoughts of the world are continually pressed upon the attention![3]

Richardson was a gifted writer, a careful editorial critic, and patient enough to do the painstaking detail work of editing a paper. These traits were evident in his background as a student and teacher of science, and as a medical doctor. Walter Scott, who possessed a great gift for overview but who was not very careful with editorial detail, saw that Dr. Richardson could be a great asset for *The Christian Evangelist*, published in Carthage, Ohio. Scott invited Richardson, a former student of his, to join the editorial staff when he was twenty-eight years old.[4] Less than two years later the young doctor was assistant to Alexander Campbell for the *Millennial Harbinger* back in Bethany. By this time, Richardson had written numerous articles over various pen names or his own initials. Later, he became the author of what is still the primary source book for the beginnings of the Restoration Movement: the two-volume *Memoirs of Alexander Campbell*. Interrupted only by several periods when his vision was not strong enough for him to continue this work, he continued his association with the journal, even after his last editorial work in 1853. In keeping with his character, he wrote a number of articles about the Holy Spirit, opposing the extreme "Word alone" theory of the most radical reformers. He also pled for a continuation of the original Restoration goal of Christian unity, and for open Communion, opposing Moses E. Lard and Benjamin Franklin, two reformers who advocated close communion.

---

[2]Robert Richardson, *Communings in the Sanctuary* (Lexington, Ky.: Transylvania Press, n.d.), 18, quoted in Stevenson, *Home to Bethphage*, 165.

[3]Ibid.

[4]Stevenson, *Home to Bethphage*, 64-65.

It is interesting to compare the theological views of the Restoration leaders regarding the doctrine of the Holy Spirit, attitudes about fellowship with non-Restoration Christians, and feelings about aesthetic questions. Richardson's openness in these areas suggests that for him these areas were intertwined.

Richardson, the physician and man of science who also had an affinity for beauty, attended carefully to precision and detail, was an alter ego for Alexander Campbell, the Lockean master of polemic who sometimes slighted detail and thought in cosmic proportions. Stevenson writes that Campbell invited Richardson to join the *Harbinger* editorial staff because "he needed someone who could be trusted to work out details after the main outlines of a task had been sketched. . . ."[5]

Richardson, the man of science and the master of detail, enlarged his life and his joy in God's created world through the arts. His youthful home life encouraged his lifelong joy in the affective thought realm where music and painting ministered to his family's humanity. Richardson's father was a practical, somewhat utilitarian man with a highly developed sense of business values. In contrast, but complementary, was the personality of his mother, Julia Logan. Julia was refined and sympathetic. Her cultivated taste was expressed in music, art, and literature. She possessed a natural air of culture and gentle strains of character.[6]

Robert's father was a vestryman in the Episcopal Church, and no doubt many of the son's ideas of decorum and reverence had their inception in the formal environment of the liturgical worship in that church. Episcopalianism had little appeal for him, but he retained the sense of order and reverence acquired there when he cast his lot with the Restoration Movement's plea for simplicity. Reinforced by the power of his mother's values, young Richardson imbibed fully the world of the arts and of learning. He had private lessons in painting, music, and French. He also learned to play the flute and violin.

So great was his aptness for music that he was even given his own Stradivarius. Sometimes he composed music for it, an enjoyment

---

[5]Ibid., 77. In his comparison of the two men, W. T. Moore, *Comprehensive History of the Disciples of Christ* (New York: Fleming Revell Co., 1909), 281, writes:
"He [Richardson] was especially a fine critic. His scientific studies were helpful to him in forming exact conclusions with respect to Biblical interpretation, and nowhere perhaps did he manifest greater ability than in the field of biblical exegesis. It was here that he was a great helper to Mr. Campbell. The latter's fondness for generalization sometimes led him into doubtful statements with respect to particular things. Not so with Dr. Richardson. He was careful about the most minute matters, and while many of his criticisms and Biblical interpretations had upon them the stamp of originality, he never, in a single instance, advocated any position which may not be defended on purely critical grounds."

[6]Stevenson, *Home to Bethphage*, 25-26.

which persisted through the years. In the same way, painting also became a hobby. His early introduction to the French language made him as much at home in this tongue and literature as in his own; he read it with ease and with pleasure and spoke it fluently.[7]

Within the framework of the Stone-Campbell Movement, Richardson benefited from two leaders whose characters reinforced the gentle traits he brought from home. The gentle Thomas Campbell was his academy teacher in the 1815-17 years. Walter Scott was Richardson's teacher and friend beginning in 1819. But Scott also brought into the young scholar's life the old-world values of Robert's mother, for he demanded perfection in French, Greek, Latin, literature, and especially the Greek New Testament.

That both men shared a continued joy in the musical art is documented by Scott's pleas for better hymns and his participation in the creation of a hymnbook, and by Richardson's use of music as a catalyst for the joyous fellowship within his own family, and a strength in his own times of difficulty. Scott had played at an almost professional level on the flute, an instrument with which Richardson had also obtained some proficiency.[8] Both men continued their joy in the musical art throughout their lives. Richardson used music as a catalyst for joyous fellowship within his family, and as a strength in times of difficulty. An typical evening at the Richardson home at Bethphage, located up a long hill from the village of Bethany, has been described:

> Music was made one of the chief attractions of this home. When young people came, it was the chief diversion. There were two guitars, a flute, a piano, and a violin, in addition to a number of good voices. Even when the family was alone, they gathered around the piano and sang hymns and popular songs. The doctor had a rich tenor voice, and usually entered heartily into these domestic concerts. Sometimes he assisted with the accompaniment by playing the flute or violin.[9]

Years later—after enduring hardships related to his eyes, the spiteful criticism of some brethren, and the ravages of the Civil War to both his country and his beloved Bethany College—Richardson still delighted in musical expression. A portrait is painted of him as patriarch and grandfather:

---

[7]Ibid., 28-29.

[8]Stevenson, *Golden Oracle*, 20.

[9]Stevenson, *Home to Bethphage*, 126.

In the music room the grown children and their guests gathered around the piano as of old to sing and to play their favorite numbers. At the family-worship circle, Father Richardson led them, as he had done for years, in the singing of his best-loved hymns: "God moves in a mysterious way," "From all that dwell below the skies," and "Jesus, and shall it ever be." The paintings on the wall, painted by Robert himself and by Mary and Julia. . . .[10]

Such activities of the heart were expressive of the happier times in the doctor's life. But even when the prospect of blindness cancelled his editorial hopes and caused deep concern for him by his entire family, music continued to be his solace. His daughter Mary wrote:

In order to endure more tolerably the hours of darkness that he felt approaching, he procured a flute and violin on which he practiced whenever he had a few minutes of leisure. This was generally in the evening between daylight and dark, and I seem to hear yet the plaintive strains of his favorite airs, such as "Life Let Us Cherish," "Oft in the Stilly Night," "Last Rose of Summer," etc., as they floated down from his study. Of course they were doubly sad and plaintive to us in view of the impending calamity.[11]

In January 1850, Richardson contributed a statement to the *Millennial Harbinger* about creativity. This article contains some of his most significant thoughts on a Christian aesthetic. As a Disciple, he refuted the Calvinist doctrine of total depravity and thus salvaged the artistic work of non-Christians as worthwhile. He agreed that their mental powers are "sullied" by sin, but believed that the image of God remains behind the good things they create.

In the same article, Richardson dealt with the problem of defining human creativity. In contrast with God's creation *ex-nihilo* (creation from nothing), human beings observe nature, learn empirically from God's created world, and then, as artists, they recombine and arrange the available materials into new statements.

Nevertheless, the powers of the human mind remain, however their brightness may be sullied, or their actions perverted and impaired. These powers are adaptations; capacities to receive, to imitate and to combine, but not to originate; abilities to abstract, to unite and to arrange, but not to create. No reason can

[10]Ibid., 226-27.

[11]Mary Richardson Chapline, "Father's Likes and Dislikes," in Stevenson, *Home to Bethphage*, 149-50.

invent the material with which it works; no fancy can imagine objects uncombined which have no prototype in nature. It is by observation and inquiry that man learns new truths, and not by intuition. . . . He differs wholly from the Deity in this, that he has no power of originating; yet this is but another statement of the fact that he is a *creature,* and cannot, therefore, be a *creator.*[12]

The inability of humans to create from nothingness, however, did not, in Richardson's mind, prevent them from being artists, and his urge to create underlines his relationship to God:

He resembles closely, however, the Deity in this: that he can combine and arrange the things of the universe presented to him, whether these be mental or material, so as to accomplish new and varied ends. We have, accordingly, the works of God, and we have the works of man. God is an artist: man is an artist also. God combines and fashions the materials which he has created. Man works with the materials and with the tools which God has furnished. Yet his skill is identical in kind—an impartation of ideas, of order, arrangement, mechanism; of connexion between means and ends; of proposition, elegance and taste.[13]

Thus the doctor, who himself created paintings, composed music, wrote prose with elegance, and performed music to express his times of great family joy and personal sorrow, freely expressed his admiration for the works of God and the works of the human artist:

How astonishing those developments of taste and skill exhibited in the magnificent painting produced from the confused colors upon the pallet; or in the beautiful statue carved from the rude and shapeless rock! The bright and glowing conceptions of the soul have here assumed those visible or tangible forms in which they may be revealed to other minds; yet these conceptions are but the combined imagery of nature; or they are the clear mental perceptions of those unities of design which she evinces when contemplated in happy moods and from favorable points of view.[14]

Richardson opposed a "dry" kind of "word alone" theory of divine truth, and accepted the reality of the Holy Spirit in the Christian's life.

[12]Richardson, "Religious Education," in *Millennial Harbinger* (1850): 16.
[13]Ibid., 16.
[14]Ibid., 17.

He has been seen as being more mystical and devotional than other members of the inner circle of the reformers. Richardson actively pleaded for a large place for the Spirit and the devotional mind, which he viewed as more important than evangelism alone.[15] His extended series of articles in the 1842-43 *Harbinger* emphasized his conviction that the Holy Spirit lives in the believer.

He accepted all people as God's children (though marred by their sins). This allowed for appreciation of aesthetically pleasing artistic expressions as man's attempts to emulate God's mighty creative act. It was Richardson's irenicism which allowed him, among the Restoration fathers, to take this positive view of humankind. He produced many an article in the *Harbinger* reflecting his broad views and his desire that the Restoration Movement would not become a legalistic sect-among-sects.

Early in his acquaintance with the Disciples movement, young Richardson observed the contrast between the different approaches to Christian thought taken by his old friend, Walter Scott, and a new friend, Alexander Campbell. Campbell appeared to have the most intellectual and logical mind that Richardson had ever known.

> Scott, too, was logical and rational; but his was a flashing brilliance, like that of a waxing and waning bonfire, depending upon a strong draft from his emotions. Campbell's mind shone like the unblinking stare of the sun, depending only upon itself for its light. Strange that these two should be drawn together! Perhaps it was because they were complementary, and that in their very difference there was a harmonious blending.[16]

This contrast foreshadowed some of the internal difficulties which the Restoration Movement experienced later in the century. Some thirty-five years later, Richardson wrote to Disciples leader Isaac Errett with concern about Campbell's cool objectivity:

> The philosophy of Locke with which Bro. Campbell's mind was deeply imbued in youth has insidiously mingled itself with almost all the great points in the reformation and has been all the while like an iceberg in the way—chilling the heart and benumbing the hands, and impeding all progress in the right direction.[17]

---

[15]Ibid.

[16]Ibid., 33.

[17]Letter to Isaac Errett from Cloyd Goodnight's transcription of Richardson's private papers, in Stevenson, *Home to Bethphage*, 123.

Richardson, as well as other first-generation Disciples leaders, could see problems for the future of Restoration Movement. Stevenson summarizes:

> Richardson could foresee the shipwreck of the Disciples on this iceberg at some future time, as the faithful wrangled within a devotionless faith and a logic of mechanical literalism—unless the danger could be melted away by the sunlight of a new insight. He labored at that time and for many years following to liberate the Disciples from this benumbing literalism. He struggled to bring a spirit of tolerance and devotion into the reformation when it seemed to be trending toward a hair-splitting, fellowship-breaking logic, too little seasoned by Christian love. As long as Alexander Campbell was alive, that great mentor was able to hold these forces in check by the sheer weight of his personality; but after he was gone, Richardson felt sure, legalism would break all controls and do its perfect work of destruction.[18]

Richardson was disappointed with Campbell's inability to respond positively to the sublime, to the grandeur of God's nature, to art, and to the warmth of Christian feeling; and yet, he respected Campbell's strength in realms of logic, the written and spoken word, and non-metaphoric experience. The "second generation" of leaders, who found all manner of reasons to divide the movement, seem to have inherited Campbell's logical thinking ability. Unfortunately, they didn't inherit Campbell's humility and sensitivity to matters of the heart and scriptural interpretation. This gentleness can be found scattered among Campbell's debates, editorial statements, and powerful comprehension of systematic structures, in many incidents which illuminate his deep humanity. The latent potential for the arts was included in the heritage Campbell left his successors.

The realm of literature, which embodies the use of words, encompasses Campbell's ability to express his deepest feelings through both the written and the spoken word. Richardson, with his sensitivity to feelings and emotions, recognized Campbell's ability to be poetically expressive as well as logical. In his biography of Campbell, Richardson wrote an eloquent account of the voyage to the New World and then recorded Campbell's deep feelings of God's creative majesty by printing the 102-line poem Campbell wrote in iambic pentameter and entitled "The Ocean."[19]

[18]Stevenson, *Home to Bethphage*, 123-24.
[19]Richardson, *Memoirs*, 1:201-2.

Next look where skies and seas converging tend;
See waters joined to waters without end;
See next thyself, borne on a mighty flood,
Supported on the floating fragile wood.
Behold thyself, the central point, and learn
The Almighty's power and goodness to discern.
Think on the depths, unfathomed yet below,
Where living myriads wander to and fro;
In liquid caves their young ones sport and play,
And through cerulean waves they wanton stray.[20]

During the previous year at the University of Glasgow, Campbell had
kept notebooks of lecture notes of his teachers, his translations from the
classics, original essays of his own, and some juvenile poems which he
had composed earlier in Ireland. Richardson, with his practiced eye in
art and literature, speaks with his customary gentleness but in a critical
mode when assessing Campbell's efforts as a creative poet:

> These [juvenile poems], however, do not possess sufficient merit
> for publication, nor did he himself ever esteem them worthy of
> it. They are deficient in rhythm and expression, and 'want
> fire'. . . . There is scarcely any one, of even ordinary taste and
> education, who does not, in the ardent period of youth, experi-
> ence something of the *afflatus poeticus.* With most, this is,
> however, but a transient influence, springing from the exuber-
> ance of youthful feeling; and though it may have its use in refin-
> ing that feeling and creating a love for poetry, it usually subsides
> amidst the sober pursuits of life.[21]

Richardson wrote in retrospect, of course, but he was firm in his belief
that Campbell did not have the tendency of mind toward "delicate analysis and minute descriptive detail" that a poet needed. Instead,
Campbell's thoughts encompassed general and wide views and "prohibited any lofty flights of fancy or of bold invention."[22] Richardson claimed
for his subject a fair degree of the "imaginative faculty," but suggested
that the application of that faculty was predominantly as an orator:

> It was in the choice of arguments, in unexpected applications
> of familiar facts, in comprehensive generalizations, widening
> the horizon of human thought and revealing new and striking

[20]Ibid., 202.
[21]Ibid., 132-33.
[22]Ibid., 133.

relations, that this faculty manifested itself; subservient always, however, to the proof of some logical proposition or to the development of some important truth.[23]

In the realm of theatrical arts and fiction, Campbell reflected a strong dose of Puritanism in this problem:

> For fiction, indeed, he had no taste whatsoever; and though he conceded, in this respect, a certain license to the distinguished poets, he used in after years often to express his wonder that any one could take an interest in works of mere invention, such as romances, when they knew, perfectly well, that not one of the things related ever happened.[24]

It is a thesis of this work that a disinterest in metaphor, a bondage to a literalism which at times became plodding, and a failure to enter into the alternative world represented by literature, visual arts, and non-vocal absolute music, may have been related to a parallel diminishing emphasis on *agape* love, the indwelling Spirit of God, and deep Christian devotion which took deeper root in later generations of Disciples. This lack drove the divisions within the Stone-Campbell Movement in its second generation.

Richardson is specific in pointing out the qualities necessary to poets which Alexander Campbell lacked:

> The true poet must possess, by nature, the most delicate perceptions of beauty and of harmony, and that vivid imagination to which these are allied, and which not only creates, but gives unity and life and action to its productions, so as to make 'things that are not' seem 'things that are.'[25]

As for Campbell, Richardson felt that his "deficiency in the musical faculty" coupled with his emphasis on reasoning powers and practical understanding restrained any poetic inclinations he may have had. Richardson may be speaking of his estimate of Campbell as a poet, or referring to his great respect for the ultimate life work of the great reformer, when he concludes:

> It is by no means to be regretted, however, that Alexander Campbell did not devote himself to poetry. He chose the more congenial pursuit of truth, and a nobler and far more important field of labor, where success was to be rewarded not by mere human

[23]Ibid.
[24]Ibid.
[25]Ibid., 134.

applause or the fading garland of the poet, but by the praise of God and the crown of immortality.[26]

Richardson included an essay that Campbell had written for a class in *Belles Lettres* at the University of Glasgow. The essay, "On the Purposes Served in our Constitution by the Reflex Sense of Beauty," suggests that "the wise author of our nature has not endowed us with any faculties of mind or body that are not useful to us." The pragmatic value system which the young Scotch-educated student carried with him into his own American college insists that, since God has endowed us with powers of receiving pleasures from the beauties of nature and art, there have to be practical reasons for that endowment. Those reasons include preparation for contemplating the joys of eternity, the means to make this life more pleasing, and the fact that beauty produces "the most refined pleasure."[27] The limitless capacity for human development of an aesthetic sense is central to the summary thought of Campbell's school essay:

> The desire for beauty is not lessened by new gratifications: in short, without it all the beauties of spring and of the blooming year, with all the variegated beauties of nature and art, would excite in us no more pleasing emotions than were all nature a mere jargon of discordances and a chaos of confusion. Whereas, on the other hand, we find a more refined pleasure in the contemplation of the color, proportion and harmony of all the works of creation and the beauties of art than in any other power or capacity with which we are endowed.[28]

The poems published in the *Harbinger* emphasized religious themes and moralist sentiments. Chosen, no doubt, more for their verbal messages than their poetic qualities, they present many budding Disciples poets together with established hymn writers and poets. Lord Byron, William Cowper, Isaac Watts, and John Greenleaf Whittier represent established authors. Some of the Disciples' entries carry titles of sentimentality (i.e., "Across the river," "The Bethany Graveyard," or "Lonely Hours of a Bereaved Mother,") or themes precious to the Stone-Campbell Restoration Movement (i.e., "An appeal to Christians," "The missionaries," or "Lines inscribed to Mrs. S. H. Campbell"). James Challen, a Kentuckian who became a leader in the Disciples missionary movement, contributed several poems among his numerous articles and letters. William Baxter, an 1845 Bethany College graduate from Pitts-

[26]Ibid.

[27]Ibid., 135-36.

[28]Ibid., 137.

burgh, probably became the most active poet from the early era Bethany student body.

President Campbell took special note of Baxter's poetic talent in the year after the younger man's graduation. In an article entitled, "Poetry," Campbell editorialized:

> We have never devoted much space on our pages to the Muses— not, indeed, because we are not amateurs of good poetry; but because we have had so much prose on hand; and because reformation is not a work of poetry, but of prose. Still we have been always resolving to give a little more poetry by way of relief.[29]

In contrast to the Lutheran Reformation, which penetrated the hearts of the German people with singing, Campbell acknowledged a secondary place of the Muse in the Restoration Movement. However, even if "by way of relief" the poet is allowed to enter the process, it is important to mark the fact that if poetry was not central, it was not excluded.

Campbell indulged in a bit of poetry criticism in his introduction to William Baxter's poetry:

> This is an age of *rhymesters* rather than of *poets*. We have among us *wooers* of the Muses, but few of their *favorites*. Now and then we discover an aspirant for their patronage, on whom they seem to cast a benignant, if not a propitious eye. Amongst those on whom they look with a partial regard, we are glad to see is our young friend BAXTER, a graduate of Bethany College. He gave us some indications of that order of genius while a student, and one specimen in the form of an epic on *Woman,* on commencement day, 1845. . . . We have seen many very respectable Odes in print over his signature, and intend occasionally to fill a corner with one of them, especially because their tendency is always moral and religious.[30]

The editor was as good as his promise, and over the next fifteen years published twenty-one of Baxter's poems. Baxter also reported from the Midwest on the progress of the reformation, in addition to contributing articles and obituaries of Disciples who died. Some of Baxter's best work never appeared in the *Harbinger,* however. His ongoing interest in worship and the arts is documented in a biography he completed in 1879, *Life of Knowles Shaw, the Singing Evangelist.*[31] A little book of

---

[29]*Millennial Harbinger* (1846): 469.

[30]Ibid.

[31]William Baxter, *Life of Knowles Shaw, the Singing Evangelist* (Cincinnati: Central Book Concern, 1879).

verse that he published in 1852 contains both religious poetry and some light-hearted verse which escapes the ponderous heroic rhetoric of the logical language of early nineteenth-century periodicals. One of the pen portraits in Baxter's *Poems* illustrates this aspect of expression:

> Kate
> Light and gay, sad and tearful,
> Hopeful, hopeless, gloomy, cheerful,
> Now all joyless, sadly singing,
> Then all joy, her sweet laugh ringing;
> Now all pensive, soon all smiling,
> Every heart to mirth beguiling;
> Be her mood as gloom or gladness,
> All must love her,—love to madness.
> Thus we see, in April weather,
> Rain and sunshine, both together;
> Pleasant both, when they come single,
> But perplexing, when they mingle;
> Still I love both shine and shower,
> Though the cloud may darkly lower,
> For when rain and sun are given,
> Then the rainbow glows in heaven.[32]

Another area of concern was the reading of fiction. Most of the Disciples leaders—as well as their non-Disciples religious colleagues—were opposed to this form of literature. Their reservation applied to novels, short stories, and even poetic sagas. The classics received a mixed review, and lyric religious poetry was acceptable. Four objections were put forward to the reading of novels by Christians, and especially by Christian young ladies:

1.   The cultivation of fantasy, the suspension of reality for the pursuit of an alternative to the world in which we live, is a dangerous panacea for human unhappiness or boredom. It implies the thought that God's created world is so unsatisfactory that writers and readers need a substitute, rather than bending their efforts toward better living in this one. Appeasing a thirst for fantasy also has a drug-like effect: satisfaction leads only to a desire for more and greater fantasy, a situation which undermines true morality, sanity, and logic.

[32]William Baxter, *Poems* (Cambridge: Metcalf & Co., Printers to the University, 1852).

2. Campbell and many of his contemporaries failed to distinguish between the business of entertainment and art. Not believing that the fiction writers had any higher motive than entertainment, they found the creation or study of novels a waste of a Christian's time and resources.

3. The old Puritan problem of practicality emerged with an American twist. "Real men don't read novels" because there are always more utilitarian needs for their time and strength: growing crops, building buildings, leading a country, and saving souls. For women, who were reputed to be particularly vulnerable to the pleasure of reading "romances," the erosion of willingness and ability to become good wives and accomplish practical work undercut their capability to carry out their primary and God-given tasks.

4. The fourth objection, perhaps, involved a sense of personal pride, together with a regret that the public held wrong value judgments. Authors like Sir Walter Scott might be mourned universally at their death, but who sheds the appropriate tears or expresses adequate admiration for the faithful but unknown Christian, the missionary preacher, or might one add, the religious reformer?

One of the earliest *Harbinger* articles which confronted the matter of fiction is a piece by Alexander Campbell in the January 1833 issue. Sir Walter Scott had died the previous year, so that Campbell commented on the real extent of the world's loss compared with the extent of the mourning by Scott's survivors:

> Sir Walter Scott, the star that beamed with such effulgence in the heavens of romance, has vanished from the gaze of mortals. The lovers of poetry and fiction are in deep mourning; and all the votaries of *Waverly* are clothed in sadness. The fall of a monarch, from the giddy heights of his ambition; or the demise of some mighty chief, who guided the destinies of nations, could not call forth such a display of sorrow, as the exit of this most accomplished story-teller. The genius, the admirable genius of the author of fifty tales of fashion, dwells upon the tongues of all the young Misses and Masters, who riot upon the delicious products of imagination.[33]

Scott was a "liberal purveyor for their amusement," and was mourned because

---

[33]"Sir Walter Scott," *Millennial Harbinger* (1833): 26-27.

The world often most admires that which has the least true merit. If some extraordinary genius, or some giant of prodigious stature, appear upon the stage, the pigmies are all amazed, and know not how to limit their admiration. But if real goodness happen to appear among us, only one in a thousand see anything divine in it.[34]

Then the editor asked, "To what taste, and to what fashion, and to what sort of minds did he devote the whole—labors of his life?" The answer: "The airy, frothy, and fantastic minds of those who live without an object, and die without a hope."[35] Noting that, like the earlier English author, Jonathan Swift, Scott "wrote some sermons," Campbell retorts, "Yes, these versatile genii have ministered to the stage, the toilet, and the pulpit with equal impartiality and *eclat.*"

Campbell lived a century and a half before the age when popular entertainers could command astronomical salaries, but he could indignantly lament:

Alas for the times! Alas, for Christian nations! When the taste and fashion, which fill the higher circles and the lofty places in society, can bestow such unmeasured praises on the inventor of a thousand fables, because he has told them in a *graceful style;* and allow to die neglected and unnoticed the sons of God, the unassuming disciples of him who assiduously went about doing good.[36]

Such regret for the waste of talent and energy upon mere fantasy was not confined to members of the Stone-Campbell Movement. An article from *The Presbyterian* was included in Campbell's 1846 *Harbinger.* The article contains warm thoughts for Sir Walter Scott the man, "so full of generosity, of hearty genial humor, and of hospitality," but it included a remark by Wilberforce about the *Waverly* novels:

I am always sorry that they should have so little moral or religious object. They remind me of a giant spending his strength in cracking nuts. I would rather go to render up my account at the last day, carrying up with me 'the Shepherd of Salisbury plains,' than bearing the load of all those volumes, full as they are of genius.[37]

---

[34]Ibid., 27.
[35]Ibid.
[36]Ibid.
[37]*Millennial Harbinger* (1846): 329.

In good Puritan spirit, the *Presbyterian* article decried the colossal waste of energy represented by the works of novelists like Scott:

> Why all this vast expenditure of so much that was rich and pre-
> cious, and that, too, without even the outward show of devotion
> manifested by her, who had expended so much of her substance
> in order to anoint her Master's feet? Were there no great living
> truths for him to defend? Were there no contests waging with
> error that called for the aid of his powerful arm? Were there no
> burning wrongs for him to expose and labor to correct, that
> he should have squandered the treasures of his mighty intellect
> in devising cunning romances for a winter evening's
> entertainment?[38]

Another selection adopted for the *Millennial Harbinger* in 1848, from the periodical *Young Lady's Guide,* warns about overdevelopment of the imagination which is exacerbated by reading works of fiction. It stated that reading novels produced an undue development of the imag-ination; and since the nervous system was connected to the brain, "mental cultivation" of the wrong sort could "increase liability to disease."[39] This remarkable theory went on to suggest that if the brain is increased through the undue excitement of reading novels and "romances," other parts of the body would be deprived of the growth they should have received. Injurious to all young people, the debilitat-ing results of fiction were most serious in the case of young women. Somehow, "frivolous reading [would] produce its correspondent effect in much less time than books of solid instruction," precisely because it excited "feelings," whereas solid instruction books opened understand-ing and enlightened judgment.[40]

Some years after her husband's death, Selina Campbell reiterated her late spouse's stand against reading or writing fiction, and punctuated his words with a militancy of her own. In her *Home Life and Reminiscences of Alexander Campbell,* she wrote:

> With an intense longing and earnest desire to instruct and
> benefit the young and rising generation by placing on these
> pages these promiscuous cullings, I shall now proceed to inter-
> est the reader by giving Mr. Campbell's views of Fiction, or, in
> other words, "The Novel Writer," with all the art and fascination
> employed to gain the attention and consume the time of immor-

[38]Ibid.
[39]*Millennial Harbinger* (1848): 273-74.
[40]Ibid., 274

tal beings, *deceiving them by the millions—beguiling them and robbing them of their precious time!* To them more valuable than gold or rubies (though they be ignorant of it) still, this is the tendency of novel reading.[41]

Assuring the reader that her own warning is based upon sixty years of consideration, Mrs. Campbell lamented:

Oh, that the young could be warned and caused to shun this injurious habit, as the baneful Upas tree that will poison and blight their life, and plunge them into innumerable sorrows, and so corrupt them as to prevent them from receiving the influences of the precious gospel into their hearts, and finally be lost eternally, yea, eternally banished from the presence of the 'Lord, and the glory of His power!'[42]

Grouping fiction with an assortment of evil worldly pleasures which detract from Christian living, she summarized:

. . . I would that I could penetrate the reader's heart with a sense of the evil, corrupting power of fiction, so that never more would the polluting pages be lifted by the young fingers to the eyesight, be they ever so fascinating, or come they from however exalted a character or gifted pen. Banish them with the ballroom, the theater, the race-grounds and, indeed, all worldly and sinful amusements, alike dishonorable to the Christian profession, and contrary to the teachings of our loving, beloved and adorable Redeemer. . . .[43]

If Mrs. Campbell and the Disciples leaders seem extreme about the evils of reading fiction, it should be noted that other thinking people of the period shared their feelings. No less a literary figure than William Wordsworth (b. 1770) expressed concern over the level of fiction writing being carried out in the early nineteenth century.[44]

Mrs. Campbell's reference to the evils of the theater frames the basic attitude of the *Harbinger* staff and subscribers toward actors and play-

[41]Selina Huntington Campbell, *Home Life and Reminiscences of Alexander Campbell by His Wife* (St. Louis: John Burns, 1882), 256-57.

[42]Ibid., 256. The upas tree is a Malaysian plant that produces a poisonous juice, sometimes used as arrow poison.

[43]Ibid.

[44]See Kenneth R. Johnston and Gene W. Ruoff, "Wordsworth: Intimations of His Immortality," in *Chronicle of Higher Education* (October 18, 1987). The article is adapted from their *The Age of William Wordsworth: Critical Essays in the Romantic Tradition* (New Brunswick, N.J.: Rutgers University Press, 1987).

wrights. English Puritans had closed the London theaters during Oliver Cromwell's administration during the eighteenth century. The same strong feelings prevailed during the Puritan era in New England. Not only did the theater share fiction's evil of representing empty fantasy, but the lifestyle of theater people—who were involved in mere entertainment, as the early Disciples perceived them—was offensive as well.

Curiously, William Shakespeare, first an actor and finally a prince of playwrights, was given a brief but mixed notice by the *Harbinger* in 1859. Twelve lines tell a brief story of Shakespeare's life, and end with a one-line summary: "Such are the meagre results of a century of research into the external life of Shakespeare." Lest the inclusion of the great theater man's life be taken as endorsement, however, the editor appended a brief evaluation: "Shakespeare lived only fifty-one years. Did he ever convert a sinner from the error of his way?"[45]

Alexander Campbell responded to an 1844 letter from an anonymous "S. C." of Pittsburgh who wondered if, when on a business trip to Philadelphia, he might not be allowed a little indulgence in forbidden things, "such as playing cards, visiting theaters, and such." The editor's reply is characteristically orthodox: a Christian's leaving his religion in the care of neighbors when leaving home is supremely ridiculous. Specifically, Campbell explained, "A Christian to be seen at the *Walnut Street Theatre,* Philadelphia! What a spectacle!"[46] Campbell here seized the occasion to make a list of temptations which the Christian should avoid at all cost:

> Balls, masquerades, routes, grand levees, sumptuous dinners, cards, wine, and theaters, are all (and most of them may justly be) regarded as 'pleasures of sin for a season,' by the great mass of sober thinkers and religious men.[47]

Campbell's objection to many of these activities is based upon concern for Christian influence rather than the intrinsic substance of any one of them, but his criticism also refers to incongruities in Christian life. In 1857, he republished a piece from the *Springfield Republican* about the theater which denied that the calling of an actor is different from the calling of a circus performer, because both are dedicated merely to amusement:

---

[45] *Millennial Harbinger* (1859): 612.

[46] *Millennial Harbinger* (1844): 378, 281. The Walnut Street Theater in Philadelphia still functions as a theater.

[47] Ibid. "Route" is an archaic expression for a fashionable evening party; "levee" in this usage refers to a formal reception, sometimes by government and political leaders.

The theater cannot live unless it pleases. It cannot please an immoral audience unless it becomes immoral. It cannot, therefore, be guided and controlled by principle in that respect. Wherein does the calling differ from that of the circus rider? Wherein is devotion to a calling like this consonant with dignity of character, with Christian principle, with noble aims of life? That now and then a genius appears, who compels the homage of the public—the good public—does not weaken our position, for he is a man who is above the theater, though standing on the stage. He has a higher aim than the public applause, and wins his reward by conquering and not by catering. This thing obtains only in exceptional instances.[48]

Campbell's son-in-law and associate editor, W. K. Pendleton, was willing to incorporate Shakespeare's words to frame his own elegantly-written article, "A plea for Peace," published in 1861. Pendleton, a graduate of the University of Virginia, apparently knew and appreciated Shakespeare in spite of the position of his friends against all things relating to the theater. The article opened with seven lines from *King John,* and called upon Shakespeare's words repeatedly and eloquently throughout the piece. His conclusion is consonant with Shakespeare's, finding resolution in the lines:

> A peace is of the nature of a conquest;
> For then both parties nobly are subdued,
> And neither party loser.[49]

Pendleton doubtless aimed at a wider audience than the usual *Millennial Harbinger* readership, a purpose which may have motivated his use of the master playwright in a wartime plea for peace.

Jonas Barish, in *The Anti-Theatrical Prejudice*, has explored the question in depth. He identifies "fallibility of human actors" as one characteristic used by critics to denigrate the stage. Fallibility of the performer undermines the rationalistic certainty pursued by logicians and empiricists; the very unpredictability of a performance injects a note of ambiguity, which was antithetical to the surefooted understanding of the world sought by the Restoration pioneers. Barish writes:

> Through all the protests runs a single thread: revulsion from the actors. The anti-theatrical prejudice battens on the stubborn centrality of the theater's human raw material, the fact that the stage must work not mainly with wood or paint or marble, or even

---

[48]"Rev. Dr. Bellows and the Theatre," *Millennial Harbinger* (1857): 387.
[49]*Millennial Harbinger* (1861): 410.

words, but with treacherous, imperfect men. Artists dream of creating something permanent, fixed, and exempt from the ravages of time, well-wrought urns and mosaic saints. Inert matter they can force to do their bidding; they can impose their wills on it, stamp it with their signatures. But how subdue human beings in the same way, who have wills of their own? How control a medium recalcitrant not with the brute heaviness of inanimate matter but with the wild rebelliousness of flesh and blood?[50]

The surrender of full control of a medium to the performers—a condition shared by playwrights and composers of music—speaks of a larger freedom in Judaeo-Christian theology. The dream of Eden, where man and woman were given the space to play out their own choices, speaks of God's unwillingness to manipulate. Calvin's concept of God as playwright and himself as actor on life's stage speaks of a major spiritual truth: "for freedom has Christ set us free" (Gal. 5:1).

Barish relates the nineteenth-century yes/no attitudes toward the theater to long-standing tensions between art and morality since the time of Saint Paul:

> From our present point of vantage in time, nineteenth-century attacks on the theater frequently have the air of a psychomania: the artistic conscience, struggling against the grossness of the physical stage, striving to free itself from the despotism of the actors, resembles the spirit warring against the flesh, the soul wrestling with the body, or the virtues launching their assault on the vices. But the persistence of the struggle seems to suggest that it is more than a temporary skirmish: it reflects an abiding tension in our natures as social beings. On the one hand we wish to license the fullest mimetic exploration of our own condition—for self-understanding, delight, and self-mastery. But to do so through the medium of other human beings like ourselves means licensing the liberation of much that we wish ultimately to control.[51]

The relationship of Christians to other forms of theater in the value system of the American reformers is not difficult to anticipate. Theater referred to "trifling plays" and entertainment rather than more substantial matters of aesthetics, literature, and philosophy. Thus, music theater, serious opera, is never even named by the various writers who

---

[50]Jonas Barish, *The Anti-Theatrical Prejudice* (Berkeley: University of California Press, 1981), 343.

[51]Ibid., 349.

contributed to either the *Millennial Harbinger* or its sister publications before the Civil War. Opera had been performed in the United States perhaps as early as 1703, definitely from 1735, and various ballad operas were given in New York during the 1750s. Italian opera was introduced in New York in 1825, and various French operas and English comedy operas were presented around the turn of the century.[52]

If the reformers from the Western Reserve or the Ohio Valley would have ventured to witness a performance during a trip to New York or Philadelphia, the offering might have been only a ballad or comedy opera, which would have reinforced the Bethany evaluation of the entire genre as "trifling entertainment." Certainly opera would have come under the same censure as any other theatrical activity, during the flowering of Verdi's art or the earlier music dramas of Richard Wagner.

Opera would have received the heavier judgment, however, because often it included dance. "Dance," in the vocabulary of the rural-oriented reformers, meant social dancing rather than art dance or ballet. About the evils of social dancing, both the reformers and their religious colleagues in other fellowships had a great deal to say. Perusal of the articles and letters relating to the dangers of such "promiscuous amusements" suggests that the dancing usually relates to the vernacular tradition, primarily folk and square dancing. "Ballroom dancing"—probably related to the non-folk "polite" tradition and cultivated society—is also regarded as a misuse of Christian time, a direct channel to other debilitating kinds of amusements such as playing cards, drunkenness, and all manner of "works of the flesh":

> We are reformers, not of ball rooms, chess boards, masquerades, tilts, and tournaments. We do not propose to convert card tables into chess boards, theaters into masquerades, ball rooms into gossip parties, farces into puppet shows, or the orgies of Bacchus into genteel tippling parties. We abjure all such worldly, carnal, and sensual practices as "the works of the flesh," and feel assured that all who delight in such amusements are not fit for the kingdom of God; and therefore, in mercy for them, and in justice to ourselves, and in honor of the Lord, on admonition and remonstrance, without reformation, they ought not to be retained as members of the church.[53]

During 1838, Editor Campbell adapted an article from the *Cross and Baptist Journal,* which, he said, "comes up to my views in every essential point." The article exhausts the biblical references to dancing, and concludes:

---

[52]Donald J. Grout, *A Short History of Opera* (New York: Columbia University Press, 1961), 500.

[53]*Millennial Harbinger* (1849): 416.

There is no instance upon record of social dancing for amusement, except that of the 'vain fellows,' devoid of shame; of the irreligious families described by Job, which produced increased piety, and ended in destruction, and of Herodias, which terminated in the rash vow of Herod, and the murder of John the Baptist.[54]

John Rogers of Kentucky published a tract against dancing in 1844, but seven years later he noted that "however that and kindred efforts from the pulpit and press may have checked the evil, most certainly it is still on the increase in this section of Kentucky."[55] In response to Rogers's call to arms against this growing cancer, Campbell provided an objective look at biblical dancing. Acknowledging the legitimate presence of dance in praise to the Lord in the Old Testament, Campbell applied the exegesis he had used in his "Sermon on the Law" to show the incongruity of dance with the New Testament spirit:

> But, in the New Testament age, we read of no religious dances, any more than of religious harps, psalteries, and trumpets. Amongst all the directions and exhortations in the New Testament, I have not found one on the subject of dancing.[56]

Lest a reader turn to James 5:13 and read, "Is any one merry? Let him dance," Campbell explained that the translation was from an "Episcopalian Testament." The King James Version reads more accurately, "Is any merry, let him sing psalms." Campbell demonstrated his tolerance from the context of his biblical exegesis:

> Still, if I saw a Christian man or woman hymning or singing psalms and dancing, I could not condemn him, because I read of one so joyful in the Lord that he entered into the temple walking, and leaping, and praising God. Besides, the Lord commanded his disciples 'to leap for joy;' but the occasion was not one of popular esteem, for it was when their 'names were cast out as evil, for the Son of Man's sake.'[57]

The article's summary, however, provides a clue for a Disciples argument against most theater-related activities:

---

[54] *Millennial Harbinger* (1838): 155-57.
[55] John Rogers, "Dancing," *Millennial Harbinger* (1851): 467.
[56] *Millennial Harbinger* (1851): 566.
[57] Ibid., 567.

Why look to Paris, the metropolis of atheism, sensuality and crime, for any other fashion or custom than those which drown men in destruction and perdition?[58]

One of Campbell's last thrusts about dancing characteristically related the activity to taste, and thus to spirituality. In a section given to "choice selections" from other sources, he reported:

At the close of a Fair held by the Freewill Baptist Society in Manchester, N. H., a few evenings since, the pastor, Mr. Davis, was asked whether dancing would be allowed. His answer was, 'No; for dancing did no good: it was a barbarous custom, and the first Baptist of whom we have any account lost his head by it.' The audience was satisfied with the reason.[59]

Although the Disciples fathers did not comment on art dance or ballet, it can be assumed from their concerns about ballroom dance that it would not have received their approval. Religious dance might have escaped censure under the circumstances Alexander Campbell described. The fact that Paris was the center of much ballet activity and development would, in itself, have placed it under a moral cloud for the Restoration leaders. The fact that it was "useless entertainment" would have raised their leftover Puritan objections, and the use of the human body itself as an art form would probably have represented a corrupting of God's temple, in their view.

The first-generation Disciples wrote little relating to the visual arts. At a time when painting and sculpture were understood in quite literal and representational terms, it is to be expected that values to be found in visual media were those of the subject. The perceived accuracy of presentation was the primary area to be evaluated, rather than expression and technique. Art was defined by Campbell in the utilitarian way of American practicality: the application of science; or it is the rules of some particular calling, or it is the practice itself.[60] The use of painting, in the period before the practical use of the daguerrotype about 1839, and for some years thereafter, was to preserve the images of important people. Campbell, fortunately, used the medium of portraiture so that we have a preservation of his appearance. On one occasion he sat for a daguerrotype portrait in New York, but was dissatisfied with the result, and consequently sat for another daguerrotype by a Bethany College

---

[58]Ibid.

[59]*Millennial Harbinger* (1855): 276.

[60]*Millennial Harbinger* (1838): 505; see also chap. 8 of this work.

student named Redmon.[61] The utilitarian function of painting, sculpture, or the infant medium of photography was appreciated, even on the Western Reserve, by the reformers in the Churches of Christ, since the heroic tradition of remembering famous men by a sculptured or painted image complemented the value system which drove their understanding. The uses of art might even be extended to the ornamentation of public and academic buildings, or the illustration of a classical theme. There seems to have been little felt need, however, for the visual representation of fantasy or "conditions contrary to fact." In an age when visual art meant representation, the cultivation of art generally shared with theater the necessity of the perceiver's accepting a metaphorical and non-literal mode of thinking.

One of the principal essays on visual art is "Moral Influence of Pictures," in an 1853 *Millennial Harbinger,* article signed merely "J.R.H." By "pictures," the author explains, he means "paintings, drawings, and engravings of every kind, representing persons, scenes, characters, etc." The author decries the moral influence exerted by the images of many pictures he finds in Christian homes, especially because of the deep, lasting, and almost indelible impression they make on the minds of children. The writer especially objected to war and battle scenes, and "most improper amatory, and other scenes, are sometimes presented in them."[62]

> For instance, I have seen hanging up in the houses of brethren, scenes of a gentleman and lady kissing, the gentleman with his arm around the lady's waist, etc! Now, what is the effect of these 'courting scenes,' but to arouse and cherish some of the most improper and immoral passions! I once saw in the house of a brother and sister, a dancing scene on the chimney screen, or screen for the fire-place! On it was a quite old looking man, with a fiddle in his hand, and dancing, and a couple of small children, a little boy and girl, dancing! What must be the effect of such pictorial examples on the minds of children, but to excite in them a love for dancing![63]

While Campbell and other religious leaders of his time were condemning the messages thus conveyed, the media by which they were conveyed were not condemned. Mrs. Campbell, in her *Home Life and Reminiscences,* relates efforts to preserve Alexander Campbell's likeness:

[61]*Millennial Harbinger* (1853): 233.
[62]*Millennial Harbinger* (1853): 212.
[63]Ibid.

Mr. Campbell was of a happy complacent disposition, and while he did not court notoriety—I may truly say, in any way—yet he was happy in yielding to the solicitations of his friends, during his travels, by sitting to have photographs taken, and on some occasions, for having busts taken of himself.[64]

Mrs. Campbell related a humorous story about one of the abortive attempts made by an artist to preserve her husband's likeness. It seems that Alexander had laid down so the artist could make a plaster mold for the bust. Apparently, the artist was not very experienced and failed to leave an opening through which Alexander could breathe so that Alexander had to jump up quickly, thereby destroying efforts to preserve an impression of his large head, neck, and shoulders.[65]

Speaking of another, but successful, effort to make a bust, she provides some background about the marble bust of her husband by Joe Hart, which was set in Bethany College. Selina wrote:

It was taken by the Kentucky artist, Mr. Joe T. Hart, at the time of the debate in Lexington, Ky., between Mr. N. L. Rice and Mr. Campbell, and was afterward taken by Mr. Hart to Florence, Italy, where he had a studio for some time. I . . . sent an order to have Mr. Hart execute it in marble. He was greatly devoted to Mr. C.'s memory, (having heard him for days in debate with Robert Owen) and was thus the better prepared to give a good impress of the lineaments of Mr. C. on the lifeless marble. In his correspondence with me during the time he was working upon it, he at one time assured me it was the first piece of marble that he ever put chisel upon free from spots, adding, 'fit emblem of that great and good man.'[66]

If the attitudes toward the arts outlined above strike the reader as Victorian, it should be remembered that they were expressed in a pre-Victorian age, and they were more representative of the religious world than atypical. The affinity of Alexander Campbell, Robert Richardson, William Pendleton, and other Restoration leaders for the realm of the heart certainly represented a counterweight to the "Word-alone" dryness and the literal legalism which pervaded much of the Protestant world in their age, and which became more pronounced in Disciples theology during later generations. As Richardson had earlier described the affinity of the younger Alexander Campbell for the exciting beauty of nature and

---

[64]Selina H. Campbell, *Home Life*, 273.
[65]Ibid.
[66]Ibid., 274.

the mystery of God's greatness, his second wife remembered this aspect of his personality as she later recalled their lives together:

> Mr. Campbell was a great admirer of the beautiful and grand. He gave a description of sunrise at sea, which I think any one who reads will admire for the beauty and grandeur of the scene as portrayed by him. . . .
>
> Mr. Campbell was a great admirer of Nature—God's works were regarded with reverence. The sun, the moon and the stars were viewed with thrilling delight, and the eighth Psalm was often quoted by him.[67]

The side of Alexander that was portrayed by Selina was not obvious to many contemporaries of Campbell and his colleagues. Some believed that the "Campbellites" were cold, spiritless, logical believers in water salvation and unemotional logic. William Warren Sweet quotes from a letter of a church worker living in Arkansas:

> The Campbellites. These are all going to heaven by water. The cold assent of the head to the proposition that 'Jesus is the Christ' and immersion in water constitutes, in their view, a full qualification for a title to eternal life.[68]

Campbell's own writings reveal how often he had to defend himself from the charges that he advocated a mere "head" religion.[69] For example, in an 1830 article on the subject of Christian Experience, Campbell wrote:

> . . . we should much regret if any sincere disciple of Jesus Christ should suppose that we opposed or disliked a religion which captivated the heart, moved the affections, purified the soul, and reformed the behavior of its votaries. So far from it, it is because of the manifest deficiency in these respects that we object to the systems, and the *experimental religion* of the popular leaders. A religion that fills not the conscience with peace, the heart with love, the affections with joy, the soul with hope, and the life with good works, is not worth an untimely fig.[70]

---

[67]Ibid., 264, 316.

[68]William Warren Sweet, *Religion on the American Frontier. The Presbyterians 1783-1840. A Collection of Source Material* (New York: Harper & Bros., 1936), 697.

[69]V. M. Powell, "Alexander Campbell and Frontier Religion," Columbia, Mo., unpublished paper (19—): 13.

[70]*Millennial Harbinger* (1830): 260.

Besides his reverent appreciation for the created works of God and the subjective changes of affections that characterize a Christian, Campbell also admired at least some of the created works of Man. His love of poetry has already been considered in this chapter; it is perhaps in the realm of music where the most ambiguities emerge in his love for the art.

Curiously, the 1860 *Harbinger* includes a brief excerpt from *Kingsley's Sermons* which the editor of the *Harbinger* must have felt merited consideration:

> There is something very wonderful in music. Words are wonderful enough, but music is even more wonderful. It speaks not to our thoughts, as words do; it speaks straight to our hearts and spirits, to the very core and root of our souls. Music soothes us, stirs us up; it puts noble feelings into us; it melts us to tears, we know not how; it is a language by itself, just as perfect, in its way, as speech, as words; just as divine, just as blessed.[71]

Intentionally or not, the editor of the *Harbinger* opened the door, at least partially, to a prevailing nineteenth-century concept: music, unlike the other arts, deals directly with the emotions, and the music which most effectively operates in this sphere is instrumental music, unencumbered by the baggage of words. Arthur Schopenhauer, archspokesman for high German Romanticism, wrote:

> Because music does not, like all the other arts, exhibit the *Ideas* or grades of the will's objectification, but directly the *will itself,* we can also explain that it acts directly on the will, i.e., the feelings, passions, and emotions of the hearer, so that it quickly raises these or even alters them.[72]

For music to speak "straight to our hearts," as Kingsley would have it, or "directly on the will," as Schopenhauer perceives it, it should not be encumbered with the extrinsic addition of verbal ideas:

> Far from being a mere aid to poetry, music is certainly an independent art; in fact, it is the most powerful of all the arts, and therefore attains its ends entirely from its own resources. Just as certainly, it does not require the words of a song or the action of an opera. Music as such knows only the tones or notes, not the causes that produce them.[73]

[71]*Millennial Harbinger* (1860): 517.

[72]Arthur Schopenhauer, *The World as Will and Representation*, tr. E.F.J. Payne (New York: Dover, 1958), 2: 448.

[73]Ibid.

In practice, the possibility of using absolute music as a metaphor for Christian worship was not a viable alternative for the American reformers. Campbell saw the use of instruments or choirs in churches as performances, or "worship by proxy." The parallel between one person leading in prayer for an entire congregation and a musician providing a musical expression in worship on behalf of other worshippers was not considered equivalent, partly because of the heavy Disciples emphasis on both cognitive words and the Word.

Living in a rural section of the Ohio Valley, Alexander Campbell and his co-reformers would rarely have enjoyed an opportunity for an orchestral concert or even solo recitals of art music. They could have encountered "absolute music" during their various travels to eastern cities, or perhaps to Cincinnati, a city whose musical development benefited greatly from its heavy German population. New York City, one of Campbell's occasional destinations, boasted a regular symphony orchestra from 1842; before that the Academy of Music had provided a potpourri of musical fare. Boston's Handel and Haydn Society dates from 1815, and even attempted to commission Ludwig van Beethoven to write an oratorio in 1823.[74] Since most instrumental folk music of the vernacular tradition smacked of dancing, the Restoration fathers might have found at least some grounds of common interest with Theodore Thomas, one of the earliest professional American conductors and, by 1871, conductor of the New York Philharmonic Orchestra:

> A symphony orchestra shows the culture of a community. . . .
> the man who does not understand Beethoven and has not been
> under his spell has not lived half his life. The masterworks of
> . . . instrumental music are the language of the soul and express
> more than those of any other art. Light music, "popular" so
> called, is the sensual side of the art and has more or less the devil
> in it.[75]

While the circle around Alexander Campbell would hardly have agreed that their lives were deprived of culture for not knowing the works of Beethoven, they might have agreed with Thomas's sentiments concerning popular music!

Alexander Campbell loved hymns, and enjoyed participating in singing hymns in his own home. His skills were apparently not equal to his enjoyment, but his joy in participation seems to have been deep. Richardson describes an evening in the Campbell household:

---

[74]John Mueller, *The American Symphony Orchestra* (Bloomington, Ind.: Indiana University Press, 1951), 115, 20.

[75]George Upton, ed., *Theodore Thomas* (Chicago: McClurg & Co., 1905), vol. 1, frontispiece.

At an early hour the entire household, domestics included, assembled in the spacious parlor, each one having hymns or some scripture lesson to recite. . . . These being briefly considered, he would call upon Mrs. Campbell, who had a good voice, to lead in singing a psalm or spiritual song, in which he himself would heartily join, and then kneeling down would most reverently and earnestly present before the throne of grace their united thanksgivings and petitions for divine guardianship and guidance. . . . In music, especially sacred music, he took great pleasure, and was visibly affected by it, often calling, when the occasion permitted, for the singing of psalms and hymns, and, though unable to carry the air alone, uniting in the singing with a clear, musical voice and evident enjoyment.[76]

Campbell practiced a life of prayer which complemented his love of worship. The numerous references to prayer in the *Millennial Harbinger*, the heavy part prayer had in personal and family devotions, and his cultivation of public prayer as an art in itself tend to counter the cliché image of Alexander Campbell as the rigid logician without heart or feeling. Indeed, the spirituality of the man expressed through prayer, hymns, and a profound appreciation for God's created world provide a counter-balance to the possible incipient legalism that could have dominated Disciples theology, even in the first generation. Together with Robert Richardson, the kindly Thomas Campbell, Walter Scott, and William K. Pendleton, a reverence for God, a sense of His majesty and His love, a sensitivity to the beauty of His creation, and a consequent generosity of fellowship were a part of Alexander Campbell's leadership of the Restoration Movement. If his doctrine of the indwelling Holy Spirit was not fully developed, and if he remained somewhat unresponsive to the intrinsic values of the arts, Campbell was not a mere logician, and this fact at least furnished a basis for a healthy balance to the young Movement. Tragically, this element was partially lost by some of the strongest leaders of the second generation of Disciples.

The degree of moral recoil from even the appearance of evil is perhaps more evident in some of the reminiscences of Selina Campbell than from any of the writings of her husband. A cousin of Alexander, Enos Campbell, followed his kinsman to the United States from Ireland, studied with the Bethany leader, tutored the children in his household, and ultimately became a leading preacher in the Disciples movement. Enos Campbell was interested in both the study of Christianity and in music. Selina tells the story:

[76]Richardson, *Memoirs*, 2:300-1, 1:117.

CAMPELL MANSION
Bethany, West Virginia

Plate 11
The Campbell Mansion (pen and ink)
BARBARA FIERS JOYCE
Courtesy Bethany College Heritage Resource Center

He was fond of music, and had procured a fine violin, quite inspiring in its resounding tones. It was practiced upon principally in the school room, in the yard adjacent to the house. Not being far from the public road, it attracted the attention of passersby. It went on very pleasantly for a little while; twice I felt a delicacy and regret to be obliged to put my veto on its continuance, but associating dancing with fiddling (and being opposed to it then, as now) and Mr. Campbell being from home on a tour, and not for a moment wishing passersby to imagine music and dancing in our domicile, I kindly requested brother Enos to take it up to the farm on the hill, at son R. Y. Henley's; he did so, and occasionally I went up to enjoy the vibrations of its spirit-stirring strains.[77]

Louis and Bess White Cochran, in their superb story of the Restoration Movement, suggest that Selina was irritated by the music and caused the young man to leave:

He [Enos Campbell] had settled at the Campbell home in Bethany until Alexander's wife, Selina, let her irritation at his fiddle playing be known in such uncertain terms that he packed up and left.[78]

Selina seems to have been torn between the same two value systems that tugged—at least gently—upon her husband. She admits to have been somewhat charmed by Enos's music—enough to make several trips up to the "back forty" at son Henley's farm to hear more of the "soul-stirring" strains. On the other hand, she was confronted with a deep obligation, growing out of her Puritan and pre-Victorian sense of propriety, to protect Alexander Campbell's name and reputation in his prolonged absence. Robert Richardson, who may not always have been Mrs. Campbell's greatest admirer, describes her very positively in terms of feminine sensitivities:

. . . Mrs. Campbell had an excellent taste, being a lady of considerable reading and culture, of a very serious and religious turn, fond of Young's "Night Thoughts," and the grave poetical and prose English authors; not at all addicted to gaiety, but on the contrary, though cheerful under the surrounding happy circumstances, possessing a constitutional tendency to melan-

---

[77]Selina H. Campbell, *Home Life*, 471-72. See Dale A. Jorgenson, "Why Did We Hide the Fiddle Player?" *The Disciple* (Sept. 19, 1982).

[78]Louis and Bess White Cochran, *Captives of the Word* (Joplin, Mo.: College Press, 1987), 126.

choly, which needed only the presence of calamity for its development.[79]

The line of Platonic tension between intellect and feeling which affected Saint Augustine, the Protestant Reformers, and Alexander Campbell was part of Selina Campbell's makeup also. In the twentieth century, psychologists speak of cognitive and affective thinking, or right brain and left brain thought. The tendency in the American Restoration Movement was to emphasize the intellectual and cognitive aspect of Christianity, but not to suffocate the emotions. Unfortunately, the heart seems to have been easily sacrificed to the intellect, and increasingly so by succeeding generations of the Stone-Campbell tradition.

Enos Campbell heard a different drummer in more than one aspect of his life and spirit. As minister of the Church of Christ in Hopkinsville, Kentucky he was instrumental in sending the second foreign missionary supported by the Restoration Movement. The bold and creative commitment which produced this action is described by the Cochrans:

> It [the Hopkinsville church] also considered the Great Commission as a command not to be disregarded, and cast about not only for a worthy man to go forth but a suitable field to which to send him. With utter disregard for conventional procedure, they chose the man among them who gave the best evidence of good logic, ready utterance and burning zeal. He was a negro slave.[80]

The man was purchased by a group of churches from his owner, trained by Enos Campbell and the church's elders for six months, and sent, with his wife and son, to Liberia. The overwhelming difficulties of the assignment and the difficult physical environment "took their toll," and Alexander Cross, the second foreign missionary of the Disciples, died after two years on the field about 1855.[81]

The passing years brought changes in the thinking of Alexander Campbell about various aspects of spirituality, culture, and social respectability. Although he never surrendered the basic framework of the reforming plea, he manifested his capacity for spiritual and intellectual growth by his ability to change his mind about "opinions."

---

[79]Richardson, *Memoirs*, 2:302. Stevenson used some notes Richardson made while preparing to write the Campbell *Memoirs* which never got into the finished manuscript: "Mrs. C.'s excessive and absurd watch over his personal movements. Its effect in weakening his memory of places, etc." See Stevenson, *Home to Bethphage*, 219.

[80]Cochran & Cochran, *Captives of the Word*, 127.

[81]Ibid.

One of the specific signs of change came about in his own home, a place noted for hospitality, stimulating conversation, and reverent family worship. The Campbell family gradually upgraded the old John Brown home Alexander had inherited from Margaret's parents to a place appropriate for the reception of honored guests and the home of one of the primary leaders in the Movement:

> But as his own wealth increased his home at Bethany began reflecting a cultural level that attracted both the wealthy and the learned. High thinking permeated every occasion. Although the appointments of the "mansion" were not ornate, they were a far cry from the crude cabin furnishings of his followers in the early days. Imported French wallpaper and gleaming silver tableware, fine linen and polished mahogany were a background for the conversational badinage of alert minds, and table talk no longer centered on the breeding habits of sheep, but ranged into metaphysical discussions, especially when distinguished visitors were present, as was the case most of the time when Mr. Campbell was in residence.[82]

The presence in his home of French wallpaper from the "heart of infidelity"—paper which has been carefully preserved by the curators of the Campbell home and is still handsome—had less sinful connotations than it might during *Christian Baptist* days, in spite of the classical Greek theme presented by the pattern. The very amenities of the Campbell home represent that delicate balance of resistance to the world with a Christian *joi de vive* which gave vitality to the young Movement.

Campbell lived to witness the end of the American Civil War. However, after his return from a trip abroad during which he suffered both a libelous imprisonment and the loss of a son who drowned in Buffalo Creek during his absence, he never quite recovered the former spark of leadership. The Civil War was a terrible shock to him, both in the carnage and tragedy of human beings, and in the threat to the unity of the fragile movement he had helped bring to existence. Additionally, the optimistic hope that the United States might be the place where constitutional freedom might lead to human improvement and redemption to the point one could be a harbinger of Christ's millennium—even a "secular millennium"—was quite thoroughly dashed. Although Campbell remained active in writing and in the College until the war years, William K. Pendleton, Robert Richardson, and for a time Isaac Errett, relieved him of a great deal of the labor involved in those responsibilities.

[82]Ibid., 152.

Barton W. Stone died in 1844, Thomas Campbell in 1854, and Walter Scott in 1861. Alexander Campbell lived until 1866, longer than the other three principal leaders of the Restoration Movement, and it is not surprising that new personalities were already supplanting the four generous spirits who had, against their own original intentions, brought into being another church group in the census of Protestant religious organizations. After the passing of leadership to others, that new group, which had been brought into being to plead for the unity of Christ's church, would itself divide and redivide.

Richardson, the biographer who knew his subject well, provides a key to the success of Campbell's work—a success based on both intellect and feeling, which clearly repudiates the accusation that his belief was a one-dimensional rationalism devoid of spiritual life:

> In Mr. Campbell's *religious* life the central thought was Jesus, the Son of God. No language can portray his lofty conceptions of the glory of Christ as of the grandeur of the spiritual system of which He is the Alpha and Omega. . . . Such was his sense of the boundless love of God in Christ that, though he possessed remarkable control over his emotional nature, the simple mention of it in his public addresses would often so affect him that for a moment or two his feelings would stop his utterance and render him unable to proceed.[83]

The values that Campbell imparted to the Movement have been neatly summarized: "More than walking with the princes of the earthly realm, he yearned in all sincerity to "walk with God."[84]

Alexander Campbell was hardly to be considered a mystic, and certainly not an aesthete. But to at least a limited extent, his life had room for both the Spirit of God and the joy of beauty. If that sense was not as great as it was in Robert Richardson, it was as genuine. The second generation leaders would have opportunity to opt for a sense of poetry with their literalism, and for a spirituality with their sometimes humanistic and logical biblicism, if they would choose to do so.

The sixteenth-century Protestant Reformation developed in the Renaissance environment of drama and theater. Then, John Calvin could perceive life as a drama acted upon the stage of reality even while rejecting the actual world of the theater. In the eighteenth and nineteenth centuries, the American frontier-oriented leaders of the Restoration Movement found it even more difficult than Calvin to find a legitimate place for works of fantasy. Buttressed further by the Puritan and Ameri-

---

[83]Richardson, *Memoirs* 2:665.
[84]Cochran and Cochran, *Captives of the Word*, 153.

can work ethic which placed primary value on practical things and productive work, the leaders of the early Disciples were able to overcome
their feelings of "tension" and be quite categorical in denigrating works
of imagination with no basis in fact. This reluctance to incorporate the
Augustinian "willing suspension of unbelief," was a real impediment to
the development of a full-blown aesthetic outlook. It contributed to a
narrow view of Thomas Campbell's category of the silence of the scriptures, to a diminished respect for personal opinions in religion, and a
literalism which often suffocated possibilities for the alternative world
required in creative thought. While Alexander Campbell was at some
pains to hold the door open, at least part way, succeeding generations
of Disciples would experience little difficulty in closing that door.
Chapter 10 describes the post-war Disciples, arguing over the door, as
"the Peripatetic Generation."

10

Reaction and Conflict:
The Peripatetic Generation

The Greek philosopher Aristotle (384-322 B.C.) studied under Plato at the academy in Athens, tutored Alexander the Great, taught in Athens as head of the Peripatetic School, and produced treatises in logic, metaphysics, natural science, ethics and politics, rhetoric, and poetics. Following his singularly creative life and work, a new generation of teachers arose who emphasized parts of his thought rather than the whole, and who were less interested in developing new understandings than in magnifying limited aspects of his work. Some of these teachers have been called the Peripatetic School. Edward Zeller (1814-1908), the German philosopher and theologian, wrote that the later Peripatetic School made no essential changes in the fundamentals of Aristotle's metaphysics or other philosophical thought, but transmitted his Peripatetic doctrines unaltered.[1]

Beginning in the ninth century A.D. there arose a movement which combined Aristotle's teachings with the mystical and intuitional tradition of the early Church fathers, especially Saint Augustine, which became known as Scholasticism. This movement was dominant in western Christian civilization until about the seventeenth century.

Using these historical developments as a model, some Restoration Movement historian-critics—in particular, George G. Beazley, Jr.—have used the term Scholasticism to denote the doctrines of the second generation of Disciples leadership. Beazley observed that, with the exception of a few creative individuals, Disciples leaders generally continued the directions set by Alexander Campbell and Walter P. Scott. Campbell and Scott had provided the great creative push, but "the views of the founding fathers tended to crystallize into a rigid legalism, and this era was dominated by a Disciple Scholasticism."[2]

Based on the preceding discussion, it is suggested that the term Peripatetic may be more descriptive than the word Scholastic. The "blowup" and magnification of first generation Disciples' "opinions"

---

[1]Edward Zeller, *Outlines of the History of Greek Philosophy,* tr. L. R. Palmer and rev. Wilhelm Nestle (New York: Dover, 1980; reprint of 1931 edition), 201.

[2]George G. Beazley, Jr., Ronald Osborne, and others use the term Scholasticism for the period c. 1866-1917. See esp. Beazley, *The Christian Church (The Disciples of Christ),* 27.

into fundamental creedal tenets resemble a distorted growth rather than petrification. The urgency of secondary issues—questions relating to church structure, methodology in carrying out the Great Commission of Christ, or in Christian social action—questions concerning who could fellowship with whom in the family of God—obscured the spirituality of Thomas Campbell.

Campbell's "Declaration and Address" indirectly rejected these secondary issues. He wrote:

> . . . our differences, at most, are about the things in which the kingdom of God does not consist, that is, about matters of private opinion as human invention. What a pity that the kingdom of God should be divided about such things![3]

The various documents of the early Restoration Movement may give the impression that the great Protestant themes of grace, sin, and the sacrifice of Christ are less vital to the Movement than procedural matters relating to "obedience to the gospel," the "ancient order," Christian unity, and personal righteousness. The latter themes, secondary to the first in a balanced system of Christian values, appeared in print much more often. However, a careful look reveals that the articles of Campbell's *Millennial Harbinger,* Stone's *Christian Messenger,* and Scott's *Evangelist* reflect a strong emphasis on Christian redemption. Even when not explicitly stated, the tenor of the articles assumes that redemption is the point of the entire Christian enterprise. Themes relating to the love of God, Christian love, and the indwelling work of the Holy Spirit *after* conversion were often studied by Richardson, Alexander Campbell, and Scott.

Walt Yancey has recently examined the heritage of the Restoration Movement. He recognizes that between 1832 and the mid-1880s the Movement continued without any overt divisions. Matters of disagreement were often hotly debated, but generally relegated to the realm of personal opinion, and fellowship between the parties continued. This is what the first generation of leaders preached and practiced. Things did not continue that way:

> However, in the second generation of the movement there arose a group of men who began to expand the list of what they considered to be fundamental Christian doctrine. There was a small group of influential editors of some of the brotherhood papers who agitated regarding these issues through their periodicals and thus kept the controversies alive. The efforts of this small group of men were instrumental in undermining the spirit of for-

[3]Thomas Campbell, "Declaration and Address" in Young, *Historical Documents,* 94.

bearance that had prevailed in the first generation leaders, sowing the seeds of the division which was to come in the third generation. Without the efforts of this small group, perhaps none of the issues would ever have caused the movement to divide.[4]

The minor issues, which became major for this editorial group, included the aesthetics of worship, the subject of entertainment, and the question of open communion. These were not new questions; all had been addressed by Alexander Campbell himself. The new dimension was the elevation of such issues to the status of Christian fundamentals. The shift which changed Thomas Campbell's definitions of "faith" and "opinion" also changed the concept of "restoring" the "ancient order." This shift produced a powerful impact on Restoration Movement aesthetics: it diminished avenues for artistic expression. The drama of redemption which had motivated the great artists of the Reformation was subordinated to issues which lacked the power to generate masterpieces in music, visual arts, or literature.

In the nineteenth century, as Garrett has aptly written, it came to be said that the Disciples did not have bishops—they had editors![5] Alexander Campbell recognized the dangers of the multitude of editorial thrones that were erected in the growing brotherhood, each with its own doctrinal hobbyhorse. As early as 1844 Campbell was bothered by inferior editorial proclamations and proposed criteria for editors of Christian publications.

> Christian editors ought, therefore, to be pious, learned, and dignified men; men of whom their readers ought not be ashamed; men capable of leading the public mind forward in the paths of learning, good taste, good manners, and Christian erudition; men of wisdom, prudence, and a perspicuous, argumentative, and forcible eloquence. —Such editors, and such only, can be really profitable to any community. . . . Invidious though it may seem, duty, nevertheless, constrains this avowal, that we have entirely too many editors, or, what is the same thing, too many periodicals. There is a sort of editorial mania abroad in the land.[6]

In 1852 Campbell became concerned about the anti-evangelical teaching of Jesse B. Ferguson of Nashville, Tennessee. Ferguson edited the *Christian Magazine* in which he presented ideas concerning Spirit-

---

[4]Walt Yancey, *Endangered Heritage: An Evaluation of Church of Christ Doctrine* (Joplin, Mo.: College Press Publishing, 1987), 59-60.

[5]Garrett, *Stone-Campbell Movement*, 409.

[6]Alexander Campbell, "The Crisis," *Millennial Harbinger* (1844): 170.

ualism and his so-called Post-mortem Gospel. Campbell addressed the problem of irresponsible brotherhood journals which were spreading unsound doctrine:

> The unlicensed press of the present day, and especially in our department of reformation, is the most fearful omen in my horizon. . . . As a community we have been the most reckless in choosing our editors, our scribes, our elders and our preachers. . . . We have had a brood of periodicals the most voluntary and irresponsible that I have ever known. We have editors just out of the shell of conversion; a youth converted this year, the next a *preacher*; the next a *scribe,* then an *editor*!![7]

Campbell's motivations may well have included a desire to protect his Bethany enterprises, so that the *Millennial Harbinger* remained the primary journal of the Movement. However, the heretical extremes in Ferguson's *Christian Messenger,* as well as polemic narrowness in other budding Disciples papers, contributed to his concern over how to control their proliferation within the freedom of the Restoration Movement. Campbell advocated establishment of three periodicals for the Movement: one weekly, one monthly, and one quarterly.

> These ably conducted, well sustained, and widely circulated, with reputable contributors from all the land, would meet the entire wants of this age, and save the community many thousands of dollars per annum for better purposes than for the readings of diluted ideas in Homeopathic doses, as we now have them dispensed in invisible pills, in the ratio of one to a gallon of water.[8]

Campbell attempted to critique the competing journals, and often felt required to pronounce some espoused doctrine to be outside the range of acceptable Christian belief. Predictably, he was accused of playing pope to the growing band of Disciples. Ferguson evidently felt he was being dealt with high-handedly and must have written that he spurned "papal authority, from Rome or Bethany" and that Campbell and other critics were attempting to crucify him, because Campbell responded that Ferguson "imagines more than he sees, and regards his best friends as about to crucify him. No one, unless superexcited, could see racks, and inquisitions, and crosses, at Pittsburg, Memphis, Cincinnati, and Bethany." Campbell wrote that he personally had authority

---

[7]Alexander Campbell, "The Christian Magazine No. 1," *Millennial Harbinger* (1852): 390.

[8]Campbell, "The Christian Magazine No. I," 391.

neither in Nashville nor in Rome, and prayed that "grace, mercy and peace, may be multiplied to them all, and to all that love our Lord Jesus Christ sincerely."[9]

Alexander Campbell occasionally made reference to serious deviations by Disciples from evangelical faith: some to Unitarianism, some to Swedenborgianism (as in the case of Jesse Ferguson), and some to Mormonism. Sidney Rigdon's defection from the young reformation to Mormon doctrine gave Campbell much heartache, as evidenced by several critiques in the *Harbinger,* and so did the similar defection of Dr. John Thomas to the Christadelphian Church.

Although Campbell and his editorial colleague, Robert Richardson, were distressed over deviations from evangelical Christian orthodoxy, they were more concerned about the frequently appearing spectre of good Disciples leaders majoring in the publication of their own personal opinions. More and more, those doctrines of personal opinion became, for some, fundamental to fellowship. Garrett observes, "there was something in the chemistry of the Movement that attracted printer's ink. Most all the leaders chose to be editors, with some more daring than others."[10] James DeForest Murch also discusses this period:

> Reactionary elements in the churches were bringing controversial issues to the fore. Among these people debates were considered to be more important than the preaching of the gospel and the salvation of souls. They regarded those who disagreed with their opinions, not as erring brethren, but as their enemies and the enemies of the truth. Incompetent leaders founded a whole flock of new reactionary journals by which they disseminated their views. Hobbies were brought to the front, subordinate and insignificant points were magnified, and the rights of churches and individuals to hold new and progressive ideas in the realm of expediency were vigorously denied.[11]

McAllister and Tucker also argue that the view taken by some of the second- and third-generation Disciples leaders was arbitrary and distorted. It emphasized Campbell's "inflexible Christian primitivism" but "virtually ignored the Lunenberg Letter which he wrote at the height of his powers." The rigid and unloving view of Campbell contributed to the rise of the Peripatetic Generation and multiplied problems which hastened the fragmentation of the Stone-Campbell Movement.[12]

[9]See ibid., 629, for Ferguson's remarks and Campbell's responses.

[10]Garrett, *Stone-Campbell Movement,* 390.

[11]James DeForest Murch, *Christians Only, A History of the Restoration Movement* (Cincinnati: Standard Publishing, 1962), 167.

[12]McAllister and Tucker, *Journey in Faith,* 158. The Lunenberg Letter is discussed in chapter 6 of this work.

Murch agrees that Campbell's death left matters in a confusing and potentially destructive state of affairs, partly due to the rigid constructions by the multiplied editors on what had earlier been considered "opinion."

> With the passing of Alexander Campbell it became clear that there was no comparable leader upon which his mantle could immediately fall. This vacuum drew several good men into prominence, largely because they were editors of journals of considerable circulation. Each operated independently and there was little agreement among them on matters of opinion. Their readers and followers in the churches were soon plunged into controversies. With no voice from Bethany to arbitrate or ameliorate the differences, a grave situation confronted the brotherhood.[13]

Missing from most of the tremendous amount of editorial discussion about the nature of the church and its problems, purposes, and structure were the classical themes which concerned the sixteenth-century Protestant reformers: redemption, grace, worship, the incarnation—and the most fundamental act of God's mercy in giving His Son for the sins of the world.

As suggested in chapter 5, a deep bonding of Christian love was hampered by emphasizing secondary matters such as the use of instrumental music in worship, proper methodology of church cooperation, and how to deal with "the sects." More importantly, in terms of this particular study, the Peripatetics failed to provide significant substance on which to base Christian celebration in worship, literature, and the arts.

Yet, it is wrong to attribute the infighting and clamor to only "ignorance, prejudice, personal ambition, reactionism, and sociological conditions." The root problem, identified by both Alexander Campbell and Robert Richardson, was a lack of commitment to Christ and inability or refusal to understand the differences between matters of opinion and matters of faith.[14]

Richardson anticipated the gradual shift in emphasis within the Restoration Movement from an inclusivist stance based upon spiritual life in Christ, to an ever-stronger demand for conformity to "the plea" and a standardized set of religious mores. This shift was generally enforced by the increasing authority of religious editors. In his booklet, *Principles and Objectives of Religious Reformation,* he wrote:

---

[13]Murch, *Christians Only*, 167.

[14]Murch agrees, and indicates that the infighting has typically, and wrongly, been attributed to "ignorance, prejudice, personal ambition, reactionism, and sociological conditions." See ibid., 158.

It is preposterous to expect that men will ever agree in their religious opinions. It is neither necessary nor desirable that they should do so. It is nowhere commanded in the Scriptures that men should be of one opinion. On the contrary, differences of opinion are distinctively recognized, and Christians are expressly commanded to receive them (Rom. 14:1). As well might we expect to conform the features of the human face to a single standard, as to secure a perfect agreement of men's minds. Hence, there can be no peace, unless there be *liberty of opinion.*[15]

The marriage of the Stone-oriented Kentucky Christians and Alexander Campbell's associates, the Disciples, remained almost intact throughout the American Civil War. To a great extent, this was because Campbell refused to condemn slaveholding as such, since he could find no direct scriptural condemnation of the institution. On the other hand, he argued that slaveholding was a blight on America and released the slaves over whom he had jurisdiction at his first opportunity to do so. This position made him personally unwelcome by both northern abolitionists and southern politicians, and he was in the painful position of having members of his family oppose each other in the Union and Confederate armies. However, by judicious compromise and the moral power of his own personal influence, he helped bring the Movement through the war in one tenuous piece. Although Campbell was aging and his effectiveness waned late in the war years, his earlier teaching about unity was influential enough to help the churches weather this most stressful of tests.

Ironically, the fellowship which had managed by and large to maintain external unity throughout the Civil War began to come apart shortly afterward. Issues which seem much less destructive to the churches than war between Americans were the foci of great controversies. Issues that stirred the most debate were open communion, the use of the title "Reverend," the "one-man system" of the pastorate, the use of the organ in worship, and organized missionary societies.

The controversy over instrumental music was visible to all and related to external aesthetics. More fundamental in shaping an ethos that related to both theology and aesthetics, however, was the concept[16] that placed those matters of "opinion" in a position of such prominence.

---

[15]Robert Richardson, *The Principles and Objects of the Religious Reformation Urged by A. Campbell and Others. Briefly Stated and Explained,* 2d ed. (Bethany: A. Campbell, 1853).

[16]The word "epistemology," which entered the English language around 1856, might be a better word to use. That is, what were the nature and grounds of the reformers' understanding, with reference to its limits and validity?

Many theses, articles and books have been written which speculate bout these issues which caused division after the Civil War.[17] Generally, the leaders of that era grouped themselves into two camps,[18] although their alignment did not constitute a clean liberal-conservative or exclusivist-inclusivist division on all issues. Some conservatives were tolerant of the Missionary Society but against instrumental music; others (such as the scholarly J. W. McGarvey) opposed the introduction of instrumental music into the churches but refused to break fellowship over the issue. The question of "close communion" does not seem to have been a highly divisive issue at any time in Disciples history, but the question of open membership (the acceptance of non-immersed members of other communions into churches of the Restoration Movement without baptism by immersion) proved to be a highly charged issue which divided the churches from late in the nineteenth century to the present.

After the conclusion of the Civil War in April 1865, and the death of Alexander Campbell in March 1866, Restoration concepts became more polarized. Much of the momentum for the polarization had begun before the war but was restrained only by the Movement's original passion for unity. After the death of Campbell, whose influence had been the glue that held the group together, debates over what was faith and what was opinion took on judgmental overtones that presaged serious trouble in the fellowship.

Some of the Peripatetic leaders adopted a more restricted approach to the silence of the Bible, with the implicit demand that matters of spiritual importance which were not directly authorized by the New Testament (or at least indirectly modeled in New Testament practice) were to be omitted from Disciples practice. Conversely, others believed that the intent of the "Declaration and Address," and more important, primitive New Testament Christianity, was to allow creative development by the churches through the leading of the Spirit to meet the exigencies of new and emerging social conditions. The second group emphasized Christian unity more than the "pattern" and the "ancient order"—terms which Campbell had used often in *The Christian Baptist.*

[17]For example, see James R. Wilburn, *The Hazard of the Die: Tolbert Fanning and the Restoration Movement* Austin, Texas: Sweet Publishing, 1969); A. T. DeGroot, *The Grounds of Division Among Disciples of Christ* (Chicago: privately published, 1940); David E. Harrell, *The Social Sources of Division in the Disciples of Christ 1865-1900* (Atlanta: Publication Systems, 1973); Forest E. Reed, *Background of Division Between Disciples of Christ and Churches of Christ* (Nashville: Disciples of Christ Historical Society, 1968): and Henry E. Webb, "Sectional Conflicts and Schism within the Disciples of Christ Following Civil War," in *Essays on New Testament Christianity*, ed. Robert Wetzel (Cincinnati: Standard Publishing, 1978).

[18]Not until 1906 did the United States government publish separate census figures for the Churches of Christ and the Christian Churches.

Plate 12
MOSES E. LARD
Courtesy Disciples of Christ Historical Society

Since the protagonists of each group were not consistent in what they were for or against, it is difficult to label one group "conservative" and the other group "liberal." The "conservatives" (on some issues) included J. W. McGarvey, Moses E. Lard, Benjamin Franklin, Tolbert Fanning, and David Lipscomb. All these men were editors and writers and most were teachers in colleges. McGarvey and Lard were both graduates of Bethany and students of Alexander Campbell. Although both opposed the Bethany positions on some divisive issues, they represented analytical biblical scholarship and could be considered "moderate" in their attitudes toward the unity of the Movement. Murch has painted a vignette of Lard:

> Moses E. Lard published a quarterly which expressed extreme conservative views. In his personality and his contentions he presented a complete contradiction. He was cordial and gracious and on occasion voiced such left-wing concepts as pacifism and universalism. But when it came to maintaining the ground that Campbell held in his *Christian Baptist* days he was adamant. In his writings he was extremely pessimistic, especially about minor concerns.[19]

Richardson mentioned an event that occurred while Lard was still at Bethany. In 1855, John B. Jeter, a highly respected Baptist minister and an old antagonist of Campbell, had written a critical book, *Campbellism Examined.* Campbell commissioned Lard to write a reply to Jeter's book. Apparently, Lard's essay was characteristic of his later editorial approach. Richardson's description seems to indicate that this was the case:

> This "Review of Campbellism Examined," forming a volume of two hundred and ninety-seven pages, appeared in 1857, with a short preface by Mr. Campbell, and was regarded generally by the Reformers as a triumphant refutation of Elder Jeter's arguments, which it discussed with unusual logical skill. Some of its expositions of Scripture, however, were considered more ingenious than correct, while the tartness and severity of its language seemed to many ill-accordant with the spirit in which religious discussion should be conducted.[20]

Lard represented the convergent school of thought which viewed any change of "apostolic practice" as an "innovation." The word "innovation" became, in Lard's usage and that of his colleagues, a term

[19]Murch, *Christians Only,* 159.
[20]Richardson, *Memoirs,* 2:624.

for disloyalty to the original "plea" and breaking ranks with the "ancient order of things" which had been advocated in the *Christian Baptist* between 1823 and 1830. The pressure for innovation, from brethren who were labelled "digressive," was considered an insidious work of Satan to capsize the Restoration Movement. Lard wrote a polemic essay, *Instrumental Music and Dancing,* which was representative of the bitter, antagonistic, and dogmatic tracts and journal articles of that period. In retrospect, it is difficult to see how such insignificant matters could occupy the time—not to mention the paper and ink—of one committed to dissemination of the gospel. Lard was among that Peripatetic Generation who raised non-essentials to the level of Christian fundamentals.[21]

Benjamin Franklin (1812-78), who published the *American Christian Review,* was probably the best known, the most travelled, and perhaps the most influential editor among the Disciples since Alexander Campbell. Franklin, largely a self-educated man of a generous spirit toward those with whom he disagreed, supported the missionary society for a time. After the Civil War and the death of Campbell, however, he became ultraconservative and violently opposed any who disagreed with him. He became opposed to missionary societies (which might destroy the autonomy of the local church); he no longer supported Bible colleges because he believed they had left the Campbellian ideals, and were instead centers for theological education and the training of preachers.

J. W. McGarvey graduated from Bethany College in 1850, where he was remembered by Alexander Campbell as one of Bethany's best and most gifted students. McGarvey diligently studied the scriptures, and for forty years he was on the faculty of the College of the Bible in Lexington, Kentucky, sixteen of which he spent as president. McGarvey wrote the definitive commentary for Disciples on the book of Acts; after a trip to the Holy Land, his experiences were recorded in his *Lands of the Bible.*

McGarvey personally opposed the use of instrumental music in the worship service, but did not want to make it a reason for breaking the unity of the Movement. This position made him "neither fish or fowl" in relation to the extreme positions taken by his brethren. As the emerging liberalism of the left began to champion biblical criticism and to question some of the fundamentals of historic Christian orthodoxy, McGarvey edited a column in the *Christian Standard*—a publication he had earlier opposed—to expose what he considered to be fallacies of the higher critics. Though his tone became quite biting and sometimes sarcastic, McGarvey's column and the journal itself have been credited as

---

[21]See Murch, *Christains Only,* Garrett, *Stone-Campbell Movement,* Richardson, *Memoirs,* and Louis and Bess Cochran, *Captives of the Word* for discussions of this generation of Restoration Movement personalities.

influential in attempting to keep the movement true to its original principles.

David Lipscomb became the second editor of the *Gospel Advocate* in Nashville, Tennessee following the founding editor, Tolbert Fanning. Lipscomb was opposed to the Christian Missionary Society, instrumental music, and "innovations" in the churches generally. He was a graduate of Tolbert Fanning's Franklin College, the forerunner of David Lipscomb College in Nashville. Both Fanning and Lipscomb exerted a strong and conservative influence on the southern churches, who for the most part followed them without question.

One can see that it is difficult to place any member of this second generation into one of two or three camps. Bess and Louis Cochran demonstrate this difficulty in the following assessment of the four conservative giants discussed above:

> By a curious bit of reasoning both Moses Lard and John McGarvey made a distinction in their war on innovations, between an innovation for "work," such as the missionary society, and an innovation for "worship," such as the organ, and they refused to join David Lipscomb and Benjamin Franklin in opposing the missionary society. But all four men stood shoulder to shoulder in their battle against corrupting the purity of the New Testament pattern of worship by the use of a musical instrument.[22]

The Peripatetic Generation included other important leaders who assumed a broader and more inclusive stance in fellowship. Among them were W. K. Pendleton, Robert Richardson, Isaac Errett, and James A. Garfield.[23] Pendleton (d. 1899) and Richardson (d. 1876) spanned the leadership generations, since each had been associated with Thomas Campbell, Alexander Campbell, and Walter Scott. Both men had participated in the editorial labors of Alexander Campbell connected with the *Millennial Harbinger*.

Pendleton became Campbell's son-in-law twice,[24] succeeded him as President of Bethany College, and inherited the position of chief editor of the *Millennial Harbinger*. In terms of intellectual and spiritual leadership, he seems to have been the logical person to take up Alexander Campbell's mantle of leadership. In a valedictory editorial of 1864, Campbell gave high praise as he turned over the journal to Pendleton:

---

[22]Louis and Bess Cochran, *Captives of the Word,* 169.

[23]Again, see Murch, *Christians Only,* Garrison and DeGroot, *Disciples of Christ: A History*; McAllister and Tucker, *Journey in Faith*; Garrett, *Stone-Campbell Movement,* Richardson, *Memoirs,* and Louis and Bess Cochran, *Captives of the Word* for discussions of these Restoration Movement personalities.

[24]His first wife, Lavina Campbell Pendleton, died five years after their marriage in 1846.

The Harbinger, henceforth, will be conducted and published by my long and well-approved associate and co-laborer in many works, Prof. W. K. Pendleton. I need not say I have the fullest confidence in his fidelity and ability. He has been my co-editor for twenty years, and it is needless for me to say anything in special commendation of his scholarship, his enlarged Christian knowledge, his sound judgment, his great prudence, his temperate disposition, his firmness and fixedness of principle, his life-long devotion to the broadest and most permanent interests of our cause, and his high moral courage in proclaiming and defending the principles of apostolic Christianity.[25]

Pendleton, however, did not have the aggressiveness and tenacity of his father-in-law. Therefore, the tenor of *Harbinger* was changed and it soon became only one among the many Disciples journals circulating in the late nineteenth century.

Pendleton is an interesting person in light of his sympathies toward the arts. He seems to have been a cultured gentleman who was fond of literature, painting, sculpture, and natural beauty. He was a student of the scriptures and could discuss them from a philosophical point of view. Nevertheless, he adopted an attitude about human nature that was then prevalent among even educated men of his time. He believed that Caucasians possessed the highest degree of perfection in moral feeling and intellectual powers, and that in other races these powers were inferior.

So, on at least one issue Pendleton must have complicated matters for his father-in-law unnecessarily, and in the process hastened the day when he himself would have to write the last farewell on behalf of the *Millennial Harbinger* (in 1870). Alexander Campbell attempted—with some success—to mediate the Northern and Southern constituencies of the Movement by assuming a moderate stance on the slavery matter. He was critical of slavery as a blot on the American conscience, but he also refused to support the militant abolitionists. He felt that his position on both sides was based on New Testament teaching.[26]

---

[25]"A. Campbell to His Readers," *Millennial Harbinger* (1864): 43-44.

[26]The demise of the *Harbinger* under Pendleton's editorship was a sort of Catch-22 situation. Before the war, Northern Disciples believed it to be biased toward the South's position on slavery because Campbell refused to join the abolitionists even though he condemned slavery. After the war began in 1861, mail service was disrupted and the *Harbinger* could not reach the very areas where its greatest support had been. After the war, the *Harbinger* was viewed as being published on the wrong side of the line and was generally out of favor in the North. See J. S. Lamar, *Memoirs of Isaac Erret*, 2 vols. (Cincinnati: Standard Publishing Co., 1893), 1: 246.

One of the most difficult questions faced by this second generation of leaders, be they liberal or conservative, was the Gordian knot of how to interpret the Disciples maxim, "where the scriptures speak, we speak; where the scriptures are silent, we are silent." The way in which these leaders understood the Disciples shibboleth, "silence of the scriptures," affected the way they viewed other theological questions. Some believed that a church was free to act in any way it chose on matters not expressly commanded or prohibited in the scriptures; others held that if the scriptures did not expressly mention a matter, the churches had no right to take any kind of action. This, of course, led to other divisions—e.g., whether a matter was or was not fully revealed in the scriptures.

One important question which was impinged upon by "silence of the scriptures" was the operation of the Holy Spirit. Was it actively guiding those who read the scriptures? Was the church still being created through the presence of the Spirit in the world? Was the "dry word alone" theory (about which Richardson had complained) the correct understanding of "God with us"? These interpretations were related to the matter of closed and convergent thought processes versus open, divergent, non-conformist thinking.

These are the kinds of questions that must have been on the mind of W. K. Pendleton in 1866 when he addressed the American Christian Missionary Society on the occasion of its eighteenth anniversary, at Cincinnati, Ohio.[27] Pendleton took a stance of freedom on "silence of the scriptures," the same stance he believed that Thomas Campbell, Alexander Campbell, John T. Johnson, Barton W. Stone, and Walter Scott had taken.

Pendleton led up to his interpretation of "silence of the scriptures" by beginning his address with a description of the ready harvests of the world and the shortage of laborers available from the Disciples of Christ. He stated that the missionary enterprise was not optional for a church that believed the Great Commission of Christ. He then cast about for reasons the Society had not been more successful. Pendleton was aware that some who were opposed to the Missionary Society believed they were speaking in the spirit of Alexander Campbell's *Christian Baptist* days. He therefore pointed out that Campbell had accepted the presidency of the Society in its first year of 1849 and held that post until his death.

He then got to the essence of the question of the silence of scripture by discussing extra-church organizations designed to carry out the church's assigned task. He agreed that there was "no special express

---

[27]The following discussion is based on "Address by W. K. Pendleton," *Millennial Harbinger* (1866): 501.

precept" in the scriptures commanding a missionary society. He then asked, "Is everything which is not scriptural, therefore wrong? Is everything, for which there is no special precept in the scriptures, therefore and necessarily unscriptural?"

Pendleton then listed three very different senses in which he believed the term "not scriptural" might be used:

> We sometimes use it positively as equivalent to antiscriptural, or literally forbidden; sometimes indefinitely in the sense of *not positively and expressly* commanded,—and yet again, inferentially to mean *not in harmony with the spirit and tenor of Scripture.* Now I need not tell the logician, that he must make his election in the beginning of the argument, which of these meanings he takes. . . . Does he say that our Missionary Society is *anti-Scriptural,* that is, especially forbidden in the Scriptures?—then we challenge him to the proof. . . . But it cannot be done. There is no such Scripture. Does he say that it is not *positively and expressly* commanded; then we demand by what canon of interpretation does he make mere *silence* prohibitory? You reply, the canon which forbids anything as a rule of Christian faith as duty, for which these cannot be expressly produced a 'Thus saith the Lord,' 'either in express terms or by approved precedent'. . . . We ask this objector then, whence came this canon? Does he find it in *express terms* in the Scriptures? He will not say so. Yet he makes it a rule of Christian duty, that is, a rule by which he regulates his conduct as a Christian. In *adopting* the canon with his restricted interpretation of it, he *violates* the canon.[28]

To drive his argument home, Pendleton pointed out that Thomas Campbell's 1809 Washington Christian Association, from which the Restoration Movement had grown, began as an extra-church organization which had officers, sent out ministers, and received contributions. Therefore, it would be inconsistent for the descendants of that association to condemn any other similar organization. He concluded that the silence of scripture on a given subject should not be taken as a positive rule of prohibition against all freedom of action or obligation of duty.

Pendleton was eloquent in showing the foolishness of a Christian who would stifle his talents and tastes by a closed, convergent interpretation of "silence of the scriptures."

> That large freedom of thought and action, and that resistless spontaneity of benevolence, which makes a Christian a living

[28]Ibid., 501-2.

power for good, wherever he goes, would be cramped and stifled by so narrow a principle, till Christianity would become a timid and cringing thing of forms, and afraid to expand itself in free and Godlike charities, lest it might startle some slumbering knight of silence into crying, 'Beware—beware—the thing is not spoken of in Scripture.'[29]

The consequences of the "silence of the scripture" position is directly related to the aesthetic-artistic possibilities for the Stone-Campbell Movement.

Pendleton's testimony concerning the attitude of the Campbells, whom he knew so intimately, has been brushed aside by some[30] who have either ignored Alexander Campbell's own activity on behalf of the missionary society or imply that he was not fully himself and was more or less forced into its leadership. Campbell's writings in the *Harbinger* after the Society's founding in 1849, however, reveal both his enthusiastic support and his full powers of reasoning.

Dr. Robert Richardson's deep commitment to unity has already been discussed in chapter 9. Richardson was inclusivist in fellowship, meek in Christian personal relationships, and spiritual in faith. He believed in the indwelling power of the Holy Spirit, and produced some of the first and richest devotional literature ever created by Disciples in his *Communings in the Sanctuary*. Not satisfied with the one-dimensional life of a man of science, he valued the arts and engaged in making both music and painting. He wrote with an elegant nineteenth-century style and showed a sensitivity for *mot juste*, which made him among the best of his colleague editors. Richardson was able to interpret articulately the Campbell plea, but was also the alter ego of Alexander Campbell[31]

[29]Ibid., 505.

[30]For example, Earl Irvin West, *The Search for the Ancient Order*, 2 vols. (Indianapolis: Earl West Religious Book Service, 1950), 2:51-53 notes Pendleton's arguments concerning the silence of the scriptures. Contending that Thomas Campbell's interest was similar to that of the opponents of innovations later in the century, he explains that at the time of the Washington Christian Association, neither Campbell nor his associates had yet come into a full realization of the implications of their own policy. West believes, "The door was now open, and human opinions, as they applied to the work and worship of the church, multiplied. To try to sweep back the avalanche by calling for divine authority was like trying to dry up the ocean with a sponge. . . . Nevertheless, an element remained to whom the call for divine authority still meant something. They believed that whatever in the practice of religion was not authorized by the word of God was wrong. The *Gospel Advocate* and the *American Christian Review* maintained this conviction down through the years. . . . These two types of thinking are responsible for even modern-day differences in religious practice. The use of instrumental music, missionary societies, and the many other practices, based on no divine authority, are but symptoms of the real trouble, which lies basically at this point."

[31]See Garrett, *Stone-Campbell Movement*, 360-61.

At least once, however, Richardson became involved in an editorial war with Tolbert Fanning of the *Gospel Advocate,* who took exception to a series by Richardson on the subject of "Faith and Philosophy." In response to Richardson's first installment, Fanning made some bold statements which denied both *a priori* and *a posteriori* knowledge, and the idea that God can be understood through nature. The discussion hinged specifically on the meaning of Rom. 1:19-20:

> Because that which may be known of God is manifest in them, for God hath shewed it unto them. For the invisible things of him from the Creation of the world, are clearly seen, being understood by the things that are made, even his eternal Power and Godhead, so that they are without excuse.

Fanning denied the orthodox interpretation, that the created external universe reveals enough of God that the Gentile world is without excuse in ignoring his word.

Fanning made several blunders which were irresistible for Richardson, who replied with some sarcasm over the errors of fact and the logical inconsistencies he found bristling in the *Advocate* editor's argument. This generated a predictable response from Fanning, which caused the aging Alexander Campbell to finally take up his pen to come out in favor of his junior editor.

Sadly, this altercation further separated and polarized the positions of the "inclusive" and "exclusive" groups on questions of scriptural silence, fellowship, spirituality, and what the "conservative" wing felt were both loss of the "original plea" and introduction of "innovations" by the "liberals." Nevertheless, the life and practice of the gentle Bethany physician exerted a strong influence toward sensitivity, devotion in worship, and intellectual openness among many, and thus helped maintain the unity of the Movement through the Peripatetic days of the late nineteenth century.

If the Campbell heir was not either Pendleton or Richardson, it may be that Isaac Errett turned out to be the true leader of the Movement after Campbell's death. Murch is enthusiastic in acknowledging the importance of Errett's understanding, insight, and broad vision during the difficult years of the Peripatetic leaders. Garret agrees with Murch, calling Errett "a special hero" in Disciples history. T. W. Grafton, who lived closer to the period, also saw Errett as one who held the Movement together.[32]

Errett was born in New York City in 1820. He was raised in a strict religious environment, and experienced hard work and great difficulties after the early death of his father and the remarriage of his mother. He had limited formal education, but was an avid reader and was able to get a start in newspaper writing by working for a Pittsburgh printer who published a paper. In his youthful leadership of a Disciples congregation in Pittsburgh, he became practiced in giving sermons, gradually growing into an excellent speaker.

Errett was a militant opponent of slavery, a position different from the mediating stance maintained by Alexander Campbell. He became the first corresponding secretary for the American Christian Missionary Society in 1857. This position placed him squarely in the center of primary issues that related to the growing numbers of Restoration churches. Some of these issues were foreign missions, congregational cooperation, and North-South differences over slavery.

In 1862 Errett's name appeared as co-editor of the *Millennial Harbinger,* along with Alexander Campbell, A. W. Campbell, and W. K. Pendleton. In 1863, Errett unwittingly drew a critical attack when, to help interpret the beliefs of his Detroit, Michigan church for the community, he published a "Synopsis of the Faith and Practice of the Church of Christ." For some reason this pamphlet caused a major-level furor among the so-called editor-bishops of various Disciples publications, who saw themselves aligned along *Christian Baptist*-oriented lines.

First, some of the smaller, Detroit-based journals took aim at Errett for his publication; then he suffered injury from the *American Christian Review* and next from *Lard's Quarterly.* The charge against Errett may have been because some thought he had attempted to make a "creed" for a Church of Christ—which violated one of the first principles of the Restoration Movement. It seems that he listed some of his church's beliefs in numerical order, i.e., I, II, III, etc. Someone complained that this was the way Protestant or Catholic creeds or confessions of faith were printed; thus, if this pamphlet were a creed, it would be unscriptural. Whether this was the major complaint against Errett—or whether

---

[32]See Murch, *Christians Only,* 165; Garrett, *Stone-Campbell Movement,* 491; and T. W. Grafton, *Men of Yesterday* (St. Louis: Christian Publishing Co., 1899), 176. For much the the biographical information about Errett, I have relied on Lamar, *Memoirs,* as cited in n. 25 above. Not all of Errett's contemporaries or descendants in the Stone-Campbell Movement have regarded him as a hero, of course. West, in his *Search for the Ancient Order,* has made this clear in the chapter about Errett's life. West acknowledges the admiration held for Errett by the present-day Disciples historians, and he might have added that most "centrists" also hold him in high regard. West warns his readers that not all historians agree concerning the merits of Isaac Errett.

there was some other undisclosed foment in progress—the pamphlet brought out intense attacks against him.

The argument cooled off when Errett finally convinced his attackers that his document was merely a *tract* and served the same purpose as a sermon or journal article on First Principles. It was the form of the presentation and not its substance which had caused the clamor.

This incident is fairly representative of the highly charged state of mind which prevailed in this Peripatetic Generation as preachers and editors felt called upon to guard "the faith once delivered to the saints," particularly as that faith had been interpreted through the focus of *The Christian Baptist*. It also underlines the need for the kind of leader Errett turned out to be at this stage of the Stone-Campbell Movement history.

In 1865, Errett was called to Hiram, Ohio as head of the biblical literature department of Western Reserve Eclectic Institute (later Hiram College). Included in the roster of the Board of Directors were James A. Garfield (1831-81), formerly head of the Hiram Eclectic Institute, and Thomas Wharton Phillips (1835-1912), a successful oil producer and friend of Alexander Campbell.[33] Errett remained there less than a year, however, for he was soon called to be the editor-in-chief of a new journal, *The Christian Standard*. Errett's associate editor was J. S. Lamar.

The new journal, under the leadership of the irenic Errett, produced a healing effect on the fragmenting Disciples movement.[34] He was able to lift the warring factions out of the mire of controversy and set their sights on the original purposes of the Restoration Movement. His intelligent and constructive articles and editorials were welcomed by many who sought unity built on the principle of the Bible as the sole rule of

---

[33]McAllister and Tucker, *Journey in Faith,* 230, write: "A one-time Disciples preacher, James A. Garfield substituted political platform for pulpit and advanced all the way to the White House. Unordained like most ministers of the Disciples in the late 1850s, he preached regularly on Sundays while engaged primarily as a teacher and then as principal at Hiram College in Ohio. Following a brief period in the Ohio senate and notable service [as a colonel] in the Union Army, he became a United States congressman in 1863 and won reelection to the House eight consecutive times. The Republican Party nominated him for President in 1880, and he defeated his Democratic opponent in the November election."

T. W. Phillips, who pioneered in developing Pennsylvania oil fields from 1861, was a member of the U. S. House of Representatives from 1893-97, and member of U. S. industrial commission from 1898-1902. The Phillips family has proved sturdy friends of various Disciples institutions of all branches, including the Disciples of Christ Historical Association Library where much of the research for this book took place.

[34]See Lamar, *Memoirs,* 315. The *Christian Standard*, like many post-war institutions, underwent great financial stress, and various schemes for its salvation were attempted. Ultimately, R. W. Carroll, a Quaker from Cincinnati, underwrote the journal and moved it from Alliance College, where Errett had been a short-term president, to Cincinnati where it still has a strong circulation and an active associated publishing house.

faith and practice. It seems ironic that the *Standard's* first issue, April 7, 1866, carried a memorial obituary for Alexander Campbell which stated that he had left no human leadership. And yet, that journal's editor, Isaac Errett, seems to be the one who partially took up Campbell's mantle.

One of the key issues with which Errett (and other Disciples leaders) had to deal was the question of whether the "pious unimmersed" could be admitted to the Lord's Table. The question, in its time, was parallel in its potential for unity or fragmentation with the present-day question of "open membership."[35]

The debate had begun in 1861 when one Richard Hawley of Michigan wrote to W. K. Pendleton of the *Harbinger* asking about "the propriety and correctness of cultivating friendly and confidential relations with all who love our Lord Jesus Christ in sincerity and truth?"[36] Errett, Richardson, and Pendleton—three "liberals"—responded in the journal to Hawley's query. Basically, they all agreed with Campbell's 1837 "Lunenberg Letter": that there are Christians among the Protestant sects.[37] Following are excerpts from the replies of Errett, Richardson, and Pendleton.

Errett contended: We are compelled . . . to recognize as Christians many who have been in error on baptism, but who in the *spirit* of obedience are Christians indeed. (See Rom. 2:28, 29.) I confess, for my own part, did I understand the position of the brethren to deny this, I would recoil from my position among them with utter disgust. It will never do to unchristianize those on whose shoulders we are standing, and because of whose previous labors we are enabled to see some truths more clearly than they.[38]

Errett, as Campbell had done numerous times,[39] refused to accept an utterly existential view of church history; nor would he assert that the church of the New Testament lacked historical continuity until the year 1809 in Washington, Pennsylvania. By acknowledging that the Restoration Movement stood on the shoulders of the Protestant Reformation, or upon other movements before Stone and the Campbells, Errett was questioning the "seven-league-boot theory" of Restoration—the idea that Stone and Campbell, by disregarding all the accretions of Christianity since the first century, had gone directly to the apostolic church with

---

[35]"Open membership," to members of the Stone-Campbell heritage, refers to admission of unimmersed members of other Christian denominations to church membership by transfer and without baptism by immersion.

[36]*Millennial Harbinger* (1861): 710.

[37]See chapter 6, pp. 131 ff. for a discussion of the "Lunenberg Letter."

[38]Errett, "Communing with the Sects," *Millennial Harbinger* (1861): 712.

[39]For one example, see the Introduction in Campbell's *The Christian System*.

no sense of obligation to anyone in the interim. Errett's position was opposed to the Restoration credo held by some of his post-war brethren, and could be expected to arouse another storm of criticism.

Robert Richardson was just as blunt in expressing his revulsion against extreme exclusivism practiced by Disciples churches and leaders. He replied to Mr. Hawley:

> I think with you that some articles in reference to the spirit in which all such matters are disposed of, would be useful; and when I read labored essays intended to build up exclusivism and Pharisaism amongst us, I often wish I had time to expose their sophistries. But I am too much occupied with my labors in the University here, and in the church, to write much at present.[40]

Richardson suggested that church leaders did not have to recognize immersed or unimmersed persons as Christians: "Our position is quite different; we neither discuss nor determine this question. We simply leave it to each individual to determine for himself." After a few years, this position became normative for both conservative and liberal Disciples. Upon it is centered the Communion announcement: we neither invite nor debar.

Pendleton's response to Hawley's query penetrated long-range issues for the young and growing Disciples fellowship. He shied away from the then-current idea of "restoration"—that Disciples congregations could and should be exact replicas of the apostolic church.[41] His usage of the word was spiritual, unity-oriented, and acknowledged the creative possibility of growth in human understanding.

> It is important to keep clearly and always before the mind the great principle of our movement in Reformation. We must remember that we are laboring, not to introduce a totally new church, but to restore the things which are wanting in one already existing; not to overthrow what is good, but to teach the way of the Lord more perfectly. Error as to ordinances may exist where there is genuine faith. Error is always injurious, but not necessarily fatal. In some points we do all offend—and in humility let us forbear.[42]

Remembering the heterogeneous makeup of the original Washington Christian Association, Pendleton asked: "Can we deny that God has

---

[40]*Millennial Harbinger* (1861): 712.

[41]Many twentieth-century followers of the Stone-Campbell Movement have discarded the concept of "restoration" because of this connotation.

[42]*Millennial Harbinger* (1861): 713.

recognized and is still recognizing the truly pious and full of faith and good works in the many divisions of professed Christians, as really and truly his people?" His answer acknowledged historic Christianity as well as a continuation of the charitable preaching of both Stone and Alexander Campbell:

> Will any one take the absurd position that the noble list of illustrious men who have been the light and ornament of religion in the ages that are past, and whose piety and learning are still the admiration and glory of the Lord's people—that all these, because of an error, not on the significancy or divine authority of baptism, but what we must be allowed to call its mode,—that all these, because of such an error, must be pushed from our ranks as reprobate—torn from our Christian affections as heretics—thrust from the communion of the body and blood of the Savior, whom for a long life they so truly loved and devotedly served, and counted no more worthy of our Christian fellowship than so many heathens and publicans! The conclusion is too monstrous for any but the hide-bound zealot of a cold and lifeless formalism. I should feel that I had injured the Christianity which I profess and which I love, could I recall that even for a moment I had allowed my head so to interpret its pleading mercy, or my heart so to restrict its wide-embracing charity.[43]

In April 1865, the very month the Civil War ended, Moses E. Lard, editor of *Lard's Quarterly*, began his own war with the *Harbinger* troika by writing an article strongly opposing the idea of "communing with the sects." His argument was:

> Let us agree to commune with the sprinkled sects around us, and soon we shall come to recognize them as Christians. Let us agree to recognize them as Christians, and immersion, with its deep significance, is buried in the grave of our folly.[44]

Although questions about baptism stirred a storm of controversy, the subject of communion did not, with but a few exceptions, become a divisive issue for Disciples. By the time Lard wrote, most congregations were practicing Richardson's exhortation to "Let each examine himself" as the primary criterion for inclusion at the Lord's Table. The underlying issue which had motivated the Lunenberg question and the Hawley question involved not only the extent to which one may fellowship with errant Christians, but whether indeed those in Protestant "sects" were

---

[43]Ibid., 714.

[44]*Lard's Quarterly* 2 (April 1865): 262.

indeed Christians. This issue has been a factor, from Campbell's baptism in 1812 until the present time, in relationships between various churches of the Stone-Campbell heritage and other Christian denominations. It is an ironic twist of history that the very position concerning the Lord's Supper which had occasioned the expulsion of Thomas Campbell from the Chartiers Presbytery of the Seceder Presbyterian Church in 1808 caused such a stir among his spiritual descendants only fifty years later.[45]

The Peripatetic Generation of Disciples leaders did not consist of only preachers and journal editors. As noted, James A. Garfield was an active Disciples church member and served on the Board of Directors of the Western Reserve Eclectic Institute.

Garfield was born November 19, 1831, in Orange Township on the Western Reserve. His parents were baptized by a Disciples preacher, Adamson Bentley, who was also a farmer and store operator. Garfield's father died later that same year, but his mother practiced her faith enthusiastically by studying the Bible, teaching her children, and walking three miles each Sunday to the closest Disciples church. Later, Mrs. Garfield gave a plot of land for the erection of a new church building closer to her home.[46]

In 1850, as a young man of about 19 or 20 years old, Garfield confessed his faith in Christ and was baptized—an experience Wasson calls his "spiritual awakening." His life became focused on his new spiritual commitment and provided the stimulus for his increasing interest in religion and education, especially for Disciples of Christ and the Western Reserve.

Garfield attended the Geauga Seminary in Chester, Ohio, where he became gradually more militant in expressing the exclusivist Restoration Movement attitudes toward other denominations. He then taught in rural Ohio schools for several years before entering the Western Eclectic Institute. He attended the Institute for three years[47] and then enrolled at Williams College in Massachusetts under the presidency and teaching of Professor Mark Hopkins. Garfield occupied his two years at Williams actively—in his courses, debating, writing articles for the *Williams Quarterly,* and in numerous kinds of student leadership. He kept several

---

[45]See chap. 1, pp. 8-10. Thomas Campbell was expelled for dispensing the Lord's Supper to non-Seceder Presbyterians.

[46]W. W. Wasson, *James A. Garfield: His Religion and Education* (Nashville: Tennessee Book Co., 1952), 12. For much of the Garfield's biographical information I have relied on Wasson, as well as McAllister & Tucker, *Journey in Faith.*

[47]He presumably left the Institute to attend Bethany College for further study under Alexander Campbell, whom he deeply admired. His own judgment, perhaps, surfaced in his decision to attend Williams instead of Bethany.

speaking engagements at scattered Disciples churches in New England and became strongly evangelistic in the process. He also began to develop an interest in politics and at the same time began to feel that Christian commitment required active resistance to slavery.

While he was a student at Williams, he heard Ralph Waldo Emerson speak. Garfield was so impressed by Emerson that he wrote the following entry in his journal:

> He is the most startlingly original thinker I ever heard. The bolt which he hurls against error, like Goethe's cannonball, goes 'fearful and straight shattering that it may reach and shatter what it reaches.' I could not sleep that night after hearing his thunderstorm of eloquent thoughts. It made *me* feel so small and insignificant to hear *him*.[48]

It is likely that Garfield's admiration for Emerson may have shaped his thinking and the way in which he encouraged the Disciples movement in future years.

In 1856 he was graduated from Williams College and taught ancient languages and literature at Western Reserve Eclectic Institute at Hiram, Ohio. As Garfield gained national prominence, he continued his activities as a lay preacher for the Disciples. Some of the incidents of his life during this time are of interest to Restoration Movement students.

One of these was his debate in 1858 with John Denton, a "freethinker" and experienced debater. The debate was held one year before publication of Charles Darwin's *Origin of Species,* and it reflected the ferment of current thought concerning the origin of the earth and mankind. Denton's presentation was entitled "Man, animals and vegetables came into existence by the operation of the laws of spontaneous generation and progressive development, and there is no direct evidence that there was ever any exercise of direct creative power on this planet." Garfield prepared thoroughly for the discussion, availing himself of all the books he could find in anthropology, geology, zoology, botany, and Christian evidences for creation.

The debate was considered by some Disciples to be a landmark, much like the 1829 debate between Alexander Campbell and Robert Owen. It occupied four days and drew capacity audiences in the Cuyahoga County town of Chagrin Falls. Although nothing definitive was decided, the Christians seemed to be pleased with Garfield's presentation, and the prestige of the Disciples grew. Garfield's preparation for the debate seems to have redirected some of his future studies, however. In an 1859 letter to a friend, Garfield wrote:

---

[48]Wasson, *James A. Garfield,* 41, from Garfield's Journal of August 22, 1854, Garfield Papers, Manuscripts Division, Library of Congress.

The battle of the evidences must now be fought on the field of natural sciences, and those who would be the leaders of their time must be armed with the weapons which the sciences afford.[49]

Although Garfield's academic emphasis had been primarily in the humanities, his new appreciation for the role of the sciences was exemplified in his emphasis on developing those studies at Hiram. The Bethany community also found a place for his new philosophy, and awarded him an honorary A.M. degree in 1861.[50] In the light of his distinguished war record in the Union Army and his election to the House of Representatives, it is not surprising that he was a welcome addition to the Bethany College Board of Trustees in 1866.[51]

Throughout his life Garfield remained a dedicated and sincere member of the Disciples fellowship, and retained his spiritual integrity. His inclination toward irenicism rather than divisiveness is evident in the encouragement he offered Isaac Errett to begin the *Christian Standard.* Even as President, he bore criticism for attending the small Disciples church on M Street and later on Vermont Street in Washington, D.C.

Nevertheless, there was a good deal of opposition by some Disciples leaders to Christian participation in any kind of political activity. David Lipscomb, editor of *The Gospel Advocate,* was one who stood firmly on the "conservative" side which condemned all political involvement by Christians (as well as involvement in "carnal" wars). Apparently, Lipscomb had suffered much during the Civil War from both the South and the North and he developed a negative attitude toward any kind of public service or public involvement to the point of even refusing to vote.[52]

Garfield's emergence from his rather parochial view of Christianity, with the limited vantage point of Hiram, to his exposure to a wider religious and philosophical spectrum, began in his decision to attend Williams College rather than Bethany. It continued through his debating, war experiences, and culminated in his years of national service in Washington, D.C. Some of Garfield's attitudes during the final period of his life suggest that he may have been more "liberal" than his *Christian Stan-*

---

[49]Wasson, *James Garfield,* quoting letter from Garfield to Burke Aaron Hinsdale, January 10, 1859 in the Garfield Papers, Manuscripts Division, Library of Congress.

[50]*Millennial Harbinger* (1861): 503.

[51]See "Extracts" from the minutes of the Bethany College Board of Trustees in *Millennial Harbinger* (July 1866). Pendleton was unanimously elected president at the same meeting, after the death of Campbell.

[52]See West, *Search for the Ancient Order,* 2:213 for a discussion of Lipscomb's attitudes.

dard friends meant by the term. Wasson believes that Garfield was sympathetic towards and maybe even in agreement with the theory of evolution, and it is highly probable that he was in accord with it. As a matter of fact, he approved applying the doctrine of evolution to the study of biology. None of this "liberal" (or to some, heretical) thinking affected Garfield's deep and abiding faith. He could see that narrow theological disagreements could not destroy the power of Christianity in the lives of believers. In his journal of 1873, Garfield wrote:

> It is clear to my mind, that the theological and formal part of Christianity has in great measure lost its power over the minds of men. But the life and Christianity of Christ are to me as precious and perfect as ever.[53]

Critical of Robert Ingersoll, the atheist, Garfield was also critical of agnosticism. He retained his faith that the New Testament was supernaturally given. With his careful study of the social sciences, he did not seem to have adopted the spirit of higher biblical criticism, a spirit which jarred other Disciples churches into further fragmentation after 1890.

Garfield had a highly developed Christian social consciousness. His activities as political leader in addressing the social needs of people may well have forecast a change in the nature of the missionary society he supported in the Disciples Movement. In an 1872 article about missionary activities directed toward the Flathead Indians, he wrote:

> We are accustomed to say that the Gospel is fitted to all classes and conditions of men. And this is probably true when we use the word in its broadest sense; but it is not true in the narrow doctrinal sense of the term. There is a gospel of clothing, of food, of shelter, of work, that should precede the theology of the pulpit. . . . For more than two centuries most of our missionary effort has been made wrong end foremost.[54]

Garfield was a champion for an open and revelatory view of restoration, rather than a view that all questions were settled and the pattern was set. In 1868, he wrote his closest friend, Aaron Hinsdale:

> Wearied with the perpetual iteration of doctrinal points of Bro. Anderson, and the intolerable denominational bigotry, arrogance and egotism, with which he puts forth the formal parts of

---

[53]Wasson, *James A. Garfield*, quoting from Garfield Papers, Manuscripts Division, Library of Congress.

[54]Wasson, *James A. Garfield*, 134, quoting Garfield, "The Indian Question," *The New York Independent* 24 (October 31, 1872).

'our plea,' I went this morning to hear a Swedenborgian, and am glad I did so. The cheerful, spiritual views of life and love and duty to which he urged his hearers, was in harmony with the beautiful freshness of this spring morning, and my heart is made glad and happy more than any study of the 'rule of faith' could have made it.

After the tragic assassination of Garfield on July 2, 1881, the Washington, D.C. Disciples congregation felt impelled to carry out Alexander Campbell's early call for a respectable meeting house. They proposed building the Garfield Memorial Church at a cost of $33,700. Lipscomb was adamantly opposed to memorializing a human being, and a year after Garfield's death, Lipscomb wrote a lament reminiscent of what Alexander Campbell wrote at the death of Sir Walter Scott:[55]

His course was one of dishonor to the church; with ability and assured success as a servant of that church, he surrendered it for service in the worldly kingdom. If Garfield's career was acceptable, why not all young men of popular talents turn from the ministry to law, war, and politics? Did I believe his course was acceptable to God, I would yet turn from the service of the church to that of the world. Is it strange when the church counts him who turned from service in her offices and works, to the work of the world, worthy of so much more honor than those who serve faithfully in her sanctuaries?[56]

Garfield's hunger for a breath of air outside the almost incestuousness of the often-repeated Disciples "pattern"—whether it be further wonders of the scriptures, a bit of beauty from the created world, or the created art of human beings—was also felt often by members of the Restoration Movement in both the nineteenth and twentieth centuries. It is interesting that, much like the Disciples poet Vachel Lindsay would do a few years later, Garfield on this occasion turned to the garbled visions of Emmanuel Swedenborg to find that fresh breath of air. The abiding question for the Restoration Movement, as it was throughout its history, is how its members may receive that draft of freedom and simultaneously retain their fidelity to the words of scripture.

Issues which were considered "innovations" by the more conservative groups of Disciples were battled by the editors from before the Civil War through the end of the nineteenth century. All of the rhetoric, in print or in the pulpit, could be categorized as interpretations of "where

---

[55]See chap. 9.

[56]David Lipscomb, "Hero Worship," *Gospel Advocate* 22, no. 26 (June 24, 1880): 401.

the scriptures speak, we speak; where the scriptures are silent, we are silent." The growing gulf between the activist understanding of scriptural silence and the passive approach was exacerbated greatly over the question of music in worship. Interestingly, Alexander Campbell's rationale for his distaste for instrumental music in worship had nothing to do with the doctrine of scriptural silence. Rather, he felt the question turned on a believer's spirituality. The scriptural silence theory which opposed all "innovations" had been tentatively outlined in the *Christian Baptist*, but became a matter considered worthy of serious controversy and eventual division beginning only in this Peripatetic, or second, generation of Stone-Campbell followers.

Two factors seem to have gradually created a demand for an instrumental support for congregational singing by the first churches which tentatively introduced it. One was the gradual growth in education, wealth, and cultural amenities by many church members. First, as the frontier moved west, the roughly hewn houses and church buildings were replaced with sturdier, more aesthetically pleasing buildings. Some farmers, stockmen, and lumbermen even built fine mansions. Wallpaper, carpeting, fine furniture, including pianos and organs, were installed. More and more, the progressives among the Disciples felt that these enhancements to worship were desirable and, while they would not compromise about matters of faith and morals, sought to honor God with their substance.

The other reason for the introduction of instrumental music into congregational worship had less lofty aims: the scandalous state of congregational singing which prevailed in many churches. The growing interest in church organs in the post-Campbellian period was the result of this experience in some churches with the abysmal level of congregational singing. Lamar describes the situation in the church at Warren, Ohio, shortly after Isaac Errett became the minister:

> One of his Sunday tribulations, when he first went to Warren, I have not yet mentioned. . . . It all originated with the singing, which at that day was not organized, but quite the reverse. It appears that a good brother, whom we may call Jasper, inasmuch as his name was not Jasper, had for years been leader of the "music"—except when Bro. Bracewell (in like manner so called) could manage to "chip" in ahead and snatch the much-coveted honor away from him. The moment a hymn was announced, the rush for the "go" between these two racers became exciting. The ungodly looked on with delight; the preacher and the sober brethren and sisters, with anxiety and distress. Sometimes in his eagerness to get ahead, Bro. Jasper would pitch the tune so high that he could not sing it himself.

Occasionally he would light into a short meter tune for long meter words, and would hold on with good heart, albeit the twists and turns which were necessary to take him through were not edifying. Bro. Bracewell had similar experiences when he was so fortunate as to get the lead. But it was when they both happened to start together, and on different tunes, and each manfully holding out—faithful to the end—that the agony of the hearers was complete. Each had his backers, who did not hesitate to declare that the other man was acting scandalously.[57]

The Warren experience, humorously described by Lamar, might also be a reminder that Errett was sympathetic to and supportive of the beginnings of women's work in the Restoration churches:

It happened once upon a time, when the tunes seemed to be unusually intractable, that a good sister, who was an excellent singer, took up the strain and led off in a clear, sweet confident voice—and thereby gave both parties mortal offense! The "leaders" closed their books with a bang, and refused to sing a note. It was manifestly wrong in her: "Your women" are to "keep silent in the churches." It created a stir. It was discussed from house to house. The "leaders" and their families were hurt; the rest of the members were glad. It brought the matter to a head, and the outcome of it all was the musical talent of the church was collected and organized, and in a very little while the singing became excellent and edifying, and both the church and the public were delighted.[58]

Walter Scott's first-generation concern that the churches study *how* to sing as they studied *what* to sing was both cogent and prophetic, and a movement in which primary leaders were concerned for the soundness of the words, but cared not at all for notes on a page or singing schools, was reaping what it had carefully sowed.

Instrumental music was first noted in a Disciples of Christ church in 1859, when Dr. L. L. Pinkerton, minister of the Church of Christ at Midway, Kentucky, introduced a melodeon into his church. Pinkerton's attitudes toward many new ideas were innovative, even "liberal" in the theological sense. Garrett suggests that the short-lived presence of the melodeon in the Midway Church was occasioned by the fact that "the singing was so deplorable that it scared the rats away. Instrumental

---

[57]Lamar, *Memoirs*, 1: 128-29.
[58]Ibid., 159.

music came to be a primary battleground for reasons having little to do with either spirituality or aesthetics.[59] Garrett suggests that from the introduction of the melodeon at Midway before the Civil War, the voice of Moses E. Lard was the only one advocating actual division over the question. The Movement was able to live with ambiguity over the issue for some years, until the "editor-bishops" injected a note of crisis into the question which called for an either-or response.[60]

The Churches of Christ ultimately became a separate body, partly over the instrumental music question. As they entered the twentieth century, the assumption that an organ in church was not only undesirable but positively sinful became standard. Walt Yancey underscores the importance of the question for traditional Church of Christ leadership when he says that, although it cannot be thought of in a category like questions of the atonement, "It is not much of an overstatement to say that we in the twentieth-century Church of Christ have made the whole Christian economy to revolve around this one issue: *a cappella* singing. We have assumed that even if some other religious group believes and practices exactly as we do regarding all other issues . . . , but they sing with the accompaniment of mechanical instruments, that they are not true Christians and they have no hope of going to Heaven. Thus we will not fellowship with such a people in any way."[61]

This latter-day rigidity is even more exclusivist than the attitudes of most of the conservatives of the Peripatetic generation following the Civil War. J. W. McGarvey opposed instrumental music, but refused to "withdraw" fellowship from the organ churches over that issue. Benjamin Franklin, highly conservative editor of the *American Christian Review,* stated, "We are free to differ but not to divide."[62]

During the 1830s, the Christians led by Barton W. Stone and the Disciples who were primarily influenced by Alexander Campbell were able to overcome their human conservatism and attempt the bold action of union. Certain that Christian unity was the will of Christ, the primary burden of their respective religious movements, the leaders of the two

---

[59]Since the melodeon, a sub-type of the harmonium, often seems to be the opening wedge for the entry of instrumental music into the nineteenth-century Restoration Movement churches, its definition is necessary for this study. Definitions are from *New Harvard Dictionary of Music* (Cambridge, Mass.), s. v. "Melodeon" and "Harmonium." *Melodeon*: A small, suction-operated reed organ of the first half of the nineteenth century (see Harmonium). *Harmonium*: Stops above the keyboard activate different sets of reeds to provide various timbres. . . . The harmonium achieved great popularity as a substitute for the pipe organ in churches and also as a household instrument. Power for the instruments' bellows was generated by foot pedals.

[60]Garrett, *Stone-Campbell Movement,* 460-61.

[61]Yancey, *Endangered Heritage,* 126-27.

[62]Garrett, *Stone-Campbell Movement,* 482.

movements both entertained concerns about the other group. But they were not yet so hardened in the belief that they had completely restored the New Testament church that they became incapable of lengthening the reach of their fellowship to overcome what Thomas Campbell had considered the scandal of denominationalism.

The tragedy of the Peripatetic generation of Disciples goes far beyond the divisions between the heirs of what had begun as a movement seeking the unity of all Christians. That sincere and honest men could attempt to define the boundaries of the Church of Christ on earth to conform to an ever-narrowing, continually hardening set of subjective biblical understandings suggests how much they had lost the spirit of the first generation Restoration Movement.

The polarity between Puritan legalism and liberal triviality was again reenacted by the Disciples of Christ. While hymnbooks were edited, church buildings in varying sizes and tastes were developed, and for the more liberal groups, the arts were cultivated as part of the church's heritage of worship, some theological vacuums created problems for serious non-verbal or literary expression by artists who accepted the Restoration thesis. Like Nathaniel Hawthorne's Reverend Dimmsdale, the ultra-conservatives failed to exult in the grace of God, the freedom of Christian redemption, and the spirituality of the love of God. Like the transcendental neighbors of Hawthorne, the future course of the ultra-liberal track seemed to lose the heady experience of knowing the supernatural, the sense of joy in experiencing freedom from personal guilt and sin, or the sustaining power Calvin had taught in the divinity of Christ, "God with us."

That neither a Rembrandt nor a Bach, neither a Cranach nor a Milton, could thrive within the extremes of Disciples liberalism or "scholastic literalism" seems understandable. The artists who have experienced power from their Disciples heritage are more likely to have drawn from the Protestant Reformation, or from the lively springs of the first-generation thoughts penned by the Campbells, Walter Scott, or Robert Richardson. The wisdom and spirituality of Isaac Errett, who kept his balance between the integrity of his biblical faith and Christian freedom, has also made possible some of the best work which has grown from the Restoration Movement.

The problems exhibited by the poet, Vachel Lindsay, present a picture of a Christian who loved his heritage of biblical foundations, Christian freedom, and unity between followers of Christ. Frustrated by both American and "Peripatetic" attitudes which deadened that heritage, Lindsay's frenzied grasping for sustaining wellsprings in Swedenborgianism or oriental thought seem to be actions of desperation.

The methodology of thought which elevated objectified trivia— opinions—to a position of fundamental importance was a methodology under which the arts can exist only with great difficulty. By contrast, artists represented in chapter 12 seem to have been able to create symbiotic relationships between their heritage of faith and the demands of their art. Since most of them are still creating and performing, the final evaluation of that symbiosis remains to be made.

Vachel Lindsay .:. Troubadour

Plate 13
VACHEL LINDSAY
Courtesy Vachel Lindsay Association, Inc.

11

Vachel Lindsay:
The Troubadour from Springfield

The life of Nicholas Vachel Lindsay (1879-1931) was a legion of contradictions. The internal tensions with which he lived are reflected in poetry that graphically mirrors his love/hate relationship with his hometown of Springfield, Illinois. His "Alexander Campbell" trilogy of poems shows his understanding of both the theological and the pragmatic dimensions of Campbellite thought. The values sung by the Midwest poet celebrate, Campbell-like, the values of mid-America, of Christ, of righteousness, of social justice. From *In Praise of Johnny Appleseed* to *General William Booth Enters into Heaven* to *The Proud Farmer*, Lindsay spoke his appreciation for Christian redemption, basic human goodness, and rural values.

Lindsay's poems also bear witness to his deep roots in Restoration doctrine. Of all artists belonging to Restoration Movement churches, Lindsay probably achieved the broadest success and recognition. He especially articulated the relationship between his Christianity—including his Disciples of Christ heritage—and the development of his art. In the same sense that the Stone-Campbell Movement is a thoroughly mid-American movement, so are the highly personal songs of Lindsay.[1]

Perry Gresham's perceptive study of Lindsay has shown that the basic spirit of Lindsay's poetry is reflective of Disciples values. Gresham's evidence of this conclusion is based on his careful research of Lindsay's works, especially the "Alexander Campbell" trilogy and the *The Broncho That Would Not Be Broken*.[2]

---

[1]See Edgar Lee Masters, "Introduction," *Vachel Lindsay: A Poet in America* (New York: Scribner's Sons, 1935), vi. Masters' biography of Lindsay is the earliest; other biographical studies include, e.g., Markham Harris, *City of Discontent: An Interpretive Biography of Vachel Lindsay*. . . (Indianapolis: Bobbs-Merrill, 1952); Eleanor Ruggles, *The West-Going Heart: A Life of Vachel Lindsay* (New York: Norton, 1959); Ann Massa, *Vachel Lindsay, Fieldworker for the American Dream* (Bloomington: Indiana University Press, 1970); and Marc Chénetier, ed., *Letters of Vachel Lindsay* (New York: Burt Franklin, 1979). Masters benefits by having been personally acquainted with Lindsay and the fact that their mothers were well-acquainted with each other. Masters' biography was written at the request of, and is based on information supplied by, Lindsay's widow. Most of my information about Lindsay is drawn from Masters' biography and Chénetier, *Letters* xvii-xxiii.

[2]See Perry E. Gresham, *The Broncho That Would Not Be Broken* (Nashville: Disciples of Christ Historical Society, 1986), 16.

Vachel Lindsay was born in Springfield on November 10, 1879, to Doctor Vachel Thomas Lindsay and Esther Catherine Frazee Lindsay. Doctor Lindsay was a medical doctor who had served as a school teacher before graduating from Miami (Ohio) Medical College in 1869. After studying in Vienna, he served as a physician in Springfield for more than forty years. His wife, the daughter of a Springfield farmer-preacher, was graduated from Glendale Female College as valedictorian. She taught mathematics at her alma mater and later studied art in Lexington, Kentucky. Both parents were active members of the Christian Church.

This terse statement of Lindsay's parentage may be factual enough, but without more information it fails to convey the family social and cultural setting which influenced the heart and mind of the poet of the Gospel of Beauty. Thus, his story must begin with the decades in which Alexander Campbell was concerned about "the inadequacy of all the present systems of education, literary and moral, to develope [*sic*] the powers of the human mind, and to prepare man for rational and social happiness."[3]

Vachel's maternal grandfather, Ephraim Samuel Frazee, was graduated from Bethany College in 1846, with a diploma signed by both Thomas and Alexander Campbell. Ephraim Samuel Frazee was one of the reported 128 students of the "orderly, circumspect, and industrious class of young men assembled from fifteen States" who studied that year at the institution which Alexander Campbell dedicated to "the development and improvement of the physical, intellectual and moral powers of man, with a reference to his whole destiny in the Universe of God."[4] In the same year, Ephraim Samuel married Frances Austen. They lived on a prosperous farm in Rush County, Indiana.[5] Ephraim Samuel Frazee was active as teacher, politician, and breeder of registered cattle in addition to his work as a pioneer Disciples preacher. Vachel spent many youthful visits with his Grandfather Frazee in Indiana.[6]

Vachel's paternal grandfather, Nicholas Lindsay, was of Scottish origin and was married in 1843 to Martha Ann Cave, a presumed descendant of Pocahontas. Nicholas was a large landowner in Kentucky before the Civil War, but when the federal government confiscated his cattle and freed his slaves because of his Southern sympathies during the war, his plantation was turned into a poor farm.[7] This fostered a life-long bitterness in Nicholas toward the government and the Northern cause.

---

[3]*Millennial Harbinger* (1830): 1:1.

[4]See my chap. 7; *Millennial Harbinger* (1846): 444-44; and Alexander Campbell, "Introductory Lecture," *Introductory Addresses: Bethany College*, 82.

[5]Chénetier, *Letters,* xvii.

[6]Masters, *Vachel Lindsay,* 12.

[7]Ibid. and Chénetier, *Letters,* xvii.

In 1866 Vachel Thomas Lindsay, the son of Nicholas and Martha Ann, began his medical practice in Cotton Hill, Illinois, near Springfield. In 1871 he married his childhood sweetheart, Olive, who died only two and one-half months after their wedding. In 1875 he sailed with his sister, Eudora, and his friend, Esther Catherine Frazee, for Europe to study medicine in Vienna. Upon their return in 1876, he married Catherine. Catherine had taught mathematics in Glendale, Ohio, and painting at Hocker College, Kentucky from 1869 until her trip abroad in 1875.

After his marriage to Catherine, Doctor Lindsay moved his medical practice to Springfield. Both he and his wife were devout Disciples and became members of the First Christian Church of Springfield. Catherine was an energetic organizer and speaker, and organized a Women's Missionary Social Union which met in her home. Throughout her life she contributed articles to religious magazines, spoke on civic subjects, and even staged miracle plays.

Lindsay's mother was without a doubt the impetus for his inclination toward art and poetry. And since the Lindsay family had brought a fine collection of books from Kentucky, Vachel grew up in an atmosphere of literature and developed a strong fascination for works of imagination. As one of his biographers observed of Lindsay:

> If ever an American poet was nurtured to sing of his land and for it in words and images deriving from nowhere except from the soil which bore him, it was Vachel Lindsay.[8]

Vachel Lindsay, the poet, was baptized by "the model, old-fashioned, Disciple preacher . . . the gray-bearded Campbellite elder," J. B. Briney, at the age of eight years.[9] His membership remained in the First Christian Church until 1927 when he was provided a transfer to Spokane, Washington.[10]

In 1897, Lindsay entered Hiram College, which was then headed by Eli Vaughn Zollars, former pastor of Springfield's Christian Church and a close friend of Vachel's father.[11] Although he was supposed to be studying subjects related to medicine, he did not do well in the sciences, mathematics, or Latin. Even so, he enjoyed his time at Hiram where he created a good deal of poetry and graphic works for various campus causes. He read widely and made numerous personal diaries in which he commented on religious, artistic, and national concerns along with his views about marriage, family, and self. He became well versed in the

---

[8]Masters, *Vachel Lindsay,* 34.

[9]Ibid., 387, from Vachel Lindsay to his cousin, Ethelin S. Coblin, February 23, 1927.

[10]The Lindsay family's membership cards are still in the records drawer of Springfield's First Christian Church. Vachel's transfer of membership is noted on his card.

[11]Ibid., 5 n.3.

works of Walt Whitman, John Ruskin, and Rudyard Kipling, among others. He kept six diaries or notebooks, and in the front of each he wrote, "This book belongs to Christ." In the book devoted to rhetoric, he wrote:

> In the world there are two forces, nature which extends through every function of man, and love whereby man may be divine in power. Two beings, God and man. No commands of Christ are impossible. Follow every commandment vigorously. Get even with the devil. Comply with the conditions by which Christ keeps possession of men. . . . I think that my first poetic impulse is for music; a second a definite conception with the ring of the universe; third clearness of exposition. . . . I hold it an especial quality in a good poem, elasticity and suggestiveness, whereby the reader may see his own emotions on a new framework.[12]

Lindsay was sensitive to the Christ-oriented curriculum at Hiram. In his book titled "Homiletics," he recorded:

> My individual allegiance is to Christ. He is my best friend, but I have grown up with him amid those who find him so, and I have never seen him take possession of those who have known him not. . . . I have supreme confidence in Christianity as a social force. . . . Laziness is cowardice.[13]

In his diary titled "Disciples of Christ," he wrote that Alexander Campbell had "brought the baptism upon which all Christendom unites; the confession on which they all unite; the repentance on which they all unite."[14]

Thus, Vachel Lindsay was thoroughly grounded in Disciples doctrine, practice, and atmosphere from his birth. However, it might seem that Lindsay failed to qualify as a son of the Stone-Campbell Movement on many counts. His aesthetic bent allowed room for playfulness, which would not have been countenanced by the logical and serious Alexander Campbell, with his Old Testament seriousness and Lockean understanding of the mind. Lindsay's children's poems, such as *What Grandpa Mouse Said* or *Drying Their Wings* in his "Moon Poems" collection,[13] suggest his ability to imagine an alternative world from the "real" world where Campbell's followers were to labor to preach the unadorned truth.

[12]See Masters, *Vachel Lindsay*, 62.
[13]Ibid., 84.
[14]Ibid., 85.
[13]See Vachel Lindsay, *Collected Poems*, (New York: Macmillan, 1925), 231-50.

Lindsay left Hiram in 1900 and returned to Springfield. Letters exchanged between him and his mother reveal his search for his calling, especially for a place where he could serve Christ, art, and his concept of beauty. The letters also reveal maternal exhortations to prepare for a medical career, but at the same time to develop and focus his art, perhaps in Christian cartooning.[16] The frantic pace of mental searching which dominated his last and academically unsuccessful year at Hiram forecast a confusion which seems to have characterized most of his adult life.

In January 1901 he moved to Chicago to take courses at the Art Institute. From September to December that year he worked in the toy department of Marshall Field's department store. He also submitted poems to various publications for consideration, and frequently went hungry from lack of money. All the while he faithfully attended the Church of the Disciples of Christ, led by Dr. Edward Scribner Ames, where he placed his membership, and even taught Sunday school.[17]

Even though his childhood Christian faith was buffeted and, at times, distored during his adult life, it was a often a steady bulwark that enabled him to endure periods of personal crisis. As a creative artist, he used it to formulate a message of hope, as seen in *Star of My Heart,* which he wrote in 1901 while in Chicago:

> Star of my heart, I follow from afar.
> Sweet Love on high, lead on where shepherds are,
> Where time is not, and only dreamers are.
> Star from of old, the Magi-Kings are dead
> And a foolish Saxon seeks the manger-bed.
> Oh, lead me to Jehovah's child
> Across this dreamland lone and wild,
> Then will I speak this prayer unsaid,
> And kiss his little haloed head—
> "My star and I, we love thee, little child."
>
> Except the Christ be born again to-night
> In dreams of all men, saints and sons of shame,
> The world will never see his kingdom bright.
> Star of all hearts, lead onward thro' the night
> Past death-block deserts, doubts without a name,
> Past hills of pain and mountains of new sin
> To that far sky where mystic births begin
> Where dreaming ears the angel-song shall win.
> Our Christmas shall be rare at dawning there,

---

[16]See Masters, *Vachel Lindsay,* chap. 5.

[17]Chénetier, *Letters,* 2, 5 n.1.

And each shall find his brother fair,
Like little child within:
All hearts of the earth shall find new birth
And wake, no more to sin.

(Collected Poems, 307-8.)

Lindsay's Gospel of Beauty differs from the gospel preached by Thomas Campbell or Barton W. Stone. And the ecumenicity he preached went far beyond the concept of Christian unity which characterized Campbell's *Declaration and Address* and the openness of the Brush Run Church. Lindsay was ready, during his ministry in the cause of Beauty, to accept some aspects of Eastern religions, the Roman Catholic mass, and the anti-Christian sentiments of Walt Whitman and Mark Twain. In 1897, while at Hiram, he made a drawing titled "The Shield of Lucifer" and wrote an accompanying poem, *The Last Son of Lucifer,*[18] which provides a shock if taken only in the context of Disciples doctrine. His theology was illuminated, to be sure, with a thorough knowledge of the Bible, but it takes turns that seem strange and scripturally untenable. His philosophy was complex; he not only expressed Christian redemption and sacrifice, but interpreted nature through the mysticism and asceticism of Buddha.[19]

Lindsay wrote poems and prose which express in a marvelously clear way some of the dilemmas faced by many serious American artists, and especially by creative individuals within the Restoration Movement. The tragic aspects of his life, which culminated in suicide at age fifty, are a witness to his sense of failure to give America, or the Midwest, or Springfield, a sense of values that made art, joy, and appreciation for the spirit first priorities. Lindsay was rooted in mid-America with mid-American education, religion, morals, and tastes. His 1911 poem *The Leaden-Eyed,* spoken on behalf of the young, might well have become a statement about his country and ultimately about himself:

Let not young souls be smothered out before
They do quaint deeds and fully flaunt their pride.
It is the world's one crime its babes grow dull,
Its poor are ox-like, limp and leaden-eyed.
Not that they starve, but starve so dreamlessly,
Not that the sow, but that they seldom reap,
Not that they serve, but have no gods to serve.
Not that they die but that they die like sheep.

(Collected Poems, 69-70)

---

[18]Chénetier, *Letters,* 2 n.4.
[19]See Masters, *Vachel Lindsay,* 298.

While in Chicago, Lindsay began reading more widely, including Milton, Dante, John Ruskin, and Walt Whitman. In 1908 he wrote that he continued to read more of Poe and had spent a good deal of time studying the English poet Algernon Charles Swinburne (1837-1909), who had been censured in 1866 for paganism. Even though Lindsay had memorized some of Swinburne's poetry, he had to write:

Yet I cannot respect the man. . . . there is something mean, uncanny and perverted in his face. . . . I would strenuously defend him to a Y.M.C.A. audience, as having a right to his liberty, and to live out his twisted personality God gave him, but I doubt if I would like to meet him.[20]

In this liberal attitude one can perhaps see Lindsay's theory of "populist" art. The basis for the "order of equals" in Lindsay's populism included cooperation, mutual respect and affection, optimism, and good humor. The quality which encompassed all of these, and to which Lindsay devoted a major portion of his life, was Beauty. Robert Sayer, in examining Lindsay's Gospel of Beauty, writes:

Beauty could only be produced in a society which was itself beautiful, in its values, common aspirations, and civic forms and functions. And in such a society, beauty in art, architecture, and letters was an expression of the whole heart and soul of its creators and audience. Secondly, Lindsay had in mind the hopes and dreams of his own Middle Western America, where the raw, hasty, and unenhanced actuality somehow made numbers of the citizens long for 'beauty' all the more.[21]

In 1902, while writing diary comments about Walt Whitman, Lindsay was still thinking about the relationship of Restoration Movement Christianity to his developing Populist art. He wrote, "Apostolic Christianity needs not so much to be changed in bone and sinew as to be clothed in a garment of humor and beauty."[22] Much of Lindsay's later poetry put the garments of beauty and humor on his undraped body of Christian beliefs.

In 1903, at the end of his studies in Chicago, Lindsay heard of the famous Robert Henri who was teaching at the Chase School of Art in New York City. He made application to study under Henri and was accepted. He arrived in New York in January 1905, and remained there until the

---

[20]Chénetier, *Letters*, 30, from Vachel Lindsay to Richard Watson Gilder of *The Century Magazine*, Nov. 6, 1908.

[21]See Robert F. Sayre, "Vachel Lindsay, an Essay," in Vachel Lindsay, *Adventures, Rhymes and Designs* (New York: Eakins Press, 1986), 25.

[22]Masters, *Vachel Lindsay*, 117.

spring of 1906, subsisting on a meager salary paid him as an art teacher for the YMCA and an occasional check from his parents. He wrote verses which he sold on the street for two cents each, visited exhibitions and galleries, and studied at the Chase School. Tension between his feelings about visual art and poetry were a strong frustration, and since he was nearing the age of thirty by this time, the pressure for decision was great.

Lindsay was troubled about the meaning and place of art in the universe more than a concern about techniques of painting or writing. On May 18, 1905, beset with what he called "private soul conflicts," Lindsay wrote to Dr. Ames at the Disciples of Christ church in Chicago and who had been his spiritual mentor for a number of years. He noted his conflict between producing visual art and poetry; he noted his interest in learning about other Christian denominations. Toward the end of his letter he wrote:

> These two things then are the largest I can *hope* for as the result of my great programme laid down three years ago. I *may* draw character sketches with sympathy. I *may* write about the Church universal with insight. . . . I *may* succeed in living for Humanity and the Church. I shall certainly be faithful to Art.[23]

It was not without a sense of guilt or failure that Lindsay embraced his gift for art and worked at developing it. In the same letter he wrote:

> The most I can hope for my verse is that it will some day become the record of my best impressions in these Churches. . . . I do not know whether you are one of those who think art is justified when it is unmoral but not immoral, wholesome but not consecrated. Sometimes I am, [but] then I have faith in art as a mission. . . . I have faith in *your* fight, . . . In a sense you are my proxy, fighting battles I wish I had the strength to undertake.[24]

Less than two weeks later, still unsettled about the role of art in the universe, Lindsay made the following diary entry:

> At half past one this morning my heart is hungering with desire to lay hold of, and live and die with the vision that possesses me. I see God in the greatness of his cold high beauty. I understand why the monks have counted their beads, why Michael Angelo carved the Night and the Morning, and painted the Sibyls. I have seen beauty that is cold as death, eternal as the voice of God, more to be desired than any earthly fire. There is peace in the

[23]Chénetier, *Letters,* 2-5, Vachel Lindsay to E. S. Ames, May 18, 1904.
[24]Ibid.

shadow of these wings. Oh, my God let me attain to them for refreshment and strength again and again—give me this thing to hold to—let my Rock of Ages be granted to me if I can only have this vision for a moment every day I can do all the things that I have been sent to do. The beauty that no man can name, deep as the ocean, high and cold as the stars.[25]

While studying under Henri, Lindsay recited his "The Tree of Laughing Bells or The Wings of the Morning" to his teacher, who was impressed with it. Later, when he read it to Henri and Henri's wife, the artist encouraged Lindsay to devote himself entirely to poetry instead of pursuing a career as a visual artist. In a letter to his former teacher, Susan Wilcox, Lindsay related this incident:

I have been surprised at the success of the Wings of the Morning. Fred Richardson and Robert Henri had fits over it, and both read it to their wives a second time. And lesser lights have taken a flattering interest in it.[26]

During the spring and summer of 1906, Lindsay engaged in the first of several walking tours. He sailed to Jacksonville, Florida and then walked back north through portions of Florida, Georgia, North Carolina, South Carolina, Tennessee, and Kentucky. He subsisted by delivering lectures, doing odd-job labor, exchanging his poems for food, and the on generosity of people along the way. He felt that the hunger, discomfort, and rudeness he experienced was balanced by the kindness of others, and the tour provided a great deal of material for his poetry. Along the way he corresponded with his friends and reported his appreciation for their friendship. In one letter he wrote:

. . . I feel that life can have other methods of happiness besides the search for Beauty, or mere pictorial and picturesque adventure, or intellectual adventure. Of course all these things are preached, and the preacher can blandly remind us that he said so, and His master said so, long ago. It is easy to be unctuous and orthodox.[27]

On the way back to Springfield, he was entertained at Lexington, Kentucky by his mother's old Bible teacher, Professor J. W. McGarvey.[28] At the end of his "tramp," as Vachel called it, his father took the family on

[25]Masters, *Vachel Lindsay,* 135.

[26]Chénetier, *Letters,* 6-8, Vachel Lindsay to Susan Wilcox, May 1, 1905.

[27]Ibid., 21, Vachel Lindsay to Susan Wilcox, April 2, 1906.

[28]See Chénetier, *Letters,* 385, letter from Lindsay to his cousin, Ethelin S. Coblin, February 23, 1927.

a pre-arranged tour of Europe. On the European tour they saw England, Holland, Germany, Belgium, and France before leaving from England. Lindsay visited many museums, including the British Museum, the Louvre, and museums in Amsterdam and The Hauge. On the way home in September 1906, Vachel experienced one of his visions and made the following entry in his diary:

> Last night I saw Immanuel singing in the New Heaven, with the church, his bride beside him, and his friends gathered round in a bright grassy place. And now I remember that at first Immanuel was singing almost alone, and the bride was a later half waking thought. The real dream was Immanuel singing wonderfully, as became a son of David. . . .[29]

Between November 10 and Christmas, 1906, Lindsay composed *I Heard Immanuel Singing* and included suggestions for singing the poem:

> The poem shows the Master with his work done, singing to free his heart in Heaven.
> This poem is intended to be half-said, half-sung, very softly, to the well-known tune:

> 'Last night I lay a-sleeping
> There cam a dream so fair,
> I stood in old Jerusalem
> Beside the temple there.—' etc.

The first and last stanzas frame the poem that sings some of the cardinal facts about the Christ, the Rose of Sharon, and the Atonement:

> I heard Immanuel singing
> Within his own good lands,
> I saw him bend above his harp.
> I watched his wandering hands
> Lost amid the harp-strings;
> Sweet, sweet I heard him play.
> His wounds were altogether healed.
> Old things had passed away.

> . . . .

---

[29]Masters, *Vachel Lindsay,* 179.

All these he sang, half-smiling
And weeping as he smiled,
Laughing, talking to his harp
As to a new-born child:—
As though the arts forgotten
But bloomed to prophecy
These careless, fearless harp-strings,
New-crying in the sky.
"When this his hour of sorrow
For flowers and arts of men
Has passed in ghostly music,"
I asked my wild heart then—
What will he sing tomorrow,
What wonder, all his own
Alone, set free, rejoicing
With a green hill for his throne?
What will he sing tomorrow
What wonder all his own Alone, set free, rejoicing,
With a green hill for his throne?

(Collected Poems, 369-70)

Between 1906 and 1909 Lindsay was back in New York teaching, lecturing, and writing. He was distinguished by his clean living, his generosity, and his congenial spirit. His diaries reveal a deep love for Christ even though there were speculative intellectual questions that sometimes pushed him far from historic orthodox Christian belief. He often rephrased his quest for his life mission. In his 1907 notebook he wrote:

> Let us seize these three ideals: Beauty, Freedom, Holiness; let us stamp them upon the innermost spirit of the land; let us write them into such perpetual phrases that future generations shall find new life in them. We must have them all.[30]

Lindsay supported himself by working as a guide for the New York Metropolitan Museum of Art and as a lecturer for the YMCA. He continued to write poetry and submit it to magazines for publication. In one letter, he mentioned that he was stirring the interest of "pious young men" from the YMCA Religious Department in art, poetry, and the Metropolitan Museum of Art. He also preached a sermon at the Rutgers Presbyterian Church on the "Holiness of Beauty."[31]

---

[30]Ibid., 187.
[31]Chénetier, *Letters*, 23, 24, Vachel Lindsay to R. W. Gilder, July 16, 1908.

Lindsay's concept of a Gospel of Beauty was wrapped up in his Gospel of Christ and attained a unity that exceeded the boundaries of the unity taught by the Restoration Movement founders or by the doctrines of other Christian groups. The Gospel of Beauty had neo-platonic overtones and even had characteristics of The One of Plotinus, or the Over-Soul of Emerson. In Lindsay's *Proclamation on the Coming of Religion, Equality and Beauty* he prophesied the union of the Church and art:

> In our new day, so soon upon us, for the first time in the history of Democracy, art and the church shall be hand in hand and equally at our service. Neither craftsmanship nor prayer shall be purely aristocratic any more, not at war with each other, nor at war with the state. The priest, the statesman and the singer shall discern one another's work more perfectly and give thanks to God.[32]

Whether or not Lindsay adopted some of the teachings of Emanuel Swedenborg (1688-1722) has been a subject of conjecture.[33] Swedenborg devoted himself to contemplation of spiritual matters and to making known to mankind the true inner doctrines of the divine Word as he claimed they were revealed to him in visions and communications with angels. He foresaw a new Church which he believed was inaugurated in 1757 to which all Christian churches belonged. Swedenborgianism has had broad definitions throughout its history, thus making it difficult to label a person as an adherent. Lindsay may have been so labelled, however, because of his habit of joining in the discussions of Springfield's "Swedenborgian" or mystical circle, which discussed not only spiritual matters but civic matters as well. Lindsay considered this group the Greenwich Village of Springfield.

Lindsay himself said, "I have never been in the least a literal Swedenborgian. But I back Willis Spaulding."[34] Lindsay used the term Swedenborgian to describe his ideal Springfield, living in harmony, but he does not seem to have adopted Swedenborg's views about God, the Trin-

---

[32]Vachel Lindsay, *Adventures, Rhymes and Designs* (New York: Eakins Press, 1986), 218.

[33]See, e.g., the biographies in n.1 above; also see Lindsay's own statements in "Adventures while Preaching Hieroglyphic Sermons," *Collected Poems*, esp. xxxvi. Massa, *Fieldworker for American Dream*, 52-58, provides insights into Lindsay's secular "Swedenborgianism."

[34]Lindsay, "Adventures Preaching Hieroglyphic Sermons," xxxvi. Spaulding was Springfield Commissioner of Public Property and belonged to Henry George's "Single Taxers" political group, which was also accused of being "Swedenborgian." It is probably in this political sense that Lindsay may be called a Swedenborgian.

ity, or other great Christian doctrines.[35] Rather, Lindsay's view of Swedenborgianism seems to be combined with his spiritualized view of
Johnny Appleseed, with the oneness of creation with beauty and art, and
for his own fuzzy focus on an American philosophy of art.

In 1908 Lindsay left New York on foot and walked through New
Jersey, Pennsylvania, and Ohio, on his way home to Springfield. After
reaching Springfield, he lectured for the Springfield and Sangamon
County YMCAs and spoke for the Temperance League. His return to
Springfield evoked strong emotions, for he wanted Springfield to
become a microcosm of his hopes for a transformed America. He made
"Blake"-like He made drawings, which included the old Springfield High
School, the First Christian Church, the Illinois State Fair Dome, and the
Church of the Immaculate Conception, to illustrate his books of poems.
In his 1925 *Collected Poems* the drawings were printed in the section
titled "Hometown," in which he included *The Springfield of the Far
Future,* the first stanza of which expresses his hope for Springfield:

> Some day our town will grow old.
> "She is wicked and raw," men say,
> "Awkward and brash and profane."
> But the years have a healing way.
> The years of God are like bread,
> Balm of Gilead and sweet.
> And the soul of this little town
> Our Father will make complete.
>
> (*Collected Poems,* 347)

Lindsay remained in Springfield, which he called "the city of my
discontent," until 1912, when he began a walking trip to California.
Along the way he distributed copies of *Rhymes to Be Traded for Bread*
and *The Gospel of Beauty* to working people; occasionally he worked
at a job to sustain himself. He kept a diary along the way in which he
recorded the kinds of receptions he received—from cold refusals to
almost sacrificial hospitality. While on the trip, he wrote *General
William Booth Enters into Heaven.* That is the poem that earned him a
$500 prize from *Poetry* magazine, and which made him famous after its
1913 publication.

After being published in *Poetry,* Lindsay met and corresponded with
other poets such as Sara Teasdale, Edwin Markham, Joyce Kilmer, and
Louis Untermeyer. In 1914 he was back in Springfield working on
several poems and collections to be published by Macmillan and Mitch-

---

[35]Even that "anti-Campbellite" and probably anti-Christian biographer, Edgar Lee Masters, acknowledged that Lindsay remained firm in his dedication to his Campbellian roots,
a fact that Masters deplored but which appears to be true.

ell Kennerly. In 1915 he recited for President Wilson's cabinet and toured all over New England and the East to recite for college English classes. By 1918 he had lectured all over the United States, not only to students but to paying audiences in Carnegie Hall.[36]

In 1919, Lindsay began a long series of appearances throughout America, which increased his fame. For several years he lived in hotels and on trains, and recited his most popular poems, *The Congo* and *General William Booth,* until he became sick of travelling and reciting. By this method, however, many children and adults living in the 1920s had the privilege of hearing a live poet, who was a keen observer of America, recite his own work, largely from memory.[37] He went to England with his mother and recited at Oxford and Cambridge, and was cordially received by poets around the world.

During this decade Lindsay's fame brought pride to his hometown of Springfield. At the same time, his pamphlets, some of his verses, and much of his personal activity brought down on his head the displeasure of many a citizen. His mother had in many ways acted as a buffer between him and Springfield society. On February 1, 1922 she died, and shortly thereafter Lindsay suffered a nervous breakdown. From this point, there was a break between the poet and the city of his "discontent."

Lindsay was forced to move from the house in which he was born because of a disagreement among Catherine Lindsay's heirs. His forced move was traumatic and underlined his sense having failed to bring the Gospel of Beauty to his hometown. Some believed the disagreement was artificial, fomented by unfriendly Springfield citizens and designed to rid the city of the poet about whom they had such ambivalent feelings. After he moved from Springfield, the poet's house became a showpiece in which people could see the room where he was born, the room where he wrote and drew, and furniture that he made himself when he was a youngster of thirteen.[38]

So Lindsay left Springfield in 1923 to become poet-in-residence at Gulf Park College, Gulfport, Mississippi, which was headed by an old friend from Hiram, Richard Cox. This assignment turned out to be a disappointment since he felt there was little genuine interest in his poetry or in the arts, and he felt spiritually isolated. Life at Gulf Park became suffocating, and he moved to Spokane, Washington, in June 1924. He stayed in Spokane until 1929, living in a hotel where his rooms became the center of an active literary circle. There he met and became a good

---

[36]See Chénetier, *Letters,* xx-xxi, and Sayre, "Vachel Lindsay, an Essay," 8.

[37]Fortunately, some of Lindsay's readings have been preserved on recordings, although those may not represent his best performances. He published altogether eight volumes of verse. See Masters, *Vachel Lindsay,* 292.

[38]See Masters, *Vachel Lindsay,* 334-38.

friend of the Australian-born pianist and composer, Percy Grainger (1882-1961). He became re-acquainted with Elizabeth Conner, whom he had met at Mills College on his 1912 western walking tour, and they were married in 1925. In 1927 his church membership was transferred from First Christian Church of Springfield to the Christian Church in Spokane, evidence that his association with the church remained alive.

In the end, Spokane also failed him when he realized that to meet the demands of those who sponsored him, he had to sacrifice freedom of thought and sponsor opinions not his own. In the spring of 1929 he and his wife and two infants moved to Springfield. Happily for him, he was able to reclaim the old home of which he had earlier been deprived. He received a cordial welcome and returned to the lecture circuit to support his family. In 1930 he was made Doctor Honoris Causa by Hiram College.[39]

By now, however, he suffered with heart disease, diabetes, and general fatigue, all of which hindered both his creative abilities and his financial ventures. He was undergoing hallucinatory experiences, taking sedative drugs, and feeling the weight of the failure of America to accept his Gospel of Beauty. The combination of physical illness and despair was too much. On the early moring of December 5, 1931, his wife heard him crawling up the stairs. When he was put to bed, he said that he had drunk Lysol. His last words were, "They tried to get me; I got them first."[40]

Vachel Lindsey died in the house in which he was born. He was buried in Springfield, close to Abraham Lincoln's tomb. His lovely old house at 603 South Fifth Street is now a registered National Historic Landmark and is a museum housing the Vachel Lindsay Association.

. . . . .

This chapter is intended to consider the relationship of his Restoration Movement roots to the work and life of the poet Vachel Lindsay, the Disciples artist, who gained international fame through his creative work. Regardless of the religious and secular by-ways he investigated in his spiritual wanderings, he remained always a son of the Restoration Movement. He acknowledged that he could never quite leave his Disciples heritage. In a letter to his cousin, Ethelin S. Coblin, he explained

---

[39]Chénetier, *Letters*, xxiii.

[40]Masters, *Vachel Lindsay*, 361.

his family's personal connection with Alexander Campbell,[41] and also explained his meaning about a certain line in his *Alexander Campbell* poem:

> I should add one more line of elucidation on the Alexander Campbell poem. One is that the statesman philosopher, the sage with high conceit, is a vague reference to men like Garfield, Lloyd George, Champ Clark, Jim Reed, R. A. Long, men living and dead, who begin to emerge or who have long emerged from the spell of little brick churches, like the church of Grassy Springs, to national or world action, and who sometimes think they have left all these things behind them. I am sure whatever changes they may deliberately make in their lives, places like the church at Grassy Springs have marked them forever, and they may trace to them some special courage or some special power, which will be a deep mystery to external and hasty biographers.[42]

Indeed, the "external and hasty biographers" seem to have been hostile to or to have misunderstood the poet.[43] This problem has been partially remedied by a lecture of Perry E. Gresham, former president of Bethany College (1953-72), (1953-72), and by doctoral dissertations available at the Disciples of Christ Historical Library in Nashville, Tennessee.[44]

Some members of Restoration Movement churches find difficulty in feeling spiritual kinship with this strange man who preached a Gospel of Beauty, who fought against commercial and financial affluence, who asked for handouts during his walking tours—and who looked into the tenets of Swedenborgian pantheism and Eastern religious philosophies. And yet, if we let Vachel speak for himself, we find that he never left his Disciples heritage, nor did it leave him. It was expressed in his art, his poetry.

---

[41]Lindsay said, "The second section is a memorial to all those who have passed from this life among my kin, one and all being members of the Disciples Church from the very earliest days of Campbell. . . . and also my memories of the great portrait of Alexander Campbell that used to hang above the fireplace at the home of my Grandfather Frazee, who studied under Campbell in his prime." See Chénetier, *Letters*, 387, Vachel Lindsay to Ethelin S. Coblin.

[42]Ibid.

[43]As noted above, Lindsay's biographer Edgar Lee Masters was not sympathetic with Lindsay's Christianity and hence presented a distorted picture of the poet's religious and theological tensions.

[44]Gresham's lecture has been published as *The Broncho That Would Not Be Broken* (Nashville: Disciples of Christ Historical Society, 1986). See n. 2 above.

As noted earlier in this chapter, Dr. E. S. Ames, who led the Chicago Church of the Disciples of Christ, was Lindsay's spiritual counselor. Dr. Ames was also professor of psychology at the University of Chicago. Lindsay seems to have felt that Dr. Ames understood him, not only as one human being understands another, but as one Disciples follower understands another in the context of the Restoration Movement. In 1904, Lindsay wrote to Dr. Ames from New York, "I am still a member of your church in Spirit," and he thanked Dr. Ames for a copy of his sermon "Living in All Good Conscience," calling it a "great strength and calming balm.[45]

Vachel lived at a time when America's social conscience had been quickened by the problems of an emerging industrial society. Leaders such as Washington Gladden (1836-1918), Josiah Strong (1847-1916), and Shailer Matthews (1863-1941) emphasized an optimistic idealism in which God was not outside the social process but within it. The term "social gospel" became popular around the turn of the century, and denominational and interdenominational social agencies arose. Many denounced concentration of wealth, unrestrained competition, and laissez faire.[46] Also at this time there were various secular political groups, large and small, which embraced differing brands of socialism; there were "single taxers" led by Henry George; there were budding labor union movements, and others. All of these movements impinged on the attitudes of Lindsay, and some of them are addressed in his poetry.

Lindsay did not embrace any of the movements wholly, but developed his own Gospel of Beauty, which contained elements of some of these movements, by which he hoped to see the world transformed into a peaceable, harmonious society. His Gospel of Beauty was based on his Disciples background and his own understanding of a "secular millennium" rather than salvation from personal sin for an eternity with God.

In his burning concern for Beauty, Lindsay felt an urgency to convert Springfield, and eventually America, to a value system that honored art and the human spirit above commercialism. Perry Gresham writes that Lindsay considered himself to be a patriot, a pacifist, and a socialist, and that his idea of socialism was that everybody should be well-fed and happy.[47]

---

[45]Chénetier, *Letters*, 2, Vachel Lindsay to E. S. Ames, May 18, 1904.

[46]See H. Shelton Smith, Robert T. Handy, and Lefferts A. Loetscher, *American Christianity: An Historical Interpretation with Representative Documents*, vol. 2 1820-1960 (New York: Scribner's, 1963), chap. 9.

[47]Perry E. Gresham, *The Broncho That Would Not be Broken* (Nashville: Disciples of Christ Historical Society, 1986), 17-18.

In a certain sense, Lindsay's so-called liberalism was an extension of his perception of the Restoration Movement emphasis on unity. But, as Gresham observes,

> Lindsay's religion was inclusive—its boundaries were man wide and God high. He always identified with the poor and the weak. He honored the Salvation Army throughout his lifetime.[48]

As a child, Lindsay was well trained in a Disciples Sunday school and as he grew up he remained a follower of Christ. Lindsay's lifelong familiarity with the scriptures can be seen in quasi-biblical phrases, many of which reflect his Restoration-oriented background. In 1909 he issued a series of *War Bulletins*, intended to shock the residents of Springfield out of their affluent complacency. In "Adventures Preaching Hieroglyphic Sermons," which introduced his 1925 *Collected Poems*, Lindsay explained the difficulty he faced while trying to impact the closed minds of Americans with a new idea:

> There is just one way to convince citizens of the United States that you are in earnest about an idea. It will do no good to be crucified for it, or burned at the stake for it. It will do no good to go to jail for it. But if you go broke for a hobby over and over again the genuine fructifying wrath and opposition is terrific. They will notice your ideas at last.[49]

Lindsay went on to relate that his broadsides had resulted in him being dropped from the YMCA work and Anti-Saloon League work he was doing in Springfield, as well as being "proscribed by the Country Club and glared at by the Chamber of Commerce."[50]

In September of 1909, Lindsay sent some of the *War Bulletins* to his friend, Ames, with the explanation that

> My best and most interested friends say that the War Bulletin number three is wild, illogical, inconsistent, anarchistic and obscure. It must be all there, for they all say so. Nevertheless, though it be a poor thing, it is my naked soul. . . .[51]

Lest Ames or his colleagues mistake his writings as anti-Christian, Lindsay went on to affirm his faith in Christ:

---

[48]Ibid., 18.

[49]Lindsay, "Adventures While Preaching Hieroglyphic Sermons," *Collected Poems*, xxxiv.

[50]Ibid., xxxv.

[51]Chénetier, *Letters*, 2, Vachel Lindsay to E. S. Ames, September 26, 1909.

You fellows get after Billy Sunday. I owe to him the line—"The Personal Savior from Sin"—. I cannot altogether reject one who gave me that. I signed his card with all my heart. Also I chose between two masters—Buddha and Christ—and thenceforth Buddha was only my brother.[52]

Lindsay's religion consistently included an affirmation of Jesus, an appreciation for Campbell's leadership in the Church, and a moderate participation in the ongoing development of the Christian Church along with the emerging Social Gospel that occupied many leading Disciples. By diffusing Christian doctrine with his Gospel of Beauty and the pantheistic doctrines of Swedenborg, to say nothing of Buddha and Eastern religious thought, the poet deprived himself of the strength that a more consistent and orthodox Christianity might have offered. Late in his life, the mounting pressure of his problems proved more than a match for his spiritual ability to cope with them. Masters, critical as he was of Christianity and especially of "Campbellism," may have been correct in spite of his bias when he wrote:

He was not in truth wholly satisfied with his Campbellite faith; if he had been his imagination would not have roamed to Catholicism and to Buddha.[53]

It seems that Lindsay recognized this at times. For example, in July of 1927, during a time of great financial deterioration, Lindsay wrote to the Canadian poet, Marguerite Wilkinson (1853-1929):

You have brought me to confessional by your article in the Y.M.C.A. Magazine. And I might as well confess *all.* It gave me a great, deep, personal 47 year old lifetime thrill to send the clipping to my lifetime friend and puzzled (but faithful) sponsor Reverend E. S. Ames, who is also the professor of Psychology at the University of Chicago.

I want this man, the most intellectual leader of the Disciples, to get your point of view about my intentions so vividly that he puts it over to all his following in the Brotherhood, that he holds so well in the hollow of his philosophic hand.

Behind this is my megalomaniac wish to bring "what I have to say". . . before the whole Disciple Brotherhood—and this without addressing or singing for any more back-breaking audiences.[54]

[52]Ibid.

[53]Masters, *Vachel Lindsay*, 177-78.

[54]Chénetier, *Letters,* 400, Vachel Lindsay to Marguerite Wilkinson, July 4, 1927.

Lindsay was a visionary with grand ideas for people to live in peace, harmony, and simplicity. In many respects that was not far from Campbell's vision of a united Christian faith based on the "ancient gospel." But the everyday problems of living in the real world caused a misery of spirit in the poet. The lack of appreciation for his work, for his evangel in the cause of Beauty, led him to believe that he was the object of enmity. In addition, he was in poor health. As he grew older he had alternating periods of optimism and despair.

On one hand Lindsay was so liberal that he translated justification in Christ into socialistic values; on the other, he seems to have adopted the legalism of the Peripatetic Generation of the Restoration. Lindsay's sincerity of faith deserves a more empathetic look by both liberals and conservatives within the Stone-Campbell Movement.

In the first place, his attachment to the Salvation Army throughout his adult life reflects both his concern for the poor and helpless and his Christian concern for evangelism. His second most requested poem, *General William Booth Enters into Heaven,* was in praise of the founder of that organization.[55] Furthermore, Lindsay was a serious worshipper in his Disciples church. Gresham relates the recollection of Mary Bourden about Lindsay's habit when he would hear Frederick W. Burnham preach:

> The poet would sit through the sermon with his head thrown back and his eyes fastened on the ceiling. When the service concluded and the last ewe of the flock had said goodby, Lindsay would go up to the pastor and say, 'Fred, let's go down to the Mission and save a soul!'[56]

Lindsay composed three poems which he placed under the heading "Alexander Campbell" in his 1925 edition of *Collected Poems.* He prefaced the collection with the closing paragraph of Campbell's last essay

---

[55]In the instructions accompanying the poem in his 1925 *Collected Works*, he wrote, "To be sung to the tune of 'The Blood of the Lamb' with indicated instrument." The "indicated instruments" were "bass drum beaten loudly," "banjos," "bass drum slower and softer," "sweet flute music," and "grand chorus of all instruments. Tambourines to the foreground," for the successive stanzas. Note however, "reverently sung, no instruments" for the last stanza, indicating perhaps that Lindsay linked unaccompanied music with reverence.

In a 1927 letter to Marguerite Wilkinson, he wrote ". . . . the first Campbellites forbid all musical instruments in church and the prejudice against having the hymn spoiled by the musician is still within me. I am against setting my chants to music, just as my fathers were. I heard it argued about before I was six." See Chénetier, *Letters*, 402. Even so, Lindsay sang, danced and celebrated exuberantly when he recited his poems publicly.

[56]Gresham, *Broncho*, 20. Burnham, later President of the American Christian Missionary Society, was minister at the First Christian Church of Springfield where Lindsay was a member. Mary Bourden, piano teacher and one time pianist for the famed evangelist, Billy Sunday, and was a member of the same church.

in the *Millennial Harbinger,* in which Campbell said "the present material universe, yet unrevealed in all its area, in all its tenantries, in all its riches, beauty and grandeur, will be wholly regenerated . . . consequently, new tenantries, new employments, new pleasures, new joys, new ecstasies. . . . a fullness of joy, a fullness of glory, and a fullness of blessedness. . . ." Perhaps it was the beauty and grandeur of the regenerated earth for which Lindsay longed.

One of the three poems in the "Alexander Campbell" collection is *A Rhymed Address to All Renegade Campbellites, Exhorting Them to Return,* which was written especially for Lindsay's brother-in-law, a missionary to China, whom Lindsay felt had edged away from the Campbellite faith.[57] Part of the poem follows:

> O prodigal son, o recreant daughter,
> When broken by the death of a child
> You called for the graybeard Campbellite elder,[58]
> Who spoke as of old in the wild.
> His voice held echoes of the deep woods of Kentucky.
> He towered in apostolic state,
> While the portrait of Campbell emerged from the dark:
> That genius beautiful and great.
> And millennial trumpets poised, half lifted,
> Millennial trumpets that wait.
>
> . . . .
>
> He stepped from out the Brush Run Meeting House
> To make the bog woods his cathedrals,
> The river his baptismal font,
> The rolling clouds his bells,
> The storming skies his waterfalls,
> His pastures and his wells.
> Despite all sternness in his word,
> Richer grew the rushing blood,
> Within our fathers' coldest thought.
> Imagination at the flood
> Made flowery all they heard.
> The deep communion cup
> of the whole South lifted up.

[57]The background for this poem was explained to Dr. Gresham by Lindsay's sister, Olive Wakefield.

[58]This is the appellation Lindsay gave to J. B. Briney, who led First Christian Church of Springfield and who baptized him. See above. Note, too, l. 7, the reference to the portrait of Campbell which was mentioned in Lindsay's correspondence. These things made a lasting impression on him.

. . . .

> He preached with faultless logic
> An American Millennium:
> The social order
> Of a realist and farmer
> With every neighbor
> Within stone wall and border.
> And the tongues of flame came down
> Almost in spite of him.
> And now all but that Pentecost is dim.
>
> *(Collected Poems,* 354)

In the last stanza above, even Lindsay recognized the tension between Campbell's Lockean intellectual religion and emphasis on cognition in an American environment which gave a particular prominence to feelings and emotions. The same internal tensions have been faced by artists of the Restoration Movement throughout its existence. He clearly spelled out this tension in his long letter to Marguerite Wilkinson:

> To all the people confused by these things the history of the highly intellectualized Disciples (Campbellites) so absolutely non-mystical, so absolutely the antithesis of the Methodists is utterly incomprehensible. They do not believe the best brains of Europe had taken to these log-cabin churches in the frontier— these churches without preachers—only elders. The idea of such pilgrims is now incredible, though it is even hinted at in Byron's eulogies of George Washington. The 'infidel' colony of New Harmony intellectuals, right there among the Indians, is remembered. But the cult of the intellectual religious log-cabin is forgotten. One of Campbell's great debates was with Robert Owen of New Harmony. I know I will make a long illustrated poem of this—sometime, with its own times.[59]

Lindsay also affirmed his Restoration roots in the Stone-Campbell Movement: "I know I am an utterly incurable follower of that high champion of the intellectual frontier 'primitive' life—Alexander Campbell." He then expressed his hope for a fair hearing from the other members of that movement:

> I wish in some far-off beautiful day of grace a Lindsay Society of about four people could get together in the Hyde Park Church Chicago—or the Disciples' Church Springfield Illinois or among the members of the Campbell Institute that are in Colum-

---

[59]Chénetier, *Letters,* 402-3, Vachel Lindsay to Marguerite Wilkinson, July 4, 1927.

bia University—and actually begin with the log-cabin churches of my ancestors when they do me the honor to play the oracle about my religion and my gospel-song. There is enough data in The Golden Book and the Alexander Campbell poem, if they cared to piece it together.[60]

The time has come, it seems, to give Lindsay that honor—by re-reading his poems in light of the log-cabin churches of his ancestors, as he requested. Lindsay loved his poetry, but he had misgivings about performing it publicly. He was disturbed that "strangers" measured his style. He wanted the public to recognize that he was not tied up with secular movements and poets, but was a son of "the hard-minded hard-studying pioneers, absolutely non-mystical but deeply Biblical, of Bethany West Virginia, Lexington Kentucky, Hiram Ohio, Eureka Illinois and the like." He complained that he was utterly unknown by his own people.[61] His vision was:

Till every citizen of the United States writes poetry happily, openly and without shame, as the Campbellites once preached—every member of the clan a preacher and every preacher a mere layman—till this comes about we will have no "leading" poets really echoing and resounding.[62]

·　·　·　·　·

Thus, consideration has been given to Vachel Lindsay, the Disciples artist who was able to make a national impact through his creative work. He is an appropriate model for this study because he was able, in prose and poetry, to articulate some fundamental relationships between art and Christian faith as understood through a Restoration emphasis. Lindsay is a problematic subject because of the inner struggle which tore at his spiritual and artistic being. The brief works of Perry E. Gresham and others have shown Lindsay's Restoration orientation. Some members of churches related to the Restoration Movement may have difficulty finding spiritual kinship with this strange many who preached a Gospel of Beauty, who fought against the basic American ideal of commerce and financial affluence, who asked for handouts during his walking tours, and—worst of all—looked beyond Christ and the Church to Swedenborg's pantheism and to Eastern philosophy. The fact remains that his personal religious and moral codes were based upon historic Christianity and in tune with the moral attitudes of Campbell. One common attitude was their opposition to war: Campbell had argued to the end against

---

[60]Ibid.

[61]Ibid., 402, 403.

[62]Ibid., 404.

the War Between the States; the outbreak of World War I elicited a pac-ifistic statement from Vachel Lindsay. Lindsay's *Abraham Lincoln Walks at Midnight (In Springfield Illinois)* is a dramatic appeal to the memory of that former Springfield resident who witnessed the American war to end human strife.

> It breaks his heart that kings must murder still,
> That all his hours of travail here for men
> Seem yet in vain. And who will bring white peace
> That he may sleep upon his hill again?
>
> (*Collected Works,* 54)

Another parallel between Campbell and Lindsay is the discourage-ment they felt from criticism, cynicism, and occasionally overt discourtesy.[63] Lindsay's poem, *The Broncho That Would Not Be Broken*. represented not only an unhappy colt in Kansas, but Vachel Lindsay as well. Gresham says, "The tender heart of Vachel Lindsay identified with the colt. . . ."[64]

> A little colt—broncho, loaned to the farm
> To be broken in time without fury or harm,
> Yet black crows flew past you, shouting alarm,
> Calling "Beware," with lugubrious singing . . .
> The butterflies there in the bush were romancing,
> The smell of the grass caught your soul in a trance,
> So why be a-fearing the spurs and the traces,
> O broncho that would not be broken of dancing?
>
> . . . .
>
> In that last afternoon your boyish heart broke.
> The hot wind came down like a sledge-hammer stroke.
> The blood-sucking flied to a rare feast awoke.
> And they searched out your wounds, your death-warrant
>   tracing.
> And the merciful men, their religion enhancing,

---

[63]Richardson, *Memoirs*, discusses discouraging persecutions and harassments expe-rienced by the reformers. One relates to sticks and stones being thrown into the water where Thomas Campbell was baptizing. Another is about his son: "As Alexander Campbell was one evening returning from an appointment, he perceived a violent storm likely to overtake him, and called at the house of a Seceder lady to seek shelter. The lady, who came to the door, desires, in the first instance, to know his name, and being informed that it was Alexander Campbell, she at once informed him that she could not admit him into her house. He was, therefore, obliged to pass on homeward, and to brave the fury of the tempest and the dangers of the timber falling across his way, which was chiefly a mere bridle-path through the woods." (1:430).

[64]Gresham, *Broncho*, 6.

Stopped the red reaper, to give you a chance.
Then you died on the prairie, and scorned all disgraces,
O broncho that would not be broken of dancing.

(*Collected Works*, 77-78)

The autobiographical parallels seem clear, though it is doubtful that in 1912 Lindsay could have anticipated his death in 1931. The refrain of the poem, however does address a primary problem faced by members of the Restoration Movement who sometimes feel they are anchored in granite. The religion of the heart, which in its expression "dances" like the little broncho, is generated neither by the trivialization of sin and forgiveness in ultra-liberal religion nor by the legalism of "neoscholastic Campbellism." The story of the violinist who was chased off the Campbell homestead[65] suggests the problem faced by the musical heart, the dancing soul.

Vachel Lindsay, physically ill and deeply discouraged, lost his battle to establish a new value system in his town and his country. And, at least to this extent, Masters was right: while the powerful faith generated through the teaching of Stone and Campbell provided substance for Lindsay's art, the cold and sometimes legalistic application of the *forms* of religion stopped the dancing. Lindsay and the broncho both died with broken hearts.

[65]See my chap. 1.

Art and Christian Commitment in the Twentieth-Century Stone-Campbell Tradition

Contemporary Stone-Campbell heirs are challenged to recognize both artistic talent and its expression as gifts of God. Not all Disciples or Church of Christ artists have experienced the stresses felt by Vachel Lindsay, but many have wrestled with the tensions in the challenge to create Christian art within the Restoration Movement tradition.

Young people who are deeply committed to Christ and who feel strongly motivated to express themselves through music, visual arts, theater, or literature can resolve the tensions once they are identified. Those who *create* art—such as painters, composers, poets, or choreographers—need to discover their intellectual and spiritual roots on a personal level. Those who *re-create* art—such as performing musicians, actors, dancers—need to understand the background of their art so they can produce a faithful representation of the artists' original ideas.

Hans Hoffman (1880-1966), the great German Expressionist painter and teacher, has spoken in depth of the relationship between the mind of the creative artist and the technique of bringing an idea to fruition. He wrote, "The depth of an artistic creation is a question of human development. The deeper the human content, the deeper the understanding of the medium."[1]

Never one to diminish the importance of technique, nor the wide differences between the various arts, Hoffman nevertheless spoke often of visual art "in the condition of music" and on the subject of creation. He wrote that the process of creation is based upon two metaphysical factors:

1. the power to experience through the faculty of empathy.

2. the spiritual interpretation of the expression-medium as a result of such powers.

Concept and execution condition each other equally. The greater the concept, the more profound and intensive will the

---

[1] Hans Hoffman, *Search for the Real and Other Essays* (Cambridge, Mass.: MIT Press, 1948), 55.

spiritual animation of the expression-medium generally be and, consequently, the greater will be the impressiveness and importance of the work.[2]

Actors, singers, dancers, and instrumental musicians, as well as visual artists, are expected to experience emotion and to possess a philosophic orientation. A singer or cellist who makes music for the glory of God should be able to combine the inner resources of the mind and heart with the technical skills required for an ideal performance. In a manner that sounds almost like Alexander Campbell speaking of the Bible, conductor Erich Leinsdorf balances the artist's need for freedom to interpret with the need for integrity to play what is written. He writes that "to discover the composer's grand design for each work is both the conductor's mission and his reward."[3] Christian artists who discover the Creator's grand design for their talents, as well as discovering the grand design of another artist's work, are able to resolve the kinds of tensions felt by Vachel Lindsay.

An impressive witness to the Christian faith is rendered by a large group of American performing artists who are thoughtful about the relationship between their faith and their art. Jerome Hines (1921-), renowned basso of the Metropolitan Opera Company, has established his international reputation by performances at Italy's La Scala, at the Wagnerian home of musical drama at Bayreuth, and the Soviet Union's Bolshoi Theatre. He has also scheduled appearances for the Salvation Army and other Christian organizations into his crowded recital calendar. He has written an opera, *I Am the Way,* about the life of Jesus. Hines's autobiography reflects both his art and his Christian witness, finding its title in the words of the well-known Christian song, *This is My Story, This is My Song.*

Christopher Parkening is an eminent classical guitarist who belongs to a Grace Community Church. He has written in a letter to the author that his motivating impulse is to play for the glory of God.

Recently, I attended a recital by Anne Martindale Williams, the principal cellist of the Pittsburgh Symphony Orchestra, and John Erickson, the church organist, at the Christ United Methodist Church in Bessel Park, Pennsylvania. After performing several movements from the standard cello repertoire, the performers presented a selection of hymns, and Ms. Williams gave her personal statement of faith and commitment in relation to her artistic powers of communication.

[2]Ibid., 61.

[3]Erich Leinsdorf, *The Composer's Advocate: A Radical Orthodoxy for Musicians* (New Haven: Yale University Press, 1981), 63.

Restoration Movement heirs are not without artistic creators and performers who wish to stimulate a symbiosis of their religious beliefs and their artistic expressions. The willingness to harmonize in an honest and meaningful way the possibilities of art and the often disturbing facts of the natural created world with the Christian faith can cause some pain for an artist. Vachel Lindsay encountered deep hurt in his effort to harmonize his artistic gifts and his social environment with his Campbell-oriented Christian faith. The spiritual hegira of Clarice True (Trudy) Jones McRae (1945-), related later in this chapter, reveals another honest wrestling with disparate facts of life and art.

The nineteenth-century Romantics sometimes speculated that the worth of a piece of art was directly related to its human cost in pain. But in any era, the enduring power of art may well reflect the genuineness of the artist's encounter with self and life which gave birth to the work. Robert Richardson's kindly critique of the somewhat self-indulgent epic poem of young Alexander Campbell,[4] as the author quantified his feelings about the magnificent ocean, misses a major issue in explaining why Campbell was not really—at least not yet—a poet. The poem, like an amateur painter's pretty picture of an idyllic landscape, unsullied by the dissonance of reality or human problem, failed to grapple with the author's questions of who or why he was.

In the twentieth century, many colleges and universities related to the Stone-Campbell Movement have followed the national trend toward establishing departments of art, music, literature, and theater. This has been helpful for young people who want to develop their artistic talents in a Christian context as they find their mission in life and consider the message of the Restoration Movement.

On the other hand, some Stone-Campbell heirs have chosen to remain ignorant of and aloof from both the generative power and the difficulties inherent in Disciples thought as it is related to art. Their solution has been similar to that of the business person who tries to separate the ethical demands of the Monday to Saturday workplace from the other-worldly ideals of the Sunday sermon. Hence, the Christian artist can try to perform as a performer and worship as a Christian. The early Stone-Campbell Movement was poorer because of its paucity of music and art. In the same way, the latter-day artist is deprived of power by a schizophrenic-like separation between artistic talents and Christian belief.

One contemporary Christian artist and writer who has recognized the void in the lives of Christians caused by neglect of the arts, cultural endeavors, and creative gifts is Franky Schaeffer. Schaeffer discusses the

[4]See chap. 9, pp. 218-19

fact that art has been "relegated to the bottom drawer of Christian consciousness, despised outright as unspiritual or unchristian." He points
out that, for too many Christians, the contents of the local Christian
bookstore-accessories-paraphernalia shop is their only criteria by which
to measure art. Schaeffer concludes his description by applying relent-
less honesty to the "Christian media":

> The airwaves as you leave the shop are jammed with a choice
> avalanche of what can generally be summed up as rubbish, ready
> to clog your television and radio set with "Christian" program-
> ming. The publishing houses church out (measured by the ton)
> a landslide of material which can scarcely be called books, often
> composed of the same themes which are viewed as spiritual,
> rehashed endlessly by writers who would be better employed in
> another trade.[5]

By neglecting the arts, Christians of all persuasions have
shortchanged themselves. Secular art has become anti-intellectual and
anti-content—artists with no spiritual or intellectual base have produced works that have no content, are expressive of nothing. What
passes for Christian art is the production of commercial enterprise with
no aesthetic base. Christians have turned away from secular non-art, but
what has taken its place? Too often it is the same kind of non-art, dressed
up with Christian themes, because both the artist and the audience have
nothing on which to base their expectations.[6]

The lack of content in concept, style, technique, and often sincerity
suggests that the voice of the *Millennial Harbinger* provides at least a
partial corrective for the flabby goodies currently served up by much of
commercial Christian enterprise. In retrospect, this stern call to integrity
and honesty may be one strong reason for the loyalty to Alexander Campbell of the poet Vachel Lindsay, as he battled the mediocrity, superfici-
ality, and banality of much of the cultural edifice of his time.

Most of the colleges and universities related to the Christian
Churches (Disciples of Christ), the Christian Churches-Churches of
Christ, and the non-instrumental Churches of Christ offer curricula

---

[5]See Franky Schaeffer, *Addicted to Mediocrity, 20th Century Christians and the Arts*
(Westchester, Ill.: Cornerstone Books, 1981), esp. 16, 21-22, 23.

[6]The twentieth-century Christian cop-out from spiritual values, especially in artistic
expression, is the religious equivalent of conditions in America's public schools described
in the *A Nation at Risk: The Imperative for Educational Reform. A Report to the Nation
by the National Commission on Excellence in Education* (Washington, D.C.: Supt. of
Docs., U.S. Govt. Printing Office, 1983).

which indicate commitment to aesthetic learning for their students.[7] Most of them provide liberal arts general studies courses in literature, music, and visual arts. Five institutions are accredited by the National Association of Schools of Music, an imprimatur which suggests a serious level of study in performance, music education, church music, or liberal studies in music. The existence of the academic programs at Restoration Movement institutions implies the presence of many faculty members who have Christian convictions and artistic abilities at a high level. Although some of these artist-teachers are not members of churches associated with the Stone-Campbell tradition, their relationship with their institutions suggests an understanding of and support for the mindset and the faith of that tradition.

Only one of the institutions is accredited by the National Association of Schools of Art and Design, suggesting that art programs are not yet as well-developed as music, and also that visual arts do not have as rich a support historically as music in the Restoration Movement. Accreditation in theater-dance has not been granted to any institutions on the list; most of the schools offer some level of theater instruction, but the institutions related to the Churches of Christ, for the most part, continue to hold reservations expressed by Alexander and Selina Campbell concerning any form of dance. Of the eighteen institutions related to the Christian Churches (Disciples of Christ), all offer some form of a major in the visual arts, two offer a major in the classics, thirteen offer a major in drama-dance, and fifteen offer a form of music major.

The study of both classic and modern literature has gone beyond the reservations held by first-generation Stone-Campbell followers in each category, as can be seen by the catalogs of the colleges and universities descended from the Stone-Campbell Movement. Most Disciples educators seem to believe that the liberating values of studying poetry, novels, essays, biographies, and short stories are substantial for students related to their respective religious traditions. For people within the Disciples heritage, the creative writing of Louis and Bess Cochran has become a fundamental part of their aesthetic and historic outlook. Louis Cochran's historical biographical novel about Alexander Campbell, *The Fool of God*, and the interpretive history, *Captives of the Word,* by Louis and Bess Cochran, are among the modern classics of the Restoration Movement.

In the professional worlds of music and theater, numerous individuals of the Stone-Campbell Movement have impacted their various media

---

[7]Some of these institutions have been accredited by the National Association of Schools of Music, and at least one has been accredited by the National Association of Schools of Art and Design.

and obtained broad recognition. Among contemporary singers who perform in opera and recital, Arlene Auger, soprano, currently a member of the Westminster First Christian Church in Westminster, California, and daughter of the church's former minister, is currently an eminent international artist known well also to those who watch the arts on public television. She is on the current roster of the Metropolitan Opera Company, and has performed in numerous opera houses in Europe. In theater, Henderson Forsyth, formerly of the Christian Church in Trenton, Missouri, and a graduate of Culver-Stockton College, has performed in numerous plays on Broadway and in New York.

Phillip Gentry Clark (1957-1982), a member of the Mountain View Church of Christ in Johnson City, Tennessee, graduated from Milligan College where as an undergraduate he was active in the theater and vocal music programs, and later attended the North Carolina School of the Arts at Winston-Salem. He also studied dance at the Martha Graham School in New York. His professional experience included a variety of roles at Virginia's Barter Theater and other regional theaters. His experience in off-Broadway and off-off-Broadway productions included performances at the Park Royal Theatre and in the Soho Rep Theatre before his untimely death in 1982. Clark's father is also an active minister in the Restoration Movement and a professor at Milligan College.

Richard Bell, who serves as head of the Department of Fine Arts at Jefferson College in Hillsboro, Missouri, gives a positive application of his Christian world view to teaching music and the arts in a state supported academic institution. Bell, who holds two degrees in vocal music education from a state university, also earned a certificate in church music from Cincinnati Bible Seminary, a school related to the "centrist" Christian Churches of the Restoration Movement. He has appeared as guest conductor and clinician for numerous choirs in the Midwest and has served as choir director for Christian churches throughout his career. He has provided leadership for numerous musical, academic, and civic associations. During 1987, Bell and his family were featured in an American Broadcasting Company news special, "A Day in the Life," with commentator Richard Threlkeld, on the theme "How the United States Constitution Touches the Everyday Lives of the American Family."

Bell spent his boyhood in a small rural community, where he was baptized in the village Christian church. The breadth of his experiences as a Christian musician, educator, and citizen is portrayed in his personal statement, which follows:

> Interpreting a phrase in Bach's *Magnificat*; motivating a lazy tenor; critiquing a recitalist; or working on a faculty staffing problem: none

of these are unusual duties in a normal day at Jefferson College as choral director and chair of the Fine Arts Department. In addition, however, to the obvious objectives of these responsibilities, I feel that they may offer some opportunities to somehow carry out an early taught and still pervasive concept of Christian evangelism.

The gospel message bore upon my early days in rural northeast Missouri as a principle which later transcended to a more aesthetic application. The teaching of the Christian Church (independent) in my hometown of Greentop, Missouri, seldom departed from the "five steps of salvation." The fifth of these steps, however, that of living the Christian life, always included the importance of discovering opportunities for evangelism as well as making moral decisions. My early church education did not include aesthetic awareness per se, but of course embraced the value of music as an aid to worship.

The most influential minister during my high school days was Leo Spurling, a quiet, scholarly man from Kirksville. His well studied sermons were unemotional yet I can remember unprecedented attentiveness from the congregation. There was, however, little allusion to the Campbells and other Restoration fathers. His solid plea was for Christian unity, together with the oft-repeated dictum, "where the scriptures speak, we speak; where they are silent, we are silent," pervaded most of his sermons. His message of restoring Christianity to its primitive origins, to "build alone upon the Apostles and Prophets, Jesus Christ himself the chief cornerstone," struck me as reasonable and indeed exciting. (It was later that I discovered the same plea in Alexander Campbell's *The Christian System*.)

Several summers of attending White Oak Christian Service Camp at Moberly, Missouri were certainly influential during my early teens. There I became aware of our many Bible colleges such as those in Joplin, Missouri; Lincoln, Illinois; and Cincinnati, Ohio. My decision was made early to dedicate one of my college years to an intense study of the scriptures and an application of music to Christian service. Cincinnati Bible Seminary was my predilection, partly because of the reputation of its music department and since R. C. Foster, Lewis Foster, and George Elliott were on the Bible faculty. (I was aware of their importance and influence in the perpetuation of the Restoration Movement.) My conscience was calling for a more knowledgeable faith in Christ and for an undeniable assurance of my own salvation.

Before Cincinnati Bible Seminary was a reality, however, I enrolled as a music education major at Kirksville State Teachers College (now Northeast Missouri State University) just ten miles from my hometown. Other occupational considerations had been osteopathic medicine and the Christian Church ministry. I felt convinced, though, that by choosing music education I could attain a broad satisfaction which would include some rewards from my other two considerations. One is in a sense, I felt, carrying out the Christian mission when teaching, effecting positive change in people's lives. Further I concluded that through music's positive influence some impact could be made on my students' *physical* well being.

My undergraduate years at Kirksville State Teachers College brought me into contact with new religious considerations such as Mormonism, Catholicism, and Lutheranism. The importance of divine authority and Christian unity became more urgent to me. Three years of excellent music education and one baccalaureate degree later, I enrolled in Cincinnati Bible Seminary for my long anticipated year of study. There was no disappointment. A sustained and intense spiritual atmosphere assuaged my conscience. It had solidified my tentative beliefs about music's potential to effect broad positive change in an individual. Feeling increasingly confident of my competence to handle the mechanics of choral conducting, much attention through my following year of graduate school at Kirksville State and several succeeding summers of post graduate work at the University of Southern California was focused on psychology, motivation techniques, and a more spiritual application of music performance.

Within the context of my broad concern with Christian evangelism, religion has impacted upon my profession in three obvious ways. The first is that I constantly feel the need to emphasize the beauty and persuasive power of the *word*. When the proper text is wedded to the communicative strength of music, a composition may affect a deep level of consciousness. Ralph Vaughn Williams' majestic *Sine Nomine* is a magnificent matching of words and music that results in a grand enriching experience. Certainly an instrumental rendition of the work is powerful, but the text gives specific direction for creative mental pictures. Whether emphasizing the veneration of the "saints" in this piece or, say, the beauty of a crimson rose in some secular composition, the mind is directed toward a focused, and in each instance, edifying experience. Penetrating and lasting truths and even purposeful information may be instilled in this manner. Thus I feel great attention should be given to the text with regard to selection of repertoire and rehearsal priorities.

Religion has also encouraged my focus on the mystery and emotion of music. Why do the lyric strains of Londonderry Air seldom fail to evoke deep feelings? The answer certainly involves more than the sum of the notes and a mere melodic or harmonic analysis. Such a consideration is analogous to religion's mystery and alliance with human emotion. Christ's death and resurrection are certainly beyond man's full comprehension; yet the gamut of human emotion is evoked. Such feelings are not to be ignored or avoided in music but rather should be sought out and emphasized. Too many artists have resisted giving attention to these important factors, perhaps in overreacting to the cheap emotionalism of certain pop and revivalistic music.

Third, my religious philosophy has helped to direct my attention in education to the reaching out to various levels of musical comprehension. Christ spoke of the diversity of man's abilities, such as in his parable of the talents in Matt. 25:14-30. He also lived, taught, and died to emphasize the worth of all men, regardless of any differences including mental capacity or achievement. The "whosoever" in John 3:16

implies the universal value of human beings. In the great cacophony of man's divergence, musical illiteracy must be included somewhere. Being encouraged in this awareness by the open-door philosophy of the modern public community college, I feel a certain persistence to reach out to all students at every level of ability, background, and achievement. A working Christian philosophy in education demands patience, understanding, and caring. At times the application is difficult, particularly with regard to select performance ensembles, but I am convinced that solutions can always be found.

My Christian Church membership has always been with small congregations. I have directed the choirs and children's musical groups in each of these churches as well as serving in various positions of Christian Education. Accepting a salary or honorarium in church music has been out of the question because I have always felt that my service should remain completely voluntary. One of the focal points of my pedagogical role is that of emphasizing the need of talented and well-trained musicians to work with their local churches, both in leadership and participatory roles.

My reaction to that Restoration call I had heard during my teens still remains "reasonable and exciting." I have found, however, that the discovery, contemplation, and application of those New Testament principles are even more reasonable and exciting.

During the twentieth century, the visual arts have also attracted the labors of individuals who were raised in the Stone-Campbell tradition. A visual artist needs a deep self-knowledge in order to harness and direct the creative process. Some artists have been unable to cope with the effort to reconcile their Restoration heritage with the demands of aesthetic thinking.

The one-time *enfant terrible* of twentieth-century painting, Robert Rauschenberg (1925-), provides one instance of a mutually unsatisfactory relationship between an artist and the conservative wing of the Restoration Movement. Rauschenberg, involved at the edge of Abstract Expressionism, was for a long time a close colleague of the musician John Cage (1912-) and the dancer-choreographer Merce Cunningham (1919-).

Rauschenberg was raised in Port Arthur, Texas; he served two and a half years in the United States Navy during World War II, after which he studied painting at the Kansas City Art Institute, in Paris, and at the Art Students League in New York City. He found encouragement through the Expressionist Jack Tworkov and Jasper Johns, and won the first prize in the Fifth International Show of Prints in Ljubljana, Yugoslavia in 1963. Durring a tour as designer with the Merce Cunningham Dance Company, he won the prestigious Venice Biennale in painting in 1964. As artist and benefactor, Rauschenberg has exerted a strong influence on art and artists throughout his mature career.

Rauschenberg's religious influence and affiliation during childhood was provided by the Church of Christ. Calvin Tomkins, popular writer for *The New Yorker,* has chronicled Rauschenberg's career in a study entitled *Off the Wall: Robert Rauschenberg and the Art World of Our Time.* In a slightly "off-the-wall" style, Tomkins wrote:

> Both the older Rauschenbergs belonged to the Church of Christ, an austere fundamentalist sect that frowned on social dancing, card-playing, movies, and almost everything else. 'Our church was so strict that it was a full-time job for any Christian just to search for evils,' according to Rauschenberg. 'Even so, I was going to be a preacher until I was about thirteen. I was really serious about it. Finally I decided I couldn't spend the rest of my life thinking everybody else was going to hell, but I kept on going to church—I still went when I was in the Navy and for some time afterward. Giving that up was a major change in my life."[8]

Rauschenberg's ultimate life style was in conflict with the biblical social standards urged by his boyhood congregation. In addition, some of his primary role models and associates, such as John Cage, were influenced by Zen Buddhism. Such association could not have been acceptable to his former brethren who found their primary norm for life in the teaching of Jesus Christ and in the New Testament. But for Rauschenberg the artist, a fundamental aesthetic conflict would have arisen in his artistic attempt to relinquish personal control of his work, to allow his materials free rein without imposing a design crafted from human intelligence on his work. Speaking of Josef Albers, a former teacher at Black Mountain College in North Carolina, Rauschenberg said:

> Albers believed that it was important to know everything there was to know about color, but he said that if you thought one color was better than another you were just expressing a personal preference. I really didn't trust my own taste, and I didn't want to do something that I knew would be just a personal preference of mine. I didn't want color to serve me, in other words—didn't want to use green to intensify red, because that would mean subordinating green.[9]

Tomkins emphasized Rauschenberg's idea that life entered certain canvases "from the outside without benefit of the artist's control."[10]

---

[8]Calvin Tomkins, *Off the Wall: Robert Rauschenberg and the Art World of Our Time* (New York, N.Y.: Penguin, 1981), 15.

[9]Ibid., 70.

[10]Ibid., 71.

314

Plate 14

Inscape I (acrylic on canvas)

TRUDY McRAE

John Cage is remembered by many for his famous non-piece 4'33",
a composition for piano in three movements consisting entirely of
silence. Cage believed that art was "purposeless play," but this play was
also an affirmation of life. It was not an attempt to bring order out of
chaos or to suggest improvements in creation. It is simply to wake up to
the very life one is living, which Cage found "so excellent once one gets
one's mind and one's desires out of its way and lets it out of its own
accord."[11]

A review of the addresses given at the opening of Bethany College
in 1841[12] is a reminder of how the first-generation Disciples pioneers
defined the commission in Genesis to "subdue the earth." Thus one can
see how Rauschenberg's and Cage's abnegation of logic, of cause and
effect, and their acceptance of utter chance rather than planned design
placed them at philosophical variance with the basic premises of the
Restoration Movement. For Rauschenberg, the ultimate estrangement
from the faith of his parents may be rooted deeper than simple theological or lifestyle differences. The contrast between his own and his
church's aesthetic roots was even greater than the divergence between
his notorious lifestyle and the ethical base he was taught as a child.

Rauschenberg's story illustrates how one artist handled the tensions
he felt between his Christian faith and development of artistic expression. Vachel Lindsay seems to have attained a relative peace with his
Christian commitments along with a latent rebellion. On the other hand,
the personal statement of Trudy Jones McRae provides a much more successful report of an artist who has been able to integrate her
"Campbellite" bent into a comprehensive understanding of serving
Christ through her painting and sculpture.

Trudy Jones McRae provides a great deal of autobiographical information in her statement which follows. She was born on a farm near
Harrodsburg, Kentucky, and attended the nearby Restoration Movement
junior college, Southeastern Christian in Winchester, Kentucky. She
then attended Georgetown College of Kentucky, and received her Master
of Fine Arts degree from the University of Alabama. She has served as a
teacher of art in several colleges and universities, and has enjoyed the
opportunity of working closely with other artists through her position
as gallery director-coordinator on two university campuses.

Mrs. McRae, like Rauschenberg, was influenced by Jack Tworkov. A
professional association with artist-in-residence at Northeast Missouri
State University. Tworkov provided Mrs. McRae with artistic encouragement enriched by the discovery of a shared personal interest in spiritual
values.

[11]Ibid., 69.
[12]See chap. 7.

Mrs. McRae has worked successively in sculpture and in painting and is currently involved—along with homemaking duties—in painting. Her exhibitions include juried shows in numerous states and at least one international exhibition.

Trudy McRae's statement effectively integrates the positive aspects and some of the problems she has experienced as a member of the Church of Christ involved in "doing art," and the comprehensive way in which she has been able to use the power of the Stone-Campbell heritage as a positive force in her integrated approach to Christian life:

The following four paragraphs is the statement which accompanies the public exhibition of my abstract acrylic paintings:

What one can put into or take from a work of art is relative to the fund of information the maker or the viewer brings to the encounter. My general fund is rooted in a rural upbringing, a liberal arts and biological science education, a graduate degree in painting and sculpture, a profession as teacher and gallery director, intermittent travel, a supportive family life, and an abiding faith in the Holy Trinity. If the experiencing of my work conveys a meaning to the viewer because he identifies with his own past experience, that is natural; it is not important that my own personal iconography be identified. My idiom of expression is deliberately nonspecific. The tangible recording of my unconscious conversation with the medium need not be tapped to produce a significant encounter; an alteration of perception is sufficient. Titles are given in retrospect much like "barn names" are given to registered dairy cows to distinguish one from another on the basis of familiarity.

As things are in a constant state of flux in nature, I feel an identity with the forces of nature in bringing about change. Subtleties of change in the surface of the raw material of unprimed canvas maintain a vivid record of the painting process. Having several paintings in progress at once increases the chance of being on "speaking terms" with at least one of them. The scale of my work is chosen to convey a feeling of open spaces that extend beyond the boundaries of the painting itself—that suggests the existence of another world in the area of the peripheral vision. Landscape, from the intimate to the sublime, is a major thematic undercurrent in my painting. Light, shadow, shape defined by the everchanging Magnolia and Redbud; soft-edged children, doves, and rabbits; angular Grackles on the wire; and clothes on the line may flow there too. Color choices are most often intuitive and less often emotional or deliberate. Formal order is the basis for compositional decisions. A successful painting has a unity of more powerful impact than any one act of alteration.

I identify with the historical concept of art in my desire to affirm my kinship with man and nature. Specifically, I relate to the forms and sensibilities of Brancusi, Moore, and Arp; the concern for nature of O'Keefe; the landscape effects of Diebenkorn, the gesture of Kline; the splashes of Pollock; the spatial manipulations of Brooks; the pattern and color of Parker; the techniques of Frankenthaler; the fluidity of Jenkins; the color quality of Louis; and concepts of Oldenburg and Morris. Artists whose exhibitions have had a marked motivational impact on me are Monet, Picasso, Klee, Matisse, Siguieros, deKooning, Tworkov, Hunt, and Kabak.

My hope is a personal synthesis of the above mentioned ideas and influences in the making of a structure that is, in its way, beautiful. My desire is to escape fulfillment of the vatication that "individuality is being lost in the pursuit of individuality."

Mrs. McRae then continues:

The wording of the preceding statement was evolved over a period of twelve years to accompany the public exhibition of my abstract acrylic paintings. The purpose was changed from satisfying oral exam requirements to putting the uncertain viewer at ease in finding his own questions and/or answers in my paintings. I have used the most recent version of the statement as an introduction to "where I am coming from." As a painter (a shower, not a teller), this project of articulating my roots in faith and art and how they interrelate is a painful but meaningful experience. I use quotes by theologians and artists who have lent structure to my concepts. I am omitting many whose spiritual impact is actually greater but is too vast to contain here.

I am a member of the Ebenezer Church which is incidentally an independent Church of Christ. My affiliation with that particular community of faith is inherited. My father was born and buried on land his parents donated for the church cemetery. His father was an itinerant preacher who raised his family here in Mercer County, Kentucky. When I read Humbert's *Compend of Alexander Campbell's Theology,* [see bibliography] I found ideas that I heretofore associated with my father's reasonable individualistic church leadership.

I will seek to identify those roots in the Stone-Campbell movement which enliven my faith. I will not dwell on those aspects which have not taken root in my personal story. Some of those traditions are pleasantly nostalgic and others irresponsibly repressive. The essential tap root of freedom to think for myself in a community of faith must suffice. I have grafted in twentieth century religious thinkers who have helped me structure my overall grasp of faith.

Alexander Campbell said that religion is a personal thing, not an assent to a theory, or a fact; but a person believing, obeying, and rejoicing in the person of Jesus Christ. For me, becoming a Christian meant accepting the love of God through Christ and the responsibility of becoming a member of Christ's body on earth—both local and universal church membership were based on acceptance of Jesus as Christ and not on denominational opinions.

In Leroy Garrett's *The Stone-Campbell Movement* is recorded the familiar plea for unity on matters of faith, liberty in matters of opinion, and love in all things. I can identify with the liberating ideals originally expressed in this uniquely American version of the Protestant Reformation; however, I chafe at the restrictive interpretations that abound in the present-day camps. That nothing is to be made a test of communion that God has not made necessary to salvation seems to have been lost in the scuffle. While diversity of individual opinion was desirable, Campbell cautioned that such is the glory of an opinionist in his own eyes that he would sometimes rather give up both his faith and knowledge than his opinion.

Campbell's dream was "to let the gospel in its own plainness, simplicity and force speak to men. Divest it of all the appendages of human philosophy, so called, and of all the traditions and dogmas of men; and in its power it will pass from heart to heart. . . from city to city, until it bless the whole earth."

He heralded the American Revolution as the precursor of an infinitely more important revolution—one in which personal accountability is made the foundation of human liberty. Campbell found the guilt of unbelief lying in the willful inattention of the sinner to the whole subject, arising from the sinner having given his heart to idols. The secret of all human inability he therefore found to be in the idolatry of the heart.

This concept of sin as idolatry was treated in Paul Tillich's *Dynamics of Faith*. Tillich defined as idolatrous that faith in which preliminary finite realities are elevated to the rank of ultimacy. He derived the term "ultimate concern" from "You shall love the Lord your God with all your heart and with all your soul and with all your might" (Deut. 5:6). This, the greatest commandment of all, was the text for Thomas Campbell's last sermon. The elder Campbell was ultimately impressed that Jesus did not call for some marvelous deed, sacrifice or penance but simply called for love of God with all that we are.

I might quibble with the term, "Restoration Movement," if it meant trying to squeeze nineteenth or twentieth century content into a first century shape. Christ was the beginning of the restoration movement, restoring the relation of mankind to God. The first century church was a prototype, a working model—not an end in itself. I believe what Thomas Campbell (Alexander's father) and Lloyd Jones (my father) perceived—that the Church of Christ upon earth is by nature already one, and that we have the duty of loving one another as Christ loved us.

Jesus Christ is the redeemer and mediator of the corporate bodies of the church just as He is of individuals. We need to find our perfection in Christ—not idolize an imperfect church. By following Christ we become self-forgetful activists manifesting an attitude of forgiveness. Christian growth results with the destruction of non-ultimate securities. Tillich pointed out that that which is based on an ultimate concern is not exposed to destruction by preliminary concerns and the lack of their fulfillment. Therefore neither the church nor the Christian should fear reform from within but view it as a necessary, on-going, life-signifying process.

Richard Niebuhr in *Christ and Culture* reminded us that all our faith is fragmentary though we do not all have the same fragments of faith: "To make our decisions in faith is to make them in view of the fact that no single man or group or historical time is the church; but that there is a church of faith in which we do our partial relative work and on which we count. It is to make them in view of the fact that Christ is risen from the dead and is not only the head of the church but the redeemer of the world. It is to make them in view of the fact that the world of culture—man's achievement—exists within the world of grace—God's Kingdom."

Niebuhr found that the humility of Christ exemplified not the moderation of keeping one's exact place in the scale of being but rather that of absolute dependence on God and absolute trust in Him. Christ spoke with authority and acted with confidence and power.

The rightness and eloquence of Martin Luther King, Jr. in *Strength to Love* struck chords of truth and beauty. Quoting Rom. 12:2 "Do not conform any longer to the pattern of this world but be transformed by the renewing of your mind," King said that nonconformity was creative when controlled and directed by a transformed life and constructive when it embraced a new mental outlook. He reminded us that we have a moral responsibility to be intelligent, avoiding prejudice by examining the facts before reaching a conclusion.

King viewed the Reformation as too pessimistic, overlooking man's capacity for goodness, as the Renaissance was too optimistic overlooking man's capacity for evil. He believed that a healthy religion rose above the idea that God wills evil—rather that God permits evil in order to preserve the freedom of man. God can bring good from evil but that does not justify the evil. To passively accept an unjust system was to co-operate in that system and to become a participant in its evil. King identified practical atheists as those who do not deny the existence of God with their lips but simply live as though there is no God. He underscored that the world will not be saved by man working alone or by God imposing His will but by man's obedience to God.

King had the gift of speaking clearly at many levels—spiritually, emotionally, and intellectually. His sermon "Three Dimensions of a Complete Life" was particularly eloquent in describing the unified life. He quoted Rev. 21:16 "The length and the breadth and heights of it are equal." He found John's description of the new city of God to be really describing ideal humanity—that life at its best was complete on all sides. We are commanded by God to get into shape. "Love your neighbor as you love yourself" (Mk 12:31). According to King the length of life was the inward concern for one's own welfare and ambitions and the breadth of life was the outward concern for the welfare of others. "Love the Lord your God with all your heart and with all your soul and with all your mind and with all your strength" (Mk 12:30). That upward reach for God was the height of life.

To live creatively we must be multidimensional. King's ideas suggested to me how to become the sound living building stone for the Church of Christ in this life referred to in II Pet. 2:4-5. "As you come to Him the living Stone—rejected by men but chosen by God—you also like living stones are being built into a spiritual house to be a holy priesthood offering sacrifices acceptable to God through Jesus Christ." As living building stones reshaped to Christian proportions, we are equally conformed to God's eternal kingdom. Only through Christ do we have the balance to grow coextensively and avoid becoming lopsided lumps.

Other "living stones" of God's "holy nation" that my roots have sought out for regular nourishment and support are C. S. Lewis, Dietrich Bonhoeffer and Keith Miller. Corrie ten Boom, Karl Barth, Carl Ketcherside, and Chuck Colson have also propped me up. I don't dare to try to generalize their profound infusion into my spiritual life. They are a "peculiar" people as a by-product of following Christ. They did not lose Christianity in the pursuit of Christianity. As Charles Colson remarked in *Loving God,* "Life isn't like a book. Life isn't logical or sensible or orderly. Life is a mess most of the time. And theology must be lived in the midst of that mess."

The common-sensical Alexander Campbell struck a contrasting aesthetic chord when he depicted mind as the differential attribute of man. He declared, "The mind is not instinct, nor mere reason, nor imagination. It is not an animal soul—a mere life. It thinks, it reasons, it wills, it loves the beautiful, the amiable, the excellent, it wonders it adores, it pants after the infinite, the eternal, the immutable. It is capable of eternal growth, of evolutionary progress, of untiring ecstasy, of ceaseless rapture."

Buckminster Fuller was more down to earth when he said that what we mean by mind is man's ability to generalize in the scientific sense. I fear that this, my statement concerning faith and art, suffers from generalization in the literary sense of trying to cover too much territory at once. I have tried to take from Fuller the courage to be a "generalist" and not allow myself to be trapped in the relative security of my specialty. Fuller's description of the co-existence of the forces of tension and compression in creating dynamic balance suggests the order of all dynamic relationships. Co-existing, sometimes paradoxical, forces are innately apparent to theologians and artists as well. Consider liberal and conservative, unity and diversity, faith and doubt, relative and absolute, good and evil, classic and romantic, freedom and obligation, rational and emotional, tension and resolution, push and pull, positive and negative, open and closed.

Art gives form to feeling. Philosopher Suzanne Langer said that life is incoherent unless we give it form: "The criterion of good art is its power to commend one's contemplation and reveal a feeling that one recognizes as real with the same click of recognition with which an artist knows that form is true. . . . The aesthetic emotion is really a pervasive feeling of exhilaration directly inspired by the perception of good art."

I feel that same intuitive "aha" when I perceive someone else's "fragment of faith" ringing true in my own life. In fact the artists to be quoted in this paper are chosen for how well they give written form to our mutual concerns and not for how closely our works relate in appearance. Hans Hoffman, Henri Matisse, and Wassily Kandinsky are legitimate roots of my painterly expression, but Ben Shahn is not.

That the relationship of art through the ages has been one of inner meaning, not outward form, was noted by Kandinsky. The same might be said of the church. Spiritual freedom is as necessary in art as it is in life. In his book, *Concerning the Spiritual in Art,* Kandinsky sounded like an Old Testament prophet when he designated the responsibility that comes with the privilege of artistic power. The artist was cautioned that his deeds, feelings, thoughts and corresponding art works create a spiritual atmosphere which should be pure as opposed to poisonous.

As a painter and erstwhile pianist, I closely relate to Kandinsky's vision "that methods of music applied to art abandon reproduction of natural phenomena in desire for rhythm in painting, for mathematical abstract construction, for repeated notes of color, for setting color in motion." I could easily categorize my own works using the two classifications Kandinsky applied to the paintings of Matisse: (1) "pictures full of great inward vitality produced by the stress of inner need; (2) pictures possessing only outer charm because they were painted on an outward impulse."

Matisse himself seems to have been a kindred spirit of Tillich when he proclaimed: "To see is itself a creative operation requiring an effort. Everything that we see in our daily lives is more or less distorted by acquired habits. . . . The effort to see things without distortion takes something very like courage."

Having the courage to see beyond "art for the sake of art" or "religion for the sake of religion" enables one to avoid elevating one of those attractive preliminary concerns to the position of ultimate concern and losing sight of God.

That the artist must maintain an attitude at once detached and deeply involved is recognized by painter Shahn in *The Shape of Content.* His social outlook paralleled that of King when Shahn said that to create anything at all in any field required nonconformity or a want of satisfaction with things as they are. He also concluded that a healthy society was one in which two opposing elements, the conservative and the creative, exist in a mutual balance. Opposing elements within the church could benefit from thus respecting their mutual necessity for a balanced dynamic relationship. My family training in "rugged individualism" has helped me adjust to my present state of being too conservative for the world of contemporary high art and too liberal for my community of faith.

My art is symbolic in that as an expression it suggests more than it says, but it does not contain specific recognizable symbols. Overcoming intellectualization was my primary lesson in graduate school painting.

Intellectualization limited me to what I could preconceive and denied me the opportunity to respond to the work of art in progress and thereby go beyond what my mind could anticipate. Likewise, over-intellectualization would limit me to what is already understood about the Bible and theology and would deny my living creatively through the questions that come in real life of faith. New concepts that evolve and ring true lose their newness and seem natural.

Art co-exists with life. Both the comfort and the adventure of day to day existence pull and distract me from the concentration needed to paint creatively; yet they provide the varied experience necessary to feed my artistic expression. In college I struggled with and explored wide-ranging sculptural styles from traditional to conceptual. Meanwhile my painting, once uncorked, flowed in a relatively smooth development. The sheer physicality of sculpture made it more of a problem and at the same time a more natural process. The act of painting remained at an intuitive and spiritual level. The processes involved in teaching art, running a gallery, having children, or managing a home seem to satisfy the creative urges that used to go into sculpture. The need to paint has at times been channeled into soul stirring reading and spiritual growth. However the basic asethetic need to make art appears with cyclical regularity. Henry Miller expressed it poetically when he said that to paint is to love again.

Although beginning a painting requires "a leap of faith" similar to religious experience, painting like faith is a steady thread in my life. Artistic creation involves the repeated destruction of the work in progress to push it to a new level of development. The trick is to catch the individual painting at a satisfactory plateau before it is overworked into an unredeemable muddle, or puddle as the case may be (I happen to use the technique of flowing saturated colors of acrylic on raw canvas). A finished painting is not technically flawless but comfortably alive.

My approach is a subtractive process of eliminating unessential possibilities, painting in the negative unoccupied spaces first in a search for the resolution of the positive space forms. I do not suffer from *horror vacui* or fear of empty spaces as did the medieval religious artist. If answers come too easily in my paintings or my theology then I suspect they stem from lack of growth and perception rather than from maturity. Van Gogh grasped the significance of the struggle when he said that being an artist meant "being in it with all my heart, always seeking without absolutely finding" as opposed to "I know, I have found it." These statements are applicable to both my art and my faith.

Hoffman, the spokesman for Abstract Expressionism in *Search for the Real,* declared that "one cannot make an artist, but one can teach art. Straining after superficialities and copying appearances destroy the inner order of the work of art." Likewise one cannot make a Christian, but one can share the grace of God. The integrity of the Christian is destroyed in straining after Christian attributes rather than allowing the Holy Spirit to keep one centered on God in Christ. The Christian life like art must be consistent within itself seeking a reality beyond imitation. As Hoffman so succinctly states that "art is greater than the sum of its parts," so also, I conclude, is faith. This statement is an open composition because it involves the ongoing and the infinite. I am grateful to Dr. Jorgenson for the opportunity to rub all of this stuff together and let it go.

The first-generation leaders of the Stone-Campbell Movement held a lofty conception of the human mind and the spoken word, a conception reinforced by their respect for the scriptures which they considered to be the Word of God. The intellectual control characteristic of their thought retained sufficient flexibility to accommodate various doctrines of the Holy Spirit, human creativity, and—though sometimes jealously—even art. The one-sided application of Restoration Moement thought to a rigid pattern resulted in the loss of the original unity plea by the Peripatetic Generation, and a mot difficult struggle by artists who were affected by Disciples scholasticism. Artists such as Robert Rauschenberg discarded both the Christian faith and Disciples epistemology in their reaction to simplistic forms of Restorationism. Vachel Lindsay pushed the boundaries of his Disciples beliefs almost beyond the borders of historic Christian faith in his struggle to assert his creative freedom. Artists such as Phillip Clark, Arlene Auger, Richard Bell, and Trudy McRae have demonstrated that a balance between the heart and the brain of the movement can yield excellent results in both Christian practice and creative performance.

13

The Heart and Brain of Restoration

> For just as the body is one and has many members, and all the members of the body, though many, are one body, so it is with Christ. For by one Spirit we were all baptized into one body— Jews or Greeks, slaves or free—and all were made to drink of one Spirit.
>
> For the body does not consist of one member, but of many. If the foot should say, "Because I am not a hand, I do not belong to the body," that would not make it any less a part of the body. And if the ear should say, "Because I am not an eye, I do not belong to the body," that would not make it any less a part of the body. If the whole body were an eye, where would be the hearing? If the whole body were an ear, where would be the sense of smell? But as it is, God arranged the organs in the body, each one of them, as he chose. If all were a single organ, where would the body be? As it is, there are many parts, yet one body.
>
> I Cor. 12:12-20 RSV

Saint Paul's introduction to the subject of Christian love and its relationship to the unity of the church is strikingly analogous to an aesthetic concept of structure and unity in art. Arthur Berndtson, in his book, *Art, Expression, and Beauty,* says:

> Structure has the oneness of the mystical whole, and the plurality of chaos; it is a one of many or many in one. Structure thus is identical with unity, which requires plurality and relations that bind the many into one. The structure of anything consists of its parts as related into the one thing, or of its wholeness diversified into related parts.[1]

Thomas Campbell spoke of "unity with diversity," as in Article Six of the "Address" in his charter document, the *Declaration and Address:*

> That although inferrences [sic] and deductions from scripture premises, when fairly inferred, may be truly called the doctrine of God's holy word, yet they are not formally binding upon the consciences of Christians farther than they perceive the connection, and evidently see that they are so; for their faith must not stand in the wisdom of men, but in the power and veracity of God. Therefore, no such deductions can be made in terms of communion, but do properly belong to the after and progressive

[1]Arthur Berndtson, *Art, Expression, and Beauty* (New York: Holt, Rinehart and Winston, 1969), 42.

edification of the Church. Hence, it is evident that no such deductions or inferential truths ought to have any place in the Church's confession.[2]

The ability to achieve a teleological overview of a matter, such as the church's mission and polity or of humanity in God's world, was one of Alexander Campbell's great strengths. It provided him with a larger view of the Restoration Movement which prevented that Movement from taking on an insular, parochial character during his lifetime, and kept his hierarchy of theological issues in tune with his Christological world view. For he *had* a world view: he choked on the term "theology," but he did maintain a Gestalt-like understanding of God, the Bible, the church, and human society. Robert Richardson said of him:

> At his bidding, the facts of scripture seemed to acquire new force and meaning; a connected train of scriptural truths and illustrations opened up unexpected and lofty views of the Divine plan of redemption; while, ascending to higher planes of thought, he left far beneath him the controversies and difficulties of all human systems, as the eagle soaring aloft in the sunlight leaves far below him the stormy clouds that darken the mountain's brow or overspread the valley with gloom and desolation.[3]

Alexander Campbell did not assert a bold position in affirming strong support for music, painting, sculpture, architecture, or literature; yet it is important that his spiritual-intellectual legacy does provide the grasp and the space for art's pursuit by those who inherited his religious understanding. The fascination and powerful magnetism of Campbell's stance have been seen to preoccupy Vachel Lindsay, even though Lindsay's theology had moved far away from Campbell's. In a similar sense, Campbell's purposiveness as well as the possibility of a larger art in search of opportunity to magnify God are reflected in the personal artistic statements of Richard Bell and Trudy Jones McRae.[4]

Although Campbell hardly articulated a unified aesthetic doctrine, his colleagues Richardson, Pendleton, and later Isaac Errett came close to doing so. Walter Scott had provided fire for the altar, but Richardson

---

[2]Thomas Campbell, "Declaration and Address," 110. Walt Yancey, *Endangered Heritage*, 138-46, suggests that the binding nature of "necessary inference" was not used by the first-generation reformers, but became established by the conservative editors of the Restoration Movement under the editorial leadership of Moses E. Lard and J. W. McGarvey. It is a standard norm in the Churches of Christ as a prohibition against instrumental music and the missionary society.

[3]Richardson, *Memoirs*, 2:106. In an earlier view of Alexander Campbell as preacher, Richardson emphasized the "lofty standpoint of his conceptions." See 2:315-16.

[4]See chap. 12 of this book.

and Pendleton put the arts in a context of total Christian life. The fragmented vision of the peripatetic editors sullied both the case for the church's unity in diversity and the use of art as a significant form of expression and communication among the churches most susceptible to the influence of those editors. A few years later, the breathtaking drama of redemption, historically the generator of powerful art forms, was diminished for that part of the Disciples Movement which elected primarily to preach a social gospel and abandon Alexander Campbell's adherence to the Bible as the Word of God.

It is the thesis of this book that the conversion of the original passion for unity with diversity to a rage for doctrinal conformity by members of the Restoration Movement was generated by the same attitude which, for people endeavoring to be artistically creative within the spirit of their faith, engendered aesthetic suffocation. This is not to say that the passion for conformity *caused* aesthetic poverty; rather, that both were parallel results of the same attitude.

The establishment of the Brush Run Church over the foundations of the heterogeneous Washington Christian Association brought into being a new religious group—by anyone's logical definition, a new Christian denomination. Resisting the truth of this simple statement required more and more retrenchment by the second-generation scholastic editors, as they moved from the founding fathers' original passion for unity into the closed circle of "Restorationism." They use "subjective cookie cutters" to define the New Testament pattern even more narrowly than most of the written creeds of the religious denominations they disparaged.

The reaction to this situation was damaging both to the Movement's significance in a Christian frame of reference, and to art. For the Campbells, Stone, Scott, and their colleagues, the Bible, as it "spoke," had been the central *raison d'etre* for the Movement. As later liberal Disciples accepted higher criticism with little reservation, the Bible became little more than a symbol of a quasi-supernaturalism dominated by a naturalistic norm.

Neither extreme developed a true Christian humanism which could exalt the *imago-Dei* of the Old Testament, the incarnation and the redemptive drama of Christ in the New Testament, to produce both a spiritual Christianity and a joyous art. Thus, it may not be too bold to ask whether Robert Richardson's deep belief in the indwelling presence of God's Holy Spirit in Christian life was not closely related to his love of art, music, poetry, and nature.

In summary, several concepts contributed to the "dry" era of Disciples teaching during the late nineteenth century which made it more difficult for Disciples to practice art. One of them had to do with what might be termed "historical existentialism"—a growing belief that somehow the Church of Christ had become dormant after the apostles—or sometime in the first century A.D.—and stayed that way until the founding of the Restoration Movement. There are still cornerstones of church buildings within the Movement which suggest that the congregation has a direct connection with the first-century church, so that there is no need to recognize a relationship to any of the intervening Christian efforts. This approach represents extreme "restorationism," disclaims any debt to the Protestant Reformers, and is a handy rationale for disclaiming fraternal relationships with "the sects."

It has been clearly shown in this work that Alexander Campbell did not endorse this view. Not only the Lunenberg Letter in the 1830s, but his introductory remarks of the *Christian System* manifest his sense of building on a foundation where Luther and the Protestant Reformers had stopped. "That glorious reformation," as he calls the sixteenth-century Protestant movement, left Campbell and his contemporaries a "rich legacy." It seems never to have occurred to him or his father to question the Reformers' basic Christianity, at least not until the question was forced on him by his most conservative Disciples brethren.

As has been suggested in chapter 2, Campbell's post-millennial concept was based on God having worked through men and women throughout history. The thought that God's providence—or the Church of Christ—had been entirely lacking on the earth since the death of the last apostle was unthinkable to him.

It is quite clear to see that the case for artistic practice was undercut by the same historic existentialism. Until late in the nineteenth century, the visual arts, music, and literature have frankly acknowledged a continuing obligation to those creative persons who preceded a given generation.

Friedrich Nietzsche's (1844-1900) concept of an alternate dominance by Dionysius and Apollo, forces of Romanticism and Classicism, acknowledged at least reaction, if not a more straight line of influence.[5] Artists, like reformers, tend to stand on each others' shoulders, and the loss of historical context implied by the extreme Restorationist theory deprived those who might have been Disciples artists of a strong sense of continuity with artistic tradition.

Campbell and his colleagues who chartered Bethany College believed in empirical knowledge and a rational way of perceiving both scripture and the world. Yet, with all their trust in Baconian empiricism, they did not give up the privilege of accepting universals from the scrip-

---

[5]For an extended exegesis of this theory, see Curt Sachs, *The Commonwealth of Art: A Lecture Delivered in the Whittall Pavillion of the Library of Congress April 15, 1949* (U.S. Govt. Printing Office, 1950).

ture as God's revealed Word.[6] The historical existentialism[7] of the Peripatetic leaders among Disciples required a total focus on the particulars of their own subjective views of scriptural teaching and "scriptural silence," and bypassed Thomas Campbell's exhortation to not bind matters on others by mere scriptural inference. It was impossible for a larger view of the world and of Christianity—let alone an artistic overview—to be developed under this condition.

The isolation from history created by second-generation Disciples Scholastics introduced a unique understanding of the scriptures as normative, but was not friendly to Christian freedom. The only passion for unity that remained was the passion for conformity to a closely defined pattern, based on subjective interpretation of both the words and the silences of the scriptures. In many cases a primary burden for souls was amended to a burden for defeating and proselytizing those whose understandings were divergent from the "pattern." This course, in addition to being less than fully Christian in motivation, was certainly defective as a generating ideal for significant art.

Since the proclamation of the principle of *sola scriptura* by the Protestant Reformers, the difficulty of creating a consensus regarding doctrinal positions has been a continuing problem.[8] The major Protestant denominations have circumvented the difficulty by establishing credal statements which bind together the constituents of their respective groups. Since the Disciples leaders rejected written creeds, the establishment of a rigid and authoritarian interpretation of scripture by editorial authority often defined lines of fellowship between dissenting groups within the movement. Honoring the scriptures as the Word of God, the Peripatetic editors sometimes confused the Word with the interpretive words of preachers and editors. If this exclusivist imposition of human interpretive authority undermined the original Movement's opportunity for unity among Christians, it also diminished

---

[6]Richardson, *Memoirs,* 2:106, writes: "Mr. Campbell strictly applied the inductive method to the Bible and made *its* facts and revelations the great basis of religious trust."

[7]For a definition of "existentialism" here I have relied on F.S. C. Northrup, *The Logic of the Sciences and the Humanities* (New York: World, 1947), 386: "Existentialism . . . is the thesis that immediately felt and apprehended reality, which is always a particular rather than a universal, is the real."

[8]To do Alexander Campbell justice concerning the centrality of the doctrine of regeneration, it is important to consult the four extra numbers of the *Harbinger* series on the the subject of remission of sins and regeneration. In opening the first such "Extra" in 1830, he placed his concept of the new birth and salvtion very much in harmony with Reformation theology: "Luther said that the doctrine of justification, or forgiveness, was the test of a standing or falling church. If right in this, she could not be very far wrong in any thing else; but if wrong here, it was not easy to suppose her right in any thing. I quote from memory, but this was the idea of the great Reformer. We agree with him in this as well as in many other sentiments." "Remission of Sins," Extra, *Millennial Harbinger* (1830): 1.

the essential space and flexibility required for the health of Christian art and metaphor.

The inroads of extreme liberalism, on the other hand, left the strongest opponents of the "Scholastics" without the basic Restoration purpose. Without scriptural norm, without a strongly centered message with authority more authentic than a humanistic social gospel, they, too, lived in an existential void. No true descendants of Stone or Campbell, they defined their *Existenz* intuitively, although their desire for unity with all Christians—except perhaps with their conservative brethren—found continued expression through their participation in the emerging ecumenical movement. Yet, the historic fact that the arts have flourished more freely among liberal groups of Disciples than among the more "scholastic" churches may well reflect the continued view of unity, of Campbell's overview of the church, which the ecumenical-minded leaders have managed to maintain. For if art requires a "oneness of the mystical whole," as Berndtson has suggested, the original plea for unity by the Restoration fathers certainly helped provide opportunity for their successors to infuse that unity with an aesthetic dimension.

The metaphoric expression of *worship* is a concept that Alexander Campbell himself does not seem to have accepted. Richardson suggests that his *preaching,* however, was not at all devoid of ornamentation, and actually depended upon simile and metaphor to at least a limited extent:

> Mr. Campbell's discourses were . . . by no means destitute of ornament. He had a correct fancy, which was rather fastidious than lovely. Hence he never employed figures of a homely character or such as were calculated to lower his subject. On the contrary, his comparisons, which were not frequent, were always such as tended to elevate it, or were at least in perfect harmony with it. These he usually drew from the scriptures, and his familiarity with the language of the Bible enabled him to employ its glowing expressions and beautiful similes with great effect.[9]

Speaking of Campbell's use of "Bible themes, Bible thoughts, Bible terms, and Bible facts," Richardson says:

> For the embellishment of these he employed scripture metaphors much more frequently than comparisons, but it was upon analogies that he seemed chiefly to rely for illustration as well as argument. These, constituting his chief imagery, were usually grand, far-reaching, and widespreading.[10]

[9]Richardson, *Memoirs*, 2:595.
[10]Ibid., 586.

But if biblical parables, analogies, and metaphors were part of the secret of Campbell's power as a preacher, his appreciation of metaphor did not extend to non-verbal forms. The use of "singing choirs" and instrumental music in worship represented for him "worship by proxy." This is evident in several passages of his writing.

Upon the publication of *The Christian Melodeon,* a book of psalms, hymns and anthems edited in 1849 by the highly esteemed "singing brother" A. S. Hayden of Ohio, Campbell gave his approbation, noting:

> This selection and adaptation of music to Christian worship, is not got up after the Bostonian style—for singing choirs and instrumental devotions—but for worshipping assemblies, not by proxy, but in person, with their hearts and their voices, exalting together the praise of the Lord.[11]

Lynn Hieronymous suggests that Campbell must be understood in the light of historical perspective in his opposition to "performances" by choirs and organs. He was "fully aware of dark ages in Christian history when the singing congregation and priesthood of believers went into oblivion. The gains of the Protestant Reformation were not to be lost again."[12] The "Boston style" of choral performance in church was "popery reasserting itself" in Campbell's watchful view.

The leading principle for which he stood in the worship through hymnody, therefor, was that of resisting the "proxy" delegation of the individual believer's right of access to God. This right could not be turned over to priest, preacher, holy men, or singing choirs. In the light of his exultation concerning the freedom and the privilege of every individual to commune directly with God, it is understandable that the American reformers did not surrender that right passively. Campbell wrote:

> Shall a choir with organs, or the whole congregation sing, are questions in doubt with some.—For my part, I vote that every Christian man, woman, and child—every professor that has one note of praise in his heart, one chord of music in his soul, should open his mouth and make a joyful noise unto the Rock of our Salvation.[13]

Hieronymous summarizes, "The possible danger in having a choir was simply the danger of religion by proxy with its consequent sickness unto

---

[11]*Millennial Harbinger* (1849): 300.

[12]Lynn Hieronymous, *What the Bible Says about Worship* (Joplin, Mo.: College Press, 1984), 239.

[13]*Millennial Harbinger* (1844): 249.

death."[14] Added to that was the danger of pride on the part of the well-trained performers who brought their art to congregational worship. Campbell's reasons for his doctrinal position had to do with the priestly privilege of individual Christians and the negative aesthetic of worship he experienced personally. They were not based primarily on common ground with the peripatetic generation's arguments for a prohibition of fellowship. Their reasoning depended on the "silence of the scriptures." Interestingly, many who opposed instrumental music in the churches later countenanced *a cappella* singing organizations in the church, and in media presentations of their worship services. In addition, the "professional" spirit of pride inevitably invaded the role of the song leader (reminiscent of Isaac Errett's experience with "brother Jasper.")

But metaphor—especially in the expression of non-cognitive experience as a vehicle of worship—was not a well-developed category in Campbell's thought. Richardson, and even Pendleton, came closer to articulating a place for non-verbal expression than Campbell, but full development of this possibility was not a part of the original Stone-Campbell heritage. Painting and sculpture were "crafts" to be used in the preservation of the appearances of people or landscapes, but the allegorical, landscape, and genre painting and the still-life works of the mid-century were still representational work.

Music, likewise, was primarily a support for the poetic word, a vehicle which could be used in a functional way as a carrier for the text, but which had no independent validity as a means of worship. In Europe, meanwhile, one of the most intensive debates in musical history was being waged between Richard Wagner and Eduard Hanslick over the communicative and expressive powers of absolute music.[15]

An area where Alexander Campbell again was more creative than some of his religious heirs related to his tolerance for ambiguity. This characteristic impacted both the goal of Christian unity and the creative possibilities open to Disciples artists.

A primary example of this attitude arose in connection with the famous Lunenberg letter in 1837. Campbell had been emphasizing the rediscovered doctrine that (a) baptism was immersion, and (b) immersion was for the remission of sins. Pressed by the lady from Lunenberg, Virginia, to state unequivocally whether there could therefore be any Christians among the "pious unimmersed," Campbell acknowledged that there doubtless were some. His reply, "Christians among the Sects," motivated a barrage of letters critical of his inclusive opinion. The affair

---

[14] Hieronymous, *What the Bible Says about Worship,* 240.

[15] Eduard Hanslick, *The Beautiful Music,* tr. Gustav Cohen (New York: Da Capo Press, 1974), argues against Richard Wagner's romantic assertion that absolute music should communicate non-musical ideas.

ran on in the *Harbinger* for several months, with Campbell continuing to explain his position and defend his consistency. In the course of an article in the December 1837 *Millennial Harbinger,* he contended that he had taught the necessity of immersion for remission of sins since the first issues of the *Christian Baptist* in 1823. He then added:

> Let me ask, in the first place, what could mean all that we have written upon the union of Christians on apostolic grounds, had we taught that all Christians in the world were already united in our own community?[16]

The rage for order and logic which occupied, even at this early date, many of the Disciples, prevented the acceptance of this apparent logical inconsistency. Leroy Garrett places the incident in its important perspective:

> Campbell obviously did some retrenching during the three-year controversy. His unambiguous stand in the Lunenberg letter was not now unambiguous. It is not that he had changed his mind, but that he had a unity movement on his hands that had reactionary elements stronger than he had supposed, and he did not want it to blow up in his face through internal disputes. Like his friend Henry Clay, he was the great pacifier who held the Movement together as long as he lived.[17]

Some of Campbell's second-generation followers could not accept his "waffling" about this question, so they refused fellowship with unimmersed members of "the sects." Moses E. Lard, for one, refused to acknowledge the fact that anyone might be a Christian who was not immersed, although some might be saved who were not Christians! Garrett comments:

> The intense debate that followed reveals an exclusivist temperament within the soul of the Movement that helps to explain the emergence of the Churches of Christ as a separate church. The dichotomy is still in evidence, for the liberal-ecumenical persuasion within the Movement is forever quoting the Lunenberg Letter, while the more exclusivistic-restorationist element seems embarrassed by it.[18]

A surprising degree of resiliency seems to have characterized Campbell's approach to scripture interpretation. Ever conscious of the

---

[16]"Any Christians among the Sects?" *Millennial Harbinger* (1837): 561.

[17]Garrett, *Stone-Campbell Movement*, 585.

[18]Ibid., 578.

difference between *scriptural truth* and his own *interpretation* of that truth, he displayed a respect for the difference which was not always present in the public exegesis practiced by his spiritual descendants. He often spoke of the sacredness and the supernatural wisdom of God with great reverence, and he exhorted followers to show honor even to the name of God, even in his concern about using the name of the Lord in material for singing schools. That reverence extended to receiving the meaning of the Bible:

> He, then, that would interpret the Oracles of God to the salvation of his soul, must approach this volume with the humility and docility of a child, and meditate upon it day and night. Like Mary, he must sit at the Master's feet, and listen to the words which fall from his lips. To such a one there is an assurance of understanding, a certainty of knowledge, to which the man of letters alone never attained, and which the mere critic never felt.[19]

An interesting situation occurred in 1857, when the editor of the *Religious Herald* thought he had detected a clear inconsistency in Campbell's positions regarding the subject of faith. In a piece entitled, "On Which Side is A. Campbell?" he charged that the *Harbinger* editor at different times had taught faith was in the belief of facts, but at other times had suggested that believing faith was not based on facts, but on the person, Jesus Christ. The *Herald* editor then summarized: "Mr. Campbell, then, with his usual perspicuity, gets on both sides of the dispute. Will he explain?"[20]

Campbell's response shows his willingness to let two aspects of a truth converge into one *Gestalt:*

> "On which side?"—! I have not noticed "in the several numbers back" of the *Herald* (for I do not file them) the two sides to which he refers: for in fact I never knew that there were two sides in our whole community, and much less two sides among our public men on any question touching faith, piety, or humanity, vulgarly called "religion and morality."[21]

Campbell made it clear that he realized a certain ambiguity of opinion was a necessary result of religious freedom in his additional comments to the *Herald* editor:

---

[19]Alexander Campbell, *The Christian System*, 16.
[20]"On Which Side is A. Campbell?" *Millennial Harbinger* (1857): 574.
[21]Ibid.

These 'two distinct and irreconcilable views of the nature of faith held amongst Reformers,' are wholly the cherished figments of his dreams and longings for such a rich banquet. We have in all communities a variety of forms and philosophies introduced into the pulpits and sometimes printed, published, and read in the periodical products of the press of all professing communities, the terms and phrases of which may not be in the best taste, nor in exact keeping with the words which the Holy Spirit spoke, or what the Apostles used in communicating the mind of the Spirit to the communities which they addressed.[22]

The "rage for order," (a concept that is sometimes used to explain the work of artists who seek to create a world different from the ambiguous and imperfect one in which they live) seems not to have consumed the first-generation reformers of the nineteenth century, as it did the peripatetic followers who sought a religious conformity through both the words and the silences of the scriptures. Robert Richardson, always the spokesman for freedom, and consequently the target of criticism from the 1860s until his retirement, acknowledged the transcendent nature of many spiritual truths for the human understanding:

We do not, however, assert that every thing contained in the Bible can be fully understood. There are some subjects too mysterious in their nature to be clearly explained in human language; some too great to be completely grasped by a finite mind; many too remote from the ordinary range of human thought, to be distinctly apprehended by the most discerning intellect. As in the natural world we have bodies so remote that they appear but as faint nebulae, and stars which can scarcely be distinguished by human vision from those which cluster around them, so have we, in the Book of God, glimmerings of spiritual systems far distant from our own, whose relationships to us we may never comprehend in our present state of being. Such must necessarily be the case in regard to communications concerning the Divine Creator and the things of an infinite, unseen spiritual world. There are subjects to be reverently pondered and contemplated only so far as, upon the heavenly scroll, we may discover their outline, or discern their more salient points. These are not things about which men may dogmatize; into which they may vainly and presumptuously intrude; or in regard to which they may insolently excommunicate and anathematize each other.[23]

---

[22]Ibid., 575.

[23]Robert Richardson, "Principles and Purposes of the Reformation," *Millennial Harbinger* (1852): 583-84.

Richardson accepted fully the Campbellite approach to the "facts" discernable in the Bible, and the logical use of a rational understanding in its interpretation. He protected carefully the difference between "faith" and "opinion," that Thomas Campbell had defined. Richardson's humility of spirit kept him from believing himself all-wise, or inflecting the private nuances of his beliefs on others as minimal requirements for fellowship. Again, it is interesting that the man of science was the premier spokesman, among all the first-generation Restoration fathers, for a spirit of openness and intellectual humility. Had Richardson's influence impacted the Disciples movement more fully, it might well have averted some of the fragmentation which occurred, and have left open a more hospitable situation for the uses of non-discursive art in the expression of Christian faith and worship.

The resistance of Alexander and Selina Campbell to works of fiction which "ignited the imagination," and thus created an insatiable appetite for a world alternative to the real one, may be partly attributed to the English and American Puritanism that fertilized their view of duty and responsibility. It is part of the American frontier spirit which they also imbibed, and it may also be a partial reaction against nineteenth-century Platonic romanticism. Born just after Wordsworth, Coleridge, and Sir Walter Scott, the same year as Lord Byron and four years before Percy Bysshe Shelley, Alexander Campbell—from the intellectual stability of his Calvinist, Scottish-Irish heritage, still heard the beat of Aristotle rather than that of Plato. Interpreted through the empiricism of Francis Bacon and the psychology of John Locke, an empirical view of reality provided a cooler basis for understanding both the Bible and the world than the feverish mindset of Campbell's contemporary English Romantics. Richardson perhaps was correct in complaining that the "dry" mindset of Locke was too much a part of Campbell's spiritual orientation; nevertheless, the dominance of the intellect over the emotions probably gave the Reformation in the West a stronger basis for a biblically ordered faith than a Pentecostal Romanticism could have provided. That the Romantic period still left its impact on Disciples, in spite of their "cool rationalism" and "Scottish common sense," is attested by George Beazley, who mentions two distinct Romantic influences:

> One of these influences is a romantic view of man, which sees nature as basically good, when not corrupted by the sophistication of an effete and cynical culture. The other is a Pietistic orientation, which lays emphasis on individual conversion and sets up a standard of conduct which seeks to perfect the individual but is largely unconcerned for the structures of society.[24]

---

[24]Beazley, *The Christian Church*, 73-74.

The *Millennial Harbinger* was started from an optimistic view of what American culture could become, an optimism which received a fatal blow from the Civil War. The Rousseau-like admiration of rural culture and primitive nature, together with faith in the general good sense of rural people over urban dwellers, was greatly diminished as the Disciples became city people in large numbers late in the nineteenth century. It does not seem accurate to suggest that Campbell and his colleagues lacked a theology of culture, as witnessed by their educational concerns, but with it they retained the Reformation concern for individual sin and salvation.

And what of the Restoration Movement as an environment for art? One of the contemporary artists who contributed to this work found some Stone-Campbell roots "nostalgic," others found them "repressive." Trudy Jones McRae chafes, along with Vachel Lindsay and others who have attempted to be creative within the Movement, at the "restrictive interpretations that abound in the present-day camps," but "can identify with the liberating ideals originally expressed in this uniquely American version of the Protestant Reformation."[25]

This is a reminder that freedom—along with unity and restoration of the primitive order—was a major ideal of the American reformation led by Stone and the Campbells. If an artist, to make an authentic statement, requires freedom and space along with significant substance, the original Disciples plea held great potential for creative artistry.

Beazley acknowledges an attitude of caution toward the arts by Disciples throughout their history. He expresses an optimism that the potential for aesthetic expression may yet be realized, though a great deal of catching up needs to be done:

> Unfortunately, the Disciples shared with the Reformed tradition a suspicion of the arts. Not only did they want a place of worship stripped of superfluous ornamentation which might distract men's and women's minds from the proclamation of the Word of God, but most of them felt that the reading of novels was not conducive to the strict morality they had set for themselves. Though, like the Puritans, they may have subconsciously reveled in the literary concreteness of the scriptural books, and though they may have savored beauty of language there and in the sermon, they would have felt that its purpose was to instruct, inform, and give the plan for man's salvation, not to be enjoyed as sensuous and imaginative pleasure. They did not have either the Anglican or the Lutheran pleasure in the esthetic quality of worship or their feel for the necessity of beautiful and graphic

[25]Trudy Jones McRae is a contemporary Christian artist. See chap. 12, pp. 316-21.

language in worship. Fortunately many present day Disciples have recognized and corrected this deprivation in their classic heritage, though even now the sense of artistic excellence would be less than the Lutheran or Anglican traditions.[26]

One aspect of beauty, incidentally, which has characterized the continuing *a cappella* singing tradition in the Churches of Christ, is the experience of hearing a large congregation artistically sing four parts, under strong leadership, of the great church hymns.

Finally, a comment needs to be made concerning the term "Restoration." Contemporary members of the Christian Church (Disciples of Christ) have almost discarded the term because of its implications for identifying a specific blueprint for the Church of Christ which is to be imposed upon every congregation. This thought implies that a single "order" prevailed in all the churches mentioned in the New Testament. Such a position is almost universally questioned, except for basic fundamentals of the faith. It also implies to many that the inspired and divine order was rediscovered by an elite body of Christians, whose prime responsibility was to get all others who would be followers of Jesus to accept their understanding of what that "ancient order" is. With a militant objection to written creeds and confessions, the Procrustean bed of beliefs imposed by the editors, academic institutions, and preachers has often become more rigid and more binding than the very credal position which forced the Restoration fathers from their Calvinist churches.[27]

There is also the question of the indwelling Spirit. It has always been a point of mere "opinion" in Disciples thought. There are many contemporary followers of the Stone-Campbell tradition who believe that the Spirit of God lives in the hearts of all Christians, and who agree with Robert Richardson and Isaac Errett that the silence of scripture provides opportunity for the creative growth of the church to respond to an ever-changing application of the gospel in a changing culture.

[26]Beazley, *The Christian Church*, 73-74.

[27]Alfred T. DeGroot's 1940 study concluded that "restorationism" is a divisive concert rather than unitive. This directly counters Thomas Campbell's hope that in the "return to the ancient order," might be found the means for uniting Christians. See DeGroot, *The Grounds of Divisions Among the Disciples of Christ* (Chicago: privately printed, 1940).

For some Disciples, however, the written Word is no longer normative.[28] Without the original Disciples faith in the Bible as more than a product of an evolving human religious awareness, and without an inspired Word that contains a Divine mandate for the faith, it would be foolish for those Disciples to speak of "Restoration." The nineteenth-century dilemma remains for both faith and art: Neither Puritan legalism nor Romantic trivialization of the problem of evil—either personal or cultural—answers the deepest need of the human race. Neither position is in tune with the first-generation fathers of the American Restoration Movement.

If the current members of the Churches of Christ, the Christian Churches-Churches of Christ, and the Christian Church (Disciples of Christ) can use the word "restore" in the light of Peter's use in the New Testament, it may yet suggest a *healing* process:

> And after you have suffered a little while, the God of all grace, who has called you to his eternal glory in Christ, will himself restore, establish, and strengthen you. To him be the dominion for ever and ever. Amen. (I Pet. 5:10)

Restoration, in words which cover the pages of the *Millennial Harbinger* in innumerable contexts, meant to the American reformers, unity, freedom, and revival of the "ancient order" to implement those goals. In a Christian context, love and freedom are words that are inextricably tied to a hope for restoration. H. R. Rookmaaker, from a Reformed viewpoint evolved from the original church of Barton W. Stone and the Campbells, interprets this hope for Christian artists:

> How is the Christian artist to fulfill this role, and to work out these lovely norms? Can he really create the lovely and the beautiful in a loving way for his fellow-men? It is a calling to promote good and to fight evil, ugliness, the negative; to hunger and thirst for righteousness; to search for the right 'finishing touch,' the right tone, the right word in the right place.

> The Christian artist has to create in an open and positive relationship to the structure of the world in which he was created

---

[28]D. Newell Williams, Professor of modern and American church history at Christian Theological Seminary, has recently underscored the shift in attitudes toward scripture alluded to here: "In the more than one hundred and twenty years since Campbell's death there have been major shifts in the assumptions of most Bible scholars regarding the character and proper use of the New Testament witness. Having generally rejected the appropriateness of Campbell's scriptural norm for determining the right order of the church, Disciples must find norms for judging the life of the church." See "The Chief Test," *The Disciple* 15, no. 4 (April 1988): 17.

by God; he has to act, on the foundation of Christ as his Lord and Saviour, in love and freedom.

He must love the people for whom the work is meant, for the material he uses, for the subject he chooses, for the truth he is going to express, for the Lord he is serving.

He must know freedom by not being bound wrongly to man-made rules. He can be traditional if he chooses and feels that to be right, he can search for new ways, new materials, new subject matter, new techniques if he feels he needs them in order to achieve his goals.

Love and freedom belong closely together, just as sin and slavery belong together. If Christians feel that they have to make all kinds of rules in a legalistic way, even if they do so with the best of intentions and aim only to preserve the good, yet they kill freedom, and in the end love is gone, and beauty has fled.[29]

The American *Zeitgeist* has moved again to a highly materialistic norm of value. Students studying the arts, literature, and the humanities are outnumbered sharply by those in business, science, computer science, and other worthy professional disciplines. These disciplines are expected to readily lead to successful careers. For Christian young people, the dual prospect of mastering the exhorbitant demands of an art form and simultaneously applying that art medium to a realization of deep Christian conviction is a burden that must give pause before even beginning. The history of the Restoration Movement might give young people in that tradition additional pause. The residue of Puritan values still alive within the Movement tends to place a much lower value on artistic accomplishment and non-material aesthetics than on athletic achievement, financial success, or political leadership. Yet, in worship, or in personal expression, the Stone-Campbell Movement includes: Christian painters and sculptors who search for more powerful means to incorporate their beliefs in physical media; architects who struggle with the human problems of form and function; singers and instrumentalists who share their gifts in worship or on stage; and actors who labor to interpret a playwright's thoughts creatively. They do this in order to help sear a hopeful path across the maze of contemporary culture—all in the Name of One who, Rembrandt reminded the world, is God Incarnate.

[29]H. R. Rookmaaker, *Modern Art and the Death of A Culture,* (Downers Grove, Il.: Inter-Varsity Press, 1970), 243-44.

Selected Bibliography

Augustine, Saint. *Confessions.* Translated by Vernon J. Bourke. Washington, D.C.: The Catholic University Press, 1953.

──────────. *Poems.* Cambridge: Metcalf and Co., Printers to the University, 1852.

Beatty, Arthur. *William Wordsworth, His Doctrines and Art in their Historical Relations.* Madison: University of Wisconsin Press, 1962.

Beazley, George G., Jr., editor. *Christian Church (Disciples of Christ): An Interpretive Examination in the Cultural Context.* St. Louis: Bethany Press, 1973.

Berndtson, Arthur. *Art, Expression, and Beauty.* New York: Holt, Rinehart & Winston, 1969.

Boll, R. H. *Truth and Grace.* Edited by J. W. Shepherd. Cincinnati: F. L. Rowe, 1917.

Bouwsma, William J. *John Calvin: A Sixteenth-Century Portrait.* New York: Oxford University Press, 1988.

Calvin, John. *Institutes of the Christian Religion.* 2 vols. Translated by Ford Lewis Battles. Philadelphia: Westminster Press, 1960.

Campbell, Alexander. *The Christian System.* Cincinnati: Standard Publishing Co., n.d.

Campbell, Selina. *Home Life and Reminiscences of Alexander Campbell.* St. Louis, John Burns, c. 1882.

Carter, Edward C. II, John C. Van Horne, and Charles Brownell, editors. *Latrobe's View of America, 1795-1820.* New Haven: Yale University Press, 1985.

Charvat, William. *The Origins of American Critical Thought, 1810-1835.* New York: A. S. Barnes & Co., 1936.

Cochran, Louis, and Bess White Cochran. *Captives of the Word.* Joplin, Mo.: College Press, 1987.

Coulton, G. G. *Art and the Reformation.* Hamden, Conn.: Archon Books, 1969.

Davis, M. M. *How the Disciples Began and Grew.* Cincinnati: Standard Publishing Co., 1915.

Dickens, A. G. *Reformation and Society in Sixteenth-Century Europe.* London: Harcourt, Brace & World, 1966.

Dixon, John W. *Nature and Grace in Art.* Chapel Hill: University of North Carolina Press, 1964.

Edwards, Jonathan. *Jonathan Edwards on Evangelism.* Edited by J. C. Wolf. Westport, Conn.: Greenwood Press, 1958.

Emerson, Ralph Waldo. *The Best of Ralph Waldo Emerson.* Edited by Gordon S. Haight. Roslyn, N.Y.: Walter J. Black, 1941.

Erdt, Terrence. *Jonathan Edwards: Art and the Sense of the Heart.* Amherst: University of Massachusetts Press, 1980.

Fitch, Alger Morton. *Alexander Campbell, Preacher of Reform and Reformer of Preaching.* Austin, Texas: Sweet Publishing Co., 1970.

Flanagan, John T. *Edgar Lee Masters: The Spoon River Poet and His Critics.* Metuchen N.J.: Scarecrow Press, 1974.

Foster, August John. *Jeffersonian America.* Westport, Conn.: Greenwood Press, 1980.

Gardner, Helen. *Art Through the Ages.* 5th rev. ed. New York: Harcourt, Brace & World, 1970.

Garrett, Leroy. *The Stone-Campbell Movement. An Anecdotal History of Three Churches.* Joplin, Mo.: College Press, 1981.

Garrison, W. E., and A. T. DeGroot. *The Disciples of Christ: A History.* St. Louis: Bethany Press, 1958.

Gilbert, Katherine, and Helmut Kuhn. *A History of Esthetics.* Bloomington: Indiana University Press, 1954.

Greaves, Richard L. *Theology and Revolution in the Scottish Reformation.* Grand Rapids: Christian University Press, 1980.

Green, John, editor. *Twentieth-Century Interpretation of the Scarlet Letter.* Englewood Cliffs, N.J.: Prentice-Hall, 1968.

Gresham, Perry E. *The Broncho That Would Not Be Broken.* Nashville: Disciples of Christ Historical Society, 1986.

_____, editor. *The Sage of Bethany: A Pioneer in Broadcloth.* St. Louis: Bethany Press, 1960.

Grout, Donald J. *A Short History of Opera.* New York: Columbia University Press, 1961.

Hanna, William Herbert. *Thomas Campbell: Seceder and Christian Union Advocate.* Joplin, Mo.: College Press, n.d.

Hanslick, Eduard. *The Beautiful Music.* Translated by Gustav Cohen. New York: DaCapo Press, 1974.

Hanson, Kenneth C. "The Theology and Hymns of the Restoration Movement." Unpublished Bachelor of Divinity thesis. Indianapolis: Christian Theological Seminary, 1951.

Hawthorne, Nathaniel. *The Scarlet Letter.* 2d ed. Edited by Scully Bradley, et al. New York: Norton & Co., 1961.

Heaton, Mary Margaret K. *The Life of Albrecht Dürer of* Nurnberg. Portland, Me.: Longwood Press, 1881.

Henson, H. Hensley. *Puritanism in England.* New York: Burt Franklin, n.d.

Hieronymous, Lynn. *What the Bible Says About Worship.* Joplin, Mo.: College Press, 1984.

Hitchcock, H. Wiley. *Music in the United States: A Historical Introduction.* Englewood Cliffs, N.J.: Prentice-Hall, 1969.

Hoelty-Nickel, Theodore. "Luther and Music" in *Luther Lectures.* Decorah, Iowa: Luther College Press, 1960.

Hoffman, Hans. *Search for the Real.* Edited by Sara T. Weeks and Bartlett H. Hayes, Jr. Cambridge: MIT Press, 1948.

Hopkins, John. "The Idea of Progress in Nineteenth-Century Disciples Preaching,"Unpublished Bachelor of Divinity thesis. Lexington, Ky.: College of the Bible, 1961.

Humbert, Royal, editor. *Compendium of Alexander Campbell's Theology*. St. Louis: Bethany Press, 1961.

Humble, Bill J. *Campbell and Controversy*. Joplin, Mo.: College Press, 1985.

Johnston, Kenneth R., and Gene W. Ruoff. *The Age of Wordsworth: Critical Essays in the Romantic Tradition*. New Brunswick: Rutgers University Press, 1987.

Jorgenson, Dale A. "Why Did We Hide the Fiddle Player?" *The Disciple* (September 19, 1982).

Jorgenson, E. L. *Faith of our Fathers*. Louisville: Word and Work, n.d.

Kandinsky, Wassily. *Governing the Spiritual in Art*. New York: Dover Publications, 1977.

Kittleson, James M. *Luther the Reformer*. Minneapolis: Augsburg Publishing House, 1986.

Koenigsberger, H. G., editor. *Luther, A Profile*. New York: Hill and Wang, 1973.

Lamar, J.S. *Memoirs of Isaac Errett with Selections from His Writings*. 2 vols. Cincinnati: Standard Publishing, 1893.

Lang, Paul Henry. *Music in Western Civilization*. Norton & Co., 1941.

Langer, Susanne K. *Feeling and Form*. New York: Scribner's Sons, 1953.

Leinsdorf, Erich. *The Composer's Advocate: A Radical Orthodoxy for Musicians*. New Haven: Yale University Press, 1981.

Leith, John H. *An Introduction to the Reformed Tradition*. Atlanta: John Knox Press, 1977.

Lindsay, Vachel. *Adventures, Rhymes and Designs*. New York: Eakins Press, 1986.

_____. *Collected Poems*. New York: Macmillan, 1925.

_____. *Letters of Vachel Lindsay*. Edited by Marc Chénetier. New York: Burt Franklin, 1979.

Locke, John. *An Essay Concerning Human Understanding*. Edited by John W. Yolton. New York: Dutton, 1978.

Lohse, Bernard. *Martin Luther: An Introduction to His Life and Work*. Translated by Robert C. Schultz. Philadelphia: Fortress Press, 1986.

Lunger, Harold L. *The Political Ethics of Alexander Campbell*. St. Louis: Bethany Press, 1954.

Luther, Martin. *Luther's Works*. Vol. 15. Edited by Hilton C. Oswald. St. Louis: Concordia Publishing House, 1972.

Masters, Edgar Lee. *Vachel Lindsay, A Poet in America*. New York: Scribner's Sons, 1935.

Masters, Hardin Warren. *Edgar Lee Masters*. Cranbury, N.J.: Associated University Presses, 1978.

Maximilian, Prinze zu Wied. *Reise in das innere Nordamerika*. Koblenz, Germany: Rhenania Buchhandlung, n.d.

McAllister, Lester. *Thomas Campbell: Man of the Book*. St. Louis: Bethany Press, 1975.

_____, and William E. Tucker. *Journey in Faith*. St. Louis: Bethany Press, 1975.

McElroy, Charles Foster. *Ministers of the First Christian Church (Disciples of Christ), Springfield, Illinois, 1833-1962*. Springfield: Bethany Press, 1962.

McLean, Archibald. *Alexander Campbell as a Preacher*. St. Louis: Christian Publishing Co., 1908.

McNeill, John T. *The History and Character of Calvinism*. New York: Oxford University Press, 1954.

Mendelowitz, David M. *A History of American Art*. New York: Holt, Rinehart & Winston, 1970.

Milton, John. *Paradise Lost and Other Poems*. Edited by Maurice Kelley. Roslyn, N.Y.: Walter J. Black, 1943.

Moore, W. T. *Comprehensive History of the Disciples of Christ*. New York: Fleming Revell Co., 1909.

Morris, Lloyd. *The Rebellious Puritan: Portrait of Mr. Hawthorne*. New York: Harcourt, Brace, 1927.

Mueller, John H. *The American Symphony Orchestra*. Bloomington: Indiana University Press, 1951.

Murch, James DeForest. *Christians Only: A History of the Restoration Movement*. Cincinnati: Standard Publishing, 1962.

Newman, Albert Henry. *A Manual of Church History*. 2 vols. Chicago: American Baptist Publication Society, 1902.

Niebuhr, H. Richard. *Christ and Culture*. New York: Harper & Row, 1957.

Northrup, F.S.C. *The Logic of the Sciences and the Humanities*. New York: World, 1947.

Opera Lutheri. D. Martini Luther: Opera Latina varii argumenti ad reformationis historiam imprimis pertinentia. 7 vols. 2d ed. Edited by H. Schmidt. Frankfurt am Main, 1865—

Pelikan, Jaroslav. *Bach Among the Theologians*. Philadelphia: Fortress Press, 1986.

Powell, V. M. "Alexander Campbell and Frontier Religion." Unpublished paper. Columbia, Mo., n.d.

Randall, Max Ward. *The Great Awakening and the Restoration Movement*. Joplin, Mo.: College Press, 1983.

Reese, Gustave. *Music in the Renaissance*. New York: Norton, 1954.

Richardson, Robert. *Memoirs of Alexander Campbell*. 2 vols. Cincinnati: Standard Publishing, 1897.

Rookmaaker, H. R. *Modern Art and the Death of a Culture*. Downers Grove, Ill.: Inter-Varsity Press, 1970.

Schade, Werner. *Cranach: A Family of Master Painters.* Translated by Helen Sebba. New York: Putnam's Sons, 1980.

Schaeffer, Franky. *Addicted to Mediocrity: 20th Century Christians and the Arts.* Westchester, Ill.: Crossway Books, 1981.

Shahn, Ben. *The Shape of Content.* New York: Vintage Books, 1957.

Schopenhauer, Arthur. *The World as Will and Representation.* 2 vols. Translated by E. F. J. Payne. New York: Dover Publications, 1958.

Schweitzer, Albert. *J. S. Bach.* 2 vols. Translated by Ernest Newman. Boston: Bruce Humphries, 1905.

Simonson, Harold P. *Jonathan Edwards: Theologian of the Heart.* Grand Rapids: Eerdmans, 1974.

Squire, Russell N. *Where is the Bible Silent?* Los Angeles: Southland Press, 1973.

Stevenson, Dwight E. *Disciple Preaching in the First Generation.* Forrest F. Reed Lecture for 1969. Nashville: Disciples of Christ Historical Society, 1969.

——————. *Home to Bethphage.* St. Louis: Christian Board of Publication, 1949.

Stone, Barton W. *Biography, Written by Himself, with Additions and Reflections by Elder John Rogers.* Cincinnati: J. A. and U. James, 1847.

Sweet, William Warren. *Religion on the American Frontier. The Presbyterians, 1783-1840. A Collection of Source Material.* New York: Harper & Bros., 1936.

Tejera, Victorino. *Art and Human Intelligence.* New York: Appleton-Century-Crofts, 1965.

Tillich, Paul. *Dynamics of Faith.* New York: Harper & Row, 1957.

Tocqueville, Alexis de. *Journey to America.* Translated by George Laurence. Edited by J. P. Mayer. Westport, Conn.: Greenwood Press, 1954.

Upton, George, editor. *Theodore Thomas.* Chicago: McClerg and Co., 1905.

Van der Leeuw, Gerardus. *Sacred and Profane Beauty: The Holy in Art.* New York: Holt, Rinehart & Winston, 1963.

Van Deusen, Kenneth. *Moses Lard, That Prince of Preachers.* Joplin, Mo.: College Press, 1987.

Vogt, Von Ogden. *Art and Religion.* Boston: Beacon Press, 1948.

Wasson, W. W. *James A. Garfield, His Religion and Education.* Nashville: Tennessee Book Co., 1952.

West, Earl Irvin. *The Search for the Ancient Order: A History of the Restoration Movement.* 3 vols. Indianapolis: Earl West Religious Book Service, 1950.

White, William Luther. *The Image of Man in C. S. Lewis.* Nashville: Abingdon Press, 1969.

Wilburn, Ralph G., editor. *The Reconstruction of Theology*. St. Louis: Bethany Press, 1963.

Yancy, Walt. *Endangered Heritage: An Evaluation of Church of Christ Doctrine*. Joplin, Mo.: College Press, 1987.

Ziff, Larzer. *Puritanism in America*. New York: Viking Press, 1973.

Early Journals of the Stone-Campbell Movement

American Christian Review. Edited by Benjamin Franklin, 1856-87.

The Christian Baptist. Edited by Alexander Campbell, 1823-30.

The Christian Evangelist (formerly *The Christian Echo*). Founding editor, James H. Garrison, 1863.

The Christian Messenger. Edited by Barton W. Stone, 1826-45.

The Christian Standard. Founding editor, Isaac Errett, 1866—

The Evangelist. Edited by Walter Scott, 1832-44.

The Gospel Advocate. Founding editors, David Lipscomb and E. G. Sewell, 1855—

The Millennial Harbinger. Edited by Alexander Campbell, 1830-64, and William K. Pendleton, 1864-70.

Index

(Names, places, and events appearing in the text are indexed. Footnote material is not indexed.)

A

Abraham Lincoln Walks at Midnight (In Springfield Illinois)" by Lindsay, 302
Acoustics in church construction, 189, 190
Adams, John Quincy, 84
Adventures Preaching Hieroglyphic Sermons by Lindsay, 296
Aesthetics
  of Calvin, 38
  Campbell critical of doggerel, 208
  in Christian colleges, 307-8
  in church life, 185-209
  definition of art by A.Campbell, 184
  slowed by Disciples, 114
  and drama of salvation, 113-14
  influenced by doctrinal differences, 146-47
  and peripatetic generation, 248
  and pride, 187
  Protestant foundation for, 34
  as reinforcement for theology, 105, 108
  and rejection of instrumental music, 204, 206
  and Restoration Movement, 34, 326
Akron Plan of church architecture, 194
Albers, Josef, 313
Alexander Campbell by Lindsay, 294, 298-99
Ambiguity
  in Stone-Campbell Movement, 137
  toleration for
    in aesthetic realm, 138
    by Campbell, 331-32
American Christian Missionary Society, 259
"American dark age,"
  described, 93
  and Second Great Awakening, 111
Ames, E. S., 286, 295, 296-97
"Ancient Gospel"
  Restoration concept, 31, 123-24
"Ancient Order"
  Restoration concept, 31
Anglican Church, 49
Anti-Burghers
  See Seceder Presbyterians
Antioch College, 152
Antrim Counrty, Ireland, 57
Architecture
  austere in Campbellian churches, 191
  Classical style, 75
  development in America, 83-84

"domed box" churches, 194
functionalism
  in Restoration Movement, 186
  in Campbellian thought, 189
Neoclassical style, 75
Picturesque style, 75
Sublime style, 75-76
vernacular tradition, 83-84, 194
A Rhymed Address to All Renegade Campbellites, Exhorting Them to Return by Lindsay, 299-300
Aristotelianism
  Campbell's view, 154
  Peripatetic school in ancient Greece, 247
Arminianism, 110
  in Church of England, 49, 50
  and Great Awakening, 111
  and Independent churches, 60
  and *sola fide, sola gratia,* 112
Art
  and Christian commitment, 303-23
  Christianity's approach to, 179
  comparison of Lutheran and Reformed, 108
  defined by A. Cmapbell, 184
  education in Christian colleges, 308
  populist, of Lindsay, 285-86
  purpose, 42
  utilitarian view, 233-34
  verbal,
    of Campbell, 329-30
    statement of Trudy McRae, 316-23
  visual,
    and Calvinism, 99, 105-8
Art, Expression and Beauty by Berndtson, 324
Art and morality, 230
Artistic standards, 46-47
Artists
  contemporary Christian, 304-6
    Cranach the Elder, 107-8
  cultivation, within Restoration Movement, 276-77
  visual
    Dürer, Albrecht, 34, 100-1
    Grünewald, Matthias, 99-100, 107
    Rembrandt van Rijn, 107-8
Arts, essential
  in Campbell's curriculum, 166
Arts, the
  Anglican view, 49
  and Bethany College curriculum, 175
  Campbell's views, 330-32
  in Christian thought, 307

as divisive factor, 22
in medieval church, 179
as "opinion," 22
Richardson's views, 211
Scott's views, 166
in Stone-Campbell Movement, 329
and tolerance for ambiguity, 138
Auger, Arlene, 307-8
Augustine, Saint, 247
Confessions, 178
Augustinian view of
artistic standards, 46-47
fiction, 46
poetry, 25
Austen, Frances
Lindsay's grandmother, 280
Austerity
in Campbellian church architecture, 191
Autonomy, congregational, 202

B

Bach, Johann Sebastian, 102-4
Bacon, Francis
Novum Organum, 152
Bacon College, 155-58
Baconianism in 19th century America, 75
Baptism
of Thomas and Alexander Campbell, 128
questioned, 129
Campbell's view, 132, 136
as church ordinance, 111
debate about between A. Campbell and J. Walker, 140
Haldanes' view, 62
in Half-Way Covenant, 110
inclusivist/exclusivist controversy, 130, 267-68
as obedience to the gospel, 123
Stone's view, 120
Baptism, believer's
adopted by Brush Run Church, 128
adopted by Disciples, 19
Campbell's defense, 136
as ordinance of Brush Run Church, 24
Baptism, doctrine of
defense, 136
and fellowship with Baptists, 138
and separation from Presbyterians, 138
Baptism, infant
in early Restorationist thought, 19
rejected by Thomas and Alexander Campbell, 128, 129
Baptists
Alexander Campbell's opinion, 139
criticized for luxurious buildings, 188
Disciples/Christians separate from, 142
in 18th century America, 111
Barish, Jonas

"The Anti-Theatrical Prejudice," 229-30
Baxter, William, 222
Beauty
See Gospel of Beauty
Beazley, George G. Jr., 63-64, 247, 335, 336
compares Stone and Campbell ethos, 124-25
on philosophy of history, 33
on Puritan aesthetic attitudes, 59-60
view of Walter Scott, 141
Bell, Richard
personal statement, 309-12
Berndtson, Arthur
Art, Expression, and Beauty, 324
Bethany College
admissions policy, 172-73
announcements about, in "Millennial Habinger," 151-76 *passim*
curriculum, 152, 159, 164-65, 170-71, 175
discipline problems at, 173
education of teachers at, 171
emphasis on natural sciences and empirical knowledge, 167
fire destroys academic buildings, 191
opening, 164-65
plans for, 159
Bethlehem, Pennsylvania
American Moravian center, 80
Bible, as authoritative norm for Restoration Movement, 38, 338
Biblical criticism, 271
Bingham, George Caleb, 82
Blair, Hugh
doctrine of sublimity, 85
Lectures on Rhetoric and Belles Lettres, 84-85
Blakemore, William, 29
Bodmer, Carl, 72-73
Boll, R. H., 121
Bonus Homo
pseudonym for Alexander Campbell, 86
Book of Common Prayer, 50, 52
Boston Symphony, 80
Bourden, Mary, 298
Bouwsma, William J., 37, 47
Briney, J. B., 281
Brown, M. Margaret
Alexander Campbell's first wife, 23, 128
The Broncho That Would Not Be Broken, by Lindsay, 302-3
Brush Run Church
founding, 24
Buffalo Academy
operated by Alexander Campbell, 140
Buffalo Seminary
opened by Alexander Campbell, 139, 140

Bunyan, John, 51, 67
  Pilgrim's Progress, 106
Burghers' Oath, 57
Burnett, D. S.
  president of Bacon College, 576
  editor of *The Christian Preacher,* 201
Burnham, Frederick W., 298
Buxtehude, Dietrich, 103
Byron, Lord
  Destruction of Sennacherib, 89

C

Cage, John, 312, 315
Calvin, John
  aesthetic practice, 38
  contributed to hymnody, 38-39
  as Protestant reformer, 36-37, 99
  Psalter, 40
  views on music, 40, 59
Calvinism
  and aesthetic expression, 105-8
  as antecedent to American Disciples
    Movement, 108
  attitudes toward aesthetics, 99, 105-8
  as basis for aesthetic values, 34, 105-8
  influence on Church of England, 49-50
  influence on Restoration leaders, 54-55
  influence on Restoration Movement, 109
  of Jonathan Edwards, 112
  rejected by Hawthorne, 114
  relationship to Restoration Movement,
    35
Campbell, Alexander, 11, 12
  appreciation of natural beauty, 235-36
  arrival in America, 23, 69
  attitude toward education, 70-71
  baptism, 19, 25, 129, 132
  birth, 16
  call for educational reform, 153
  contradictory views of church history,
    30-31
  conversion, 122
  curriculum criteria, 153-54
  death, 253
  death of son, 243
  debate with Robert Owen, 65
  debates vs. concept of unity, 129
  deficient in musical faculty, 220
  doctrine of Holy Spirit, 121
  dualistic dimensions, 95, 154
  edited hymnals, 198-99
  education, 150
  educational philosophy, 156
  endorsement of Bacon College, 158
  eschatology, 43
  essays, 86-87, 90
  essays on education, 151-76 *passim5*
  essays on ministerial character, 179

  evolutionary philosophy of education,
    150
  evolving attitude toward Bacon College,
    156-58
  first meeting with Barton W. Stone, 143
  at Glasgow University, 62, 89, 219, 221
  home life, 243
  hymnal, 207-8
  imprisonment, 243
  literary criticism, 91
  literary principles, 86
  lover of hymns, 238
  mature thought about "opinions," 241
  member of Virginia constitutional con-
    vention, 163
  musical deficiency of, 220
  plans for Bethany College, 150-51, 162
  poetry, 45, 89
  post-millennialist view, 87-88
  preaching style, 50-51, 77, 181
  president of Bethany College, 160
  professor of Mental Philosophy, 170
  pseudonyms used by, 86
  quoted by Lindsay, 298-99
  rationalism, 217
  as Renaissance man, 149
  scriptural basis for theology, 43
  sermon at his own baptism, 128
  speech on epistemology and psychology,
    154
  teaching career, 140
  and tension between poetical/logical
    tendencies, 90-91
  use of language, 45-46
  view of Lord's Supper, 56
  view of Protestant Reformation, 31-32,
    123-24
  view of "proxy" musical expression, 330
  view of sin and justification, 121-24
Campbell, Dorothea
  Alexander's sister, 128
Campbell, Enos,
  Alexander's uncle, 240-41, 242
Campbell, Henley
  son of Alexander and Selina, 241
Campbell, Selina, 48
  attitude towards fiction, 46
  comments on architectural simplicity,
    194-95
  opinions on visual arts, 234-35
  opposition, to fiction, theater, etc.,
    226-28
  story of Enos Campbell, 239-40
Campbell, Thomas
  arrival in America, 15-17, 69
  baptism, 19, 25, 129
  birthplace, 58
  and Chartiers Presbytery, 17

chairman of board of Bethany College, 160
death, 243
decision to organize independent church, 111
development of aesthetic values, 58
development of religious attitudes, 58
dismissed from Seceder Presbyterians, 16
inclusivist stance, 130
literary principles, 86
ministry in Ireland, 16
reply to Lunenburg letter, 131-32
sermon at his own baptism, 128
teacher of Richardson, 214
Campbell, Thomas (1777-1824)
Scottish poet; not father of Alexander, 89
Campbellian Movement
See Stone-Campbell Movement
Campbellite Movement
See Stone-Campbell Movement
Camp meetings, 119-20
Cane Ridge revival, 120-21
Captives of the Word by Louis and Bess Cochran, 308
Carlstadt, Andreas
rejection of church music, 35
Cartwright, Thomas, 53
Catechism (of John Calvin)
and definition of Church, 37
Catlin, George, 82
Cave, Martha Ann
Vachel Lindsay's grandmother, 280
Challen, James, 202, 221
Channing, Edward Tyrell, 84
Channing, W. C., 174
Chartiers Presbytery, 17
Charvat, William
on American literary criticism, 86
Chase School of Art, 285-86
Chorales
and Martin Luther, 35
by Lindsay, 292
The Christian Baptist
Campbell's editorship, 92
content, 122
discontinued, 140, 142
emphases, 124
essays on "Ancient Gospel," 130
establishment, 30
inauguration, 140
sarcasm in, 135
Christian Churches-Churches of Christ, 12
Christian Churches (Disciples of Christ), 12
Christian Hymn Book used in singing schools, 206-7
The Christian Magazine, 249
The Christian Melodeon, 330

The Christian Messenger, 143
Christianos
pseudonym of Archibald McKeever, 134
The Christian System
by Alexander Campbell, 121
statement on Protestant Reformation, 32
"Christian Scheme of Education"
by Alexander Campbell, 151
Christ United Methodist Church
Bethel Park, Pa., 305
Church
founded on Word of God, 38
Restorationist view, 19
visible and invisible, 37
Church, Frederic, 82
Churches, independent
influence, on Campbells, 60
Churches of Christ
ecumenical roots, 135
separation from Disciples, 275
Churches of Christ (non-instrumental), 12
Church growth
not primary concern of early Movement, 141
Church history
Campbell's view, 30, 33
Errert's view, 265-66
Church membership
and Half-Way Covenant, 110
Church of England
influenced by Calvinism, 49
Church of Scotland, 55
Church Ordinances
See Baptism; Lord's Supper
Cincinnati
music in, 238
Cincinnati Gazette, 193
Clarinda
pseudonym for Alexander Campbell, 86
Clark, Phillip Gentry, 309
Classics
A. F. Ross's arguments favoring, 167-68
Campbell's attitude toward, 152-53
Coblin, Ethelin S.
cousin of Vachel Lindsay, 293-94
Cochran, Louis and Bess, 241, 257, 307-8
Coed education
Campbell's arguments for, 152
Cole, Thomas, 82
College of Professional Teachers at Cincinnati, 154
College of Teachers in Cincinnati, 157
Common-Sense philosophy
affect on American aesthetics, 84
influence on Alexander Campbell, 24
Communion
See Lord's Supper
Confessions of faith

early Restorationist views, 18
The Congo by Lindsay, 292
Congregational autonomy
  in public worship, 202
Congregational Churches
  in 18th century America, 111
Conner, Elizabeth
  wife of Vachel Lindsay, 293
Copley, John Singleton, 82
Corneigle, Jane
  wife of Thomas Campbell, 16
Coulton, G. G., 101
Cowper, William, 89, 221
  Task-Book, 181
Cox, Richard, 202
Cranach, Lucas the Elder, 34, 101-2
Cranmer, Thomas
  objections to *Book of Common Prayer,*
  52
Creativity
  concepts, 184
  Richardson's thoughts about, 215-16
Creeds
  rejected by Disciples leaders, 328
Cromwell, Oliver, 50-51, 227
Cross, Alexander
  missionary to Liberia, 241
"Cultured" and "vernacular" traditions
  in American arts, 79-86

D

Danbury, Connecticut
  Site of church founded by Sandeman, 61
Dancing
  censured as trifling, 231-33
David, King of Judah
  and penitential psalms, 97-98
Davies, Samuel, 109
Debates of Alexander Campbell
  about baptism, 129
  with John Walker, 140
  with Robert Owen, 65
Declaration and Address by Thomas
  Campbell, 23
  central theme, 19
  and concept of unity through restoration,
  127
  early plans for, 18
  on "opinion," 247
  theme of unity in, 130
Deism, 110
Dentler, Howard E., 94
Denton, John
  debate with James A. Garfield, 269
Dewey, John, 184
"Dialogue on the Holy Spirit"
  by Alexander Campbell, 65-66
Disciples

architecture of worship buildings, 84
rationalistic roots, 135
and relationships of Bible, Christ, Spirit
  and Word, 42
united with Kentucky churches, 31
Disciples of Christ Historical Library, 294
Disciples of Christ Historical Society, 12
Döring, Christian, 102
Doctrine development in early Restoration
  Movement, 127-28, 129
Doctrine, development of
  in early Movement, 141
Donohue, Agnes McNeill, 116
Down County, Ireland, 57
Drama
  Augustinian view, 46-47
  Disciples view, 46
  Calvin's view, 47-48
  of salvation, 107
  of sin and redemption, 98
Drying Their Wings by Lindsay, 282
Dürer, Albrecht, 34, 100-1

E

Eaton, W. W., 163
Economy, Pennsylvania, 72-73
Ecumenicity
  of Barton W. Stone, 24
  of Stone's followers, 31
Edict of Nantes, 58
Editors of religious journals
  qualifications for, 248
Education
  attitudes of first-generation leaders, 149
  Campbell's views, 140, 151-54
  Disciples attitudes toward, 55
  lack of financial support for, 161-62
  Scottish Presbyterian attitudes toward,
  55
Edwards, Jonathan, 109-10
  concept of evil and sin, 113
  "Faithful Narrative" of Great Awakening,
  111
  "Judging Persons' Experiences," 115-16
  "Sinners in the Hands of an Angry God,"
  112
  "Treatise on Grace, 112
Emerson, Ralph Waldo
  Garfield's impression, 269
  "Self-Reliance," 117
  "The Over-Soul," 117
  Transcendentalist clergyman, 117-18
Emmons, Francis W., 201-2
Empiricism, 327
Enlightenment, English
  and aesthetics, 66
  influence on Restoration leaders, 63
Erastianism, 56

Erickson, John, 305
Errett, Isaac, 243, 257, 325
  letter from Richardson, 217
  peripatetic generation leader, 262-63
  "Synopsis of the Faith and Practice of the
    Church of Christ," 263-64
Essay
  used by early Restoration leaders, 90
Essay Concerning Human Understanding
  by Locke, 21-22, 67
Essay Concerning Toleration,
  by Locke, 63, 64
"Essays on Education"
  by Alexander Campbell, 154
Eucharist
  See Lord's Supper
Eurpoean Evangelistic Society for the Study
  of Christian Origins, 12
Evangelism
  characteristic of Kentucky Christians,
    141
  by early Disciples, 142
  not primary concern of early Movement,
    141
Evolution, theory of
  Garfield's view, 270-71
Ewing, Grevill, 62
Exclusivism
  condemned by Richardson, 266
  in early Restoration Movement, 133

F

Faith
  operative, 123
  and opinion
    in Lockean thought, 151
  and reason, 64-65
    shift in definition, 248
  vs. "opinion," 19-20, 21
"Faith and Philosophy"
  by Robert Richardson, 262
Fanning, Tolbert, 255, 257, 262
Federal style architecture, 83
Ferguson, Jesse B., 198-99, 249-50
Fiction
  attitudes of Disciples toward, 46
  Augustinian view, 46
  criticism, 223-28
  in 19th century America, 90
Fitch, Alger Morton, Jr., 63, 180
Forsyth, Henderson, 309
Foster, Augustus John, 69, 70
Four Apostles by Albrecht Dürer
Franklin, Benjamin
  advocated close communion, 212
  American Christian Review, 55-56
  on instrumental music, 275
Frazee, Ephraim Samuel

Vachel Lindsay's grandfather, 280
Frazee, Esther Catherine
  Vachel Lindsay's mother, 281
Frederick the Wise, Elector, 102
Free will
  in Disciples theology, 113
  vs. predestination in Restoration Move-
    ment, 137
Frontier of America
  social ferment, 94-95
  spiritual condition, 93
Functionalism
  in Campbellian theology and architec-
    ture, 189

G

Gardner, Helen, 99-100
Garfield, James A., 257
  aesthetic views, 272
  assassination, 27
  biographical information, 268-72
  debate on evolution, 269
  teacher at Western Reserve Eclectic Insti-
    tute, 269
Garfield Memorial Church
  Washington, D.C., 272
Garrett, Leroy, 135, 136, 145, 248, 263,
  275, 332
Garrison, Winfred, 159
Geauga Seminary, 268
*General William Booth Enters into
  Heaven* by Lindsay, 291, 292, 298
Geneva, Switzerland city government, 44
Georgetown College (Baptist), 155
Gilbert, Katherine, 66-67, 179
Gladden, Washington, 295
Glas, John, 61
Glasgow University, 85
God, doctrine of, 91
Gospel
  anticipated in Old Testament, 97
  drama, 98
Gospel of Beauty
  development, 295
  Lindsay's concept, 284, 290
Gothic architecture, 191
Gottschalk, Louis Moreau, 80-81
Goudimel, Claude, 40
Grainger, Percy, 292-93
Great Awakening, 109, 111
  See also Second Great Awakening
Greaves, Richard L., 55
Greek Revival architecture, 83
Gresham, Perry E., 294-96, 298, 301, 302
  *The Broncho That Would Not Be Bro-
    ken,* 279
Grimke, Thomas Smith, 152
Grünewald, Matthias, 99-100, 107

Guilt, concept of
in *Scarlet Letter,* 114-15
Gulf Park College, 292

H

Haggard, Rice, 109
Haldane, James Alexander and Robert, 61-62
Half-Way Covenant
in colonial New England, 109-10
Handel and Hayden Society of Boston, 238
Hanson, Kenneth C., 196
Hart, Joe T., 23 5
Harvard College, 111
Harvard University, 175
Hastings, Thomas, 80
Hawley, Richard, 26 5
Hawthorne, Nathaniel, 276
religious view, 114
Scarlet Letter, 114-15
Hayden, A. S., 330
Heaton, Mary M., 100-1
Heaven and hell
described by Jonathan Edwards, 113-14
Henri, Robert, 285-87
Hieronymous, Lynn, 54, 330, 331
Hill Street Christian Church, Lexington, Ky., 144
Hines, Jerome, 305
autobiography, *This is My Story, This is My Song,* 305
opera, *I Am the Way,* 305
Hinsdale, Aaron, 271
Hiram College, 264
attended by Lindsay, 282
Historical existentialism, 327, 328
History of the Church
See Church history
Hodge, William, 119
Hoelty-Nickel, Theodore, 103
Hoffman, Hans, 303-4
"Holiness of Beauty," sermon by Lindsay, 289
Holy Spirit
and aesthetics, 213
Campbell's doctrine, 239
Campbell's writing on, 137
in contemporary Christianity, 337
indwelling
emphasized in Stone-Campbell journals, 247
in Restoration Movement theology, 66
and scriptural silence, 259
Stone's view, 121
Hooper, John, 50
Houdon, Jean-Anotine, 83
Humble, Bill J., 129
Hymnals
of Stone, Johnson, Scott, and Campbell, 200
Hymnody, 195-96
Hymns of Martin Luther, 35

I

I Am the Way, by Hines, 305
I Heard Immanuel Singing, by Lindsay, 288-89
Images in sixteenth-century, 41
Immersion
See Baptism; Baptism, believers; Baptism, doctrine of
Inclusivism/exclusivism
in peripatetic generation, 255-58
Independent churches
influence, on Campbells, 63
Infant baptism
See Baptism, infant
Ingersoll, Robert, 271
Innovations
examined, 272-73
term used for "disloyalty," 256
Institutes of the Christian Religion, by Calvin, 36
Isenheim Altarpiece by Grünewald, 99

J

Jesus Christ and the Word
in scholastic Disciples' thought, 42
Jeter, John B.
"Campbellism Examined," 255
Johnny Appleseed
Lindsay's view, 291
Johnson, John T., 144
"Judging Persons' Experiences" by Edwards, 115-16
Justification
Campbell's doctrine, 121-24
drama, 98
in Lutheran and Calvinist theology, 112-13
and Luther's tower experience, 99
in *Scarlet Letter,* 114-15
Stone's view, 121

K

Kate by William Baxter, 223
Kentucky
and Second Great Awakening, 111
Kilmer, Joyce, 291
Kingdom of God
doctrine, 43-44
Kingsley's Sermons on music, 237
Knox, John, 44, 50, 55, 56
Kuhn, Helmut, 66-67, 179
Kuhnau, Johann, 103

L

Lamar, J. S., 273-74
Lands of the Bible by McGarvey, 256
Lang, Paul Henry, 59
Language
  and aesthetic sensitivity, 181
  logical, in Campbell's use, 182
Lard, Moses E., 255-56, 275, 332
  advocated close communion, 212
  exclusivist position, 267
  "Instrumental Music and Dancing," 256
Lasso, Orlando di, 98
Latrobe, Benjamin Henry
  Classic revivalist architecture, 83
  "Essay on Landscape," 75
  work and travels in America, 73-77
Legalism
  contrasted to liberal triviality, 276
  as distortion of Campbellian heritage, 91
  endangered early Restoration Movement, 133
  slowed development of Restoration aesthetics, 114
Leinsdorf, Erich, 305
Leith, John H., 42, 46
Leonard, Silas, 206-7
Liberalism
  affected Stone-Campbell Movement, 329
  in Colonial religious life, 112-13
  as distortion of Campbellian heritage, 91
Life of Knowles Shaw, the Singing Evangelist by Baxter, 222-23
Lindsay, Nicholas
  Vachel Lindsay's grandfather, 280
Lindsay, Olive
  Vachel Thomas Lindsay's first wife, 281
Lindsay, Vachel, 1, 2, 89, 279-303
  affirmed Campbellian beliefs, 300-1
  art education in New York, 285-86
  church membership, 293
  compared to Robert Rauschenberg, 313
  compared to Alexander Campbell, 301-2
  education, 281-82
  honoray doctorate from Hiram College, 293
  illness and death, 293
  lecturership, 291-92
  letters to Marguerite Wilkinson, 297, 300
  move to Chicago, 283
  parents, 280
  philosophy, 298
  recital for Wilson's cabinet, 291
  relationship with Springfield, 292
  religious training, 296
  religious views, 297
  sermon, 289
  suicide, 284, 303

teaching career, 289
tensions about art and poetry, 286-87
travel to England, 289
  travel to Europe, 288
walking tours, 287-88, 291-92
Lindsay, Vachel Thomas
  Vachel Lindsay's father, 281
Lipscomb, David, 255, 257
  critical of Garfield, 270
Literalism, 229
Literary criticism
  principle, 90
  in 19th century America, 86, 90
Literature
  Campbell's attitude toward, 154
  Campbell's contribution to, 219
  Campbell's remarks about, 183-84
  in Christian colleges, 308
  development in America, 84-85
Liturgy
  of Martin Luther, 35
  Puritan view, 53
  rejected by American Protestants, 53
  as "worship by proxy," 202-3
Locke, John
  empirical method, 64
  influence on Restoration ethos, 34
  Essay Concerning Human Understanding, 21-22, 67
  Essay Concerning Toleration, 63, 64
  "No Innate Principles in the Mind" 151
Lockean philosophy
  in Campbell's thought, 151
  influence on Alexander Campbell, 24, 63
  influence on Restoration theology, 63, 65
  influence in Restoration Movement, 11
Logic
  and aesthetic development, 146-47
  Campbell's dependence on, 24, 136
  in Campbell's Lunenburg Letter reply, 132
Lollards, 51
Lord Byron, 221
Lord's Supper
  admission to, 266
  as church ordinance, 56, 111
  and Half-Way Covenant, 110
  as ordinance of Brush Run Church, 24
  question about admission to, 265
  theological function, 55-56
  visual and theological centrality, 189, 191
Luce, Matthias, 138
  baptized Campbells, 128
Lunenburg Letter of 1837, 265
  and history of the church, 137

Campbell's second reply to, 134
in *Millennial Harbinger*, 131
Lunenburg Question, 331-32
Luther, Martin
aesthetic values, 34-35
biographical sketch, 98-99
Lutheran Reformation
as model for aesthetic expression, 104-5
Mahoning Baptist Association, 141
Male chauvinism
Campbell's heritage, 180
Mann, Horace, 150, 152
Markham, Edwin, 201
Mason, Lowell, 80
Massachusetts State Board of Education, 150
Masters, Edgar Lee
critical of Christianity, 297
Matthews, Shailer, 295
Maximilian, Prince, 72-73
Mayer, Frederick, 175
McAllister, Lester, 24, 57, 88, 156, 250
McEwen, James S., 55-56
McGarvey, J. W., 255
columnist for *Christian Standard,* 256-57
entertains Vachel Lidsay, 287
on instrumental music, 275
Lands of the Bible, 256
McGready, James
Stone influenced by, 119-20
McGuffy, William Holmes, 157
McKever, Archibald
Alexander Campbell's brother-in-law, 134
McLean, Archibald, 181-82
McNeill, John T., 36, 45
McRae, Clarice True Jones (Trudy), 316-23, 336
contemporary Christian artist, 305
Merrell, James L., 1-2
The Millennial Harbinger
content, 122
articles on sin, justification, and salvation, 121-22
Campbell's editorship, 92
establishment, 87
poetry in, 89-90
Millennium
Campbell's view, 33-34, 87
Miller, Samuel, 90
Milton, John, 51, 67
Paradise Lost, 105-6
Mirror of Taste and Dramatic Censor, 90
Missions
divisive subject among Disciples, 200
Moravian musical culture, 80
Mourner's bench

removed by Barton W. Stone, 177
Mueller, John, 82
Munro, Andrew, 19
Murch, James DeForest, 250, 255, 262
Music
ambiguity of Campbell about, 236-37
Campbellian view, 166, 331
cultured and vernacular traditions, 79-81
development in 19th century America, 79-81, 81-82
of early Disciples, 81
and Luther, 35
polyphonic, 98
of Richardson, 214-15
as a science, 166
and scriptural silence argument, 203-4
as source of sectarianism, 200
in worship, 80
Music, instrumental
basis for Campbellian rejection, 204
Calvin's view, 40
Campbell's objection not based on scriptural silence, 273
controversy over, 253-54, 275
first introduced in Disciples congregation, 273-74
opposed in peripatetic generation, 255-56
viewed as "proxy worship," 237-38
vocal, 39
Musical instruments, 54
Musical notation
emotional objections to, 199
omitted from early Disciples hymnals, 197-98
Music in Western Civilization
by Lang, 59

N

Nathan the Prophet
and David's sin, 97
National Association of Schools of Music
accreditation, for Christian colleges, 306-7
Nature
affinity of Restoration leaders to, 235
and understanding of God, 262
New Athens College, 183
New Testament
primacy in Stone-Campbell Movement, 42
New York Academy of Music, 238
New York Philharmonic Orchestra, 238
New York Philharmonic Symphony Society, 80
New York Symphony Society, 80
Nietzsche, Friedrich, 327

"No Innate Principles in the Mind" by
Locke, 151
Northampton, Mass.
colonial religion in, 109-10

O

Oberlin College, 152
*Off the Wall: Robert Rauschenberg and the
Art World of Our Time* by Tomkins,
313-14
Old Main at Bethany College
architecture praised, 193
Olson, Lani L., 194
Open membership
as contemporary issue, 265
permitted by liberal Stone-Campbell
churchs, 137
Operative faith
See Faith, operative
Opinion
"full freedom," 24
vs faith, 19-20, 21
Opinions
published as doctrines, 250
vs. scriptural facts, 131
Optimism
in Campbell's writing, 87
as literary principle, 87
Ordination
questions regarding, 129-30
Original sin
Augustinian view, 113
opposed to doctrine of free will, 113
Osborne, Ronald E., 32, 63, 91, 150
Owen, Robert, 65

P

Paedobaptism
See Baptism, infant
Painting
Campbellian view, 331
development in America, 82
heroic style, 81
Paradise Lost by Milton, 105-6
Parkening, Christopher, 305
Patronage Act in 18th century Scotland,
56-57
Paul, Apostle
on sin and redemption, 97
Pelikan, Jaroslav, 104
Pendleton William K., 243, 257, 325
appreciated Shakespeare, 229
literary principles, 86
on missionary societies, 260
opening address at Bethany College,
169-70
as primary leader of Restoration Movement, 169-70

professor at Bethany College, 163
racist views, 258-29
on scriptural silence, 259-61
sympathetic to arts, 258
Penitential psalms, 97-98
as inspiration for Orlando di Lasso, 98
as poetry, 98
Peripatetic generation, 247-77
and aesthetics of worship, 248
contribution of Campbell to, 251
controversial climate, 264-65
divisive issues, 252-53
historical existentialism, 328
shift in emphasis and doctrine, 251-53
Phrenology
Campbell's hopes for, 154
Pilgrim's Progress, by Bunyan, 106, 108
Pinkerton, L. L., 275
Pittsburgh Symphony Orchestra, 305
Plato
Augustine's comments on, 178-795
Poetry
of Alexander Campbell, 219, 305
Augustinian view, 25, 46
Calvin and Campbell compared, 44-45
Campbell's views, 139-40
of Disciples hymnody, 195-96
of 19th century America, 88
in *Millennial Harbinger,* 221
not excluded from Campbellian thought,
222
Platonic view, 25, 46
of Lindsay, 286
Poetry Magazine, 291
Portraiture
in 19th century America, 82
used by Restoration leaders, 233
Prayer
Campbell's practice, 239
Preaching
Campbellian view, 53
in early Restoration Movement, 178-79
emphasized in Independent churches,
60
Puritan approach to, 50-51
style of Alexander Campbell, 77, 181,
183
Predestination
rejected by Restoration Movement leaders, 35-36
rejected by Stone, 121
vs. free will in Restoration Movement,
137
Pre-existence of Christ
not believed by Stone, 143
Presbyterianism
as basis for aesthetic values, 34
in Ireland and Scotland, 55

in 18th century America, 111-12
in 18th century Ulster, 58
See also Seceder Presbyterians
Pride and aesthetic taste, 189
Principles and Objectives of Religious Reformation, by Richardson, 252
Proclamation of the Coming of Religion, Equality and Beauty, by Lindsay, 290
Psalm singing
of Genevan reformers, 38
in Puritanism, 53
Psalter of Sternhold and Hopkins, 53, 56
Puritanism
Calvinist influences on, 50
church polity, 51
condemned by Hawthorne, 114
development, 50
influence in America, 54, 109
influence on Christian faith, 67
influence on Restoration Movement, 109
influence on Stone-Campbell Movement, 51

Q
Quaker architecture, 188

R
"Rage for order" concept, 334
Randall, Max Ward, 92-93, 109, 121, 124-25
Rapp, George, 72
Rationalism
influence on Campbells, 24
as roots of Restoration Movement, 135
Rauschenberg, Robert, 312-15
Ray, Joseph, 157
Reason and scripture interpretation, 24
Redemption emphasized in Stone-Campbell journals, 247
Redstone Baptist Association, 138-39, 140
Reformed (Calvinist) theology
influence on Restoration Movement, 36
Reformed Churches
See Calvinism
Reid, Thomas, 84
Rembrandt van Rijn, 107-8
Return of the Prodigal, 108
Restoration
concept, 266
early emphasis on, 127-28
in early Stone-Campbell Movement, 11
implications of the term, 337-38
Restoration Movement.
affinity with Protestant Reformation, 31
as applied to the Church, 29
and Bible as Word of God, 38
Campbell's view, 30
contemporary status, 12

doctrine development, 129
early change in emphases, 124-25
polarization within, 253-54
relationship to the arts, 336
roots of in historic Christianity, 327
Scott's claim for, 30
shift in emphasis, 177
See also Stone-Campbell Movement, 12
Restoration of "ancient order"
as basis for Washington Christian Association
See also Unity, 18
Return of the Prodigal, by Rembrandt, 108
"Review of Archippus, No. III" in *Millennial Harbinger,* 123
Revivalism
in rural Kentucky, 159
in Stone Movement, 124-25
Rhau-Grunenberg, Johann, 102
Rhetoric, 67
Rhymes to Be Traded for Bread by Lindsay, 291
Richardson, Robert,
aesthetics, 105, 211-18, 216, 325-26
on ambiguity, 334
artistic inclinations and training, 213-14
background, 212
on believer's baptism, 128
blindness, 215
board member of Bethany College, 160
comments on Campbell's use of language, 45
Communings in the Sanctuary, 261-62
doctrine of Holy Spirit, 217
dual intersts of science and aesthetics, 78
on faith and opinion 33 , 143, 243
flautist, 214
inclusivist stance, 261
literary principles, 86
as member of peripatetic generation, 257
on nature of Holy Spirit, 66
opening address at Bethany College, 168-69
opinions on public worship, 201-2
professor at Bethany College, 163
talents, 212-13
view of unity, 20
writing style, 77-78
Rogers, John, 232
Romanticism in poetry, 88
Rookmaaker, H.R., 338
Ross, A. F., 163, 165-68

S
Sacrament
See Church Ordinances
Sacred Harp hymnal, 198

Saint Paul's Church, New York, 187
Salvation Army Lindsay's view, 298
Sandeman, Robert, 61
Sarcasm
    Campbell's use and defense, 135-36
    in *The Christian Baptist,* 140
Scarlet Letter
    by Hawthorne, 114-15
Schade, Wermer, 102
Schaeffer, Franky, 305
Scholastic Disciples
    and Jesus Christ and the Word, 42
    and "primitive pattern," 24
    uncompromising views, 136-37
Scholasticism
    of early Church Fathers, 247
    early development in Restoration Movement, 134
    of Stone-Campbell movement, 328
Schopenhauer, Arthur, 237
Schweitzer, Albert, 102-3
Scott, Sir Walter (Scottish author)
    Waverly, 90, 224-25
    criticized in *The Presbyterian,* 225-26
Scott, Walter
    appointed as Baptist evangelist, 124, 141
    associated with Haldane congregation, 62
    curriculum design for Bacon College, 155
    death, 243
    education, 150
    emphasized art in curriculum, 166
    encouraged singing, 196
    evangelization by, 149
    flautist, 214
    frontier religious work, 93-94
    The Gospel Restored, 30, 71
    hymnal, 199
    literary principles, 86
    president of Bethany College, 151
    synergistic/humanistic presentation of gospel, 142
    teacher of Richardson, 214
Scriptural silence
    and ambiguity, 177
    and relation to aesthetic-artistic concerns, 261
    inclusivist/exclusive polarization about, 262
    not basis of Campbell's rejection of instrumental music, 204, 205, 208
    and peripatetic generation, 259-61
    and simplicity in worship, 100
    and sufficiency of scripture, 51-52
Scripture
    as authorative for Campbell, 140
    interpretation, 328-29, 333

sufficiency, as Campbellian norm, 52
Sculpture
    Campbellian view, 331
    development in America, 83-84
Seceder Presbyterians
    and Burgher/Anti-Burgher schism, 16, 57
    in Scotland, 15
Second Great Awakening, 109, 111
    and Barton W. Stone, 94
    influenced Stone movement, 124
    See also Great Awakening
Sectarianism
    in early Restoration Movement, 133
Self-Reliance by Emerson, 117
Shakespeare, William, 47, 228
Shape note hymn books, 81
Silence of scripture
    and aesthetics, 19
    introduction of concept, 19
    as source of division, 25
    and sufficiency of scripture, 51-52
Simonson, Harold P., 113
Sin
    Campbell's doctrine, 121-24
    differentiation between physical and moral evil, 97
    and redemption, 97-125
    Reformation view vs. transcendental view, 118
    relationship to grace and law, 114
    Restoration view, 118
Sin and redemption
    anticipated in Old Testament, 97
Singing,
    a cappella, 275
    congregational, 39
    encouraged by Puritan minister, 196
    encouraged by Walter Scott, 196
    polyphonic
        Calvin's view of, 40-41
        Reformed view of, 50-53
        Restoration view of, 40
Singing schools, 198
    Campbell's disapproval of hymnals in, 206-7
"Sinners in the Hands of an Angry God by Edwards, 112
Skepticism (theological), 110
Smith, "Racoon" John, 144, 159, 180, 182
Social gospel
    of 19th century, 295
    emphasized by Alexander Campbell, 71
Sola fide, sola gratia
    Campbell's objection to, 123
    as defense against Arminianism, 112
    as focus of Luther's reformation, 99
Sola scriptura
    Prostant concept, 42

and Puritanism, 52
Southern Harmony and Musical Companion by Walker, 198
Sovereignty of God in Calvinist thought, 112
Sports, competitive
Campbell's attitude toward, 159
Springfield, Illinois
Lindsay's hometown, 291
Sprinkling
See Baptism, infant
Squire, Russell N., 203-4
Star of My Heart by Lindsay, 283-84
Sternhold and Hopkins *Psalter,* 53, 56
Stevenson, Dwight E., 63, 199, 211, 212, 218
Stewardship
and aesthetic taste, 187
and entertainment, 230-32
Stoddard, Solomon, 109-10, 111
Stone, Barton W., 11
antitrinitarian views, 143
belief about pre-existence of Christ, 143
at Cane Ridge, 109
conversion, 120
death, 243
dedication to Christian unity, 94
development of doctrine, 118-19
difference with Campbell about Holy Spirit, 121
ecumenical spirit, 24
education, 150
first meeting with Alexander Campbell, 143
frontier religious work, 93-94
leader of Kentucky churches, 31
and Second Great Awakening, 109
and Western Awakening, 119-21
Stone-Campbell affiliation
in Civil War, 253
Stone-Campbell Movement
Alexander Campbell's view, 137
approach to a music ethos, 41
consolidation, 143
purpose, 11
union of Christians and Disciples, 276
See also Restoration Movement
Strong, Josiah, 295
Stuart, Charles, 163
Stuart, Gilbert, 82
Sublimity
Blair's concept, 85-86
aesthetic use, 75-76
Campbell's use, 85-86, 89
Swedenborgianism
influence on Lindsay, 290-91
interest of Garfield, 272
Sweet, William Warren, 236

Swinburne, Algernon Charles, 285
Symbolism
in Campbellian church architecture, 190
Symmes, Thomas, 196

T

Teasdale, Sara, 291
Teleman, G. P., 103
Theater
attitudes of Disciples toward, 46
criticized by Campbell, 228
This is My Story, This is My Song. autobiography of Hines, 305
Thoreau, David, 116
Tocqueville, Alexis de,
Journey to America, 70-71
Tomkins, Calvin, 313-14
Trancendentalism
influence, on Disciples, 117-18
Transubstantion, in Knox's theology, 56
Transylvania College, Lexington, Ky.
descendant of Bacon College, 158
"Treatise on Grace," by Edwards, 112
Trinity
as "opinion" in Campbell's theology, 143
Stone's view, 91
Tucker, William E., 24, 57, 88, 156, 250
Tworkov, Jack, 316

U

Ulster Plantation by King James I, 57
Ulster Scots
migration, to America, 58
Union
of Disciples and Christians, 144-45
Unity, Christian
articles by Stone and Campbell, 143-44
and the arts, 329
as basis for Washington Christian Association
and disunity in Movement, 145-47
with diversity, in Campbell's thought, 324
as divisive source, 20
with diversity, in Campbell's thought, 324
in early Stone-Campbell Movement, 11
Lindsay's concept, 290
vs. Restoration, 24, 124, 127
in writings of Thomas Campbell, 130
Ussher, James, Archbishop, 57
Utility
as key concept of Bethany College, 165

V

Van der Leeuw, Gerardus, 104
Vernacular tradition

emphasized at Bethany College, 174
Vogt, Von Ogden, 54

W

Walker, William, 198
Walther, Johann, 103
War Bulletins of Lindsay, 296
Washington Christian Association
    decision to organize into a church, 23,
        111
    organizational meeting, 18
Watts, Isaac, 221
Waverly, by Sir Walter Scott, 90
Wesley, John, 60
West, Benjamin, 82
Western Eclectic Institute, 264, 268
    See also Hiram College
Western Literary Institute, 154
What Grandpa Mouse Said by Lindsay, 282
White, Benjamin Franklin, 198
Whitefield, George (1714-76), 60
Whitgift, John, Archbishop of Canterbury,
        53
Whittier, John Greenleaf, 89, 221
Wilburn, Ralph G., 29, 63
Wilcox, Susan, 287
Wilkinson, Marguerite, 297, 300
Williams, Anne Martindale, 305
Williams College, 268
Wishart, George, 55
Women
    education for, 152
    work of in Restoration churches, 274
Wood carving
    vernacular tradition of American sculp-
        ture, 83
Word of God
    as authorative norm, 43
    Calvinist thought on, 43
    primacy, in Stone-Campbell Movement,
        42
Wordsworth, William, 227
    influenced by Hugh Blair's ideas, 85
    influence on American poetry criticism,
        88

World Convention of Churches of Christ,
        12
Worship
    "by proxy," 203
    congregatinal autonomy in, 202
    congregational freedom in, 200
    dignity in, 202
    public, 201
Wrather, Eva Jane, 149
Wycliffism, 51

Y

Yale College, 111
Yale University, 175
Yancey, Walt, 142, 247, 275
Young, Charles, 19
Young Lady's Guide, 226

Z

Zeller, Edward, 247
Zollars, Eli Vaughn, 281

Selected Scripture References

All scripture quotations are from the Revised Standard Version.

Ps. 51:1-2, 97
Ps. 51:3-4a, 98
Matt. 1:21, 97
Acts 2:38, 130
Acts 2:42, 201
Rom. 1:17, 98
Rom. 1:19-20, 262
Rom. 2:28-29, 262
Rom. 5:1-2, 97
1 Cor. 12:12-20, 324
1 Cor 15:28, 44
Eph. 6:17, 42
2 Timothy, 27
2 Tim 3:14-15, 42
2 Tim. 4:2, 42
1 Pet. 5:10, 338
John 1:1, 143
John 1:3, 42
John 1:14, 42
John 17:21, 119